Alchemists of Loss

How Modern Finance and Government Intervention Crashed the Financial System

KEVIN DOWD

and

MARTIN HUTCHINSON

A John Wiley and Sons, Ltd, Publication

This edition first published in 2010
© 2010 John Wiley & Sons, Ltd

Registered office
John Wiley & Sons Ltd, The Atrium, Southern Gate, Chichester, West Sussex, PO19 8SQ, United Kingdom

For details of our global editorial offices, for customer services and for information about how to apply for permission to reuse the copyright material in this book please see our website at www.wiley.com.

Wiley also publishes its books in a variety of electronic formats. Some content that appears in print may not be available in electronic books.

A catalogue record for this book is available from the British Library.

ISBN 978-0-470-68915-8

Set in Bembo by Sparks – www.sparkspublishing.com
Printed in the United States by Courier Westford

Contents

11 Loose Money   247
12 Government Meddling in the Financial System   269

Part Five: Götterdämmerung   **295**

13 Bubble, Burst, and Panic   297
14 The Slope Down Which We're Heading   331

Part Six: Charting a New Way Forward   **349**

15 The Math of Proper Risk Management   351
16 Back to the Future – A New Vision of Finance   373
17 A Blueprint for Reform   389
18 Lessons to Take Away   403

    Bibliography   407
    Index   413

Acknowledgements & Dedication

It is a great pleasure to thank the many people who have contributed to this book. We thank the former editor of *Financial Engineering News*, Jim Finnegan, who first brought the two of us together. We thank Martin Walker for his splendid Foreword, and Philip Booth, Jim Dorn, Steve Hanke, Alberto Mingardi and Andrew Stuttaford for their generous endorsements. We thank the Wiley and Sparks teams, especially Pete Baker, Aimee Dibbens and Viv Wickham, for their work and support in this project. We also thank the following for all manner of diverse contributions: Mark Billings, David Blake, Carlos Blanco, Chris O' Brien, Andrew Cairns, Dave Campbell, John Cotter, Roger Field, Chris Humphrey, Anwar Khan, Duncan Kitchin, Bill Lee, Anneliese Osterspey, Dave Owen, Stan Szynkaruk, Margaret Woods, Basil Zafiriou and Martin's colleagues at Reuters BreakingViews and Agora Publishing, both fertile sources of good ideas and inspiration. Finally, thanks to Heather Maizels, whose inspiration led to the cover design. Most of all, we thank our long suffering families – most especially Mahjabeen Raadhiyah and Safiah on Kevin's part, and Anna and Rumen on Martin's.

★★★

Dedication

Kevin: to Mahjabeen, Raadhiyah and Safiah.

Martin: To Brian, Jean, Virginia, Anna and Rumen,
the Hutchinson family.

★★★

Foreword

This book will startle readers. So it should. The scale and breadth of the latest financial crisis justify a fundamental re-assessment of the way that economic affairs are managed. And there could hardly be anything more fundamental than the authors' recommendations. They advocate a return to the classic form of banking developed in 18th century Scotland; the abolition of state guarantees of bank deposits and of home mortgage tax relief; the eradication of the World Bank and International Monetary Fund and a return to the gold standard, or some commodity-based equivalent. They also propose a tax on US banks whose assets are greater than $360 billion (2.5% of US GDP), in order to shrink them to manageable size. The six largest US banks are their target.

They do not suggest that Wall Street and the City of London will disappear. They do, however, maintain that their fate will resemble that of the American rustbelt; Wall Street will be like the Cleveland, Ohio, of the 1970s and they see its skyscrapers becoming ghost buildings. London is condemned to become the Youngstown, Ohio, of the 1980s, "an excellent market for rottweilers, wire mesh and tattooed thugs." The author's pungent opinions, uncompromising analyses and muscular prose style make this an entertaining and provocative as well as an instructive read.

Perhaps the most striking feature of this book's full-blooded defense of genuine free market economics is that so many of its proposals have already been espoused by more conventional economists. Its call for a tax on financial transactions to discourage trading was originally framed by the Nobel prize-winner James Tobin. Its insistence that no bank should be permitted to become too big to fail has been echoed by the former chief economist of the IMF, Simon Johnson, who also maintains that the profound political influence of the big banks in the American political system can be seen as a kind of coup d'etat. Like another Nobel laureate, Paul Krugman, this book argues that the financial sector had become a classic example of rent-seeking. And the gold standard has many defenders, including former Federal Reserve chairman Alan Greenspan. He is hailed in this book for calling the bubble fifteen years ago with his warning of "irrational exuberance, and excoriated for doing nothing about it. In that, too, these authors are in good company.

It should come as no great surprise that serious economists, whatever their political leanings, can agree on crucial issues. There are absolute truths in economics, and it is the great merit of this book to restate them, and to recall to mind that Ur-text of economic wisdom, Rudyard Kipling's poem 'The Gods of the Copybook Headings.' It reminds us of the wisdom of our grandmothers, who warned us that all that glitters is not gold, that we should save for a rainy day, and that if something sounds too good to be true then it probably is. A mortgage for 125 percent of a house's value, with no deposit and amounting to six times the applicant's annual income, is certainly too good to be true. And yet these were the terms being advertised by the British bank Northern Rock shortly before its collapse and rescue by the British taxpayer. There could have been few clearer signs of an unsustainable bubble.

There were many such signs. The fall of the US personal savings rate below zero in 2006 was one. The rise in personal debt to over 100 percent of national income was another. The way chronic imbalances between Chinese surpluses and US deficits became routine should have been yet another. The dangers of a European monetary union without the assurance of a responsible sovereignty to support it was yet another. The emergence of "the Greenspan put," in which financiers were encouraged to assume by the Fed that any financial crisis would be met by a rescuing surge of liquidity, should also have sounded an alarm. It changed the essential balance between risk and reward. To put it another way, it encouraged greed while reducing fear. It encouraged bankers to throw caution to the winds, since in the immortal words of Citibank chief Chuck Prince in 2007, "As long as the music is playing, you've got to get up and dance."

Bankers should not speak and far less act like this. Bankers should be sober men in a reliable and even boring business, cautious custodians of other peoples' money. We have heard this before, most memorably from Walter Bagehot, a polymath who wrote on physics and philosophy and literature, edited *The Economist* and produced in *Lombard Street* (1873) the first classic book on banking. His advice on the role of central banks in financial panics and crises has never been bettered: "to avert panic, central banks should lend early and freely, to solvent firms, against good collateral, and at high rates." These three essential conditions have been signally and perilously flouted in our current crisis. Central banks have lent to the insolvent, against toxic collateral and at the lowest of rates. We will pay dearly for the temporary and unconvincing relief the Fed's actions have delivered.

Bagehot argued, in a remark that neatly encapsulates the core argument of this book, that "The business of banking ought to be simple; if it is hard, it is wrong." The Alchemists who are the targets of this book made the business of banking and credit and debt management into something not only hard, but well-nigh impenetrable. Their algorithms and quants and Gaussian models and Efficient Market hypotheses turned finance into an arm of higher mathematics and bamboozled investors and bankers in the process. Their mumbo-jumbo perfectly embodied George Bernard Shaw's remark that "any profession is a conspiracy against the laity." It also failed its first real market test, with the Long Term Capital Management fiasco of 1998, a warning that was ignored, thanks to a brisk exercise of the Greenspan put.

The authors predicate a (somewhat) mythical golden age of finance, characterized by "the importance of trust, integrity and saving, the need to invest for the long term," and proceed to contrast it with Modern Finance. This is defined as "a focus on marketing and sales, form over substance, and never mind the client; an obsession on the short-term and the next bonus; a preference for speculation and trading over long-term investment; stratospheric remuneration for practitioners, paid for through exploitation of clients and taxpayers."

Modern finance and its mathematician-alchemists are the targets of this book, but the authors identify a single arch-villain it is the eminent

British economist John Maynard Keynes, characterized here as "the sublime Paracelsus of economic alchemy." And yet Keynes is cited with approval for his famous remark on the founder of the Soviet Union in *Economic Consequences of the Peace*: "Lenin was certainly right. There is no subtler, no surer means of over-turning the existing basis of society than to debauch the currency... By a continuing process of inflation, governments can confiscate, secretly and unobserved, an important part of the wealth of their citizens."

Because of the actions taken over the past two years by governments and central banks, a new inflation is almost certainly coming. Between them government with over $3 trillion in deficit spending and central banks with another $4 trillion in liquidity creation have pumped over 10 percent of global GDP into a heroic effort to fend off a new Great Depression. As a result, the level of government debt in most developed countries is now approaching or exceeding 100 percent of GDP. There are three ways to deal with such debt. The first is to grow out of it. The second is to default. The third, and easiest for governments to deliver, is to inflate it away. For all their criticisms of Keynes, the authors of this book whole-heartedly endorse his warning.

The real trouble with Keynes, of course, is the Keynesians in government who donned his mantle and claimed to be enacting his precepts when they went into deficit to invigorate a temporarily sluggish economy. Keynes advocated extraordinary spending by government in times of emergency. Politicians of all parties quickly misapplied his theories to justify borrowing money in ordinary times to give gentle boosts to an economy, usually in time to produce an artificial boom before an election. Such Keynesians gave Keynes a bad name. "We are all Keynesians now," a phrase originally attributed to Milton Friedman in a *Time* magazine interview in1965, has come to be associated with President Richard Nixon in 1971. It is sometimes forgotten that it was Nixon, a Republican president, who took state intervention in the economy to its greatest extreme in US peacetime history. In the weekend of August 14, 1971, Nixon imposed a wage and price freeze, an import surcharge, and finally severed the dollar's link to gold and abandoned the Bretton Woods system (which Keynes had devised). The Great Inflation of the 1970s followed.

Our financial crisis has been brought about by an unholy combination of model-crazed mathematicians, dancing bankers, profligate central banks and politicians who believed their own rhetoric about their ability to manage and to deliver economic growth. Nixon was but an extreme example of this hubris, one particularly ugly sub-peak in a very long and rising trend. In 1901, the revenues of the federal government of the United States were just under 3 percent of GDP, and being in modest surplus it spent rather less. In 2010, the federal government will spend 28 percent of GDP. Add in the 8 percent spent by the individual states, and government as a whole in the US approaches that 40–50 percent of GDP routinely arrogated by the welfare state governments of Europe.

These swollen governments have meddled increasingly in national and international economics. They impose taxes in order to enact social goals and political targets, from generous pensions to subsidized health care and education and housing. The intentions were usually admirable; the unintended consequences less so. The current financial crisis first became apparent in 2007 in the sub-prime mortgage sector. A major reason for this was that the US Congress had required that the two government-sponsored enterprises in housing, Fannie Mae and Freddie Mac, should make 55 percent of their loans to borrowers at or below the median income level.

Unless restrained, the role of government is almost certain to grow in the aftermath of the current crisis. For the first time, the developed economies are starting to feel the pinch of baby-boom retirement. The four eurozone countries in the most trouble, Portugal, Italy, Greece and Spain, have the most difficult demographics of any of Europe's OECD countries; that is, the lowest birth rates combined with a swelling population of retirees. There are not enough workers coming into the system to pay for the pensioners leaving it. This is starting to hit countries world-wide, including the United States, Japan and China. It makes the crisis of public finances, after the massive deficit spending and money creation of the last two years, look even more intractable. We shall all pay for this, through the nose. And the best reason to read this book is that the authors were among that select and disregarded band who saw it coming.

Martin Walker, Washington DC, March 2010
Senior Director, Global Business Policy Council, AT Kearney

Part One

Past Successes and Disasters

1

Introduction

Towards the end of his *General Theory of Employment, Interest and Money*, published in 1936, John Maynard Keynes wrote that:

> "… the ideas of economists and political philosophers, both when they are right and when they are wrong, are more powerful than is commonly understood. Indeed the world is ruled by little else. Practical men, who believe themselves to be quite exempt from any intellectual influences, are usually the slaves of some defunct economist. Madmen in authority, who hear voices in the air, are distilling their frenzy from some academic scribbler of a few years back. I am sure that the power of vested interests is vastly exaggerated compared with the gradual encroachment of ideas."[1]

In this book we suggest that the key to understanding the recent financial crisis is to appreciate the impact of two belief systems, at first sight unconnected. Both of these belief systems originated from economic theories propounded by "defunct economists."

The first of these is Modern Finance. At its broadest level, Modern Finance consists of a set of attitudes and practices, perhaps best understood by comparing it to what went before. In the past, finance emphasized old-fashioned values: the importance of trust, integrity and

---

[1] Keynes, 1936, p. 383.

saving; the need to build long-term relationships and invest for the long term; modest remuneration for practitioners and a focus on the interests of their clients; and tight governance and a sense of harmonized interests and mutual benefit. All of these dovetailed together into a coherent whole.

Modern Finance emphasizes the opposite: a focus on marketing and sales, form over substance, and never mind the client; an obsession with the short-term and the next bonus; a preference for speculation and trading over long-term investment; stratospheric remuneration levels for practitioners, paid for through exploitation of clients and taxpayers, or "rent seeking"[2]; the erosion of the old governance mechanisms and out-of-control conflicts of interest.

Underpinning much of Modern Finance is a vast intellectual corpus, the formidable mathematical "Modern Financial Theory." This includes Modern Portfolio Theory developed in the 1950s; the Efficient Market Hypothesis and the Capital Asset Pricing Model developed in the 1960s; the weird and wonderful universe of financial derivatives pricing models, including notably the Black-Scholes-Merton equation for valuing options, developed in the early 1970s, and its many derivatives; and financial risk management or, more accurately, the modern quantitative theory of financial risk management, which emerged in the 1990s.

Modern Financial Theory soon became widely accepted; those who questioned it were, for the most part, drummed out of the finance profession. It became even more respectable with the award, to date, of no fewer than seven Economics Nobels, ample proof of its scientific respectability.

Modern Finance was big on promises. We were assured that it would provide us with the ever-expanding benefits of "financial innovation" and sophisticated new financial "services," and not just at the level of the corporation, but trickling down to the retail level, benefiting individual savers and investors in their everyday lives. The evidence for this was, allegedly, the much greater range of choice of financial services available and the expanding size of the financial serv-

---

[2] The phrase "rent seeking" is economists' jargon for self-serving activities that capture resources without providing any economic benefit in return, such as the activities of the Mafia or of crooked politicians. Unlike most economic jargon, this term is actually useful: rent seeking is one of the main themes of the book.

ices sector as a percentage of GDP. At the same time, improvements in financial risk management meant that we could sleep easily in our beds, knowing our hard-earned money was safe in the hands of financial institutions working on our behalf. Or so we were led to believe.

Yet, intellectually impressive as it is, most of this theoretical edifice was based on a deeply flawed understanding of the way the world actually works. Like medieval alchemy, it was an elegant and internally consistent intellectual structure based on flawed assumptions.

One of these was that stock price movements obey a Gaussian distribution. While the Gaussian distribution is the best-known distribution, it is only one of many, and has the special property that its "tails" are very thin – i.e. that events from outside the norm are truly rare, never-in-the-history-of-the-universe rare. History tells us that's not right; markets surprise us quite often.

Among some of the other common but manifestly indefensible claims of Modern Finance are that:

- modern "free markets" ensure that financial innovation is a good thing, which benefits consumers and makes the financial system more stable;
- risks are foreseeable and, incredibly, that you can assess risks using a risk measure, the Value-at-Risk or VaR, that gives you no idea of what might happen if a bad event actually occurs;
- highly complex models based on unrealistic assumptions give us reliable means of valuing complicated positions and of assessing the risks they entail;
- high leverage (or borrowing) doesn't matter and is in any case tax-efficient; and
- the regulatory system or the government will protect you if some "bad apple" in the financial services industry rips you off, as happens all too often.

The invention and dissemination of Modern Financial Theory is a startling example of the ability to achieve fame and fortune through the propagation of error that becomes generally accepted. In this, it is eerily reminiscent of the work of the Soviet biologist Trofim Denisovich Lysenko, a man of modest education whose career began when he claimed to be able to fertilize fields without using fertilizer.

Instead of being dismissed as so much fertilizer themselves, Lysenko's claims were highly convenient to the authorities in the Soviet Union, and he was elevated to a position of great power and influence. He went on to espouse a theory, "Lysenkoism," that flatly contradicted the emerging science of genetics and was raised to the level of a virtual scientific state religion. Those who opposed his theories were persecuted, often harshly. Lysenko's theories of agricultural alchemy in the end proved highly damaging and indeed embarrassing to Soviet science, and Lysenko himself died in disgrace.

Of course, the analogy is not perfect: proponents of Modern Financial Theory did not rely on Stalin to promote their ideas and silence their opponents, nor did they rely on the prison camps. Instead, their critics were sidelined and had great difficulty getting their work published in top journals, so ending up teaching in the academic "gulag" of less influential, lower-tier schools. But what the two systems share in common is a demonstrably false ideology raised to a dominant position where it inflicted massive damage, and an illusion of "scientific" respectability combined with a very unscientific unwillingness to listen to criticism.

For its part, the financial services industry eagerly adopted Modern Financial Theory, not because it was "true" in any meaningful sense (as if anyone in the industry really cared!) but because the theory served the interests of key industry groups. After the investment debacles of 1966–74, investment managers wanted a scientific-seeming basis to persuade clients to entrust their money to them. The options and derivatives markets, growing up after 1973, wanted a mechanism to value complicated positions so that traders could make money on them. Securities designers wanted mechanisms by which their extremely profitable derivatives-based wrinkles could be managed internally and sold to the public. Housing securitizers wanted a theory that reassured investors and rating agencies about the risks of large packages of home mortgages, allowing those packages to get favorable credit ratings. Back-office types and proprietary traders wanted models that would provide plausibly high values for the illiquid securities they had bought, allowing them to be marked upwards in financial statements and provide new profits and bonus potential. Most of all, Wall Street wanted a paradigm that would disguise naked rent seeking as the normal and benign workings of a free market.

With this level of potential support, it's not surprising that Modern Financial Theory was readily adopted by Wall Street and became dominant there, even though crises as early as 1987 demonstrated that it was hugely flawed. It didn't hurt that, in parts of the business, the universal adoption of Modern Finance techniques tended to validate them, as options prices arbitraged themselves towards their Black-Scholes-Merton value, for example. After 1995, the loosening of monetary conditions for a time created an apparently eternal "Great Moderation" bull market environment in which Modern Finance techniques appeared to work well, but then broke down completely when they were really needed.

Nevertheless, for those with open eyes, it has been apparent for some time that Modern Financial Theory wasn't delivering what was promised on its behalf. The industry was benefiting, to be sure: its remuneration skyrocketed, and perhaps that had something to do with its expanding share of GDP. But what about everyone else? What exactly were these new financial services that were benefiting us all? More credit than we could afford to repay? Subprime mortgages? Unwelcome cold calls at dinner time from our bank pestering us to buy expensive "products" we didn't want? Or, at the corporate level, credit derivatives perhaps? And if risk management was working so well, why were there so many risk management disasters over the last two decades? Something was going wrong.

For a long time the problems were explained away or swept under the rug, and critics were dismissed as coming from the fringe: if you held your nose and didn't look too hard at what was going wrong, you could perhaps still just about persuade yourself that it really was working. Occasional problems were, after all, only to be expected.

But there eventually came a point where denial was no longer an option: as institution after institution suffered unimaginably unlikely losses in 2007 and 2008 and much of the banking system simply collapsed, the edifice of Modern Financial Theory (and especially Modern Financial Risk Management) collapsed with it.

And, to any flat-earther who denies what is self-evident to everyone else, we would ask: if the events of 2007–08 do not constitute a failure of Modern Financial Theory, then what exactly would?

Yet, even after this debacle, Modern Financial Theory remains in daily use throughout Wall Street. Its models are still used to manage investments, value derivatives, price risk, and generate additional profits, just as if the crash had never happened. Needless to say, this refusal to recognize reality is deeply unhealthy, although the costs will probably be borne yet again by taxpayers and the global economy in general rather than by Wall Street's denizens themselves. A new paradigm is urgently needed.

The second belief system that led to financial disaster is one which celebrates the benefits of state intervention into the economy. Of course, there are many such belief systems, but the one most directly relevant when seeking to understand the current financial crisis is Keynesian economics. The "defunct economist," in this case, is Keynes himself.

Keynesian economics came to dominate economic thinking in the 1930s, as people tried to come to terms with the calamity of the Great Depression. It maintained that the free market economy was inherently unstable, and that the solution to this instability was for the government to manage the macro economy: to apply stimulus when the economy was going down, and put on the brakes when it was booming excessively.

In his *General Theory*, Keynes explicitly put himself in the dubious tradition of the monetary cranks, the "funny money" merchants of old, who had been dismissed before then. He sneered at the Gladstonian notion that the government should manage its finances like a household and instead offered a macroeconomics founded on paradox – in particular, the "paradox of thrift," a notorious idea infamously espoused by Bernard Mandeville in his *Fable of the Bees: or, Private Vices, Publick Benefits* (1714) that caused great offence when it was first suggested and was aptly described later as a cynical system of morality made attractive by ingenious paradoxes. The gist of it was that we can somehow spend ourselves rich. Keynes not only resurrected the idea and made it "respectable," but enthroned it as the centerpiece of his new theory of macroeconomics.

Keynes liberated us from old-fashioned notions about the need for the government to manage its finances responsibly, inadvertently perhaps also paving the way for the more recent belief, widespread before the current crisis, that we as individuals didn't need to be responsible for our own finances either.

Keynesianism ruled the roost for a generation or more. In practice, Keynesian policies almost always boiled down to more stimulus, typically greater government spending and/or expansionary monetary policy.

The result was inflation, low at first, but by the late 1960s a major problem. Keynesianism never really came to terms with this problem, and its most significant attempt to do so – the treacherous Phillips curve, interpreted by Keynesians as a trade-off between inflation and unemployment – was refuted by Milton Friedman in his famous presidential address to the American Economics Association in 1967. In the long term, no such trade-off existed.

Yet policymakers were reluctant to embrace Friedman's position that bringing inflation down required tight monetary policy – lower monetary growth and higher short-term interest rates – which was likely to produce short-term recession as a side effect. Policymakers were hooked on "stimulus." In any case, if inflation ever did get out of hand, they could always apply brute force or wage and price controls to contain it, and they ignored the warnings of Friedman and his monetarist followers that controls wouldn't work either.

Keynesian economics reached the apogee of its influence after World War II in both the United States and Britain, then ran into serious trouble in both countries after 1970. After the 1970s' Keynesian-driven stagflation, a move towards much tighter money eventually worked. Inflation was brought down and seemed to be conquered for good.

Yet slowly, quietly, Keynesianism made its comeback. Most economists and policymakers had never entirely given up on the idea that policy should have some element of "lean against the wind," even if they acknowledged that "old" Keynesianism had gone too far. Moreover, as the memories of past inflation horrors began to dim, the Federal Reserve in particular slowly began to squander the inflation credibility it had earned with such difficulty and cost in the Paul Volcker[3] years of tight money in the late 1970s and early 1980s. In the meantime, Volcker had been replaced by Alan Greenspan,[4] who began in the mid-1990s to pursue the easy-money policy demanded by politicians and the stock market. For over a decade the Fed pushed interest rates down, and its 'accommodating' – that is to say, expansionary – monetary policy fueled a series of ever more damaging boom-bust cycles in

---

[3] Federal Reserve Chairman, 1979–87.
[4] Federal Reserve Chairman, 1987–2006.

asset markets, the worst (so far) of which culminated in the outbreak of crisis in the late summer of 2007.

More ominously, the policy response to the most acute crisis since the Great Depression was massive stimulus – deficit spending on an unprecedented scale; even more accommodating monetary policy, with interest rates pushed down to zero; and massive taxpayer bailouts of financial institutions and of the bankers who had led them to ruin. Keynesianism was now back with a vengeance. Thus, in another one of those Keynesian paradoxes, the Keynesian medicine that had helped fuel the crisis was now, in huge doses, the only solution to it. The irony was lost on most policymakers.

One of the few exceptions who didn't lose his mind in the panic was the social democrat German finance minister, Peer Steinbrück. In December 2008, he expressed the bewilderment of many when he observed how

> "The same people who would never touch deficit spending are now tossing around billions [and, indeed, much more]. The switch from decades of supply-side politics all the way to a crass Keynesianism is breathtaking. When I ask about the origins of the crisis, economists I respect tell me it is the credit-financed growth of recent years and decades. Isn't this the same mistake everyone is suddenly making again …?"[5]

Indeed it is.

Both these ideologies, Modern Financial Theory and Keynesian economics, have proven themselves vulnerable to the revenge of the gods of the Copybook Headings, in the words of Rudyard Kipling's poem. Kipling wrote it in 1919, at a time of sadness and disillusionment after losing a son in World War I. Its central theme is that whatever temporary beliefs we may acquire through market fluctuations or fashionable collectivist nostrums, eventually the old eternal truths of the children's copybook return to punish us for having departed from them:

---

[5] *Newsweek* interview, December 6, 2008, in magazine dated December 15, 2008.

"Then the Gods of the Market tumbled, and their smooth-
tongued wizards withdrew
And the hearts of the meanest were humbled and began to
believe it was true
That All is not Gold that Glitters and Two and Two make
Four
And the Gods of the Copybook Headings limped up to explain
it once more." [6]

Kipling was an instinctive economist; this verse of the poem describes
exactly how the wizards of the tech boom and the housing boom
withdrew at the peak of the market, when the gods of the Copybook
Headings reawakened and took their revenge. Traditional truths about
the market that had been thought outdated and irrelevant were then
revealed to have been in control all along.

Copybook Headings whose gods have already come back to haunt
us include the following, out of many others:

"Speculation always ends in tears." This is the oldest Copybook
Heading of all, and we have all known about this since the foolish
Tulip Mania in Holland in 1636–37, when at one point 12 acres of
prime farmland was allegedly offered for a single tulip bulb – needless to say, a painful crash followed. A recurring feature of speculative
manias is how, as the market peaks, those involved reassure themselves
that some new paradigm is now in control that guarantees that, this
time, the laws of economics no longer hold and the market can only
go up and up. We saw this at the peak of the tech bubble when "new
economy" proponents assured us that internet stocks obeyed a different set of rules, free of the constraints of old economics. The central
premise of Pets.com, that money could be made by express shipping
catfood around the US, was so risible that a moment's reality therapy
should have exposed it, but there was no reality in that market. We
saw it again in 2006–07, when believers in the Great Moderation fal-
lacy assured us that the vagaries of the business cycle had finally been
conquered, shortly before a very immoderate crisis broke loose. The
god of this Copybook Heading is particularly powerful and vengeful,
with a long memory.

---

[6] First published in the *Sunday Pictorial*, October 26, 1919.

"Whoever makes a loan has responsibility if it goes wrong afterwards." One of the most important gods of traditional banking, this one was widely flouted in the securitization markets, in which loan originators were able to escape responsibility for poor credit decisions. The result was an orgy of poor housing lending, involving not simply poor credit decisions but outright fraud, connived in by loan originators who collected their fees and passed the fraudulent paper on to Wall Street and international investors. In this disaster, Wall Street was self-deluded, drunk with excessive money supply, aided and abetted by mortgage brokers whose ethics would have made used-car salesmen blush.

"Don't take risks that you don't understand." Flouted openly in most bubbles, this god was drugged during this one by perverted science, most egregiously, by "Value-at-Risk" risk management methods, which controlled risk just fine provided that the markets involved were not in fact particularly risky.

"The maximum safe leverage is 10 to 1 for banks and 15 to 1 for brokers dealing in liquid instruments." This Copybook Heading was widely ignored, most openly by investment banks operating at leverage ratios of over 30 to 1 by the end of 2007, the sin made worse by banks hiding their risks by pushing assets off their balance sheet by use of "structured investment vehicles" funded by commercial paper that was apt to become illiquid when most needed. This god's revenge is traditionally very painful and is proving so again.

"Investments should be recorded in the books at the lower of cost or market value until they are sold." This time around the accounting profession adopted "mark-to-market" accounting, which allowed investments to be "marked up" on rises in value, with mark-up earnings reported and bonuses paid even when the investments had not been sold. Wall Street is now bleating about "mark-to-market" because it requires mark-downs of investments that have fallen in value; the real reason why it should be dropped is its enabling of spurious mark-ups, of which the Street took full advantage. Mark-to-market is highly pro-cyclical and provides counterproductive incentives to fallible and greedy bankers. But as this Copybook Heading god is rather young and junior, it is not yet clear how severe his revenge will be.

"Don't inflate broad money much faster then real GDP." This very mild version of the Sound Money Copybook Heading seeks to ensure stable prices and suppress asset bubbles. It was followed by Paul Volcker and by Alan Greenspan in his first seven years in office, then abandoned in early 1995, since when money supply has soared ahead of real GDP. Its abandonment resulted in series of asset bubbles, the more dangerous of which was that in housing because of the debt involved. Its god is something of a Rip Van Winkle, having allowed 12 years of misbehavior whilst he slept soundly from 1995 to 2007, but is exceptionally powerful and malignant when roused, as we discovered in 2008, but may need to learn again.

"Save for a rainy day." One of the oldest and most venerable Copybook Headings, this articulates the notion that long-term prosperity requires that we restrain our impulse to spend everything today, and be especially careful about living on credit. Keynes and his followers took particular delight in teasing its god with their arguments that prosperity required spending rather than saving. This god is famously slow to anger, but his revenge is devastating when it comes: his specialty is a disappearing act, when all that credit-fuelled prosperity suddenly vanishes and those who defy him discover to their dismay that they are thrown out on their ears, stark naked, like Adam and Eve expelled from the Garden of Eden.

As well as the above gods, whose revenge has already become partly or fully apparent, recent events have flouted further Copybook Headings that will in due course no doubt produce further retribution:

"Allow capital to flow to its most productive uses." This Heading is always flouted during bubbles, when capital is allocated to innumerable unproductive dotcoms or ugly undesirable McMansions. It is sometimes also flouted during downturns, when the government rescues failing industries, devoting capital to the dying and unproductive. Examples abound, notably in Britain in the 1960s and 1970s and in France in the 1980s and 1990s. In the present crisis, there is not just the $700 billion debt bailout, but the $400 billion rescue of Fannie Mae and Freddie Mac, the $50 billion rescue of the automobile industry, and the clearly impending bailouts of overseas governments and various states and municipalities in the US to be considered. In downturns, capital is especially scarce; hence flouting this Copybook Heading during a downturn produces a much nastier revenge by its god, killing off far more new and productive investments than it would in a boom and slowing long-term economic growth to a crawl.

"Keep the fiscal deficit to a level that prevents the public debt/GDP ratio from rising." This, originally propounded by Gordon Brown, when UK Chancellor of the Exchequer and before his recent apostasy, for which he will certainly be called to account, is the wimpiest possible version of the Copybook Heading warning against budget deficits. The stricter and more substantial versions of Gladstone's time mandated low levels of government debt and prohibited deficits altogether. The Brownian version is the bare minimum, and even that is defied now more than ever before, both in the short term through $1 trillion plus deficits from recession and bailouts and in the long term through the actuarial problems in Social Security and Medicare. The revenge of this god is exquisitely cruel; he turns the country into Argentina.

We can speculate why the last decade has seen such a record level of Copybook Heading flouting. Maybe the Baby Boom generation, who have been in charge, were affected so badly by the permissive theories of Dr. Spock and the "flower-power" 1960s that rejecting conventional wisdom in the form of the Copybook Headings became second nature to them. But be that as it may, the gods are clearly not happy and, as the Chinese might say, there are interesting times ahead.

In the remainder of this book, we will begin with history, move on to financial analysis, show how the theory intersected the reality, add the element of monetary policy, and demonstrate how the result was market chaos and meltdown. Having anatomized the disaster, we will suggest some solutions, theoretical, institutional, and practical, as well as examining the financial services business's likely future.

The next two chapters are historical. Chapter 2 looks at the traditional financial system, in London and New York, and discusses why it worked, in particular what mechanisms it had to ensure its long-term continuance and the financial system's overall stability. Chapter 3 anatomizes previous market meltdowns, drawing lessons as appropriate that throw light on recent events and on our current situation. Current difficulties have their reflections in past crises, and anatomizing a broad range of such crises is the best way to analyze the present. Useful past history is *not* limited to the Great Depression.

Part Two is the analytical core of the book. It begins (Chapter 4) by setting out the principles of Modern Financial Theory, along with a light-hearted gallery of the financial alchemists involved, seven Nobel prizes and all. It then (Chapter 5) examines the assumption flaws underlying the theories, why they were unrealistic, and why their lack of realism caused the theories themselves to be hopelessly fallible when applied in practice. Finally (Chapter 6), this section examines the theory of risk management, that new science, whose principles were derived from Modern Financial Theory, which gave practitioners and regulators alike a spurious sense that all was rationally controlled. Since the theories underlying risk management techniques were themselves flawed, risk management likewise broke down. Indeed, commonly practiced modern risk management turned out to be a perfect paradigm of error, focusing risk managers' attention away from the periods during which major risks arose, and failing utterly when it was most needed.

Part Three examines the interaction of theory and practice, how modern financial theory migrated to Wall Street, and why it was given vastly more attention and resources than is granted to most professorial maunderings.

The first chapter (7) details changes in the business environment from the 1960s that both accompanied the introduction of Modern Finance and made the financial services business especially receptive to it. Chapter 8 details the process by which sector after sector of Wall Street found elements of modern theory exceedingly useful, whether as sales techniques, as spuriously precise valuation methodologies, or as generators of new opportunities to make remarkable profits producing "products" that had little or no social value or were just downright dangerous. Chapter 9 looks at the other side of the coin – how the adoption of Modern Financial Theory modified Wall Street itself. It looks at how the incentives of Wall Street interacted with the techniques of Modern Finance and captive regulators to produce a system that enlarged risk rather than controlling it, and led to unprecedented levels of rent seeking and crony capitalism. Chapter 10 then takes a closer look at the litany of financial disasters that have occurred in Wall Street's wake.

Part Four looks at how policy, captured by Wall Street during these years, interacted with the financial markets to make matters worse. Chapter 11 looks at monetary policy, and how it metamorphosed in the last three decades, and how the long period of excessive monetary expansion since the mid-1990s fuelled a series of boom-bust cycles, so creating the perfect environment for Wall Street's excesses. Chapter

12 looks at how the regulatory system not only failed, but actively contributed to these excesses.

Part Five, Chapters 13 and 14 looks at the events of 2007–09, the bursting of the bubbles and the market, and the public reactions to that bursting. Chapter 13 also suggests alternative steps that could have been taken at various points during the crisis, which might well have mitigated the losses for taxpayers and would certainly have reduced the crisis' overall costs to the global economy. In the official responses to crisis, remnants of belief in the Modern Finance chimera mingled with anti-Wall Street populism, but there were very few practicable suggestions of how we might move towards a financial system that would actually work. In Chapter 14 we outline the nightmare scenario that will unfold if no substantial reform steps are taken.

Finally, in Part Six we turn to possible solutions. Chapters 15 and 16 return to first principles and discuss how financial alchemy might be turned into reality-based chemistry, the first chapter dealing with quantitative risk management methods, and the other with the needed institutional changes for the finance industry. Chapter 17 suggests some policy reforms to provide a legal and monetary framework within which the finance industry especially and the economy generally can be returned to health; underpinning this is the need to rein in rampant cronyism and restore the moral authority of the capitalist system. The last chapter offers some final thoughts on what we might learn from the dreadful experiences of recent years.

This book details how a misguided alchemy-like corpus of Modern Financial Theory combined with a wishful-thinking Keynesian mindset, ever present greed, and inept monetary and regulatory policy to produce a "perfect storm" of financial meltdown. Global prosperity, endangered in any case by the inexorable rise in population and the not unreasonable demands of the new billions for Western living standards, mandates that we learn deeply and permanently how to avoid a similar comedy of errors in the future.

2

Pre-Modern Finance

Finance is not naturally particularly risky, nor is it exceptionally profitable. Before the emergence of Modern Finance it was a stable, even slightly dull, activity whose institutional participants tended to last a couple of centuries and whose leaders were not exceptionally rich. As John D. Rockefeller reputedly said in 1913 when learning of the $100 million legacy of J. Pierpont Morgan, by far the greatest financier of his time: "Well, and to think that Mr Morgan was not even a wealthy man!"[1]

Before we examine today's finance, it is worth examining what finance used to be like. In doing so, we quickly notice that there are two distinct eras of "pre-Modern Finance." There was the period before 1914, when finance and trade became globalized, and there was by later standards very little government control, financial regulation or taxation. Then after a "broken" period including the two World Wars, finance revived in the late 1950s, but on a much more controlled basis, in a more protectionist and restricted world. It was also organized around the reality of very high personal tax levels in both Britain and the US. This second era lasted until roughly 1980, after which the Modern Finance revolution took hold and turned the practice of finance on its head.

---

[1] Quoted by Paul Johnson, *Forbes*, October 11, 2004.

The financial world before 1914 evolved as a system of specialists, their specialties reflecting their origins. London merchants evolved into merchant bankers, their initial role of financing international trade later encompassing the financing of overseas governments as well. British merchant banks did not, however, generally arrange finance for domestic industry – that was done primarily by brokers.

Brokers had evolved as promoters of new companies at the time of the South Sea Bubble in 1720. They, in turn, dealt with company promoters, typically small operations headed by a flamboyant personality, which later evolved into specialists.

The London Stock Market also emerged at around the same time, and the actual trading (or "market making") was done by jobbers. This split between brokers and jobbers was felt to protect market integrity, and to limit insider trading practices such as the "front running" of large investor orders.

In England, banking (the taking of deposits and making loans) was typically done by private banks. These were much the same size as merchant banks but evolved out of the wealthier domestic merchants in a community rather than out of any foreign trade connection. After their legal restriction to a maximum of six partners was removed in 1826, these banks grew in size, many of them taking advantage of the joint-stock (or limited liability) corporate form, especially after the Companies Act of 1862. The retail banks were involved in the low-complexity end of the business, since their principal functions were to act as risk-free homes for deposits and to finance local businesses.

In the United States, the large agglomerations of capital necessary for private banking did not exist outside the international trading community. Thus joint-stock banks on the British model, primarily oriented to retail business, never became very important. Instead, the merchant banks did both banking and broking (or issue business), and the distinction between banks that took retail deposits and banks that did primarily issue business never became so firm. So, for example, both J.P. Morgan (with a few retail clients) and First National Bank (the nucleus of Citigroup, which had a large international branch network quite early) combined some level of retail banking services with a full range of wholesale banking services. Making markets in shares, however, was in New York as in London separate from the sales function, being carried out by specialists in the New York Stock Exchange.

Other countries had somewhat different models. Paris, the third leading financial centre of the period, had "banques d'affaires" that were involved in venture capital to an extent unimaginable among the London merchant banks or even in New York. The result was a less well developed public equity market, than in the other two centers, but a financial system that if anything was rather better at developing new industrial and infrastructure ventures.

Nevertheless there was a considerable commonality about the division of labor in all three centers. All three had leaders – the merchant banks in London, the leading "universal" banks in New York, and the banques d'affaires in Paris – who arranged deals and essentially ran the system. In all three centers the brokerage function – matching buyers and sellers in securities – was regarded as secondary. And in all three centers retail banking – the taking of deposits and the making of domestic loans – was regarded as a backwater, considerably less well remunerated and less well regarded than the more dashing deal arrangement function.

At this distant perspective, it is clear that the nineteenth century had two pre-eminent financiers, at opposite ends of the century: Nathan Meyer Rothschild (1777–1836) and John Pierpont Morgan (1837–1913). Finance evolved considerably between their eras, but both were revolutionary in their impact on its practice. It is therefore instructive to examine their careers in a little more detail.

Rothschild, the son of the Frankfurt banker Mayer Amschel Rothschild (1744–1812), began in the textile business in Manchester, then in 1804 moved to London and began dealing in foreign bills, government bonds, and gold. He and four brothers coordinated a system of money transfers across the continent of Europe during the latter stages of the Napoleonic wars. After the war, he used his brothers' international network to push Barings from its previous position of pre-eminence and establish Rothschilds as the leading house in continental bond finance, as well as in the trade finance in which his house specialized.

Morgan was also the son of a successful banker, Junius Spencer Morgan (1814–1891) a New England merchant who took over the London merchant bank that became Morgan Grenfell. He began in 1860 as New York agent for his father's firm, then in 1871 formed a partnership with the Drexels of Philadelphia, which after 1893 he controlled outright, renaming it J.P. Morgan & Co. He made his initial fortune through bullion dealing during the US Civil War, then moved into railroad finance, where he was active in a number of reorganizations.

After 1880, Morgan moved from railroads into industrial finance, carrying out the merger that formed General Electric in 1892 and the merger that became US Steel in 1901. During the financial crisis of 1895, he bailed out the US Treasury by arranging a syndicate that provided it with a gold loan of $65 million. Most famously – and this was before the advent of the Federal Reserve System, when the US had no central bank – he played the leading role in ending the Panic of 1907 when he orchestrated the rescue of the New York trust banks and arranged the emergency sale of the Tennessee Coal, Iron and Railroad Company to US Steel.

Both Rothschild and Morgan bore certain resemblances to modern investment bankers or hedge fund managers. Both employed leverage to great effect. Both were expert insider traders, who did not hesitate to engage in "principal trading" for their own account as they arranged deals. They also leveraged their knowledge of corporate operations, political and military developments and funds flows to make profits that were unavailable to less-informed outsiders.

Today, by contrast, insider trading on corporate information is illegal, but insider trading based on inside knowledge of political developments remains common in the shadowy "crony capitalism" nexus between finance and government. As for insider trading based on knowledge of funds flows, now mechanized through computerized "automated trading programs," it has become one of the most important profit sources for the market leaders.

In one way, Rothschild but not Morgan resembled his distant successors. Rothschild's business was oriented much more towards markets than most merchant bankers of his day or the succeeding century, and he did not finance industrial companies except in their short-term trading activities. Hence client relationships played only a modest role in his activities. There was however one notable exception: his activities for the British government in ensuring the bullion flow to pay the Duke of Wellington's armies in the Peninsula required close relationships with the War Office and the Treasury, and were sufficiently well known as to make his name in Britain and also make a considerable portion of his fortune.

For Morgan, by contrast, client relationships were paramount. He would have been unable to put together General Electric and U.S. Steel without a network second to none, and client service was his principal raison d'être. Morgan was a consummate market operator, but his market operations almost always had a client-driven rationale and a clear industrial logic. Above all, Morgan emphasized the quality of the advice he gave: this was key to getting deal mandates, which were the principal drivers of his firm's profits. His advice was also much sought after, and those who sought it included a succession of Presidents, British prime ministers and other international statesmen, and the titans of American industry.

One key difference between Rothschild and Morgan and their modern equivalents was the time horizon on which they operated. For Rothschild, this was partly a matter of technology; as a major trader and trade financier, he was constrained by the limited communications of the day. Nevertheless his strategic sense in building up his business and in developing client relationships indicated that his priority was not next quarter's profit, but to build a business that his descendants could take over. For Morgan, the long time horizon was even more explicit. By his time, communications had improved, so that instantaneous transmission of information across the Atlantic was possible. Nevertheless he worked closely with his father in his earlier years and his son in later years to build the power of the Morgan house, and create a bank with a market position that would outlast him for a very long time.

Another difference was that Morgan and Rothschild both relied on remuneration structures that were economically rational, in the sense that their incentives were much better aligned with those of the outside capital they deployed. Even if they got free shares in deals, there was no question of "incentive compensation" payouts until deals were finally sold. Nor was there any question of them taking a share of the profits in the good times whilst avoiding the losses in the bad, in the way of a modern private equity fund or hedge fund.

But probably the most important distinction between Rothschild and Morgan and their modern counterparts was the partnership structure of their operations, and consequent unlimited liability. In Rothschild's time, limited liability was very restricted indeed; an Act of Parliament was necessary to obtain it. For Morgan, limited liability was an option, but one of which he did not avail himself either in

New York or London. When Morgan Grenfell was reorganized in 1909 it remained a partnership, with the New York house being a 50% partner. Even in New York, where the major commercial banks with which Morgan competed had limited liability, Morgan still chose to keep the partnership form.

Both Rothschild and Morgan had full liability for their risks, and this liability extended to their own personal fortunes. Nineteenth century bankruptcies such as Pole Thornton in 1825 demonstrated the harsh reality of this liability: there was no safety net for either the bank or its partners if things went badly wrong. They were therefore highly unlikely to take on businesses that produced short-term profits with the danger of major long-term risks to the institution. And, of course, their willingness to bear the risks of unlimited liability was a key factor in reassuring their counterparties that their money would be well looked after.

Finally, Morgan and Rothschild employed the ethos of "gentlemanly capitalism" in which their word was trusted, and they expected business partners to be trustworthy as well. They took the motto "My word is my bond" with deadly seriousness. For his part, Rothschild realized that a reputation for probity was essential and he fought the anti-Semitism common at the time to establish a business that was highly ethical by contemporary standards and grudgingly acknowledged as such. Morgan's ethos of gentlemanly capitalism was most famously expounded in his exchange with Samuel Untermyer, counsel to the 1912 Pujo Committee, at the end of his life:

> Untermyer: Is not commercial credit based primarily on money or property?
> Morgan: No sir, the first thing is character.
> Untermyer: Before money or property?
> Morgan: Before money or anything else. Money cannot buy it. ... Because a man I do not trust could not get money from me on all the bonds in Christendom.[2]

It was a maxim that today's bankers could usefully follow.

---

[2] Quoted in Chernow, 1991, p. 154.

The (fairly) free market financial system came to an abrupt end on the outbreak of war in 1914. The governments of belligerent countries promptly suspended the gold standard and took control over their countries' financial systems for war purposes. After 1918, Britain no longer had the financial strength to act as entrepôt of the world, and the Bank of England restricted British houses in their international lending.

Their internationally inexperienced cousins in New York were happy to fill the gap and seized former British clients in Latin America and Europe with enthusiasm untempered by much prudence. Inevitably, they overreached themselves and, when the next downturn happened after 1929, the result was mass defaults, and a subsequent refusal by US investors to place money overseas. With the US running massive protectionist trade surpluses in the 1930s and Britain unwilling to lend outside its Empire, the system of international finance seized up altogether. The new crisis also brought down the partially restored gold standard of the 1920s, and the resulting exchange rate instability added further to the miseries of the 1930s.

But not all developments after 1914 were unhealthy. In Britain, the London merchant banks, restricted from international lending, began to take a sustained interest in domestic corporate bonds and shares, so bringing them into line with their New York cousins. This was a highly desirable development; in the era of the company "promoters" before 1914 new British companies had been forced to run a terrifying gauntlet of shysters and conmen before they could establish themselves properly on the Stock Exchange. Only a few major names, such as Guinness, floated by Barings in 1886 with immense success, had managed to circumvent this decided deterrent to public listing. In addition, though international lending remained restricted, domestic debt and equity markets were active after the worst of the depression passed, and southern England in particular enjoyed an astonishing economic boom in the mid- to late 1930s before war came.

By comparison, the financial services business in the US was under a deep cloud in the 1930s. It was widely blamed for the 1929 stock market crash, which was itself widely believed to have been responsible for the Great Depression. (Modern scholarship has pretty decisively refuted both these claims, but they still persist.) It was also widely believed (and this is another claim rebutted by later scholarship) that banks' stock underwriting activities had led them to take excessive risks. To remedy this alleged evil, the US Congress passed the Glass–Steagall Act in 1933 splitting commercial banking (that is, deposit-taking) from investment banking (or stock underwriting).

Unfortunately, no thought had been given as to where investment banks would get their capital. Consequently the US investment banks were set up in the depth of deep depression with woefully inadequate capital, a problem that would persist until the 1970s. Investment bank undercapitalization had baleful results; the volume of new corporate financings, debt, and equity in the New York market was much lower in the late 1930s than at the depths of the early 1920s recession[3] – the investment banks simply didn't have the ability to take substantial risk, never mind the appetite. Indeed, this shortfall in corporate issue volume, caused by misguided government action, must bear some of the blame for the US Great Depression's extraordinary persistence.

As well as splitting the commercial banks, the 1930s reforms in the US distorted the financial system in other ways, some of which were to have baleful consequences decades later. The new Securities and Exchange Commission (SEC), set up in 1934, bureaucratized the issue process, adding to its costs and intensifying the issue drought caused by Glass–Steagall. It also established the superficially appealing but in fact highly damaging principle of "investor protection." The Federal Deposit Insurance Corporation was set up in 1933, following the epidemic of bank failures in 1930–33, to ensure that consumers no longer had to worry about their banks' solvency, by insuring deposits up to $5,000. The National Housing Act of 1934 set up a parallel institution, the Federal Savings and Loan Insurance Corporation, which guaranteed the deposits of US Savings and Loans institutions to the same amount. The reassurance to depositors provided by federal deposit insurance may have helped to end the runs of the 1930s, but it introduced a huge element of "moral hazard" into banking that was to weaken banks severely later on, contributing greatly to later crises and costing taxpayers very dearly.

The New Deal also saw the creation of the Federal National Mortgage Association (Fannie Mae), originally set up to trade mortgages

---

[3] See St Louis Fed, FRASER (Federal Reserve System for Archival Research), *Federal Reserve Bulletin* 1931–40.

issued under the Federal Home Mortgage Association, but quickly becoming a mortgage guarantor. "Privatized" in 1968 and joined by its sister Freddie Mac, these agencies greatly distorted the US housing market and were to play major roles in later crises, most especially in that of 2008.

After 1945, the British financial sector was flat on its back for a decade. Not only did the country have exchange controls, preventing most international business, but commodities and options trading were also prohibited, the latter until 1958. In New York, the investment banks were heavily undercapitalized, and wholly un-oriented to international operations. Furthermore two new institutions, the International Monetary Fund and the World Bank, had been set up under the 1944 Bretton Woods Agreement. These were to take a moderate percentage of the traditional merchant banking capital raising business. They also took a huge percentage of their emerging markets advisory work, since acceptance of their advice was generally the condition not just for IMF and World Bank credit, but also for many government to government credits as well. Only the large New York commercial banks remained in place, with substantial international branch networks and the ability to lend; the 1950s were their glory decade.

Slowly, the system started to open up again, and the period from about 1955 onwards saw considerable financial innovation, the majority of which originated in London merchant banks. These innovations included Eurodollar deposits, Eurobonds, syndicated loans, currency swaps, contested takeovers, and floating rate notes. The model that evolved was one where the London merchant banks and US investment banks tended to lead financings, with the big European and US commercial banks acting as co-managers.

It was thought that medium-sized houses had a comparative advantage as lead managers. Thus there was a short-lived fashion in the early 1970s for the big banks to set up "consortium banks" – medium-sized houses jointly owned by several banks – that hoped to combine the believed IQ and nimbleness of merchant banks with the placing power of large commercial and universal banks. This structure, with innovation taking place on a modest scale in medium-sized houses, the bugs being ironed out, and the big banks then scaling up new transaction types only once the innovation was seen to be sound, helped protect the system against the danger of unsafe innovations – such as the credit default swaps of the post-Millennium period – that might endanger the system as a whole.

The markets during this period operated with tight restrictions, however. With exchange controls remaining in force in Britain until 1979, there were tight restrictions on international activity by London houses. Other wealthy economies such as France and Japan had exchange controls until well into the 1980s, with the same Balkanizing effects on capital markets. In the US, by contrast, there was an Interest Equalization Tax imposed by the US authorities on holdings of non-US domiciled bonds. In addition, until 1980 the Federal Reserve controlled interest rates through regulation Q, preventing a free market growing up in bank obligations, and Glass-Steagall was to remain in force until 1999.

The most debilitating feature of the 1955–80 period was the grossly excessive level of personal taxation, combined with substantial and, in Britain, dangerous levels of inflation. In Britain, this de-capitalized the entire system. Jobbers, subject to personal tax because of their unlimited liability, went out of business at a steady rate throughout the period, and by 1980 were far too undercapitalized to make markets in the size required by the institutions. Merchant banks, by now subject to lower corporate levels of tax, nevertheless saw the value of their capital bases eroded by high inflation and the weakness of sterling. By 1980 they were reduced to minnows that, in retrospect, were doomed to be swallowed up by larger, predator banks. Thus taxation and inflation perpetrated in Britain the same disastrous erosion of the capital available for the issues market as had the Glass-Steagall legislation in the US a generation earlier. Inevitably, perhaps, the punitive levels of tax levied on merchant bank senior staff led to a slackening of effort and a resulting preoccupation with those wonderful lunches in the bank dining rooms ...

Both the financial systems of 1955–80 and 1864–1914 had a number of advantages over today's system.

First, client relationships were paramount and long-term in nature, stretching over decades. It was unnecessary for large companies to employ large financial staffs, let alone set up their finance department as a profit centre, because they knew they would do financing business with a limited number of houses, and that their most important business – large share issues and mergers – would be carried out by their lead financial advisor. Conversely, since they had a long-term relationship with that advisor, clients were confident of getting its best endeavors in deal structuring, syndication, innovative ideas, and pricing (and commission structures were generally standard, which reduced the scope for conflict). The financial system operated with far lower staffing levels than is thought necessary today, without any obvious downside in terms of lower useful output.

These long-term relationships affected investor decisions also. The largest institutional investors had long-term relationships with the issuing houses and so tended automatically to buy paper issued by those houses (though the relationship was sweetened by such investors receiving preferential allocations of "hot" deals). Investors without such close relationships nevertheless relied on the issuing house's name on the paper as a guarantee of its quality and soundness. There was less need for detailed scrutiny of the issuer's financial statements, which in the nineteenth century were in any case rudimentary. For their part, the issuing house took great care to protect its "name" in the market and to avoid issuing unsound securities, since a tarnished reputation would make it much more difficult for it to attract new clients or to sell paper in the future.

While there was always a certain amount of trading activity in merchant banks, merchant bankers regarded investment as a long-term process, and there was little pressure to make short-term market moves. In any case, in Britain in the later period, transactions carried a hefty stamp duty, making short-term trading prohibitively expensive. Insider trading was legal but limited, and was most common in the (not so respectable) "bucket shop" fringe brokerages. The major houses practiced it on occasion, but usually limited it to protect their long-term relationships with issuers and investors. When Sir Kenneth Keith said to Martin in 1978 "they're making insider trading illegal; I don't know how you *young* chaps will make any money at all,"[4] he reflected the ethos of his youthful exploits at Philip Hill Investment Trust, not those of the major (and highly respectable) merchant bank of which he was by then Chairman.

---

[4] Sir Kenneth Keith (later Lord Keith of Castleacre), personal conversation, Hill Samuel & Co. Limited Christmas party, 1978.

Products were generally simple and readily comprehensible to clients and investors alike. There were no "black boxes" spitting out estimates of pricing or valuation to be taken on trust. Indeed, since there were no readily available means to assess the value of complex financial products, such products were essentially unsalable. Innovation was generally handled by medium-sized houses (with the exception of J.P. Morgan & Co., under the great man himself) and was therefore undertaken on a moderate scale, with no danger of systemic failure from misguided product design.

In any case, until at least the 1930s, most merchant banks remained partnerships and the partnership structure created little temptation for firms to over-extend themselves through pushing innovation too hard, either in products or in clientele. A product innovation such as the credit default swap, in which the profitability was substantial but the risks more or less unlimited, could never have got started in this system. It would have needed the merchant banks to get it going, and they would have had no interest in potentially immolating their entire business and fortunes.

Large deals were arranged by the merchant banks through their network of contacts among pools of capital, including the large British and international banks, insurance companies, pension funds, and (later on) mutual funds. The merchant banks themselves took only moderate underwriting risks, in line with their capital bases, and institutions underwrote deals based on the reputation of the bank concerned and the deal flow they had seen from it.

Thus one really bad deal or a succession of sour deals could weaken a bank's underwriting capability for several years, as Barings found in the 1890s after its earlier adventures in Argentina turned sour. At the same time, the need for broad underwriting of transactions and the long-term nature of the relationships concerned helped to weaken conflicts of interest between the merchant bank's role as issuing house and investor, or between the bank and its individual partners.

Risks in merchant banks were managed by agreement between the partners, who while the partnership structure remained were jointly and severally liable. Their liability made partners very reluctant to delegate decision-making on large risks. Thus if a particular department was undertaking a large underwriting or a shareholding in respect of a takeover, the other partners would expect to know about it.

The partnership structure was undoubtedly more risk-averse than a modern behemoth corporation, but this was no bad thing; the risks taken were moderate and carefully considered. Larger risks could be taken through formal underwriting, a cumbersome and difficult process but not in most market conditions an impossible one. It also helped greatly that even in the 1970s these were relatively small and stable institutions in terms of personnel – job-hopping between the different merchant banks was both frowned upon and rare.

Remuneration was much more heavily based on salaries, with bonuses (where they existed at all) only moderate. Of course, partners earned additional remuneration from their profits share, and the re-alignment of partnership shares at regular intervals was a matter of intense interest and, doubtless, bickering. However, partnership shares were essentially collegial and long-term in nature, and partners expected to benefit from the firm's collective endeavors over the long term.

The situation was broadly comparable on the retail side. The local bank manager was a pillar of the community, and the banking profession was highly respected. You could trust your local bank manager to give you impartial advice without the suspicion that he was trying to sell you a financial product you didn't want or even need. Their customers, depositors and borrowers alike, were expected to behave financially responsibly if they were to obtain bank credit or even maintain an account. If you wanted a mortgage, you had to save up a considerable amount as a down payment and build up a long-term relationship with the bank involved, a process that could take a long time. No chance here of the "liar loans" of more recent times.

There were also important differences in the nature of the regulatory systems under which financial institutions operated. By about 1900, both Britain and the US had evolved largely informal "regulatory" (or more accurately, supervisory) structures, in which lead institutions and key figures provided an oligarchic leadership that called the shots without formal regulatory powers. It was taken for granted that the big institutions had public duties even though they were private institutions.

In both countries, a banking crisis would be resolved by the leading player or players either allowing a weak institution to fail (as Overend Gurney & Co was allowed to fail in London in 1866) or calling on other members to assist in an orchestrated rescue (as in the Bank of

England's "lifeboat" rescue of Barings Bros in 1890, or J.P. Morgan's handling of the crisis of 1907).

The weakness of the system was that it created the potential for moral hazard – institutions might take risks in the expectation of being bailed out if they got into difficulties – but the system worked well by modern standards, and the leaders of these banking "clubs" sought to control moral hazard (with some success, too) by limiting access to the club to "respectable" institutions who knew how to obey the club's informal "rules." Membership of the club was a much sought-after privilege.

The US soon moved away from this informal club approach, first with the foundation of the Federal Reserve System in 1914 and then with the establishment of the great federal regulatory bodies such as the FDIC, the FSLIC, and the SEC in the 1930s. These bodies, with their vast rigid rulebooks and formalized intervention into the market (for example, in the form of deposit insurance and investor protection rules), were to be the pattern for more modern times.

In Britain, by contrast, the informal bank club approach continued for a long time. The towering figure was the Governor of the Bank of England who, it was said, would merely have to waggle his eyebrows to express disapproval, thereby bringing even the chairmen of the largest banks, the clearing banks, into line, even though by this time the resources of the clearing banks were vastly bigger than those of the Bank itself.

The Bank's powers over the system was demonstrated by its success in orchestrating the rescue of Barings in 1890. When the unexpected news came in November 1890 that the (still) great house of Barings was in imminent danger of default, the Governor of the Bank, William Lidderdale, quickly called a meeting of the leading London financial institutions and persuaded them to participate in a fund to guarantee Barings' liabilities. The market soon settled down when news of the rescue operation was announced.

But what is interesting here is how the Bank persuaded the other banks to participate, against the interests of their own shareholders. In this context, there is a City tradition that the chairman of one of the joint-stock banks later had second thoughts and attempted to renege on his obligations under the agreement. Lidderdale, with characteristic decisiveness, promptly summoned him and informed him that if he did not adhere to the agreement he would close his bank's account with the Bank and announce the fact to the London evening newspapers, giving him an hour to make up his mind. The poor man gave the matter further thought and then decided that perhaps his shareholders wouldn't mind so much after all.[5]

A further innovation in the British banking club system was the establishment of the Accepting Houses Committee in 1914, the membership privileges of which included the assurance of their "acceptances" (trade bills) being guaranteed by the Bank of England.

Membership of the Accepting Houses Committee was a privilege that was jealously guarded. It was granted only grudgingly to S.G. Warburg in 1957, when it bought the Accepting House Seligman Brothers,[6] and to Harry Kissin when he merged Lewis and Peat with the Accepting House Guinness Mahon in 1972.[7] Only after an eight-year delay did Kenneth Keith at Philip Hill, Higginson gain entry in 1959.[8] When Edward du Cann, already Chairman of the 1922 Committee of the Conservative Party and soon to feature prominently in Margaret Thatcher's elevation to political power, requested membership for Keyser Ullmann in 1973 he was rejected altogether.[9] ("They do not like some of your colleagues," as Sir Leslie O'Brien, Governor of the Bank of England, bluntly told du Cann.) Only the most reputable were allowed into the sanctum sanctorum.

The Bank's control over the system stemmed from privileges of membership and the Bank's ability to withhold it. The Bank and the AHC then used the system to stiffen behavioral rules of conduct and offset the problem of cowboys and heavily capitalized outsiders weakening the bonds of mutual trust and common principles of conduct on which the London market was based. The AHC system also helped to offset the funding cost disadvantage of the medium-sized houses, the natural homes of innovation, compared to the large deposit banks.

However, the system was also an attempt to counter the increasing internationalization of the London market. When its time came, it was

---

[5] Powell, 1915, pp. 526–7.
[6] Kynaston, 2002, p. 80.
[7] Ibid., p. 124.
[8] Ibid., p. 240.
[9] Ibid., p. 491.

rapidly swept away by the forces unleashed by the "level playing field" reforms of the 1980s and the intrusive regulatory reforms of the Financial Services Act of 1986. The old City of London – the old firms of jobbers and brokers, the old money market firms and the independent investment banks – was gone.

3

Lessons from Past Financial Crises

Much commentary on the 2007–09 financial crisis and subsequent recession has compared it with the Great Depression of the 1930s. Indeed, the intent to avoid a repetition of that event was the intellectual inspiration behind the policies of Fed Chairman Ben Bernanke. However, the analogy is simplistic: recent events bear little resemblance to the Great Depression, either in their causes or their denouement.

In analyzing the recent events, it is much more fruitful to look at the broader range of major crises since the emergence of financial markets 300 years ago. Examination of these crises reveals some unexpected parallels to recent events. We find that there are distinct types of crises, some centering on the stock market, others on banking or liquidity problems, others on the financial consequences of macroeconomic policies or shocks, and a few involving more than one or even all of these elements.

The reactions of political leaders and policymakers to financial crises are often blinkered by their own limited sense of history. If they learn from history at all, they learn from relatively recent crises, or from major events still close to living memory, but ignore lessons that can be learned from foreign crises, while regarding those of a century and more ago as being too distant to be relevant. Thus, Bernanke himself is only too willing to take lessons from the Great Depression, but has learned little from the Japanese crisis of 1990 or the British crisis of 1973–74, even though they are more relevant to recent events.

As we look through the history of financial crises, we see a number of recurring themes – the impacts of rampant speculation, government involvement or poor governmental responses, misguided monetary policies, ill-designed regulation and misunderstood new financial technology, as well as the oft-repeated failure on the part of policy-makers and legislators to draw the appropriate lessons from painful experiences. Perhaps the biggest mistake repeatedly made is the belief that crises require more rather than less government involvement. On the contrary, the historical record suggests that government responses to crises have often contributed greatly to them and sown the seeds of further problems down the road.

We propose to discuss the financial crises of the last three centuries in reverse order. This will lead readers from the more familiar to the less familiar, in terms of technology, thought processes and regulatory environment. By establishing the characteristics of recent crises, parallels with forgotten ones will be illuminated, while the unfamiliarity of the technological, social, and economic environment in earlier crises will be less obtrusive.

★★★

The most recent financial crisis large enough to be reasonably compared with the 2007–08 meltdown was the bursting of the Japanese stock market and real estate bubble in 1990.

Japan had enjoyed remarkable economic growth for 40 years before its 1990 crash, with only one minor interruption at the time of the 1974–75 oil crisis. The rapidity with which Japan bounced back from that crisis was itself a testimony to the resilience of the Japanese economy, already wealthy and more dependent than any of its competitors on imports of Middle Eastern oil. In the ebullient markets of the late 1980s, Japanese equities seemed a one-way bet.

So did Japanese real estate. The settlable area of the Japanese archipelago was limited – not least by numerous laws limiting redevelopment – and the Japanese population was at that stage still increasing quite rapidly.

Throughout this period, the Bank of Japan kept interest rates low in an effort to slow the currency's inexorable rise, and there was little danger of inflation with productivity increases so rapid and the currency appreciating in world markets.

With interest rates and spreads low, the ability of Japanese borrowers to service mortgages soared, and real estate prices soared to an even greater extent. By late 1989, according to one well-publicized calculation, the grounds of the Imperial Palace in Tokyo, at prevailing real estate values, were worth more than the entire state of California. The Tokyo real estate industry then came up with a global first – the 100-year mortgage, the only way by which a Japanese "sarariman" (salaryman, or less politely, corporate wage-slave) could service the mortgage on a small Tokyo apartment costing $1 million or more – a sure sign of impending problems. It is perhaps no wonder that the Japanese "sarariman" became prone to "karoshi," death by overwork.

For their part, Japanese banks were highly liquid after the early 1980s, while Japanese exporters had become less dependent on bank sources of capital as stock markets and international bond markets had opened up to them. Bank capital had steadily increased, as most Japanese banks had large shareholdings in client companies that could be sold at a profit to increase capital and produce whatever earnings were deemed desirable.

On the corporate side, growth in reported profits was necessary to boost stock prices, and the stock price growth became a matter of intense competition in prestige. At the same time, traditional valuation metrics were held to be irrelevant – most Japanese companies at this time did not publish consolidated accounts, so profit figures were easily manipulated and highly unreliable. All this fed into stock market speculation, the funding for which could be obtained exceptionally cheaply from international markets, where investors would accept bond issues with equity warrants at near-zero interest rates, and the cost of the warrants was not at that time expressly reflected in financial statements. Hence conservative companies could issue warrant-bonds and invest in conservative long-term bonds; aggressive companies could issue warrant-bonds and invest in the stock market. Either way, profits could be reported, thereby increasing the issuing company's stock price and further feeding the stock market boom.

This simple process was dressed up as "zaitech," in effect speculative financial engineering, and a number of companies formed separate
"tokkin" funds to increase the funding for stock market speculation.
With accounting slack and over-flexible, profits from "zaitech" activity were much easier to achieve, legitimately or illegitimately, than
profits from regular operations.

This combination of market gambling and slack accounting was
to prove lethal after the markets finally turned down in 1990. Many
Japanese banks responded to the downturn by looking to financial engineering to hide their losses and postpone the day of reckoning. They
were soon desperate for derivatives transactions that would allow them
to generate paper profits before tax-year end to disguise their losses;
it was someone else's problem down the road when the real losses
emerged and the skeleton fell out of the closet years later. Notable
among these was an alleged deal involving Morgan Stanley nicknamed
the MX, after Ronald Reagan's favorite toy. Like a rocket, this landed
on the bank's balance sheet where it generated an instant paper profit,
but was programmed to blow up some twenty years later when the
underlying hidden, but by then much greater, losses would reveal
themselves. It cost the client a fortune – and was said to be Morgan
Stanley's most profitable deal to date – but the client was delighted.[1]

The length of the downturn, unprecedented in global economic
history outside pathological cases such as Argentina, was largely determined by the volume of bad assets accumulated in the bubble, and by
the reluctance of Japanese banks, companies, and regulators to own up
to their losses – as a result of which, those old toxic assets continue to
haunt the Japanese economy twenty years later. Banks also had loans
against overvalued real estate, both residential and commercial, companies still had underwater "tokkin" funds, and bank capital was eroded
by the steady decline in the value of their equity stakes in companies.

The downturn itself was a slow process; the Nikkei index, which
had peaked around 39,000 on the last day of 1989, remained above
20,000 until 1993 and did not hit its final low of 7,600 until March,
2003. Gross Domestic Product growth virtually stopped for two decades, but productivity improved as rapidly as in the US, indicating the
underlying strength of Japan's economy.

---

[1] Partnoy, 1998, Chapter 10.

Japan's problems were made worse by misguided macroeconomic policies, notably an excess of fiscal "stimulus" investment in infrastructure projects. It was only after 2001, when Junichiro Koizumi forced the banks to mark their loans to market and recognize losses, that the system finally stabilized. Regrettably, the Koizumi liberalization of Japan's financial and economic system proved unpopular, at least among his own party's Diet members, so after his departure in 2006 there was considerable policy backsliding.

The depth of Japan's downturn was unexceptional; its extraordinary and debilitating length, devastating the careers of an entire generation of Japanese, was caused by two factors: a refusal to face up to reality in asset valuations, and an ill-judged interventionist policy response.

Proponents of low interest rates might also note that Japan's near-zero interest rates didn't seem to help either. Indeed, it is highly likely that low interest rates were a key factor behind the remarkable fall in Japanese savings rates after 1990s – now down almost to American levels. Far from promoting economic recovery as Keynesian macro-economics suggests, low interest rates seem to have had the opposite effect by hindering the long-term rebuilding of the Japanese financial system.

★★★

The savings and loan meltdown of 1989–91 was a somewhat more complicated occurrence, from which lessons were only partially being drawn in the crisis twenty years later. The S&Ls got into difficulty in the late 1970s, when US interest rates rose sharply as the Federal Reserve chairman Paul Volcker sought to bring US inflation back under control. The rise in interest rates, necessary in itself, was a disaster for the S&Ls, which were now paying much more on their deposits than they were getting on their mortgages. However, S&Ls were able to keep afloat by raising rates on brokered deposits, which flooded in from across the country, taking advantage of federal deposit insurance, thanks to which depositors were concerned only with the high rates on their deposits and not their risks. By the end of the tight money period in 1982, most of the S&Ls were insolvent, reduced to zombies, propped up by brokered deposits and deposit insurance, and only continuing in operation thanks to an indulgent regulator that should have been closing them down.

The Garn–St.Germain Act of 1982 then freed them from previous lending restrictions. The financial system needed to be deregulated, but in the context of deposit insurance, this measure merely increased their opportunities to gamble at other people's expense. They then went big-time into real estate lending in general, in which they had little expertise, and their losses escalated. Needless to say, a number of crooks joined in the action, bribing US Senators as they did so to keep the regulators and law enforcement off their backs.

The point eventually came where Congress had to admit that the S&Ls had to be closed down to stop losses escalating even further. Congress set up the Resolution Trust Corporation for this purpose, and appointed the chairman of the Federal Deposit Insurance Corporation, L. William Seidman, to run it. It was estimated that the cost of resolving the S&L could be $500 billion or more.[2]

It was an inspired appointment. Seidman was given until 1995 to carry out an unprecedented task with goals that were, he said, "forever in conflict": to sell the shopping centers, vacant office buildings, residential developments, and other assets of failed S&Ls quickly, for maximum value, and with minimal impact to the larger market, using an agency he had to build from scratch.

"The job combined all the best aspects of an undertaker, an IRS agent, and a garbage collector," Seidman wrote later. "Each savings and loan arrived with records in disarray, key personnel gone, lawsuits by the hundreds, and a management that was still mismanaging or had departed and left the cupboard bare."

Seidman took a market-oriented approach, selling dodgy real estate and mortgages as quickly as possible for whatever they would fetch, not worrying that their buyers might make a killing: the top priorities were to move quickly and close deals. At its peak, the RTC was sorting out about seven S&Ls a week. By the time it closed in 1995, the RTC had closed or otherwise resolved 747 institutions, with total assets of $394 billion, at a cost to taxpayers of $152.9 billion – far less than had been feared.

"What we did, we took over the bank, nationalized it, fired the management, took out the bad assets, and put a good bank back in the system," Seidman said on CNBC in January 2009, not long before he died.

---

[2] For example Silk, 1990.

As a result, the US financial system was not left burdened by use-less decaying assets, so helping the US economy to avoid Japan's fate, a long period of stagnation. Seidman's approach should form a model for future crisis resolution; it has notably not been followed by Hank Paulson or Tim Geithner in the recent unpleasantness.

★★★

The last true credit crunch was that of 1973–74, which was not con-fined to Britain but was most severe there. In May 1971, the Bank of England's Competition and Credit Control reforms had ended the ear-lier system of quantitative credit controls, with the intention of moving to a market-based allocation of credit based on market-clearing interest rates. The problem, however, was that the British monetary authorities did not know how to manage the new system; they kept interest rates too low, and bank lending (and, on the other side of the banks' balance sheets, deposits, that is to say, the money supply) began to grow rapidly. The timing of this reform was also particularly unfortunate, in that it coincided with the death throes of the Bretton Woods exchange rate system and, hence, the end of the constraints that system had earlier imposed on loose monetary policy. The Heath administration, fed up with Britain's laggardly postwar economic growth rates, was now free to embark on its disastrous "dash for growth," fuelled by massive fiscal as well as monetary expansion.

Both the large British clearing banks and the traditional merchant banks were at this time conservative institutions, not inclined to reck-less pursuit of short-term profits. However, the smaller "secondary" banks, formed in the wake of earlier banking deregulation, were dif-ferent, and soon indulged themselves in an orgy of high-risk lending, borrowing heavily in the wholesale money markets that had sprung up in the 1960s. The result was a classic bubble, encompassing the stock and especially property markets, fueled by cheap money and easy finance. By the end of 1973, the secondary banks had displaced the clearing banks as the major providers of property finance, in the process becoming heavily over-exposed to the property market, compromis-ing themselves further by running maturity mismatched books and funding fixed rate loans at variable rates.

The property market started to rumble in the spring of 1973 and international bond market conditions became difficult after June.

Meanwhile, inflation had soared, and the government belatedly responded to this problem by raising interest rates, which doubled during
the second half of 1973, reaching then unheard-of levels of 13% in
November. By the end of the year, the Bank of England had reintro-
duced quantitative controls, in the form of the Supplementary Special
Deposits scheme, appropriately known as the "Corset."

The rise in interest rates took institutions by surprise and many suffered heavy losses. A full blown liquidity crisis rapidly ensued, a "flight
to quality" in which deposits were withdrawn from the secondary
banks and re-deposited with the primary banks; the latter, too, sought
to reduce exposure to the secondary banks, whose difficulties were by
now obvious for everyone to see. The economic climate deteriorated
further the following spring when property values collapsed; and then
the stock market slumped, further depressing the market values of investment portfolios.

The secondary banks soon began to fail. The first was London and
County Securities, which went into insolvency on November 30; the
cascade of bankruptcies that followed was rapid and very severe.

The Bank of England, deeply alarmed, responded by organizing
a "lifeboat" rescue modeled on Governor Lidderdale's earlier rescue
of Barings in 1890, with the major institutions roped in as reluctant
partners. The purpose of this was to protect what was left of market
liquidity and organize an orderly liquidation of the fringe banks' portfolios. Initially, this was organized around First National Finance,
itself a secondary bank but more conservatively run than London and
County; however, within a month, First National was itself caught up
in the maelstrom. Another casualty was the homebuilder Northern
Developments, brought down less by property exposure than by its
dependence on bank lending. The scale and scope of the lifeboat operation steadily grew over the next year; at its peak no fewer than 30
banks were on life support, and at one point there was even fear that
the gigantic National Westminster Bank might go under.

The British economy had two dreadful years in 1974 and 1975,
with inflation peaking at 25%, unemployment peaking at more than a
million and deep industrial unrest, itself prompted by the Heath Government's unwise and ineffective attempts to impose wage and price
controls. This unrest led, in turn, to a damaging miners' strike and a
three-day workweek; the prime minister then called a "who governs

Britain?" election, which he lost. By the end of 1974, the country was governed by a hard-left Labour administration, the policies of which, especially its reluctance to discard policies of massive fiscal and monetary expansionism, were to take the country to the brink in 1976, when it was finally rescued by the International Monetary Fund and Keynesianism was officially abandoned.

Many people at the time felt the economy was disintegrating. The stock market seemed to agree: the *Financial Times* share index dropped from its 1969 and 1972 peaks of over 500, and around 400 in late 1973 to a low of 150 in January 1975, a drop of 70% in nominal terms and a lower level in real terms than its nadir of 40.4 after the 1940 evacuation of Dunkirk.

Overseas, a particularly unfortunate event, another by-product of the credit crunch, was the unexpected bankruptcy of the medium sized German bank I.D. Herstatt, which took place on June 26, 1974. Normally a relatively minor event such as this would have caused only a modest ripple internationally, but the German authorities foolishly closed the bank in mid-afternoon, while New York was still trading. This decision had dreadful consequences. A number of banks, including Martin's then employer the merchant bank Hill Samuel, had entered into spot foreign exchange transactions, and had paid deutschemarks into Herstatt, expecting to receive dollars from Chase Manhattan, Herstatt's New York correspondent. The dollars were never paid. This proved to be utterly destructive of international banking confidence; a period of illiquidity followed that was similar only to that after the Creditanstalt failure of 1931. Japanese trust banks, a highly solid and well-behaved bunch, were forced to borrow at 2% above LIBOR for around a year, making their funding cost 2% higher than the best US and European banks. The US banking system was also badly affected, with the Franklin National Bank, a major institution that had invented the bank credit card in 1952, being forced into insolvency on October 8, 1974.

The credit crunch persisted until the end of 1975, lasting for around two and a half years in all, and bankrupted most of the entrepreneurial financial institutions in the City of London, including notably Jessel Securities, a major fund manager, and Slater Walker, which until 1973 had been the pre-eminent financial innovator of its day. Both these firms were internationally diversified and neither was significantly involved in commercial real estate lending; nor was either aggressively run – indeed Jim Slater had begun de-leveraging a year before the crash, as he saw trouble coming – and no wrongdoing was proved against the head of either organization. Yet by the end of 1975 both very substantial companies had gone bankrupt and neither founder played a significant further role in the British financial sector. This was a great pity: in losing Jessel and Slater, Britain had lost not only their able founders but the most aggressive entrepreneurial teams in the City of London, who might have been best able to compete against the foreign invasion that took place after the British "big bang" opened the doors to the invaders in 1986.

The merchant banks were also gravely hit by the inflation of the 1970s, which halved their capital base in dollar terms, making them too small to compete effectively against larger foreign institutions. Hill Samuel's Kenneth Keith, the best long-term strategist of that generation's merchant bankers, had foreseen the problem as early as 1970, attempting to gain a larger inflation-proof capital base through merger with the real estate company MEPC. However the problem was not at that stage extreme; as of December 1973 Hill Samuel had a larger capital base than Salomon Brothers, already among the most aggressive forces on Wall Street. By 1980 the position was very different; Salomon Brothers alone made $500 million in profits in 1982, more than the entire banking and broking City of London; the British banks were now piranha fodder.

More clearly than the later crises in Japan and the United States, the British secondary banking crisis showed the debilitating effects of over-lax monetary policy. As in the US housing bubble of the 2000s, this did not produce a surge in productive investment, nor in innovation, but instead a collapse in lending standards in the most intellectually undemanding sector of the market. As in the US in 2008, the collapse was economically devastating. It was mitigated in the worst possible way by the damaging high inflation of the period, which imposed a gigantic tax on the thrifty and prudent in favor of the spendthrift and profligate, while at the same time saving the government's bacon by reflating the housing market. Americans may yet find Ben Bernanke's monetary policies imposing the same solution in 2010–12.

★★★

The financial services sector from the 1930s to 1970, in the United States and Britain, was both over-regulated and quiescent. Hence, while there were several economic downturns, none of them had a specifically financial cause. Going backwards, the next major downturn we come to is thus the Daddy of them all, the Great Depression, the poster child of Keynesian economics.

The Great Depression is still much misunderstood. Perhaps the most important reason for this was the influence of the Keynesian revolution in the 1930s and 1940s, which established the view, still widely held today, that the Great Depression was "proof" of the inherent instability of free markets, and of the need for the government to counter that instability by managing the economy through interventionist macroeconomic policy. In practice, this usually boils down to the one-sided policy prescription that the government should inject "stimulus" whenever the economy seems to be going down.

The Keynesian belief system has profoundly distorted the way in which the Great Depression is remembered and interpreted. In essence, the followers of Keynes established the simplistic myth that the Great Depression was primarily caused by the 1929 stock market crash, itself caused by excesses of speculation and inequality in the free-market 1920s, a view popularized by J.K. Galbraith in his entertaining 1954 best-seller.[3]

Yet the stock market crash itself can largely be absolved of guilt. The 50% drop in the Dow Jones index in the autumn of 1929 was no larger than several other declines, before and since. Large stock market declines, on their own, don't generally trigger Great Depressions. In any case, the 1929 stock market was not especially overvalued by modern standards. The valuation of Radio Corporation of America, the premier growth stock of the era – think Google, Cisco, or Microsoft – never got above 28 times earnings, and in terms of the economy's size the market never became anything like as overblown as Japan in 1989 or the US in 2000. The 1929 stock bubble was in itself therefore no more likely to lead to a major economic depression than the more overvalued 2000 stock bubble, or indeed the now forgotten overvalued stock bubble of 1968.

---

[3] Galbraith, 1954.

Neither were 1920s monetary and financial policies to blame. Fiscal policy of the time was exceptionally austere, producing budget surpluses, public spending decline, and steady expansion. Monetary policy was expansionary but not excessively so on domestic considerations. However, the global monetary system had been imbalanced by Britain's 1925 return to the Gold Standard at an overvalued parity, the effect of which had been to flood the New York market with London's liquidity.

A more immediate trigger for the Great Depression was the banking crash of 1930–31, which was triggered on December 11, 1930 by the collapse of the Bank of United States, the third largest bank in New York and 28th largest in the US. At this point, the Fed should have done what it was set up to do – support the financial system by expanding liquidity. Instead, it failed to do so, and the Fed's restrictive policy led to a liquidity crisis on both sides of the Atlantic, leading in May 1931 to the collapse of the Austrian bank Creditanstalt, which then triggered a major international financial crisis that culminated in Britain being forced off the Gold Standard in September. After this the pound fell in value by about 30%, relieving pressure in the London money market but increasing that in New York.

In the US, the banking crisis spread: waves of bank failures followed over the next two years, the money supply sharply declined, and the economy went into freefall. By early 1933 the crisis had become a national emergency and state after state declared banking holidays in which the banks were closed, whilst regulators hurriedly decided which ones could be safely allowed to reopen, culminating in the decision by the incoming Roosevelt administration to declare a nationwide banking holiday and temporarily shut the whole banking system down.

As the landmark work of Friedman and Schwartz[4] was later to show, the failure on the part of the Fed to support the banking system was the principal factor that turned what would have likely been a minor downturn in a major depression. However, there were many other policy responses that also greatly contributed both to the severity and the length of the downturn. During the Hoover administration, the most significant of these were the protectionist Smoot-Hawley tariff of June 1930, the Hoover tax increase of 1932, increasing the top

---

[4] Friedman and Schwarz, 1963.

marginal income tax rate from 25% to 63%, and the Reconstruction Finance Corporation's activity in propping up politically connected large corporations.

After Franklin Roosevelt became President in March 1933, further actions prolonging the downturn were the National Recovery Act of 1933, which set minimum wage levels throughout industry, the Glass-Steagall Act of 1933, which established federal deposit insurance and split the investment banks from commercial banks leaving the former hugely undercapitalized, the Wagner Act of 1935, which imposed union wage scales and restrictive practices on vast portions of industry, the Social Security Act of 1935, which sucked out premiums from the US economy for three full years before benefits began to be paid in 1940, and the ill-judged increases in Fed reserve requirements for banks in 1936 and 1937, which knocked the stuffing out of the nascent economic recovery. Despite all the hype about the New Deal, the Depression was to last into the 1940s, to be ended courtesy of the Japanese Imperial Navy when it attacked Pearl Harbor.[5]

★★★

The precedent for financial sector policymakers in 1929–33 was, or rather, should have been, the Panic of 1907. This crisis was almost entirely a banking system liquidity problem, itself a consequence of the onerous restrictions of the National Banking System legislative framework under which US banks had been operating since the Civil War. These restrictions made it difficult for the banking system to respond to seasonal increases in the demand for liquidity, leading to repeated liquidity crises that were either unique to, or much more severe in, the United States. This happened in 1873, 1884, 1890, 1893 and 1907.

In each case, money market rates suddenly rose to extraordinary heights, liquidity became extremely tight, and many vulnerable firms failed. Over time, bankers gradually evolved an effective response to these shortages of liquidity – they established clearinghouse associations

---

[5] The impacts of some of these policy errors have been cogently articulated by some of the 'revisionist' studies of the Depression. We strongly recommend, for example, Timberlake, *Monetary Policy in the United States*; Smiley, *Rethinking the Great Depression*; Powell, *FDR's Folly*; Schlaes, *The Forgotten Man*; Meltzer, *A History of the Federal Reserve, Vol. 1 (1914–1951)* and, of course, Friedman and Schwartz.

that would grant emergency loans to firms that they considered sound, whilst throwing the rest to the wolves; they also issued clearinghouse loan certificates, in effect, illegal emergency currency, which the public readily accepted and which the legal authorities tacitly condoned because even they could see that it helped allay the crisis.

At the same time, leading bankers would respond by resolving the crisis themselves. In 1907, J.P. Morgan took the lead. He decided not to rescue the Knickerbocker Trust, the failure of which was the immediate cause of the panic. Knickerbocker had been using customer deposits for speculation in the copper market, a practice of which Morgan rightly disapproved. In the tense days that followed, he arranged the takeover of the Tennessee Coal, Iron and Railroad Company by US Steel, which he effectively controlled. In so doing, Morgan injected liquidity into the system, doing what the Fed failed to do in 1930–31, so restoring confidence and ending the panic.

Effective as it was, the resolution of the 1907 crisis made the US political establishment deeply uncomfortable. They were uncomfortable with the notion that the private sector could resolve financial crises, even though it had clearly demonstrated that it could; but they were also uncomfortable with the fact that the private-sector resolution of the crisis had involved illegal private-sector emergency currency, and with the fact that Morgan's actions, though effective, had been in breach of the Sherman Anti-Trust Act. However, rather than make the emergency currency legal and repeal the Sherman Act, or even just continue to look the other way, the politicians afterwards decided that the US needed its own central bank to manage any future crisis on an "official" rather than private/illegal basis.

The new central bank, the Federal Reserve, was, nonetheless, supposed to take its lead from Morgan's response to the 1907 crisis – thus to resolve a future liquidity crisis by injecting emergency liquidity into the system. But, as we have seen, it was the Fed's failure to follow this mandate when the time came that was the key factor that turned the relatively minor downturn of 1929 into the catastrophe of the 1930s Depression.

★★★

A little earlier, on the other side of the Atlantic, we come to the first central bank bailout of a banking organization – and the first case of "too big to fail" – the (first) Barings crisis of 1890. Unlike Barings' subsequent 1995 disaster, this was not caused by new technology, nor by a rogue junior employee. Instead it was caused by Barings' premier business of sovereign bond issues, and by its Chairman, Edward Baring, first Baron Revelstoke. Revelstoke had been working at Barings since 1853, but he lacked the business judgment of his illustrious forbears, and he was personally lazy but over-aggressive, concerned to keep Barings a leader among the London merchant banks, even at risk of its capital. Sometimes Revelstoke's aggression worked, as in the initial public offering for the Guinness brewery in 1886, one of the first successful industrial IPOs led by a merchant bank. More often, it didn't.

In particular, Barings failed to exercise adequate control over the foreign borrowings of its client Argentina. It allowed its advisory duty as Argentina's merchant banker to be overridden by a plausible client seeking, as Argentina has always done, to develop its economy using other people's money rather than generating an adequate domestic savings base of its own. The resulting over-expansion then led to a downturn and a looming Argentine default. Against this background, "the appalling intelligence was [suddenly] made known that [the] great house [of Baring Brothers] was in the extremest danger of stopping payment ... and that the most energetic measures must be taken without a moment's delay to avert the catastrophe."[6]

The Governor of the Bank of England, William Lidderdale, quickly decided that a house of Barings' stature could not be allowed to default. He therefore acted swiftly to call a meeting of the leading London financial institutions, and cajoled them to participate in a fund to guarantee Barings' liabilities, with the Bank itself providing for the firm's immediate obligations. The settlement was promptly announced and the market soon settled down.

The Barings crisis was to be the first of many similar later cases, in which a financial institution was suddenly discovered to be in imminent danger of collapse, and the central bank faced a crisis that demanded immediate resolution, either by letting the institution fail or by organizing a rescue operation. The former risked a shock to market confidence and the danger of the crisis spreading, but the latter sent a bad signal for the future – that is, it signaled that banks could take risks

---

[6] MacLeod, 1896, p. 167.

and if they turned sour hope that the central bank would rescue them too from the adverse consequences of their own risk-taking. In the case of the first Barings crisis, the Bank opted for short-term damage limitation, but it was acknowledged even at the time that this had set a dangerous precedent.

The rescue of Barings meant that some banks were now (or even might in future be) considered too big or too important to fail, and the problem of how to rein in the moral hazard this created was to be a recurring (and indeed, worsening) headache in the second half of the twentieth century and beyond.

★★★

Going further back in time, we come to the quintessential bank failure of the Victorian period, the 1866 collapse of the banking house Overend & Gurney.[7]

Overend & Gurney grew out of a Norwich banking house controlled by the immensely wealthy Gurney family. It was not itself primarily a bank, but a discount house that traded bills of exchange, generally of 90 days or shorter maturity, drawn on the numerous London and country banks. It was therefore at the centre of the London money market, which was itself the centre of the London financial system, and was to remain so until the 1980s. It was a private partnership with unlimited liability until just before its demise. Under the steady management of Samuel Gurney, who died in 1856, Overend & Gurney became the most important financial institution in the London market, known affectionately as the "Corner House." It was central to the financing of British trade, which was typically financed by merchants issuing bills that were then "accepted" or guaranteed by local banks.

Discount houses tended to get into trouble during the periodic liquidity crises, such as those of 1836, 1847, and 1857. After Samuel Gurney died, the Corner House was run by his nephew, David Barclay Chapman, a man of an altogether different character. Chapman had attempted to cover up a serious loss from taking fraudulent security in

---

[7] The Overend & Gurney story is well told in Geoffrey Elliott's *The Mystery of Overend & Gurney*. Its 1857 and 1860 confrontations with the Bank of England are described in detail in Kynaston, 1995, pp. 192–202.

1853, as a result of which he was known not-so-affectionately in the City as "Gurney's Liar." In the crisis of 1857 he recklessly attempted to bring the Bank of England down by presenting large quantities of Bank notes for immediate redemption in gold, in the hope that the Bank did not have the gold in its vaults to meet those commitments. But the Bank survived and won the battle, in part by calling on the Chancellor of the Exchequer to suspend temporarily the restrictions on its note issue imposed by the Bank Charter Act of 1844, and which had made the Bank more vulnerable to attack. David Barclay Chapman was then forced into retirement, to be succeeded by his son, David Ward Chapman.

The younger Chapman was more like his father than his great-uncle. He had a lifestyle altogether flashier than most bankers of his day, with a large new house at Princes Gate, a fashionable wife, and a penchant for lavish entertaining. He was also very ambitious and, in spite of spending only five hours a day in the City,[8] he pushed the limits of Overend & Gurney's business to increase profitability.

His most dangerous diversification was into private equity investment, including a shipping line that attempted to lay the first transatlantic cable, a Greek Mediterranean shipping line of doubtful provenance, and a shipyard that built Isambard Kingdom Brunel's steamship *Great Eastern*. As usual, some of these investments were fraudulent, some were mildly promising, and some were simply unsuccessful. This move into private equity investment was financed through a highly risky innovation: he financed the entire portfolio by three-month bank bills, rolling them over frantically as necessary. (Modern Financiers: before you mock, don't forget asset-backed commercial paper or Northern Rock.) Thus, as with Northern Rock later, the company was highly exposed to liquidity risk.

Ward Chapman's other folly was to follow in his father's footsteps by taking on the Bank of England again, in 1860. After the Bank had refused to buy discount house paper from him, Ward Chapman arranged for a syndicate to withdraw £2 million of £1,000 notes from the Bank within 24 hours. There followed a sinister anonymous message to the Bank: "Overends can pull out every note you have; the writer can inform you that from their own family assistance they can

---

[8] Xenos, 1869, p. 64.

nurse *seven* millions." But again, the bold coup failed; needless to say the Bank was now thoroughly alienated. As a consequence, when Overend & Gurney began to run into real trouble, the Bank and its supporters (which comprised most of the City of London) sat on their hands and watched.

Ward Chapman then attempted to rectify Overend & Gurney's deteriorating position by a novel tactic. He took advantage of the new Companies Act of 1862 to convert the Overend & Gurney partnership into a limited company – Overend, Gurney & Co. – and float it in July 1865 through the dodgiest of the new share promoters, Baron Grant, later the model for Anthony Trollope's scoundrel Melmotte.[9] The issue was remarkably successful, however, selling 100,000 £50 shares and moving to a premium. Had the shares been fully paid up, this huge £5 million of new capital might have rescued the bank's fortunes, but regrettably following the custom of the time the shares had been issued with only 30% paid upfront. After the hefty issue commissions and expenses had been met, this provided nothing like enough new money, and so on May 10, 1866, "Black Friday," Overend, Gurney & Co. was forced to close its doors, prompting another crisis in the London money market.

The shareholders' fury at finding their ten-month old paper worthless was only compounded when the liquidators came to them and demanded subscription of the unpaid 70% of the issue amount to which they had unwisely committed themselves. Their money did however ensure that the creditors were eventually paid in full. For his part, the anti-hero of the episode, David Ward Chapman, was bankrupted and fled to the Continent to avoid the bailiffs hot on his heels.

The Overend & Gurney failure has a number of parallels with recent events. Its main protagonist led a flashy lifestyle more reminiscent of modern Wall Street than of the conservative bankers of his time (though most modern bankers don't get away with a five-hour day!). It involved misguided high-tech investment and a massive quasi-fraudulent share issue, made on the basis of questionable accounts. It was generated by a novel financing technique that was not properly understood and whose risks were poorly managed, and which led to sudden crisis when liquidity ran short. Its collapse also had important systemic

---

[9] Trollope, 1873.

effects, because of the bank's network of connections throughout the discount market.

★★★

Further back in time, we come to the most misunderstood period in US financial and monetary history: the period of the late 1830s and early 1840s, an earlier Great Depression also caused by misguided policies. This is a period that modern economists have been particularly apt to misunderstand, because most of them take the necessity of a central bank for granted and the US had no central bank after 1836. Standard textbooks dismiss this as a period when unsound "wildcat banking" flourished: crooked banks were said to issue notes redeemable "where the wildcats roamed." Their noteholders, fearful of wildcats, were then reluctant to demand redemption, and the notes would trade at heavy discounts relative to their notional par values. Both these, however – the necessity of a central bank and the characterization of the banks of the period as "wildcats" – are myths, albeit the latter an entertaining one.

The background to this period is a combination of protracted policy controversy, legal restrictions, and tight money. The controversy centered around the question of whether the federally chartered Bank of the United States should have its charter renewed. This institution is known to historians as the Second Bank of the United States, as its unfortunate predecessor, the First Bank of the United States, had expired after the renewal of its charter had been blocked in 1811. Opponents of both institutions had argued, rightly in our view, that they were unconstitutional, based on a strict interpretation of the Constitution under which the federal government had no authority to charter a bank. The most vociferous, even rabid, opponent of the Bank was the President, Andrew Jackson, who had based his 1832 re-election campaign on a platform opposed to the Bank's re-charter. The Bank War, the prolonged conflict between the President of the United States and the President of the Bank of the United States, Nicholas Biddle, went on for years.

The Second Bank was a quasi-central bank. Chartered in 1816, its notes were legal tender for all payments to the government, and it acted as the federal government's bursar and depository. Its history was however somewhat checkered. It had single-handedly triggered a previous panic early in its life, in 1819, by irresponsibly expanding credit on an unchecked basis. But it was well managed under Nicholas Biddle, President of the Second Bank from 1822, a damn good banker who in different circumstances might have created a US equivalent of Rothschilds or Barings.

In the US economy of the period, the principal advantage of Biddle's Bank was its nationwide branch network, which made its notes acceptable at par for payments across the rapidly expanding United States. Unfortunately, the Bank was also the only institution legally permitted to operate across the whole country, because all other banks were chartered by the states. State charters not only prevented them operating inter-state, but often restricted them to operate only within a single county. The state charter system was also notoriously corrupt, the charter to operate being a privilege that was often sold by state legislators.

The controversy raged against a background of tightening money, itself a partial consequence of the war between Jackson and Biddle. Specie (gold and silver) was in increasingly short supply, a shortage that would continue to intensify until the California gold discoveries of 1849. Monetary tightness in the US was intensified further by two Jackson decisions. First, he withdrew government deposits from the Bank in 1833 and re-deposited them with politically favored state banks – Jackson's "pet banks" – effectively reducing the monetary base of the time. Second, his Specie Circular of 1836 stipulated that payments for government land sales, then a huge source of government revenue, should be made in specie – the surge in demand for specie to which this led tightened money even further.

The Bank War culminated in victory for Jackson, who successfully vetoed the renewal of the Bank's charter, which lapsed in 1836.

The lapsing of the Bank's charter meant the withdrawal from the financial system of the currency that the Bank had hitherto provided, leading to a fall in the money supply of perhaps a third. This had a profound deflationary impact, and was a key contributing factor to the panic that broke out in May 1837, which led to a nationwide suspension of specie payments that lasted a number of years in some states. Notes fell to a discount against gold, and discounts varied dramatically at different times and places.

No longer could a Mississippi merchant pay for Massachusetts goods with Second Bank paper; instead he could use only his local bank paper, which traded in New York or Boston at a discount of up to 50%. It was as if the currency union between the states had been dissolved, an economically devastating event paralleling the collapse of central Europe's economy after Austria-Hungary dissolved in 1918–19 into mini-states with their own fluctuating currencies.

This monetary disruption led in turn to a huge and prolonged depression, notwithstanding a temporary recovery in 1838–39, with no fewer than eight states defaulting on their bonds in the years that followed, and innumerable bank failures, including the remnants of Biddle's Second Bank in 1841.

Milton Friedman gave a memorable assessment of these events, drawing a direct analogy to the miserable 1930s:

"The banking panic of 1837 was followed by exceedingly disturbed economic conditions and a long contraction to 1843 that was interrupted only by a brief recovery from 1838 to 1839. This Great Depression is ... the only depression on record comparable in severity and scope to the Great Depression of the 1930s, and its monetary concomitants largely duplicate those of its later mate. In both, a substantial fraction of the banks in the United States went out of existence through suspension or merger – around one quarter in the earlier and over one-third in the later contraction – and the stock of money fell by about one-third. There is no other contraction that even closely approaches this dismal record. In both cases, erratic or unwise government policy with respect to money played an important part."[10]

Many writers have suggested that Jackson's veto of the Bank's charter was a major mistake. We would suggest a somewhat differenct explanation: that the blocking of the Bank's charter, while desirable in principle, was highly questionable in a context where legal restrictions prevented other banks from providing their own nationwide branching networks and issuing their own paper denominated in the gold US

---

[10] Friedman, 1960, p. 10.

dollar and accepted across the country. In effect, the US government had given the Bank a monopoly of an important, indeed indispensable role – the provision of a nationwide payments system – and then abolished not the monopoly but the monopol*ist*, in the process plunging the country into monetary chaos.

This was a classic instance of the theory of the second best, a sadly recurring theme in the history of economic policy, in which a measure that is good in an otherwise first best world can be detrimental in a second best world. In this case, the first best would have been to have no legal restrictions and no Bank of the United States. However, keeping the legal restrictions and abolishing the Bank might well be a third best policy compared to the second best policy of keeping the Bank in the presence of the legal restrictions.

There was to be no central bank, quasi- or otherwise, until the establishment of the Federal Reserve System on the eve of World War I. For its part, from 1837 until the outbreak of the Civil War in 1861, the federal government did the monetary and financial system a great service by staying out of it. At the state level, there followed a period of experimentation, with different states experimenting with different legislative regimes – the experience of this period was that liberal regimes were broadly successful and that heavy-handed ones were not. By the eve of the Civil War, most states of the union were operating successful and stable systems of "free banking," subject to little government intervention. The infamous "wildcats" were as factual as the Loch Ness Monster.

★★★

The crisis of 1825 was England's worst ever financial crisis, at least until 2007–08, and shook the English financial system to its core; by contrast, Scotland, with its relatively free banking system, was hardly affected. It took place against a restrictive legislative environment in which English, though not Scottish, banks were limited to partnerships of no more than six partners each, a restriction intended to enhance the monopoly privileges of the Bank of England, but which made English banks, especially outside London, artificially small and vulnerable.

One cause was excessive speculation in the early 1820s in what might be called "subprime" South American bond issues, including one "liar loan" bond issue in 1822 for a country, Poyais, said to be somewhere near Honduras, but which did not actually exist.[11] There was also a proliferation of new joint-stock corporations offering their shares to London investors. As one contemporary put it, "bubble schemes came out in shoals like herring from the Polar Seas." Some 624 companies were floated in 1824 and 1825 alone. The expansion was fueled by exceptional monetary ease and the stock market boomed, reaching its peak in April 1825.[12]

Monetary contraction and falling asset values thereafter helped bring on the jitters, and country banks began to experience payments problems. The pressure was aggravated by seasonal liquidity strains, and country bank failures began to mount. The failure of two major London banks (Wentworth, Chaloner & Rishworth and Pole, Thornton & Co.) in December then forced dozens of country banks to suspend payments. This prompted a general run on the country banks, which responded by going to their London bankers for cash; they in turn went to the Bank of England. The Bank responded by issuing more notes where these were accepted and, where they were not, by paying out in gold. The Bank itself came within an ace of failure and it was said afterwards that the country had come within 24 hours of reverting to barter. But by the end of December, the crisis had run its course and was starting to abate.

A large number of banks had failed and a massive wave of bankruptcies and a painful recession followed. By 1827, only 127 of the companies formed in 1824 and 1825 remained, and their combined capital was down by 70%.

There were angry recriminations, many of them against the legal privileges of the Bank of England, which had done so much to weaken the English banking system. Indeed, so strong were feelings against the Bank in the years that followed that the Bank was lucky to get its charter renewed in 1833.

But the crisis did lead to useful liberalizing reforms. The six-partner rule was repealed, and English banks were now allowed to form joint-stock companies and partnerships with more than six partners,

---

[11] The issue's publicity material was however very plausible: Poyais' purported capital Saint Joseph boasted "broad boulevards, colonnaded buildings and a splendid domed cathedral." See Reinhart and Rogoff, 2009, p. 93.

[12] Neal, 1998, p. 64.

provided they were established beyond a 65-mile radius from London, and the partners were still subject to unlimited liability. The limitations of the Bubble Act of 1720 were also repealed, which had prevented joint-stock companies from engaging in any activities other than those specified in their charters. These and other reforms were to lead to a major positive transformation in English banking in later decades, as they allowed the English banking system to begin to consolidate and strengthen and, eventually, to reap the benefits of a nationwide branch banking system.

★★★

Finally, we come to the granddaddy of all financial crises: the twin crises caused by the Mississippi Scheme in France and the South Sea Bubble in Britain (yes, we're aware of the 1637 Dutch tulip-bulb disaster, but florists don't count as financial institutions!).[13] Both involved attempts to pay off the national debts of the respective countries by converting them into equity holdings sold to gullible investors, utilizing inflated bubble-market valuations. Unsurprisingly, the scheme that was more effective in doing so, the Mississippi Scheme, caused far more long-term economic damage. Both were dodgy schemes dreamed up by inventive but shady financiers, aligned with governments eager to reduce their burden of debt and crooked politicians all too happy to receive personal handouts for their support.

The Mississippi Scheme began when an émigré Scottish economist and financier of dubious repute, John Law, acting with the connivance of the French Regent, Philippe d'Orleans, set up a bank capitalized with government debt in 1716 and then took over the then-dormant Mississippi colonization company the next year. In 1718 his bank became the Banque Royale, effectively France's central bank with notes, un-backed by gold, guaranteed by the monarch – thus making Law the inventor[14] of an inconvertible paper money system. The Mississippi Company's shares then took off, and were used to acquire the whole of

---

[13] By far the best account of both schemes, and of the Dutch tulip-bulb mania is in Charles Mackay's 1841 classic *Extraordinary Popular Delusions and the Madness of Crowds*. It avoids the modern delusion that Law was a genius economic innovator.

[14] Or re-inventor. Song Dynasty China had one, which worked quite well until the Mongol conquest – the Mongol emperors took the Ben Bernanke approach to money creation.

the government debt. In 1720, the Mississippi Company acquired the Banque Royale for yet more shares, at which point it owned France's national debt and issued its paper currency. However the company had few resources of its own except its holdings of government debt. Its stock, having been massively overvalued at its peak, soon collapsed in value and the company was bankrupt by 1721. Shareholders lost most of their investment and the public were left with worthless paper currency. John Law became a wanted man and fled the country, it was said by dead of night, living in exile until his death in 1729. For its part, the government had had its national debt financed on favorable terms but had lost its ability to raise credit in the future.

Moving over to Britain, the South Sea Company had been founded in 1711 by the Lord Treasurer, Robert Harley, ostensibly as a (primarily, slave) trading company but in reality as a vehicle to fund the purchase of government debt incurred during the War of the Spanish Succession. The government granted the company a monopoly of trade with Spain's South American colonies, the term "South Seas" referring in those days to the seas around South America. The company promised high profits from this trade, but purchased successive large amounts of government debt. Investors anticipated high trading returns, but were guaranteed at least the annuity payments on the company's holdings of government debt. The government benefited from lower interest on its debt.

The company effectively bribed influential people – senior politicians, the King's mistresses and so on – into becoming stockholders, using their influence and names to give it an aura of respectability that then attracted other investors. It then talked up its stocks with "the most extravagant rumors" of its future trades and so created a frenzy of speculation. Its share price rocked from about £100 a share in January 1720 to nearly £1,000 in August, and large numbers of people from all walks of life rushed into the frenzy. The price then fell back down to about £100 again by year-end, and thousands of individuals were ruined in the process.

The consequences of the two bubbles were very different. In France, Philippe d'Orleans remained in office until his death in 1723, and the disaster was conveniently blamed on the fugitive foreigner, Law. Other guilty parties, including the Regent himself, went free. The mercantile class, the principal holders of both Banque Royale notes and Mississippi Company shares, was severely damaged, and the French public was left with an abiding sense of the horrors of finance and paper money that was to last a very long time. The nascent French financial system had been crippled and the government's creditworthiness destroyed, making it difficult for France to finance its wars for the remainder of the century and putting the country at a major disadvantage relative to Britain in their subsequent wars.

In Britain on the other hand there had been no note issue, the losses of South Sea shareholders had been contained, at least, and there was an accounting afterwards. In response to public indignation, Sir Robert Walpole orchestrated a House of Commons investigation against those responsible that revealed widespread fraud amongst the Company directors and considerable corruption in the Cabinet. Heads rolled. The South Sea Company directors were deprived of their estates to pay the victims; its cashier Robert Knight fled into exile; the Chancellor of the Exchequer John Aislabie was expelled from the House of Commons and subsequently imprisoned; the Postmaster General, James Craggs the elder, committed suicide; his son, James Craggs the younger, died in disgrace in exile; and the de facto prime minister of the time, Earl Stanhope, was saved from impeachment only by his death.

The financiers didn't come out of it looking too well either: a resolution was subsequently proposed in Parliament that they be tied up in sacks filled with snakes and thrown into the Thames.

Stanhope was replaced by Walpole, who was not implicated in the South Sea Bubble itself and was credited for sorting the mess out. Confidence in the British political and economic system was thereby restored, and there followed 20 years of peace, prosperity and stability under Walpole's leadership.

★★★

The discussion above has shown there are only a few – in fact, five – basic causes of financial disaster, which recur again and again. Any crisis involves at least one and usually more (and sometimes all) of these five ingredients:

Rampant speculation is one of the classic tell-tale signs of an approaching crisis, and was present in most of the cases we discussed: in Japan in the 1980s, in the US S&Ls, in the secondary banking crash, in 1929, in the run-up to 1825, and, of course, in the Mississippi and South Sea crises.

Government involvement: in the cases of the Mississippi and South Sea crises, government misconduct was arguably the key problem; in 1837, government action caused the Panic; in the cases of the Japanese recession after 1990 and the Great Depression, the governments' responses greatly worsened and prolonged the problems they sought to alleviate; in other cases, the government response to one crisis sowed the seeds of later ones: a case in point is how the federal deposit insurance introduced in the Depression became one of the causes of the S&L crisis in the 1980s.

It is also interesting to note that crises without significant direct government involvement are generally quite mild in their economic effects, like 1825, Barings in 1890, the panic of 1907 and Overend & Gurney.

Misguided monetary policy played a major role in the banking crisis of the early 1930s, which was the true driver of the Great Depression, in the onset of the Panic of 1837, in the British secondary banking crisis of 1973, in the savings and loan debacle, and in many other crises. Generally speaking, excessively loose monetary policy causes price instability and an orgy of speculation, while sudden tightening of monetary policy can send the banking system over the cliff and cause a major downturn.

Misguided regulation or legislation was responsible for the S&L debacle and played a major role in both the Japanese and secondary banking crises. Going further back, beyond living memory, it was misguided legislative restrictions that made the US vulnerable to the crises of the pre-1914 period and made the English financial system vulnerable to the 1825 crisis.

Many financial crises involved *new financial technology*, often imperfectly understood and misapplied: certainly, this was a major cause of the Mississippi and South Sea disasters, but was also fundamental to Overend & Gurney, and the Japanese debacle of 1990.

All five of these factors – rampant speculation, government, misguided monetary policy, poor regulation/legislation, and misunderstood new financial technology – were highly significant in the run-up to the recent crisis.

★★★

In examining how financial crashes were handled, we also saw a cor-
nucopia of failed approaches that didn't work, either doing no good or
making matters worse, and only a small number of cases where policymakers' responses seem genuinely to have helped in resolving the
crisis.

Apart from Bill Seidman's limited but successful resolution of the
savings and loan crisis in 1989–91, only three statesmen stand out who
instinctively understood how to deal with financial crises, one per century.

The first was Sir Robert Walpole. Unlike his French contem-
poraries, Walpole recognized in late 1720 that the situation required
pragmatic damage limitation. He determined that this would best be
achieved if the bankruptcy of the South Sea Company could be avoided, and produced a rescue plan that allowed the Company to continue
in business without inflicting further losses on its shareholders. It was a
"least bad" solution to a problem that the government itself had done
much to create. Nor was it opposed by free market economists, as free
market economics had yet to be invented!

To preserve Britain's political stability in the face of public anger aroused by the Bubble scandal, Walpole discreetly "managed" the
House of Commons inquiry to provide appropriate scapegoats without
stigmatizing the entire political class, as would strictly speaking have
been appropriate: this was, after all, the High Age of Parliamentary
corruption, when virtually every MP was on someone's payroll. It was
whispered that Walpole may also have ensured that Robert Knight,
the South Sea Chief Cashier whose information could have caused
much embarrassment, was safely kept out of the country in the Austrian Netherlands (Belgium) until 1742.

Finally, Walpole recognized that restoration of public finances
required a lengthy period of sound administration and government
economy, without wars, and this he was able to provide. His success
was reflected in declining interest rates and the Government's improving creditworthiness; these were good in themselves but also useful to
the Government when the wars with France resumed in 1740.

The second successful crisis manager was Robert Banks Jenkinson,
Lord Liverpool, the British Prime Minister at the time of the 1825
crisis. He was one of very few political leaders in recorded history who
denounced a bubble while it was still in progress and made it quite clear

there would be no bailouts. In May 1825 he made a major speech to the House of Lords in which he voiced his concern about the "general spirit of speculation, which was going beyond all bounds and was likely to bring the greatest mischief on numerous individuals." He "wished it to be clearly understood that those persons who now engaged in joint-stock companies or other enterprises, entered on their speculations at their own peril and risk." He also thought it his duty to declare that he would "never advise the introduction of any bill for their relief; on the contrary, if any such measure were proposed, he would oppose it" and hoped Parliament would reject it.

When the bubble burst in December 1825, he was as good as his word, offering neither government help nor even advice to the Bank of England as it struggled with the effects of the crisis, instead simply giving permission under an 1822 law for the Bank to make emergency issues of £1 and £2 notes to alleviate the shortage of liquidity.

Liverpool was also alert to the need for reform in the aftermath of the crisis. His initial reaction was to assign some of the blame to the country banks' expanding note issue in the run-up to the crisis, and he therefore proposed to abolish the £1 note. His proposal to abolish the £1 note was ill-judged, however, and nearly caused a rebellion in Scotland, where the free banking system centered on Scottish pound notes had worked very well. The leader of the discontents was Sir Walter Scott, the author of *Ivanhoe*, writing under the evocative pen name of Malachi Malagrowther. Liverpool had the good sense to back down on the Scottish pound note, but he was also well aware of the need to rein in the privileges of the Bank of England and reform English banking in general. Accordingly, he pushed for reforms to remove the six-partner rule, he forced the Bank to open up branches around the country to improve the working of the payments system, and he repealed the Bubble Act.

The third proponent of sound solutions to a financial crisis was Andrew Mellon, US Secretary of the Treasury 1920–32, and by his lifetime achievements easily the most distinguished ever occupant of that office. Regrettably the President at the time of the Crash was no longer "Silent Cal," Calvin Coolidge, a free-marketer with whom Mellon had worked well, but the interventionist Herbert Hoover. Mellon produced a blueprint for handling the downturn, representing a free market approach that had worked in 1921–22 and would doubtless have worked again. But Hoover followed none of Mellon's policies, instead moving in the opposite, statist direction, to be followed in 1933 by even more statist Franklin Delano Roosevelt. The combination of Roosevelt's "New Deal" and bad Federal Reserve policy then prolonged the Depression right up to the point when the United States entered World War II in 1941.

Mellon favored a "liquidationist" approach to economic downturn. His philosophy, as described in Hoover's memoirs, was to "liquidate labor, liquidate stocks, liquidate the farmers, liquidate real estate ... It will purge the rottenness out of the system. High costs of living and high living will come down. People will work harder, live a more moral life. Values will be adjusted, and enterprising people will pick up the wrecks from less competent people." Thus he opposed fiscal stimulus and government bailouts of the banking system, proposing instead in 1931 the private sector solution of a National Credit Corporation, underwritten by the large banks, that would buy up some of the assets of the failing banks – the proposal failed because the Fed refused to accept NCC obligations as eligible paper for the discount window.[15] As the state-sponsored monopoly issuer of emergency currency, the Federal Reserve, charged with the responsibility to protect the banking system in just this sort of eventuality, stood by paralyzed by its own inept leadership.

Our discussion suggests that the best responses to financial market crises are those that work with, rather than against, market forces. Politically difficult as they might be, especially in a modern democracy when the government is expected to "do something," the best policy when a crisis hits is often one of sloth and inaction, relying on natural market forces to rectify the problem.

During non-crisis periods it is, needless to say, of the utmost importance to avoid government policies that might produce a financial crisis in the future.

And perhaps the most important conclusion is simply this: crises will always be damaging, but only with government assistance before, during, or after their climacteric do they become truly economically devastating.

---

[15] Meltzer, 2003, p. 425. Meltzer believes that "if Mellon's proposal had been implemented, many of the bank failures and the resulting financial crisis could have been avoided."

Part Two

The Modern Financial Theory Engine

4

Theoretical Foundations of Modern Finance

To quote Keynes again, "Too large a proportion of recent 'mathematical' economics are mere concoctions, as imprecise as the initial assumptions they rest on, which allow the author to lose sight of the complexities and interdependencies of the real world in a maze of pretentious and unhelpful symbols."[1]

From about 1965, the business and financial environment in the United States underwent a number of structural changes, described in detail in Chapter 7. Modern Financial Theory, which emerged in stages from the 1950s, was a key enabling feature in these developments. Once the structural changes were underway, the demand on Wall Street for Modern Financial Theory expanded remarkably, as described in Chapter 8. Before discussing the metamorphosis of Wall Street, therefore, we must examine the theory that energized that metamorphosis and, in many cases, greatly contributed to it.

In essence, Modern Financial Theory can be summarized as the application of the theories of mathematical statistics to finance. The techniques involved soon became known colloquially as "rocket science," although in fact real rocket science is a lot simpler.

---

[1] Keynes, 1936, p. 298.

The process of quantifying finance began over a century ago (over two centuries ago if one includes actuarial science: actuaries were quantifying financial risk long before anyone even heard of financial risk management) and was to result in a string of no fewer than seven Nobel Prizes for its principal developers, including (among others) Harry Markowitz in 1990 and Robert Merton and Myron Scholes in 1997. By the mid-1990s it was said that there were more PhD physicists working as "quants" in the research departments of investment banks than were working in physics itself.

★★★

A good starting point and one of the key pillars of Modern Finance is the 1958 Modigliani-Miller Theorem, developed at Carnegie-Mellon by Franco Modigliani and Merton Miller. This stated that under a set of hypothetical conditions – which included (i) no taxes, (ii) no difference between the rates at which individuals and corporations could borrow, (iii) zero transactions costs, and (iv) the complete absence of agency costs (no conflicts of interest) – then the value of a company is invariant as to its capital structure. In other words, capital structure, the balance between debt and equity, is irrelevant.

The Theorem was quickly extended to take account of the tax-deductibility of debt and the double taxation of equity dividends in the US system to show that, for a US company, the theoretically optimal level of leverage was infinite and the optimum dividend payout from earnings was zero.

This theorem, which spread quickly through the nation's business schools,[2] was an incredibly popular result with corporate management, remunerated increasingly with stock options. It justified both excessive leverage, which jacked up the growth rate on equity investments, and

---

[2] Martin was taught Modigliani-Miller as "revealed truth" in first year Finance at Harvard in 1972. The theory conflicted with the traditionally conservative view of debt taken by Harvard's Investment Banking course, taught by a bow-tied old-school professor, who had been an expert witness in the 1947 anti-trust Investment Bankers' Case. When doing a financial analysis, you had to remember which professor you were doing it for! Later students (including Kevin ten years later at the University of Western Ontario) were taught the Theorem without opposition from bow-tied traditionalists.

cutting dividends, which were unattractive drains of equity value for those holding stock options.

As with most of Modern Financial Theory, the flaws in Modigliani/Miller were primarily in the assumptions. Notoriously, taxes exist. Individuals cannot borrow at the same rates as companies, and borrowing rates are not the same as lending rates. However, the greatest problems in Modigliani-Miller's assumptions lie in ignoring transactions costs and agency issues. While brokerage costs may be low, and borrowing costs for debt relatively so, the cost of bankruptcy, both to the company itself, to the economy, and to the company's employees and customers, is gigantic – far in excess of the minor savings from over-leveraging. Hence, to the extent it works at all, Modigliani-Miller works only in times of very cheap money, when debt is particularly inexpensive and bankruptcy particularly unlikely. Of course, from 1995–2008, that is exactly what we had.[3] But even then, Modigliani-Miller was completely at odds with the increasing agency disconnect between management and shareholders, which worsened considerably after 1970.

A second key pillar was Modern Portfolio Theory, which was first developed in the early 1950s. The underlying ideas were simple; the application of those ideas, however, was anything but straightforward.

Imagine an enterprising trader who runs a market stall by an English seaside. Our trader can afford a certain outlay and has to choose which of two goods to sell, but is concerned about the day-to-day fluctuations in his income.

He begins by selling ice cream and sunglasses. This works really well when the sun is shining and everyone wants ice cream and protection against the sun: on such days, sales of both boom. However, this being England, there are many days when it rains, so on those days people want neither and he sells nothing. So he either makes a lot of money or he makes nothing, depending on the weather, and the English weather is very uncertain.

He then has the bright idea of switching from sunglasses to umbrellas. When he does so, he then finds when the sun comes out, he does

---

[3] We are not suggesting that Modligliani-Miller is complete rubbish. Were the assumptions valid, then the results in the theorem would follow with mathematical certainty. The issue is what to make of it, and our main criticism is simply that it does not justify high leverage in the real world.

well on the ice cream but not on the umbrellas; and when it rains, he does badly on the ice cream but well on the umbrellas. His income is now much steadier, even though the weather is as unpredictable as it was before. Our trader has diversified his risks.

In the one case, the lines of business had a strong positive correlation, meaning that if one did well, the other was also likely to: both depended on the sun being out. In the second case, the two lines of business had a strong negative correlation: one did well if the sun came out, and the other did well if it rained.

The lesson is to search for lines of business that are negatively correlated and so have risks that offset each other.

Modern Portfolio Theory applies this idea to an investor managing the risks of an equity portfolio. Our investor has to choose which shares to buy, but it is concerned with the unpredictability of his returns. We can measure this unpredictability by the volatilities of those returns, which itself is often measured by their statistical standard deviations. These volatilities are known in the trade as *sigmas*, after the Greek letter "s." We have the sigmas of the individual positions in the portfolio, and we have the sigmas of the portfolio as a whole. Like our seaside trader, the investor is not especially concerned with the individual sigmas as such; he is really concerned with the sigma of the portfolio and wants to choose positions that produce a low portfolio sigma.

At the same time, our investor also wants a good expected return on his portfolio. In short, he wants a portfolio with a low risk, and a high expected return.

The inventor of portfolio theory, Harry Markowitz, realized that this problem could be solved using statistics. To do so, one needs to make certain statistical assumptions – the usual ones being that individual returns follow Gaussian distributions and that the investor has reliable estimates of their expected returns, known as *mu* after the Greek letter "m," their sigmas, and the correlations between them.

Granted these assumptions, Markowitz showed that it was possible to design an efficient portfolio in which the investor could maximize expected return for any given level of portfolio risk, or minimize risk for any given expected return. This translated into a trade-off: if he wanted more return, he needed to take on more risks. A conservative investor would choose a relatively safe portfolio with a low expected return and low risk; a more adventurous investor would choose a portfolio with a higher expected return and higher risk.

This new portfolio theory appeared to put investment theory on a firm quantitative basis. If one set out the investment choices available in terms of the mus, sigmas, and correlations, one could write out equations showing the optimal combinations of investments, and all the investor would need to do is select his preferred trade-off between expected return and risk.

The Markowitz approach also told an investor with an existing portfolio what additional investments to look for. A potential new investment could be judged in terms of two features:

- The first was how the new position would affect the riskiness of the existing portfolio, if added to it. This additional risk had its own Greek name, *beta*. The beta takes account of the volatilities and correlations of the positions involved. A high beta position adds a lot to existing risks and a low beta position adds little risk.
- The second was how the new position would affect the expected portfolio return, independently of the impact of its beta on the portfolio. This impact was known as the *alpha*.

A good additional investment was therefore one that involved a low beta and/or a high alpha, the former indicating low risk and the latter a high expected return. Investors' search for such investment assets then created an insatiable demand for new asset classes, which was in time met by the expanding universe of securitized assets and the prospect of ever greater opportunities for portfolio diversification.

But this is to run well ahead of ourselves. When Markowitz set out his theory in his PhD dissertation in the early 1950s, even his examining committee did not know what to make of it. Milton Friedman commented that he couldn't see any mistake in the mathematics, but it wasn't economics and he couldn't give it an economics PhD. Nor was it mathematics, and it certainly wasn't literature. It was in fact something new, Modern Financial Theory, and Markowitz got his PhD in it.

Markowitz's work was an impressive intellectual accomplishment, but its implementation was problematic. The immediate problem was simply computational cost. With the state of computing at the time, the cost of a single portfolio optimization exercise could be enormous. This problem was to haunt Modern Portfolio Theory for a long time, but would in time be overcome with the advent of much more powerful modern computers.

A second and less amenable problem was the number of correlations. If there are two assets in a portfolio, A and B, then there is only one correlation involved, the correlation between the returns to A and B. If there are three assets, then we have three correlations – those between A and B, A and C, and B and C. With four assets, we have six different correlations; with five assets, we have ten correlations, and so on. The problem is that the number of different correlations grows very rapidly as the number of assets increases. More generally, with n assets, we have $n(n-1)/2$ different correlations. So if we have 100 different positions, by no means a particularly large portfolio, then we have 4,950 different correlations, and if we have 1,000 assets, we would have almost half a million correlations. You do not need to be a statistician to realize that, in practice, we just don't have enough historical market data to estimate nearly so many reliably.

The bottom line is that when Modern Portfolio Theory was first propounded, it was just that: theory.

The need to make portfolio theory implementable led, in the early 1960s, to a simplified version of Modern Portfolio Theory that came to be called the Capital Asset Pricing Model (CAPM). The key to the CAPM was to ask what would happen if everyone practiced Modern Portfolio Theory: the result would be an equilibrium in which the CAPM would hold. In essence, it would be "as if" everyone held a combination of some hypothetical "market portfolio" and a risk-free asset. The expected return to *any* asset (not just stocks!) would be given by a simple equation depending on the expected returns to the market portfolio and the risk-free asset, and on the beta between the asset and the market portfolio.

Each asset now had its own *single* beta, which told us how risky it was.

Needless to say, this beta was assumed to be stable, and the CAPM launched a cottage industry of analysts who would produce beta estimates for their clients – a snake-oil industry that is still going strong, long after the model itself has been discredited.

The CAPM was to dominate academic finance for a long time. The key to its success was its unreserved adoption by the financial economists of the Chicago school, in conjunction with the closely related notion of the Efficient Markets Hypothesis (of which more below). They defended the CAPM with religious zeal, and most business schools were soon teaching it as established orthodoxy, cranking out tens of thousands of MBAs a year who didn't really understand the CAPM but who knew nothing better.

Nonetheless, doubts emerged about the CAPM soon after it was first set out. One obvious objection was common sense – for example, in capital budgeting, do you really believe that a company should use the CAPM to decide if it should purchase a photocopier? Many practitioners also voiced their doubts, not least because it would, if accepted, make much traditional investment analysis, and not just capital budgeting analysis, redundant.

A string of "anomalies" – results that that the CAPM could not explain – also emerged. There was the large firm effect, the Monday effect, the end of the month effect, the end of the year effect, the bank holiday effect, even the Yom Kippur effect, and many others. These "anomalies" steadily accumulated, but were explained away as minor "departures" from a position that was just *assumed* to be sound, never mind any annoying evidence to the contrary. To make matters worse, there was also mounting evidence that estimated betas were unreliable.

In 1977 Richard Roll published a devastating critique[4] that undermined the CAPM by showing that the market portfolio could never be reliably identified.[5] Roll soon had people asking if beta was dead,[6] but still the CAPM orthodoxy dismissed him as a spoilsport and the CAPM party continued for a little while longer.

The end finally came with a study by Eugene Fama and Kenneth French published in 1993, which showed that the beta was not related to stock market returns. This refuted the most basic prediction of the CAPM, namely, that stock market returns should be positively related

---

[4] Roll, 1977.

[5] This market portfolio was typically identified with one or more stock markets, but the theory itself was meant to be all-encompassing: the "market portfolio" was, therefore, the stock of everything, all assets included. No wonder empirical researchers couldn't find it.

[6] Wallace, 1980.

to their betas. The bloody beta was *useless*. People were now mischie-vously asking if beta was dead, again.[7]

From a purely scientific point of view, the Fama and French study was merely the latest in a long series of studies that undermined the sci-entific respectability of the CAPM. Its significance however was not in its results – although it should have been – but in its authorship. Fama, the inventor of the Efficient Markets Hypothesis, of which more be-low, was a key figure in the development of the CAPM itself. Thus, one of the key pillars of Modern Financial Theory was renounced by one of its principal creators.

The Efficient Markets Hypothesis was closely related to the CAPM. Its essence was the claim that market prices were "efficient" in the sense that they "fully reflected" all available information: markets are "efficient" because they get prices right. This hypothesis was the per-fect embodiment of the notion of "rational economic man" that ruled the economics textbooks: efficient markets was rational economic man in the stock market.

Large amounts of empirical evidence were soon being collected that seemed to support the Efficient Markets Hypothesis. Doubts and evidence against it were generally ignored and academics who opposed it were railroaded: the Efficient Markets Hypothesis bandwagon had taken off like its CAPM cousin.

The Efficient Markets Hypothesis goes beyond the self-evident truth that, on average, you can't expect to beat the market. It is one thing to say the market is hard to beat, as good investment gurus had maintained since at least Benjamin Graham,[8] another to say that market prices are, somehow, "right."

Yet the Efficient Markets Hypothesis was clearly inadequate. This was especially so for the "strong form" of the Efficient Markets Hy-pothesis, which maintained that prices fully reflect all information, both public and private. For one thing, *how exactly* does the information in one person's head become instantaneously known to everyone else

---

[7] Grinold, 1993.

[8] Benjamin Graham (1894–1976), author of *Security Analysis* (1934), generally known as "Graham and Dodd" after the 1940 second edition, of which David Dodd was co-author. Father of "fundamental" investment analysis. Friend and mentor of the youthful Warren Buffett.

in the market? And, if the strong-form Efficient Markets Hypothesis does hold, then what incentive would anyone have to collect any more information? If prices fully reflected the information available, then it would be economically irrational to spend resources collecting it. In that case, the investment advice industry shouldn't exist at all. But it did. There would be little reason to trade either.

There was also the awkward implication, usually glossed over by its proponents, that if markets were truly efficient, then why do market prices move so much? If markets are efficient, then changes in market prices must reflect new information becoming available to the market. If so, what was the information that became available on October 19, 1987 that caused the New York Stock Exchange to fall by 23% that day?

The Efficient Markets Hypothesis therefore goes too far. A more defensible position is perhaps to say that if you are to expect to beat the market, you must have an informational or analytical edge over it.

Information is also useless without analysis. Early in Martin's banking career he had a very senior colleague with excellent market connections, but – shall we say – limited analytical capability. Every day this colleague would talk to the heads of syndication at all the major houses and then, armed with priceless up-to-the-second market information, puff on his pipe and apply his limited powers to figuring out what it all meant.

Martin, snotty youth that he was, quickly figured out that this guy could be used as an anti-Warren Buffett. If Buffett can consistently beat the market, then there must be people who consistently fall short. By and large, these will not be little old ladies, who, lacking knowledge, can be expected to invest largely at random, thereby matching the market, but bankers with excellent connections but below-average analytical abilities. So when Martin wanted to give a client his best guess on where the market was going, he would consult this oracle and then tell the client the opposite. Very useful chap, the oracle was – and a lot cheaper than Warren Buffett!

This said, the Efficient Markets Hypothesis did serve one useful purpose. It highlighted the social value of investment advice: it suggested that the average social value of investment advice was zero (or, more accurately, zero if you ignored the costs involved and less than zero if you took them into account). The better financial economists and the investment industry have been at war ever since on this issue, but the overwhelming evidence, from study after study, suggests that the financial economists are right, for once: all that advice telling you how to beat the market is so much financial snake oil.

But we could have deduced this anyway from Ben Graham: if on average, you can't beat the average, then the average value of all that advice telling you how to beat the average is, at best, zero.

The next stage in our story was the development in the early 1970s of models to value financial derivatives. The centerpiece of the story is the problem of how to value or price a European call option,[9] a very simple form of derivative compared to many of those that came later.

The starting point was the notion of Brownian motion, named after the nineteenth century Scottish botanist Robert Brown, who observed how small particles suspended in liquid would randomly move over time – a process known as diffusion. In 1900, Louis Bachelier suggested that this sort of process could be applied to stock prices, but the model he proposed, known as arithmetic Brownian motion, was superseded by the model of geometric Brownian motion proposed by Albert Einstein in his doctoral thesis of 1905, the same year in which he also proposed the Special Theory of Relativity.

However, the problem of how to value a call option was only solved much later by Fischer Black, Myron Scholes and Robert Merton in the early 1970s.

Pricing the option involved the use of a "risk-neutral" pricing methodology, based on a hypothetical world with a whole bunch of unrealistic assumptions: trading was costless, liquidity was perfect, there were no short-selling restrictions, the stock price never jumped and had a constant volatility, you could borrow at a constant risk-free rate, and so on; *and* all the "laws of motion" were assumed to be known with certainty. The value of the option was then determined by a formidable stochastic differential equation, the solution to which came when Black, Scholes, and Merton realized that their equation was related to the heat transfer equation in physics, whose solution was already known.

---

[9] A European call option on a security gives the holder the right but not the obligation to buy the security at a fixed price on a specified date in the future.

The Black-Scholes-Merton call option formula was eagerly adopted by the early option traders and other options pricing models soon followed. These included alternative models of the simple European call option, such as stochastic volatility models, which allowed the volatility to be random, and jump-diffusion models, which allowed for the stock price to jump suddenly. They also included models of other options, such as barrier options, which, depending on their type, were either activated or deactivated when the underlying random variable on which the option is predicated hit (or perhaps exceeded) a specified barrier, and American options, which allowed the holder to exercise the option not just at the end of the option's life but any time before. If you think these are complicated, there were then the large numbers of "exotics" in the 1980s and afterwards.

New options were also invented for new types of risk factor that were, in general, also more difficult to model. The original options predicated on share prices were soon joined by others predicated on exchange rates, commodities, interest rates, and, later, credit risk factors. Eventually, options appeared on more or less anything that could be measured.

Yet the process of building these models was by no means easy, even for the quantitative specialists: formulae for even the simplest American options were difficult to obtain, because of the additional complications created by their early exercise feature; and it took another 20 years after Black-Scholes-Merton to produce the Heath-Jarrow-Morton pricing model for interest-rate derivatives, which was able to take account of the ferocious complications created by the interest-rate term structure. Then, there were the credit derivatives, but more of them later.

It was no surprise, then, that Wall Street and the City of London were soon vacuuming up quantitative science PhDs to build ever more elaborate models. After the fall of the Berlin Wall, the best graduates of Moscow State University could always find gainful employment building more complicated financial models. A new discipline, financial engineering, had been born.

In theory, all this derivatives rocket science was only for the good. The models were becoming better and gradually driving out the poorer ones. Markets were becoming more "complete," meaning, in essence, that more and more risks were becoming quantifiable and hence manageable by the expanding tools of modern quantitative risk management. Corporate clients had more opportunities to hedge their risks, and investors had more opportunities to diversify their risks and optimize their "risk–return trade-offs." According to Wall Street's partisans, the ongoing process of financial innovation was, without doubt, a great benefit to society: new financial "products" were good for customers, and the rapidly expanding universe of financial derivatives created ever greater opportunities for risk management.

The reality was very different: the real incentive to design a new model was to sell new attractive-looking financial products to customers who, for the most part, had no idea what they really involved. You needed either a better model of an existing instrument, or a model of new type of instrument, or a model that covered a new type of risk factor. You only needed to make a few big trades and you had made your money. Once everyone else piled in, in a matter of perhaps only months, your margins had gone and you moved on to design next year's attractive new model.

The only margins that did not disappear quickly were those driven by the desire to circumvent the system, where the instrument enabled a bank to evade some rule, to enter forbidden markets, hide losses, avoid taxes or reduce regulatory capital requirements.

Then things started to go wrong. The crash of October 1987 was to show that this rocket science wasn't really working as it should: more of this in the next chapter. Then a steady stream of derivatives disasters started rolling in, in the early 1990s, by which time cynics began wondering if the physics PhDs were now building financial hydrogen bombs instead of real ones.

Nor were these the only problems. The models were only one part of an unholy financial trinity, each part of which was only moderately damaging on its own, but which together were to be cumulatively devastating in their impact, and allow insiders to extract rents on a massive scale.

The first element we shall encounter in Chapter 7, the short-term oriented bonus culture, with its focus on rewarding (apparent) short-term results. The second element is the models, which provide a means, the theoretical or empirical "correctness" of which is not relevant here, to value complicated positions. These two elements create a potent mix: you use the models to create notional values and you pay yourself extravagant bonuses based on the "profits" your models say you created. The scope for fiddling and other forms of chicanery is too obvious to need explaining, especially when everyone else is playing the same game, all benefiting to the detriment of shareholders and customers who are only dimly aware of what is going on and unable to do much about it anyway.

Now add the third element, the wonderfully misnamed "fair value" accounting, and the mix becomes truly explosive. You can now use your models to assign allegedly "fair" values to almost any position, whether a market really exists in it or not. The black box nature of the models then combines splendidly with the inconsistencies and complexities of the accounting standards themselves to create fictitious valuations and hence fictitious profits. These fictitious profits can then be used to produce very non-fictitious bonuses for those involved – yet another form of financial alchemy, and perhaps its ultimate achievement – without any real profits ever having been made. The parties involved then pocket the money and what happens down the road is not their problem.

At the same time, it is difficult to believe that such naked looting would be allowed to take place without some ideology to give it a fig leaf of respectability and the appearance, at least, of benefiting the rest of society. And so it was: we were constantly assured of the benefits of new financial innovation, of greater "risk-sharing" opportunities, and of the availability of more and more investment outlets. But underlying these claims was a deeper vision, the underlying foundation of the ideology of modern quantitative finance. The key to this was the notion of expanding market completeness, the idea that more and more risks are being brought into the market arena and hence shared between willing participants, to everyone's mutual benefit. Nowhere was this more clearly expressed than in Robert Shiller's much acclaimed 2003 book, *The New Financial Order.*[10]

In this book, Shiller outlines a vision of greatly enhanced risk-sharing resulting in much greater economic security and hence greater personal fulfillment for us all. He envisions the "democratization" of finance and the risk-sharing benefits enjoyed by the clients of Wall Street being brought to the customers of Wal-Mart. At the same time, he envisions the establishment of "macro markets" operating on a huge

---

[10] Shiller, 2003.

scale, trading long-term claims on macroeconomic variables such as national and even world GDP – and, in principle, any random economic variable that might matter.

Underpinning this would be a new global financial architecture and a vast expansion in risk-sharing activity involving, paradoxically, not so much the expansion of "free" markets in which private agents freely "share" their risks, but a vast expansion in government activities across the world. Much of this would entail government-to-government derivatives trading on behalf of their citizens, who are implicitly assumed, if these arrangements are to be for their benefit, to be unable to trade on their own behalf. Consequently, the New Financial Order has a distinctly statist and paternalist tone, and one which, taken to its logical conclusion, implies the establishment of nothing less than a world government with the power to redistribute most of our income at will.

The retail or micro side of the New Financial Order is nicely illustrated by Shiller's example of a young woman from India who wishes to become a professional violinist, but has difficulty borrowing the money for her training. Shiller's solution is for her to take out a loan contingent on the future incomes of professional violinists, financed by investors willing to take on some of her risk exposure to partake of the benefits of her future success; with their financial support, she can now go ahead to realize her ambitions; everyone benefits.

All very heartwarming. But this begs the issue of why she had difficulty borrowing in the first place. If she has no collateral, investors would be right to be cautious. After all, she might simply be a bad risk: she might drop out, might not be good enough, or be unable to repay. Shiller's investors would be naive if they ignored these possibilities; they might not even be doing her any good by saddling her with costly obligations. Perhaps she should just go into another career. Not all stories can have a Bollywood ending.

Shiller's ship runs aground, as it were, on the reef of credit risk. The mistake is to think that these and other barriers to risk-sharing arrangements are merely "imperfections" that will disappear as the market (inevitably?) becomes more "perfect." On the contrary, these barriers are intrinsic to the underlying economics of the situation, and this does not go away.

Then there is the macro side to the New Financial Order involving government-to-government risk transfer. An example is Shiller's proposal for GDP swaps, in which two countries agree to exchange part of their countries' uncertain future Gross Domestic Products. He discusses how, for example, back in 1965, Argentina and South Korea might have agreed a real GDP swap in 1965, when Argentina was a relatively rich country and South Korea a relatively poor one.

Shiller claims that they would both have been better off, as viewed then, because they would be sharing their relative economic performance risks. In theory, this can be correct, but only if you make a whole bunch of untenable assumptions, the most important being that any difference in GDP could be ascribed to random "luck" *and* if you can ignore all the political economy complications involved: minor details such as the disincentive effects of very high taxes and the government trampling on property rights. Since 1965, Argentina's real per capita GDP has fallen, whereas South Korea's has risen by more than 500%, so South Korea would have ended up paying a very substantial proportion of its GDP as a transfer to Argentina.

The problem with this arrangement is surely obvious, so much so that it is hard to imagine an example that better illustrates the problems with Shiller's case. Can one really imagine South Korean voters taking the view that they should hand over the fruits of their labor to compensate their "unlucky" counterparts in Argentina – as if their greater prosperity owed nothing to their own hard work or the Argentine government's record of chronic economic mismanagement? The scale of the transfers would dwarf the infamous reparations imposed on Germany after the Treaty of Versailles and which ended up paying the victorious Allies next to nothing anyway. Instead, South Korea would presumably have taken a leaf out of Argentina's own financial history book and reneged on the deal, and, absent a world government – how else to overcome the problem of sovereign risk in such circumstances? – there would have been little that Argentina could have done about it.

But even if we throw out the government-to-government level of the New Financial Order and revert to its retail level, we still face the problems that arise with our Indian violinist: some risks are much more difficult to "share" than others, and the obstacles to such risk-sharing cannot be assumed away as annoying market "imperfections" that will eventually disappear. Some risk-sharing contracts are simply not feasible.

The vision of financial "market completeness" – that financial markets can become perfect and share any measurable risk – *might* look good on paper, if you focused only on the risk-sharing benefits and ignored the many problems involved. It is, however, like all utopian ideals, away with the pixies.

★★★

Appendix 1: Some Leading Financial Alchemists ...

Louis Bachelier (France, 1870–1946)

Grandfather of modern financial alchemy. A mediocre student at the Sorbonne, his 1900 PhD thesis "Theorie de la Speculation" laid out a mathematical description of Brownian motion (the motion visible under a microscope through vibrating molecules randomly bashing dust particles), but applied it to stock market prices rather than particle physics, as would have been natural. In spite of patronage by his instructor Henri Poincaré, France's leading mathematician, the thesis only drew the grade of "honorable." Albert Einstein later improved the Brownian motion mathematics, publishing it in 1905 with its proper physical application. Bachelier later had an academic career that might be politely described as peripatetic, interrupted by service as a private on the Western Front.

By applying a perfectly good physics model to finance, and assuming Gaussian randomness of prices and zero net expectation in markets, Bachelier was inadvertently the creator of a new discipline that ultimately led to multi-trillion dollar losses more than a century later. His work was obscure but not entirely forgotten, influencing the Soviet mathematician Andrei Kolmogorov (1903–87) and then becoming a source for the work of **Benoit Mandelbrot** and **Franco Modigliani**, both of whom studied in Paris in their youth.

Fischer Black (1938–95)

A third of the Black-Scholes-Merton options valuation equation. Degree and PhD in applied mathematics from Harvard, after which he spent some time at Arthur D. Little. Joined the University of Chicago in 1971, where he did some interesting work on the theory of moneyless monetary systems and propounded the remarkable theory that monetary policy was irrelevant to the economy's movements. His most famous work, with **Myron Scholes**, the eponymous option valuation equation, was published in a paper "The pricing of options and corporate liabilities" in January 1973. This was just in time for the explosion in options trading, and enabled him to move to a lucrative position with Goldman Sachs in 1984. He was unlucky enough to die of throat cancer two years before the work leading to his equation was honored with the 1997 Nobel Prize.

Robert F. Engle (1942–)
Inventor of Autoregressive Conditional Heteroskedasticity (ARCH) methods of volatility forecasting, initially applied to the UK inflation rate; this subsequently generalized by his former student Tim Bollerslev to create the GARCH model, which was then widely applied to financial volatilities. Co-founder of the Society for Financial Econometrics. BS in Physics (MS in Physics, Williams, PhD in Economics (Cornell). Professor at UC San Diego, 1975–2003. The co-inventor, with Clive Granger, of the theory of cointegration, which models equilibrium relationships between trended variables.

Eugene Fama (1939–)
Propounded the Efficient Market Hypothesis in his 1965 doctoral thesis "The behavior of stock market prices." PhD in Economics from University of Chicago, with **Benoit Mandelbrot** as doctoral supervisor. He also played a leading role in the development of the Capital Asset Pricing Model, before putting it out of its misery a generation later in a landmark paper with Kenneth French. Apart from Black, Bachelier, and Gauss (all dead), he is the only leading Financial Alchemist not to get the Nobel. It is unclear why he has been snubbed in this way; it's not as if any of the other financial alchemists' theories worked either.

Carl Friedrich Gauss (1777–1855)
Son of a gardener in Brunswick, Germany, he is ranked in the "objective scoring system" of Charles Murray's *Human Accomplishments* as the

fourth greatest mathematician of all time.[11] He was reputedly the last mathematician to know all of the mathematics of his day. Inventor of the famous Gaussian probability distribution, often mislabeled the "normal distribution," which is a lot less normal than its proponents normally suggest. Also invented modular arithmetic and proved the fundamental theorem of algebra showing that any polynomial in a single variable has at least one root. His calculations enabled astronomers to identify Ceres, the first identified asteroid. Identified a method for representing the unit of magnetism (the Gauss). Disliked teaching and was not a prolific writer.

Gauss married twice and had six children, but maintained poor relations with his two sons, whom he would not allow to become mathematicians "for fear of sullying the family name."

Gauss would have rejoiced in the practical and lucrative uses to which his probability distribution has since been put. However, as a highly rigorous yet intuitive mathematician, he would undoubtedly have spotted the fundamental flaws underlying Modern Financial Theory the moment he saw it.

Harry Markowitz (1927–)

Inventor of Modern Portfolio Theory, published in the *Journal of Finance* in 1952. PhD, University of Chicago in Economics. Developed the Markowitz frontier, under which the risk/expected return function of all securities in an optimal portfolio lies on a single Markowitz Efficient Frontier curve, which helped pave the way for the later Capital Asset Pricing Model. Worked at Rand Corporation, founded CACI International, pioneer in computer simulation and a well-read and open-minded polymath. Professor at UC San Diego. Awarded Nobel Prize in 1990 for development of portfolio theory, along with **Merton Miller** and **William F. Sharpe**.

Robert F. Merton (1944–)

Generalized the Black-Scholes options valuation equation and then produced an inter-temporal version of the Capital Asset Pricing Model. Hailed by Paul Samuelson as the Isaac Newton of Modern Finance,

---

[11] Murray, 2003. Murray's scoring system is based on citations in scholarly encyclopedias and references in later scientific papers. Gauss ranks below Euler, Newton, and Euclid.

which, since Newton was a keen alchemist, is only appropriate. Professor at MIT Sloan School of Management, 1970–88, Harvard Business School, 1998–. Spectacularly eventful consulting career. With **Myron T. Scholes**, was a Director of Long-Term Capital Management, which slid famously into collapse in 1998, causing a major crisis and triggering a panicked bailout led by the Federal Reserve. Chief Science Officer of Trinsum Group, a financial advisory firm that filed for bankruptcy protection in January 2009. Awarded Nobel Prize jointly with **Myron T. Scholes** for their work on options valuation.

Merton Miller (1923–2000)

Co-author with **Franco Modigliani** of Modigliani-Miller theorem, which proposed the irrelevance of debt-equity structure. PhD in Economics from Johns Hopkins University, 1952. At Carnegie Institute of Technology in 1958, jointly authored paper "The cost of capital corporate finance and the theory of investment" propounding the Modigliani-Miller theorem, which was sometimes used to give a spurious respectability for grossly excessive leverage in US financial and corporate systems, and among US consumers. A leading advocate of the benefits of financial derivatives – he often claimed that financial derivatives made the world a safer place rather than a more dangerous one – and free financial markets. Professor, University of Chicago, 1961–93. Nobel Prize, 1990 with **Harry Markowitz** and **William F. Sharpe**.

Franco Modigliani (Italy/US, 1918–2003)

Primarily a macro-economist. Co-author with **Merton Miller** of Modigliani-Miller theorem, allegedly after he and Miller had been assigned to teach corporate finance to business school students, and as good economists determined that the existing texts were internally contradictory. Modigliani also propounded the life-cycle theory of saving in the economy, in parallel to Milton Friedman's "permanent income" theory, which supposed that consumers would aim for a stable level of consumption through their lifetime, saving in early years to fund their retirement. Left Italy in 1939 for France, then went to the US in 1942. D.Soc.Sci., New School for Social Research. Professor, Carnegie-Mellon, then MIT 1962–2003. Nobel Prize, 1985.

Myron T. Scholes (Canada/US, 1941–)

Co-author with **Fischer Black** of Black-Scholes option valuation model. BA Economics McMaster University, PhD/MBA, University of Chicago. Professor, MIT 1968–73, University of Chicago, 1973–81, Stanford, 1981–96. Director of Long-Term Capital Management with **Robert F. Merton**, which collapsed in spectacular fashion in 1998. From 1999, Chairman of Platinum Grove Asset Management, $5 billion hedge fund which was forced to suspend withdrawals in October 2008 after a 38% loss, then lost another 11% in March 2009 and by October 2009 was in a Special Rebalancing Situation. Nobel Prize 1997 with **Robert F. Merton** for the European call option valuation model.

William F. Sharpe (1934–)

Devised the Capital Asset Pricing Model, published as "Capital asset prices – a theory of market equilibrium under conditions of risk" in the *Journal of Finance* in 1964. MA, PhD in Economics from UCLA. Professor, Stanford, 1970–89. Also devised the Sharpe ratio measuring the return of a security in relation to its risk. One of his doctoral students Howard Sosin founded AIG Financial Products, whose activities in the CDS market were a major contributor to the recent financial crisis. Co-founder of the consulting firm Financial Engines, which encourages its clients to save more for the retirement that, thanks to Modern Finance, many of them will never live to see. Nobel Prize, 1990 with **Harry Markowitz** and **Merton Miller**

Appendix 2: ... And Some Non-alchemists

Augustin Louis, Baron Cauchy (France, 1789–1857)

Father of the Cauchy distribution, the ultimate long-tailed risk. Born into a Royalist family and spent his first five years hiding from the French revolutionaries deep in the countryside. Educated at the new Bonapartist École Polytechnique, where he objected to the military discipline, then became an engineer. After a few years of engineering, he returned to Paris in 1812 and switched to mathematics. Three years later, when Napoleon fell and the Bourbons were restored, as a well-known Royalist he was appointed a professor at the reorganized École Polytechnique in December 1815 and a member of the Academie des Sciences the following year.

As a professor, he was not entirely successful, since he took his students through higher mathematics at a brisk, rigorous trot that baffled all but the best of even the École Polytechnique's elite. He designed the Cauchy stress tensor, central to the theory of elasticity, and Cauchy's integral theorem, which led to the development of the theory of complex functions and his proof of Taylor's theorem, central to calculus. In mathematical papers produced, he was second only to Leonhard Euler.

Then in 1830, disaster struck. The reactionary Charles X was overthrown and Cauchy went into exile, refusing to swear an oath of allegiance to the new regime of Louis Philippe. In exile he was for five years tutor to the legitimist heir Henri d'Artois, Duke of Bordeaux, an exercise that left the Duke with a lifelong hatred of mathematics and Cauchy with a legitimist (and therefore, alas, legally unofficial) barony. He was only readmitted to the École Polytechnique after Louis Philippe was himself overthrown.

Cauchy was an eccentric reactionary,[12] but a very great mathematician; he ranks eighteenth all-time among mathematicians (above Fibonacci and Archimedes) in Charles Murray's *Human Accomplishments*.

Benoit Mandelbrot (France/US 1924–)
Should be thought of as the Robert Boyle or Antoine Lavoisier, who began to move the world of finance beyond alchemy. PhD, Mathematical Sciences, Paris. Centre National de la Recherche Scientifique, 1949–57; Institute for Advanced Study, Princeton, 1953–54. Moved to US in 1958. Fellow, IBM Research Centre, 1958–90. Also taught as Visiting Professor at Harvard and Yale. Mandelbrot discovered as early as 1962 that financial market prices did not follow a Gaussian distribution: cotton prices in fact followed a Levy stable distribution with constant of 1.7 instead of 2 as in a Gaussian.[13]

---

[12] Gauss, only twelve years older than Cauchy, was also a Royalist but a less fanatical one.

[13] Mandelbrot, 1962.

Mandelbrot invented fractal geometry, which he named in 1975, publishing *The Fractal Geometry of Nature* in 1982, Chapter 37 of which is "Scaling and price change in Economics." His 1997 book *Fractals and Scaling in Finance* and his 2004 book (with Richard L. Hudson) *The (Mis-) Behaviour of Markets* exploded many of the axioms of Modern Finance, without posing a wholly satisfactory alternative paradigm.

The only possible excuse the Nobel people have for not having awarded him one or two Nobel Prizes is the lack of a Nobel Prize for Mathematics. Even so, he is a gap in the Economics Nobel line-up.

★★★

Alternatively, it might be more appropriate if the Sveriges Riksbank would end the Economics Nobel Prize as a failure: strictly, it is isn't a true Nobel at all; it was not part of Alfred Nobel's legacy, but a much later add-on to pander to the economics profession's vain pretensions of scientific respectability. If we judge a science by the hallmark of predictability, then the predictions of economists are no better than those of ancient Roman augurs or modern taxi drivers; alternatively, we can judge it by its contribution to "scientific" knowledge, in which case the contribution that financial economics has made makes us wonder if the agricultural alchemist Lysenko shouldn't have got a Nobel himself; or we can judge it by its contribution to the welfare of society at large, in which case the undermining of the capitalist system, the repeated disasters of the last twenty years, the immiseration of millions of innocent workers and savers, and the trillion dollar losses of recent years surely speak for themselves.

5

Modern Financial Theory's Hideous Flaws

Hideous Flaw I: Assumption of Gaussianity

Constructing the edifice of Modern Financial Theory was a great intellectual achievement. It was, nonetheless, also a deeply flawed one.

Perhaps the most glaring problem was the assumption of Gaussianity – the assumption that financial returns could be adequately described by the Gaussian or normal probability distribution, often known as the bell curve.

Unlike most others, the Gaussian distribution is very tractable and has the attraction of being underpinned by a key principle of statistics, the Central Limit Theorem. This states that if one takes a large number of independent random variables from some unknown but "well-behaved" (a lovely statistical caveat emptor, allowing awkward complications to be swept under the rug!) probability distribution, then their mean will be approximately Gaussian. For this reason, undergraduates are commonly taught in applied statistics classes that if they don't know what the true distribution really is, they can often get away with assuming that it is Gaussian.

This is highly convenient, but for many purposes, simply not true. The most compelling evidence comes from looking at extreme events.

A Gaussian distribution is shown in Figure 1. This figure shows the probability density function of a random variable, according to this distribution. The distribution is centered around the mean, implying that the most likely values are those clustered around the mean. The degree of dispersion, or uncertainty, is determined by the distribution's standard deviation (or sigma). Outcomes further away from the mean are less likely than outcomes closer to it, and the distinctive feature of the Gaussian is the way in which the "tails" slope off rapidly, making extreme outcomes very unlikely.

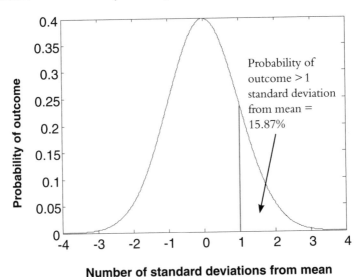

Number of standard deviations from mean

Figure 1: A Gaussian Distribution

The probability of an outcome occurring within any given range depends on the area under the curve over that range. So, for example, the figure shows that the probability of an outcome 1 standard deviation or more greater than the mean – a "1-sigma event" – is 15.87%. Table 1 shows the probability of various other outcomes under the Gaussian distribution. The probability of a 2-sigma event is 2.275%; the probability of a 3-sigma event is 0.135%, the probability of a 4-sigma event is 0.00317%, and so on.[1] Note how rapidly these probabilities fall as the number of sigmas increases: the tail probabilities run into a headwind, and rapidly go toward zero.

Table 1: Probabilities of k Sigma Events Under the Gaussian Distribution

k	Probability in Any Given Day	Expected Occurrence: Once in Every
2	2.275%	43.96 days
3	0.135%	741 days
4	0.00317%	31,560 days
5	0.000029%	3,483,046 days
6	0.000000099%	1,009,976,678 days
7	0.000000000129%	(about) 776,000,000,000 days

Translated into financial terms, the Gaussian tells us that extreme returns are *extremely* unlikely. If returns are Gaussian, then the probability of a 5-sigma loss on any given day is 0.000029%. The waiting time associated with such a loss, the length of time we would expect to have to wait to observe such a loss, is almost 3.5 *million* days or (at 250 trading days to a year) about 14,000 years, much longer than the period of time that has elapsed since civilization evolved. By contrast, the waiting period associated with a 10-sigma event, in years, is about 5.2 but with the decimal point moved 20 twenty places: 5.249 e+20 in scientific notation, a period that is vastly bigger than the age of the universe itself. And the waiting period associated with a 20-sigma event is a number, in years, that considerably exceeds recent estimates of the number of particles in the known universe. It is no exaggeration, therefore, to say that the probabilities of high-sigma events are inconceivably small.

Losses such as the 22- or 23-sigma event of October 19, 1987, are thus to all intents and purposes impossible under the Gaussian. The fact that even a single loss of this magnitude occurred at all – and, in

---

[1] All the figures quoted here are taken from Dowd et al., 2008.

fact, these sorts of events seems to occur at least every few years – conclusively proves that the Gaussian distribution does not provide an adequate model of financial returns. So when Goldman Sachs Chief Financial Officer David Viniar famously admitted to being puzzled by a sequence of "25-standard deviation moves" in August 2007,[2] it might have occurred to him and others, but apparently didn't, that Wall Street's risk management methods even at the best-run institutions were hopelessly inadequate.

There are also good reasons to expect financial returns *not* to be Gaussian. The Gaussian presumes that stock prices move continuously and do not jump around: they behave like random particles moving around in fluid. Implicitly, this assumes that market prices are somehow *given* to traders – that traders have to take prices as given – but this is manifestly not so. In fact, market prices are determined by traders themselves and often greatly affected by individual trades. Prices are determined by the complex dynamics of traders trading on information, trying to get the better of each other.

For instance, if traders perceive that a particular trader *has* to sell, they will mercilessly take advantage and offer that trader worse terms or, more damaging still, they might refuse to trade at all until they have a better idea what is happening: the unfortunate distressed trader then falls into a liquidity black hole. Other times, operators will deliberately trigger price falls by appearing to be distressed, so that they can then buy later on at lower prices. And the opportunities for these sorts of games only increased when barrier options came along in the 1980s, options which knocked out or knocked in when certain barriers were hit. A whole new range of ploys were then developed to trigger or avoid prices hitting the barriers; these destabilized short run market dynamics even further, but at least they made a lot of money for the traders.

Consequently, market prices are far more volatile than the Gaussian allows.

The point here is that the Gaussian applies to certain types of random variables but not others. If we are interested in the distribution of

---

[2] "We were seeing things that were 25-standard-deviation moves, several days in a row. There have been issues in some of the other quantitative spaces. But nothing like what we saw last week." Viniar, quoted in *Financial Times*, August 13, 2007.

human heights, then the Gaussian provides a reasonable fit: the chances of meeting an adult human who is twice the population average height are negligible. However, there are *many* other random variables that cannot be described by a Gaussian. An example is individual net worth: the chances of meeting someone with the twice or even ten or a hundred times the population average net worth are far from negligible.

In his book *The Black Swan*, Nasim Taleb[3] makes the distinction very relevant here between two alternative domains. The first, Mediocristan, is where large shocks are very rare and have little impact even when they happen. Mediocristan is predictable. In our earlier example, meeting a very tall person would make little difference to our estimates of average human height. Variables like human height, IQ, and dentists' incomes all belong to Mediocristan. Then there is unpredictable Extremistan, where extreme events (or "black swans") are common. Besides wealth, Extremistan also includes many other random variables, such as book sales per author, company sizes, traders' incomes, and commodity prices. Mediocristan and Extremistan are *very* different.

Extremistan is governed by a very non-Gaussian randomness known as Mandelbrotian randomness after its discoverer, Benoit Mandelbrot. This notion of randomness is closely related to fractals, which are the way in which geometric patterns repeat themselves at different scales: if you keep increasing the resolution in a picture, you see the same basic patterns repeating again and again. It turns out that fractals are one of the great "laws" of nature. Mandelbrot's book on the subject, *The Fractal Geometry of Nature*,[4] made a sensation when it came out in 1982, and his work has since had a profound impact on disciplines ranging from aesthetics and architecture to computer and natural science, as well as mathematics. Mandelbrot's fractals also helped to pave the way for the later development of the new science of chaos and complexity.

Mandelbrotian randomness is illustrated in the following stylized example.[5] Suppose that there are 1 in 62.5 people in the US with a net worth of more than $1 million. Then there are:

---

[3] Taleb, 2007.
[4] Mandelbrot, 1982.
[5] Borrowed from Taleb, op. cit., pp. 232–3.

- 1 in 250 with a net worth of more than $2 million.
- 1 in 1,000 with a net worth of more than $4 million.
- 1 in 4,000 with a net worth of more than $8 million.
- 1 in 16,000 with a net worth of more than $16 million.
- 1 in 64,000 with a net worth of more than $32 million.
- And so forth.

Notice the pattern: double the net worth threshold, no matter what it is, and you cut the incidence by a factor of four. The size of the tail falls at a constant rate: unlike the Gaussian, there is no headwind to slow the tail down. This property is known as scalability.

Scalability reflects a "power law," which stipulates that, if x is some tail value, then the probability of an observation exceeding x declines in proportion to x raised to the power of one plus alpha (hence the term power law). Equivalently, the probability is proportional to $x^{-(1+\text{alpha})}$. (This parameter alpha is not to be confused with the alpha we encountered when discussing portfolio theory in Chapter 5, the risk-free return: there are after all only so many Greek letters to go around!) The alpha parameter takes a value between 0 and 2, the latter limiting case being equivalent to the Gaussian.

This type of distribution is often known as a stable Paretian, after the great Italian economist and statistician Vilfredo Pareto (1848–1923), who discovered it in the course of his studies of the distribution of wealth. Our earlier example of the distribution of US net worth is, in fact, based on an assumed value of alpha = 1, a value chosen because it illustrates scalability and the power law most clearly.

Leaving aside the (unrealistic) special case where alpha = 2, where the Gaussian and stable Paretian distributions coincide, these distributions differ not just in their scalability and tail behavior, but also in their tractability: the Gaussian is comparatively easy to fit, whereas the alpha parameter in a stable Paretian is much more difficult to estimate. More ominously, they also differ in that a single very extreme observation – like a "25-sigma event" – is enough to disprove the Gaussian, whereas a stable Paretian with alpha of less than 2 can plausibly accommodate any large event.

Underlying this difference is that the standard deviation is finite in the Gaussian but infinite in the stable Paretian with alpha less than 2.

This latter property does *not* mean that a sample from a stable Paretian will have an infinite standard deviation; instead, it means that if we keep drawing random observations from a stable Paretian, add each new drawing to our existing sample, and estimate the sample standard deviation anew each time, then the estimated sample standard deviation is likely to grow and grow, without limit.

This arcane property is of great significance. After all, how can we use sigma for portfolio management if it is theoretically infinite? It is therefore significant because it torpedoes the sigma and everything built on it. If we accept that price movements follow a stable Paretian, then the whole edifice of modern portfolio theory (including the CAPM, the beta, etc.) collapses. From the perspective of Gaussian portfolio theory, this is heresy.

Mandelbrot first applied the stable Paretian to the study of cotton price returns in the early 1960s: his analysis suggested an alpha of about 1.7. This work was initially well received and led to him being offered a professorship at the University of Chicago Graduate School of Business. However, once the implications sank in, the initial welcome turned to hostility and the job offer was withdrawn: the Modern Finance mafia was having none of it. Mandelbrot's work was dismissed – after all, you can get other results with other data sets, especially ones with no rare events in them – and the Gaussian party went on.

Among the family of stable Paretians, a particularly significant special case occurs when alpha = 0: the Cauchy distribution.

Imagine a rifleman with an infinitely powerful rifle, poised on a turntable ten feet from a wall of infinite length. Every minute his turntable is rotated (we assume he is not subject to dizziness!) and he fires a shot in a random direction. Naturally, half the shots miss the wall altogether. The other half hit the wall, mostly close to the spot opposite the rifleman, but some are far away, and a few almost infinitely far away. After many shots, the probability distribution of bullet marks on the wall approaches a Cauchy distribution.

The Cauchy distribution is shown in Figure 2 and is compared with the Gaussian "bell curve" distribution.

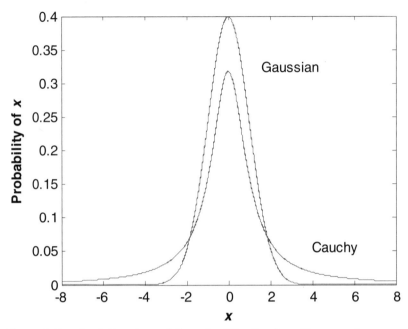

Figure 2: Standard Cauchy and Gaussian Distributions Compared

What is most striking about the Cauchy is its long drawn out tails, implying that extreme losses are much much more likely than under the Gaussian; indeed, being based on the lowest possible value of alpha = 0, the Cauchy generates the most extreme tails of any stable Pare-tian.

The Cauchy distribution is a result of a random process, just as the Gaussian distribution is, but it has very different properties. It could re-sult not from a random walk but from a "random warp", with each step consisting of a jump through a science-fiction warp drive that could take you infinitely far across the universe but generally doesn't. Those with knowledge of stock market behavior in turbulent periods can see that a "random warp" is in many respects a better description of it in those periods than the conventional "random walk" – the price jumps are not of approximately equal size but can be arbitrarily large.

To illustrate, under the Gaussian shown in the figure, a loss of x = 4.47 (a 4.47-sigma event under the Gaussian) would occur one day in just over 1,000 years. Under the Cauchy, by comparison, we would expect the same loss to occur in just over 14 trading *days*, and the wait-ing time for a 25-sigma event is a mere *two and a half months*.

This is however almost certainly too extreme: 25-sigma events don't occur *that* frequently. There is, presumably, a happy medium somewhere between the countless billions of years we would wait under the Gaussian (alpha = 2) and the two and a half months we would wait under the Cauchy (alpha = 0).

There are further reasons to prefer stable Paretians. The interconnectedness of network interactions often gives rise to distributions that have stable Paretian characteristics. Many crises are characterized by a system that is stressed by a failure in a key node that then produces a cascade of further failures in its wake. Examples would be power outages and fires caused by hot dry weather, but we often see the same in financial systems: the entire system gets stressed and a key element fails, starting off a chain reaction of further failures. In the financial context, a stable Paretian will often provide a good model of the losses involved.

Interestingly, The Options Clearing Corporation, an options clearing house whose incentives are to set trading margins for participants high rather than low, uses a stable Pareto distribution with alpha = 0.5 to set trading margins. It had found in the crash of 1987 that setting options margins using a Gaussian formula had made them far too low, leaving OCC very exposed when volatility increased.[6] So at least some practitioners were aware of this problem, but then they also had an incentive to be.

And, to bring the discussion back full circle, the failure to acknowledge the interconnectedness of networks highlights a very common failing often witnessed during the latest crisis: adverse events will often be treated as if they were independent, when in reality they share a common cause. To give an example, in January 2008, Citigroup CEO Vikram Pandit explained his bank's almost $10 billion loss the previous quarter as being due to two factors: significant losses on its subprime portfolio and an increase in credit costs.[7] But these are not independent, as both were affected by the housing market and, at a deeper level, by the bank's own previous policies, which left it exposed in the first place. This gives the misleading impression that Citigroup was merely

---

[6] www.optionsclearing.com/risk-management/margins/default.jsp (accessed 25 January 2010).

[7] Citigroup press release, January 15, 2008.

unlucky – because two bad things happened to it – whereas the reality was rather different.

The worst example of this fallacious thinking was when Robert Rubin, President Clinton's former Secretary of the Treasury, described the 2008 crisis as "a perfect storm … an extremely unlikely event with huge consequences."[8] The phrase "perfect storm" suggests that financial institutions were very unlucky to get hit by a variety of adverse independent events at the same time. This is, of course, just "25- sigma" again, a pathetic excuse of the "the dog ate my homework" variety to allow those responsible to dodge the blame.

Hideous Flaw II: Assumption of Stable Underlying Laws

A second key problem with modern quantified finance relates to the underlying maintained belief that we can carry over quantitative methods from the natural sciences, and most especially physics, and apply them mechanically to social and economic problems. This belief is naive for a number of reasons.

Perhaps the most obvious reason is that the processes governing the operation of financial markets (and more generally, any social systems) are not immutable "laws" comparable, say, to the laws of physics. Any social system is changing all the time – as the Greek philosopher Heraclitus put it, you can never step into the same river twice. In social systems, time-invariant phenomena, if they exist at all, are the exception rather than the rule.

Indeed, in contrast to the hundreds of "laws" that operate in the natural sciences, the only real quantitative law in quantitative finance is the law of one price – the "law" that two securities or portfolios with the same payoffs should have the same value – and even this is often violated and holds only as a rough approximation.

One reason is that the broader environment in which we operate is itself always changing. A second reason is because the ways in which we respond to the environment and interact with each other are always changing. Pricing relationships fluctuate with supply and demand

---

[8] Interview with F. Zakaria, CNN, October 26, 2008.

conditions, of course, and other relationships are simply the temporary consequences of unusual conditions (such as high water prices in a drought). Still others are the product of artifice, such as a marketing strategy to break into a new market. And then there are changes due to changes in policy, such as a switch from a fixed to a floating exchange rate, or a sudden change in monetary policy. We should be wary, therefore, about relying too much on any perceived trends or relationships continuing indefinitely in the future.

In addition, in physics, the phenomena being measured mostly do not change with the measurement itself or with the ways that the observer uses those measurements. The well-known exception, the Heisenberg Uncertainty Principle, is a feature of subatomic particle physics, but it is an exception and does not affect cosmology or those problems where Newtonian physics gives good answers. In finance, by contrast, the financial equivalent of the Heisenberg principle is much more prevalent. The act of modeling a financial process over time – such as the movement of a stock price – will often lead observers to react in ways that affect the process itself. For example, if enough risk managers adopt a risk management strategy such as portfolio insurance, then that strategy will affect the stock price dynamics and so undermine the strategy itself. These sorts of problems are always present to some extent in financial systems, but can become more pronounced in a crisis.

There is, relatedly, a great danger of identifying spurious but superficially plausible patterns that are little more than accidental and have no serious predictive value. Indeed, one of the many scams in finance is the cottage industry of self-described "technical analysts" who claim to be able to detect the patterns in stock prices and profit from them. They treat the charts as some kind of ouija board that magically reveals the secrets of the market. The trick is to identify the pattern – a "head and shoulders," a "reverse duck tail and pheasant," or whatever – and then use it to predict where prices are going. The patterns might be there, temporarily, but they are at best frustratingly ephemeral and, more often than not, exist only in the eye of the beholder: predictions as useful as those of Old Mother Shipton.[9] In modern American parlance, "technical analysis" is a crock.

This problem of spurious but superficially plausible patterns has plagued risk management from the word go, and one does have to wonder whether risk forecasting is, in substance, any different from chartism. Take a risk manager, give him data and a model, and he will come up with risk estimates that mainly reflect his data set (and to a lesser extent, the assumptions on which the model is based). Now take a dozen risk managers and they are likely to come up with much the same risk estimates as the first risk manager. This seems to have been what happened with the Amaranth hedge fund, which went belly-up in September 2006 with the biggest (up to then) trading losses of all time, almost $7 billion, a few days after it reassured its investors that its team of risk managers had concluded that the hedge fund was safe. Amaranth is Greek for "undying." Nice touch, that: the firm was only founded in 2000 and didn't last seven years before it self-destructed.

Nonetheless, one feature that one can confidently identify in financial markets is the apparently random oscillation between "normal" periods in which markets are stable and "crisis" periods in which markets are anything but. Most of the time, markets are fairly stable: volatilities and correlations are fairly low, pricing relationships are steady, spreads are low, markets are fairly liquid, credit is both cheap and easily available, and returns are good. In short, everything functions pretty well.

Then, once in a while, all hell breaks loose and all the above phenomena disappear: volatilities rise, correlations radicalize, earlier relationships suddenly break down, credit and liquidity become scarce or dry up altogether, risk management strategies that had previously seemed to work well unravel and bring pandemonium in their wake, financial institutions suffer very high losses, and there are many bankruptcies.

Financial markets have fluctuated between these alternate states since time immemorial. The markets in crisis are completely different

---

[9] Ursula Shipton, née Southeil (1488–1561), soothsayer born in Knaresborough, Yorkshire, and a better one than Nostradamus – but then, Kevin and Martin both being Yorkshiremen (at least by ancestry), would say that, wouldn't we? She is said to have foretold the Great Fire of London in 1666 and World War I; she also predicted that the world would end in 1993, thus causing many sleepless nights for Kevin as a young boy.

from what they were in normal states, and you cannot predict what will happen in the one state from what happened in the other.

A good analogy may be with fluid dynamics; markets generally follow a pattern of streamlined flow, obeying one set of equations, with only local instances of turbulence where those equations break down, but in extreme circumstances such as those of 2007–08 the turbulence spreads throughout markets, causing a general breakdown of systems that had hitherto seemed to work well.

Finally, and of most importance, a key difference between physical and social models of behavior is that physical models ignore the ways in which thinking agents react to and try to anticipate (and outdo) each other. We have already encountered this when we discussed how traders try to get the better of each other.

From this perspective, the basic physical model can be described as a "game against nature": the intelligent human agent interacts with nature and nature responds predictably (and unintelligently) in accordance with its own laws. Unraveling those laws has kept scientists busy for many centuries, of course, but the important point here is simply that the scientist or engineer pushes the buttons and nature responds as predicted. Unfortunately, social systems don't work that way, and the physical "game against nature" is a poor analogy for many important problems in economics, finance, and indeed in social science generally.

A simple example is how to model a duopoly: how do we model the behavior of firms in a two-firm market? This deceptively simple problem has never been properly solved, even although models of duopolies abound. Each duopolist has to take account of what the other might do, but it all depends on what you assume. There is any number of models and they all give different answers. Or you might forget all this economic theory and assume they get together quietly and agree not to do each other down: better to rig the market and rip off the customer instead.

The point is that there are any number of possible outcomes and no way in which we can plausibly eliminate most of them. So, ex ante, we cannot predict what will happen. This type of uncertainty – strategic uncertainty – pervades many situations encountered in economics and finance.

A famous example is the beauty contest described by John Maynard Keynes in Chapter 12 of his *General Theory*. There he likens the process of professional investment, with considerable justification, to:

> "... those newspaper competitions in which the competitors have to pick out the six prettiest faces from a hundred photographs, the prize being awarded to the competitor whose choice most nearly corresponds to the average preferences of the competitors as a whole."[10]

At first sight, the obvious response is to choose the six prettiest faces, but this will not do at all. As Keynes explains:

> "... each competitor has to pick, not those faces which he himself finds prettiest, but those which he thinks likeliest to catch the fancy of the other competitors, all of whom are looking at the problem from the same point of view. It is not a case of choosing those which, to the best of one's judgment, are really the prettiest, nor even those which average opinion genuinely thinks the prettiest. We have reached the third degree where we devote our intelligences to anticipating what average opinion expects the average opinion to be. And there are some, I believe, who practice the fourth, fifth and higher degrees."[11]

To attempt to think through these problems like this is to blow your mind away. A few years later, John von Neumann and Oskar Morgenstern were to give them the name, "economic games," in their 1944 book *The Theory of Games and Economic Behavior*. Games could be solved if you assumed that the parties involved followed particular rules, but you can never anticipate in advance which rules they would follow. Economic games are characterized by a particular sort of non-statistical uncertainty, strategic uncertainty, which is fundamentally unpredictable. And they are everywhere.

---

[10] Keynes, 1936, p. 156.
[11] Loc. cit.

Hideous Flaw III: Parameter Problems

Then there are the parameter problems.

The key parameters are the volatilities and the correlations of financial returns, the expected returns, and, more recently, the parameters associated with credit risk models.

The simplest case is the estimation of volatilities of financial returns, and yet even this is problematic. Let's suppose that we select a model and there are many to choose from, ranging from a simple constant volatility model to a sophisticated Generalized Autoregressive Conditional Heteroskedastic model (thankfully, usually referred to by its acronym, GARCH).

We then collect a suitable data set, but often find that the available data is quite limited. We can get a good run of NYSE stock price data, but data is much more limited for newly emerging markets and new financial instruments. But even if we have the luxury of a long enough data set, how long should our sample be? To answer this question, we need to make a subjective judgment about sample relevance. In essence, we know that our model is not a particularly good fit, because market conditions are always changing, so we choose a sample short and relevant enough to give us a rough approximation, but long enough, hopefully, to give us some accuracy. But there is no easy answer to how long that should be. In practice, whatever model we use, volatility estimates tend to alternate between periods of high volatility and periods of low volatility, and one can rarely tell in advance when the switch will take place: the estimated volatilities are themselves highly volatile.

The correlations are harder to estimate, but, to the extent we can estimate them, the one stylized fact about them that stands out is the way in which they can radicalize in crises. Estimated correlations can chug along for years in the range -0.5 to +0.5, or thereabouts; then suddenly, when a crisis hits, they jump towards plus or minus 1. The significance of this is twofold:

- It means that a hitherto well-diversified portfolio suddenly loses its diversification just when it really matters, suggesting that a diversified portfolio management strategy might protect us against the small market moves that do not really matter, but can fail spectacularly in the face of the large market moves that do. As the recent

crisis confirmed, much "portfolio management" has all the usefulness of a chocolate teapot.

• It can mean that risk estimates based on samples from the "good"
times can be way off the mark in the "bad" times: losses can be way
in excess of what our risk models predicted.

Another problem is that many correlations are merely temporary
phenomena, usually a product of policy. A standard example is the
correlation between two exchange rates that depends on their central
banks' monetary or exchange rate policies. Accordingly, an exchange
rate can be very stable for years and then suddenly jump when the
central bank of one country changes its policy, usually in response to a
crisis. This has happened repeatedly with the Mexican peso, for example: peso crises repeatedly caught US financial institutions off-guard,
having fallen asleep at the wheel and having made the naive assumption that the US dollar-peso exchange rate would remain fixed simply
because it had been fixed over the recent past.

A more recent example occurred in the dollar/yen foreign exchange market, where traders were in 2005–07 prone to engage in
the "carry trade," borrowing yen at very low rates, lending dollars or
other high-rate currencies, leveraging up, and profiting from the interest rate differential. After a lengthy period from July 2005 of yen/dollar
exchange rate fluctuations only in the 110–120 yen to the dollar range,
giving "carry traders" an apparently assured profit with apparently little
risk, in November 2007 the yen broke sharply out of this trading range
and within a year was above 90 yen to the dollar, in the process inflicting large losses on the carry traders who had naively assumed the yen
would stay within its earlier range.

Even where an underlying stable relationship actually exists, the
relationship between two variables is often much more complex than
a simple correlation would suggest. The "correct" way to handle this
problem is therefore to set out the deeper underlying relationship, but
of course, in practice, one usually has, at best, only a vague sense of
what that might be. As Douglas W. Hubbard nicely puts it, this can be
the difference between knowing someone's IQ and knowing how the
brain works.[12]

---

[12] Hubbard, 2009, p. 190.

A final problem with correlations is that we have to forecast not an individual correlation but a whole correlation matrix involving a potentially vast number, $n(n-1)/2$, separate correlations for n assets. Leaving aside other problems (having enough data, etc.), these forecasts are often very inaccurate – so much so, in fact, that correlation errors frequently drown out the impact of other factors such as market movements. Estimated correlation matrices are therefore not to be trusted.

Then there are the problems involved in estimating expected returns. A whole cottage industry has grown up around this problem. Leaving aside those who would attempt, with greater or lesser success (usually the latter), to estimate individual stock alphas – that is to say, the CAPM alphas, not the alpha parameters in stable Paretian distributions – this usually boils down to estimating the "equity premium," the extent to which average stock returns are likely to beat returns on bonds.

The consensus over the last few years seems to be that the equity premium in the future is likely to be less than it was in the post-War period. So the best future projections suggest that *no* recent historical sample is likely to give us the most likely outcome, but we *can* get a plausible forecast by taking past data and tweaking it. The debate over the equity premium tells us that sometimes we have to use a lot of subjective judgment to calibrate our models and, if necessary, tweak historical estimates in light of how we think the future might be different from the past. But no one really knows.

Yet these problems pale besides those associated with the estimation of the parameters of credit models. The main parameters here are the default probabilities and their correlations.

How do you estimate the probability that a particular firm, which has (typically) not yet gone bust, is likely to do so over the next year or so? You might, perhaps, collect data on the default histories of other, apparently similar firms, but no two firms are the same and often such data are very limited anyway. But even if you have the luxury to choose, what is the relevant historical period? Defaults tend to follow the business cycle, and if you choose a relatively benign historical sample period, your results will give you little sense of what to expect if the economy tanks.

To make matters worse, we also need estimates of *their* correlations and these are even harder to pin down. How do you determine the correlation between the probability that both firm A and firm B will default, when neither have yet defaulted? About the only sensible thing you can do is try to build a model of how defaults (including the possibility of multiple defaults) might be related to common factors such as the state of the business cycle, monetary policy, and lending standards. Then you still have the problem of finding suitable data and choosing a relevant sample period. Good luck.

Given these daunting problems, the assumption often made is that default events are independent. This, however, is a very questionable assumption, in part, because there is no reason to believe it: defaults are related to the underlying common causes that might lead two or more firms to default.

It is also a very dangerous assumption, because the values of credit derivatives are often extremely sensitive to these elusive factors. To give a simple example, which also illustrates what went wrong with Collateralized Debt Obligations (CDOs) in 2007–08: we have, say, a portfolio of 100 mortgages, all roughly comparable, and we think the probability of default on any one of them is, say, 4% a year. We build a CDO with a set of tranched claims against it, with the lowest tranche absorbing, let's say, the first ten defaults. If we now make the (all too!) convenient assumption that defaults are independent, then we can invoke the binomial distribution to calculate that the odds of the lowest tranche experiencing ten defaults are 0.22%.[13] This looks pretty safe. Similarly, if the second tranche is exposed to the next ten defaults, then the odds of it experiencing such an event are 0.00000004%, which looks very safe indeed. And the more senior tranches are apparently even safer. So it is no wonder these securities seemed to be so safe, on paper.

The reality is that the very circumstances that would lead one mortgage to default are likely to lead others to default as well. To be on the safe side, we might assume that the default correlation is 1. (This is to be biased the other way – as the true correlation is likely to be between 0 and 1 – but this is also much closer to what we have experienced in the recent US housing market.) In this case the probability that *all* of them default is 4%. Moreover, since we probably didn't take account

---

[13] This probability is easily calculated using binomial functions in Excel or, say, MATLAB. This particular one is obtained using the MATLAB command "1-binocdf(10,100,.04)".

of downturn conditions, the true probability of any default is more likely to be 10% or 20% if we are talking subprime, in which case, the true probability of all the mortgages defaulting is 10% or 20% as well.

In the one case, the CDOs seemed to be extremely safe, but in the other, their true riskiness is revealed: it all depends on what you assume about default probabilities and their correlations.

These problems go to the heart of what was wrong with the calibration of credit derivatives models. No wonder credit derivative portfolios collapsed in value when the crisis hit!

Hideous Flaw IV: Behavioral and Institutional Obstacles

Finally, most of the models used in Modern Finance fail to account for human and institutional factors. The first of these are "irrational" behavioral biases identified by the relatively new and increasingly influential fields of behavioral finance and biological economics. These have refuted the notion of the rational economic man, homo economicus, which is the bedrock of the traditional economics and finance, including notably the Efficient Market Hypothesis and endless numbers of valuation models and investment management paradigms. It turns out that we are not quite as rational as economists previously thought we were. Instead, both for biological reasons and because of our millennia hunting woolly mammoths and fending off attacks by saber-toothed cats, it appears we humans have a number of hard-wired brain impulses that override economic rationality in one way or another. Examples include:

• Confirmation bias, which causes us to overweight information that confirms our viewpoint. This leaves us blind to disconcerting (but often useful) information suggesting we are wrong.
• Availability bias, which causes the most recent information to be heaviest weighted, and hindsight bias, by which we rewrite history to convince ourselves that "we always knew that." So, for example, we all now believe that we had known all along that housing was a bubble. And so the economists, journalists, and policymakers who were entirely oblivious of the housing bubble while it was in

progress are now telling us that they should be taken as the experts on the subject, and many of us believe them. A related bias is that we fail to learn from experience, and so we rely on the very people who got us into this mess to get us out of it.

- We overrate what we think we know. Nowhere is this more evident than in the fanciful belief systems we set up to comfort ourselves. The fertile minds of the ancient Egyptians imagined the sun god Ra in his daily cycle across the heavens; the Pharaohs performed daily devotions to Amun to preserve their precious harmonious order, ma'at, from the ever present threats of the evil god Set who would bring chaos in his wake. For his part, the modern risk manager tries to keep Set's financial equivalent at bay by building a VaR model. The difference is that the Pharaoh's daily devotions generally worked – ancient Egypt only experienced disaster every few hundred years – whereas the inadequacies of VaR were already very apparent early on, when the VaR on Nick Leeson's positions at Barings in February 1995 indicated zero risk two days before those same positions caused the bank to go bust, and in 1998, when LTCM's VaR model indicated that the firm was perfectly safe just weeks before it spiraled into collapse.

- We are also very bad at judging the magnitude and severity of low-probability high-impact events. Our ancestors might have been terrified of attacks by saber-toothed cats, but (thankfully) didn't experience enough of them to get a good sense of how likely they were and how damaging they were likely to be. Instead, the terror they evoked in our ancestors often clouds our ability to think clearly about the magnitude and odds of the dangers facing us, so we lie in bed imagining the unlikeliest terrors lurking in the closet. Yet, at other times, there may be a fairly obvious danger right in front of us and we can be oblivious to it. Subprime mortgages were a case in point.

- Another is a propensity to overconfidence. Indeed we need a fair amount of confidence in order to get through our day successfully. Psychologists have demonstrated that our natural state is to imagine ourselves more capable than we really are, imminently about to make the big breakthrough in our careers, able to forecast with more than usual accuracy which investments will do best for us. While it is notoriously the case that most institutional investors fail to beat the averages over the very long term, it is inescapably the fact that most private investors do even worse, buying high, selling low, being absurdly prone to following fashion, and missing the performance of the stock averages by a substantial margin. The only thing that prevents us falling into terminal depression is that most of us are too lazy or poor at record keeping to benchmark our performance properly against the indices.

The investment management and brokerage industries flourish through our optimism; that's why most market commentary is relentlessly bullish. Of course, over the last 25 years, relentlessly bullish market commentary has been right most of the time, with only the occasional regrettable lacuna in 1989–91 or 2000–02. Brokers, whose worst nightmare is the investor who sticks his money into an index fund and forgets about it, have made large fortunes over that period by convincing us that their bright new strategy is the one that will infallibly lead us to riches. Institutions themselves are not immune; otherwise the hedge fund and private equity fund industries, distinguished more for the size of their fees than for the superiority of their returns, would have no customers.

At the top of the cycle, of course, the perpetual optimists have credibility – also money. Ken Fisher, the broker whose perpetually bullish commentary infests the Internet, is, according to *Forbes*, a billionaire. In his new book, annoyingly advertised by email, he claims investors believe a number of falsehoods, the most significant of which is that high price-earnings ratios make stocks more risky. We would argue that this "incorrect" belief is in fact one of the bedrock principles of economic understanding. However, he's a billionaire and we're not, so let's pass on. As we said, optimism sells …

Confidence and salesmanship are particularly lucrative in the more high-tech portions of the financial market, where disclosure is limited and understanding even more so. Products such as securitization and derivatives have enabled deals to be done that would have been impossible in days when lenders knew their borrower the old-fashioned way.

The entire subprime mortgage market rested on this. In the days of savings banks lending directly to homeowners, the lending officer was responsible for the credit risk, so the Wal-Mart cashier trying to buy a $700,000 home didn't get a mortgage. Today the people who have some chance of meeting the Wal-Mart cashier, the mortgage broker and the loan origination officer, have no interest in anything beyond ringing up an extra fee. Meanwhile the originating company and its investment banks are mostly sales conduits whose responsibility is diluted by the large number of loans in the packages they sell. The ultimate investors haven't the faintest idea what they are buying, but buy it because it offers a high yield and their competitors are buying similar junk. With confidence, the wheels of commerce are well oiled and everybody is happy.

As investors, we are particularly prone to make mistakes that are governed by our biology. We choose the popular, reinforcing our biases by doing so. We listen to the advice of our broker, always cheerful and upbeat about the market. In this respect, previous generations were much luckier. A dour (usually Scottish) conservative bank manager, rejecting risky ventures firmly and nagging clients to save more, both gave better investment advice and interacted better with our biological failings than the cheery but crooked salespeople we rely upon today.

Then are there those factors associated with limited human lifetime and limited human memory. The experiences we have lived through have a major impact on us: someone who has lived through the Great Depression of the 1930s or World War II will have a different worldview than someone who has not. Those who were born afterwards can read about it but it's not the same. Another, very different, example is the 1960s: as they say, if you can remember it, you weren't there.

At the same time, the big defining events, thankfully, do not occur that frequently. So most of us have only a limited experience of crises of any kind. To quote one famous mariner, drawing on his by-then fifty years' experience at sea:

> "… in all my experience, I have never been in any accident … of any sort worth speaking about. I have seen but one vessel in distress in all my years at sea. I never saw a wreck and never have been wrecked nor was I ever in any predicament that threatened to end in disaster of any sort."[14]

---

[14] Quoted in Taleb, op. cit., p. 42.

The author of these words was E.J. Smith, the Captain of the *Titanic*.

Much the same goes for a typical banker, who has only seen a small number of crises at most, meaning that the collective memory of those working in financial institutions is very short.

It is also becoming shorter. In the City of London of the 1950s, Morgan Grenfell Chairman Vivian Hugh Smith, Lord Bicester, had begun his City career in 1890. He had joined the firm as a partner, recruited as fresh new blood by J. Pierpont Morgan himself, in 1905, so by the end of his career he had 65 years' experience, 50 in a senior position. He could give his younger colleagues a first-hand account not just of the 1929 crash, but of its predecessors in 1890 and 1907; and a good second-hand account of crises back to the US Civil War. Conversely, at the start of the recent unpleasantness, on August 3, 2007, Sam Molinaro, CFO of Bear Stearns described market conditions as "the worst he'd ever seen."[15] Maybe so, but the poor soul's career had only begun in 1985, after the end of the last big recession. People have difficulty experiencing the possibility of outcomes they have never experienced or even heard second-hand.

And, lastly, there are institutional issues. In the old days, J. Pierpont Morgan could not only ride out crises, but ride in to resolve them, because he had both deep pockets and the comfort of being able to take a longer-term view. With the rare exception of investors such as Warren Buffett, who are comparably placed, most modern financiers are under great short-term pressure and can seldom afford to buck the trend for long. A banker who refuses to join the herd will forgo easy short-term profits and will come under pressure from those to whom he reports to go after the apparently easy money. Yet longer-term profitability, not to mention solvency, requires that a banker resist the urge the follow the rest of the herd if he (or she) suspects they are going to go over the cliff. A banker who is too conservative for too long will lose their job, even it turns out they were right all along. As the saying has it, the market can stay irrational longer than you can stay solvent.

This saying is reminiscent of one of another apt and unusually prescient aphorism by Keynes, and one that captures the very essence of modern banking: he once defined a "sound banker [as] not one who foresees danger and avoids it, but one who when he is ruined, is ruined

---

[15] "Bear Stearns bares its soul," *Forbes*, 3 August 2007.

in a conventional and orthodox way along with his fellows, so that no one can really blame him."[16]

To give an example from a seasoned risk veteran, after a "period of time, everyone has pretty similar trades. After ten successful years, everyone is doing the Thai baht carry trade. Why? Because even though you think it might be a risky trade, all your friends are getting rich doing it, and after a while it becomes difficult to resist the pull. You don't want to be the only person at the hedge fund cocktail party who is not doing the trade du jour. Plus, the statistics show that it's a risk-free trade. After eight years, it's an immutable fact – Thailand doesn't devalue. So you begin to look like a person who is not scientific – you're a victim of your own unfounded insecurity, a man of the past. All your friends are getting wealthy. Why don't you, too, take on these risk-free trades?"[17]

As astute readers will have guessed, this was written in 1998, in the aftermath of the bloodbath caused by the Thai devaluation in 1997, which triggered the East Asia crisis. Those risk-free trades were not so risk-free after all!

This type of problem is real enough, but is not due to any intrinsic property of the market, but the rather to the modern institutional structure, with its obsessive focus on the short term.

★★★

In short, Modern Financial Theory is a very impressive intellectual edifice, but one based on the shakiest of real-world foundations. The above are some of its major flaws, but this modest list by no means exhausts them – we will meet others in Chapter 15. It is, in essence, a self-serving belief-system. In Chapter 8, we will consider how the ideology of Modern Financial Theory helped to transform the practice of finance, with devastating consequences.

---

[16] Keynes, 1931, p. 176.
[17] S. Jonas, quoted in *Derivatives Strategy*, April 1998, p. 20.

6

Risk Management: Daft Theory, Dodgy Practice

"In theory, there is no difference between theory and practice; but in practice, there is."

(Old engineering motto and the epitaph of modern financial risk management)

Traditionally, risk management in banks was simple. Banks' main risks were credit risks, and managing these boiled down to a few rules of thumb that bankers understood well: you lend conservatively, be careful who you lend to, build long-term relationships, and so on. The only quantitative rule that mattered was the hallowed 3-6-3 rule, the basis of banking: borrow at 3%, lend at 6%, and be on the golf course by 3 p.m.

The main source of market risk for the banks – the risk of loss due to changes in market prices or rates – was their exposure to changing interest rates. This had caused major problems in periods of high inflation and volatile monetary policy in the 1970s and 1980s, but banks had learned to handle this risk using stress tests and interest rate swaps. Beyond that, their main exposure to market risk arose from the securities they held on their money market desk, linked to their funding and liquidity activities. Internationally active banks also had considerable foreign exchange positions, and others had equity positions. However, the risks involved were simple and well understood, and each desk could be handled on its own.

Nonetheless, in the late 1980s, the expanding international behemoths found themselves in a changing environment. They had offices all over the world, and their holdings of marketable securities were rapidly increasing and becoming more complicated. It was no longer considered acceptable to handle desks on a standalone basis – banks wanted to know how their London equity risks were related to their New York bond risks, and so on. It became increasingly important to take a holistic view of the risks being taken and aggregate risks across different desks. This would allow for the correlations between them and so lead to better risk management and more efficient use of capital.

This required a model of aggregate risks and a suitable risk measure. The models subsequently developed were inspired by Modern Portfolio Theory and, indeed, are perhaps best understood as an attempt to extend its principles, hitherto applied mainly to equity risks, to the whole range of measurable market risks: equities, fixed-income, commodities, foreign exchange risks, and even derivatives risks. The risk measure chosen was one that was virtually unknown as late as 1990, but which shot to fame in the early 1990s: the Value-at-Risk (VaR), loosely speaking, the maximum *likely* loss.

The most famous of these models was the RiskMetrics model developed by J.P. Morgan. The construction of this model and others like it involved a vast amount of work: measurement conventions had to be agreed, data had to collected and standardized, procedures had to be agreed to estimate volatilities and correlations, and many other practical problems had to be resolved. Nonetheless, the basic model was in place and working by about 1990 and was unveiled at J.P. Morgan's research conference in 1993, where it aroused a great deal of interest.

The RiskMetrics model, a simplified version of J.P. Morgan's in-house model, was then published on the web in October 1994. It was an overnight sensation; soon everyone wanted their own VaR model.

The RiskMetrics model was firmly rooted in the tradition of Modern Portfolio Theory and was, in many ways, its ultimate triumph.[1] It involved a multivariate Gaussian distribution with (by the time of the fourth Risk Metrics Technical Document in December 1996) 480 benchmark assets. The parameters of the model, including all 480 variances and $480 \times 479/2 = 114,960$ different correlations were updated daily.[2]

To use the model, you specified your portfolio as closely as you could in terms of the benchmark assets in a process known as mapping: so much in the NYSE, so much in one-month US Treasuries, and so on – and the model gave you your VaR.

More formally, the VaR tells us the most you can lose over a chosen horizon period at a certain probability. So if your horizon is the next trading day and your probability is 95%, then you have a 95% chance of losing no more than the VaR. If we assume a Gaussian with a zero mean and a standard deviation of 1, then the VaR at the 95% percentile, or 95% VaR for short, is equal to 1.645. Hence, on 95 "good" days out of 100, we can expect to do no worse than make a loss of 1.645; on the remaining five "bad" days, on the other hand, we can expect to make a loss bigger than the VaR.

VaR had many attractions as a risk measure: it was easy to understand and communicate; it was denominated in an easily understood unit, namely, "lost money"; it could be applied to many different types of financial risk (such as interest rate as well as equity risks, and in principle even derivatives risks); it could aggregate over different risk

---

[1] RiskMetrics also involved a solution to the awkward problem of matrix invertibility. This involved the assumption that all returns followed the same process over time, a process known as an exponentially weighted moving average. Everyone knew that this was an oversimplification and would involve some degree of error, relative to a more sophisticated alternative; however, it was transparent, at least, and it ensured that the system would always work once you inputted the latest day's data to it. This (or something like it) was essential if the system was to be reliable in real-time, and allow the daily '4:15' VaR report to be on the boss's desk in time. The exponentially weighted moving average also implicitly allows observations to "age" over time, giving them less weight as they get older, which gives a solution of sorts to the problem of how long the sample period should be: in this case, the answer is to use as long a sample as possible, but let older observations become increasingly discounted relative to new ones. For more on these issues, see, e.g., Dowd, 2005, chapter 4.

[2] See J.P. Morgan/Reuters, 1996, p. 97.

factors taking account of how they were correlated; and it could even take account of leverage. Most important of all, the VaR was the best risk measure, allegedly, that modern *quantitative* finance could offer, and gave risk managers the mantle of quantitative, almost scientific, respectability.

The VaR, with its cloaking of statistical respectability, also seemed to be much superior to older risk measures such the loss outcomes generated by stress tests. The problem with these was that the stress event – the "what if?" scenario – was entirely subjective: the usefulness of the exercise depended entirely on the skill or otherwise of the stress tester. By contrast, the VaR appeared to be more objective and, of course, required a fully fledged VaR model; stress testing was, in comparison, *so* primitive. The attitude was, "Those who can, do, and those who can't, do stress testing."

The adoption of the VaR as the preferred risk measure also served the interests of risk managers. For one, the VaR *seemed* like a panacea, and could easily be justified in terms of moderately conservative risk management. Based firmly on principles taught in all the best business schools, and endorsed officially into the Basel capital adequacy rules in 1996, it fulfilled the "never get fired for buying IBM" mantra that ensures your back is covered.

At the same time, it wasn't *too* conservative. Excessive conservatism would lose them their jobs, because traders – who as revenue generators would always have more corporate clout – would bitch and moan to get them replaced. In particular, with the rest of Wall Street also using VaR, it would have been almost impossible for a risk manager to use a more conservative model and survive the inevitable corporate caterwauling from the "unfairly" restricted traders, not to mention the pressure from senior management living off the traders' profits.

And, finally, precisely because it was so widely accepted, VaR offered risk managers the chance of preserving their jobs even if it failed. Since any VaR failure would affect most or all of the major houses on Wall Street, they had a decent chance of being able to explain it away as a 25-sigma or "perfect storm" event that could not possibly have been predicted; the risk managers, who ought to have prevented the disaster, could with luck and good in-house politicking escape significant blame.

Implementing the VaR requires the user to specify the forecast horizon period and percentile. Since the VaR was to be applied to market risks, the usual rule of thumb was the time needed to make an orderly liquidation – a matter of days. And, since the model was to be used to manage day-to-day risks over a quarterly or annual reporting cycle, most institutions chose a percentile that would be exceeded somewhere between once a month and once a year, suggesting a percentile in the range of 95% to 99%. Unfortunately, a VaR predicated over these horizons and percentiles tells us nothing about the most important risk: that of insolvency or our capital being wiped out.

To give a significant example, the Amended Basel Accord in the mid-1990s soon allowed banks to use their VaR models to set their market risk capital requirements. To do so, the regulators had to specify the VaR parameters and they settled on a ten-day horizon period and a 99% probability, parameters that have been ossified in the Basel regulations ever since. Were the regulatory capital requirements simply equal to the 99% VaR over a ten-day horizon, the position would (assuming the model were "correct") wipe out its capital in one ten-day period out of 99 such periods – that is to say, about once every three years.

A regulatory capital requirement that allows a position that blows up every three years is, to say the least, a little unconservative. To get around this problem, the regulators invented a fudge: the regulatory capital requirement would be equal to this VaR times a fudge factor, quickly dubbed the "hysteria factor." The hysteria factor was an arbitrary number, somewhere between 3 and 4, imposed on a bank by its local regulator based on their assessment of the bank's risk model.

Let's assume that the bank regulator is very conservative and imposes a hysteria factor of 4, the maximum possible. Let's assume, too, that they allow the bank to use a Gaussian model, such as the RiskMetrics one. Assuming the model is correct, the resulting capital requirement is then sufficient to meet a $4 \times 2.232 = 8.928$-sigma ten-day loss event, an event so remote it would never happen. The regulatory capital requirements were thus reassuringly conservative.

But then again, maybe not. Recall that the Gaussian is not reliable in the tails, so let's replace it with some more tail-oriented distribution – say, the Cauchy. In that case, the probability of the capital being wiped out in any given ten-day period turns out to be 3.55%. This is a whole lot *less* conservative: it suggests we could expect to see the capital wiped out more than once a year.

So the length of time we would have to wait to see the regulatory capital wiped out is somewhere between a little under a year and infinity – that is to say, we have no idea.

The bottom line is that moderate risks and extreme risks are very different animals and we can't really extrapolate from one to the other. To borrow an analogy from Riccardo Rebonato, no study of the height of hamsters, however careful, will tell us much about the height of giraffes, especially if we no real idea of how tall giraffes might be in the first place.[3]

It was just as well, perhaps, that the banks' trading positions were still small relative to the rest of their balance sheets.

Leaving aside these difficulties, the VaR also has a serious, indeed, fatal, weakness – at least if we are interested in tail risks rather than the more regular monthly or quarterly ups and downs. The VaR tells us the worst we can expect on the 99 (or whatever) good days out of 100, but it tells us *nothing* about what might happen on those remaining bad day(s), when the loss might be anything – a little bigger than the VaR, perhaps, or catastrophic. Anything can happen and the VaR does not tell us.

The "tail blindness" of the VaR is a truly fatal drawback in financial risk management, because it is the tail risks, the possibilities of very high losses, that really matter. It is no good telling me that I will be OK on so many days out of 100 or 1,000, whilst omitting to tell me that any one of the remaining days might easily be lethal: I need to know what's in the tail and the VaR does not tell me.[4]

The defects of VaR become even more apparent when "tranched" securitization is considered, in which loans are commingled into a pool and different slices of risk are sold to different investors. For each slice the risk of loss is zero if the overall pool has only small losses. Then beyond the point at which the previous tranche is exhausted, the loss rises on a leveraged basis, much more rapidly than losses on a pool of conventional mortgages. The high-risk tranches would appear to have

---

[3] Rebonato, 2007, p. 180.

[4] Moreover, these sorts of problems have been known about for a long time too, but most practitioners didn't want to know. See, for example, Artzner et al, 1999. Admittedly, this article is not the easiest read, couched as it is in the difficult language of mathematical measure theory, but many others, including both Kevin and Martin, have been saying similar things for years.

relatively modest losses in good times, but would suffer very heavily on a leveraged basis when trouble hit.

Even more dangerous were AAA-rated securitization tranches. These traded like top quality corporate bonds in good times, so making their VAR low, but were subject to wild price risk once the internal correlations between their underlying asset risks were exposed and it became clear that they bore risk far in excess of traditional AAA-rated securities. Add multiple tiers of securitization, such as in the notorious "CDO-squared", and it is clear that the tails of the distribution, to which the VaR is completely blind, become "fat" to an explosive degree and the VaR becomes ever more misleading. Even without the level of mortgage fraud that was being committed, these babies would have caused huge trouble at some stage: the risks involved couldn't be hidden forever.

Furthermore, the margins on complex high-risk derivatives, double securitizations, and the like are higher than those on simpler, more liquid products. Their greater profit margins then combined lethally with their greater disguised riskiness to ensure that these pathological products were *favored* over simpler less profitable but less risky alternatives, itself a highly pathological outcome.

And, finally, the VaR is especially bad when used in conjunction with the Gaussian distribution, as it often was: one underestimates the tail itself and the other is blind to what is in it. This makes for a splendid combination that could have been purpose-built to produce disaster: one has the cliff in the wrong place the other underestimates the length of the drop when one then inadvertently goes over the edge.

On the other hand, the people using it were not all fools, so one has to ask what purpose the Gaussian VaR models really served. The answer is depressing: if the VaR was to be used to set regulatory capital requirements (which it was), and if the aim of the exercise was to keep these as low as possible (which it also was, with rare exceptions), then the Gaussian VaR was in fact just right after all. But this is not really risk management.

Fortunately, there are good alternatives to the VaR. These have many of the attractions of the VaR, but, unlike the VaR, helpfully give us some indication of how bad bad might be:

- There is the Probable Maximum Loss, the worst loss we can expect on one day out of 100 or 1,000, or whatever.
- There is Expected Shortfall, which tells us what we can expect to lose if a tail event occurs. This tells us something about what might happen in the tail, unlike the VaR, and has been used by actuaries for many years (although, actuaries being actuaries, they would insist on giving it a string of confusing names: Tail Conditional Expectation, Tail VaR, Tail Conditional VaR and so on; the worst was Worst Conditional Expectation).
- There is the outcome of a humble stress test: "what if?" is a much underrated question in risk management. A good stress test will often reveal problems that no other method could identify, such as taking account of what might happen in a crisis, where normal market conditions break down.

These risk measures were much better than the VaR, but they never really displaced it among practitioners. Apart from anything else, they were more conservative[5] and would have damped risk-taking and produced higher capital requirements. Who wanted that?

Given these problems with the VaR, it is almost churlish for us to add that VaR models were, in practice, enormously inaccurate – so much so, in fact, that many reported VaR numbers were virtually meaningless. These problems became apparent very early on, too. In one well cited study, an experiment was carried out in which a number of different firms implementing the same risk system were asked to estimate the VaRs of various specified positions: the estimates VaRs of theoretically identical positions often differed remarkably, and no two firms ever reported the same VaRs for the same position.[6] Another study looked at the sophisticated (and expensive!) VaR models used by leading US banks and found that these were highly inaccurate and, indeed, less accurate than much simpler, almost rules-of-thumb, VaR forecasts. This appears to be at least in part due to inaccuracies of the forecasted correlation matrices on which the more sophisticated models depended; all that extra time, effort, and money spent building a fancy VaR model was wasted.[7]

---

[5] Strictly speaking, stress tests can be more or less conservative than the VaR depending on the severity of the stress, but we ignore stress tests that are less conservative than the VaR as of no real value.

[6] Marshall and Siegel, 1997.

[7] Berkowitz and O'Brien, 2002.

An additional measurement problem was that VaR systems were not in practice sufficiently accurate to distinguish sharply between simple products, on which competition was fierce and spreads narrow, and more complex products, whose spreads were broader and which under VaR appeared little more risky. Competitors that avoided complex products or maintained only moderate leverage then found their businesses increasingly commoditized and their returns skimpy – resulting in demands from shareholders for more aggressive policies. Most important, since bonuses were paid based on annual earnings rather than on long-term returns, it paid to leverage as much and take as much risk as VaR calculations would permit.

In short, it was apparent from early on not just that VaR was deeply flawed in principle, but that VaR models were very inaccurate in practice. But like much else in Modern Finance, these inconvenient truths were swept under the rug and the party went on.

Leaving aside the risk measure, there is also the question of which statistical distribution to fit to our data. Ideally, we are looking for a distribution that has suitable properties for the purpose at hand and fits the data reasonably well.

However, from a risk management perspective, it is the tails that matter and so the Gaussian, despite it tractability, should be avoided at all costs. Instead, we should choose distributions such as the stable Paretians, which are suited to the tails, because of their scalability and power-law properties.

And if we are interested in *extreme* tails, as we might be from a solvency perspective, we can draw on the impressive corpus of Extreme Value analysis. As we push further into the tails, we go from power laws into the even less familiar domain of the Extreme Value Theorem, which tells us how we should expect the *maximum* value of a sample to behave.[8] The Extreme Value Theorem is an estranged cousin of the more familiar Central Limit Theorem. The Central Limit Theorem deals with the central mass of a distribution (and more particularly, a sample *mean*) while the Extreme Value Theorem deals with the extremes (and more particularly, a sample *maximum*). Needless to say, EV distributions are *very* non-Gaussian.

---

[8] For more on Extreme Value, see, e.g., Bassi et al., 1998, Focardi and Fabozzi, 2003, or Cotter, 2001.

The impetus to EV analysis came from an unfortunate disaster, a flood in the Dutch provinces of Holland and Zeeland on February 1, 1953, in which the sea dykes protecting the country were breached and over 1,800 people were killed. As a result, the Dutch government set up the Delta Committee under the renowned mathematician David van Dantzig and asked it to determine how high the walls needed to be to ensure that a comparable disaster would only occur once in every 10,000 years. Their attempt to answer this difficult question gave birth to EV analysis as a practical discipline.

EV analysis tells us what distribution to fit to the (extreme tail) data, how to estimate its parameters, and how to use the fitted tail to extrapolate well beyond our sample range. It can tell us, in theory, how high the sea walls must be to reduce the probability of a repeat flood in Holland (or in Bangladesh) to a 1 in 10,000 year event, equivalent in financial terms to an annual VaR at the 99.99% percentile. From a statistical point of view, this is the best we can do and yet it can only take us so far.

We should keep in mind that the Dutch only had, at most, perhaps 300 annual observations or so to go on, most of which were not tail observations anyway; and when the sea walls were rebuilt, no one at the time considered the possibility that the sea level might be slowly rising, and this undermined a key premise on which their analysis was predicated.

The idea that we can reliably estimate 1 in 10,000 or even 1 in 1,000 year events is therefore essentially hubris. Or, to quote the great physicist Richard Feynman's immortal observation on the Challenger disaster, "If some guys tells me that the probability of failure is 1 in 10^5, I know he's full of crap." [9]

In any case, we can never in practice be sure we have the "right" distribution (though we can be confident, with tails, that it is not the Gaussian), we can never be certain how relevant our data set might be to the future (which is unforeseeable and we never have enough data anyway), and our parameter estimates will always be inaccurate (especially those that relate specifically to the tail). Hence our best-fitting curve will be little better than educated guesswork and the further we extrapolate into the tail, the less reliable our results will be. As anyone who has ever climbed a tree and gone out onto a limb will know, the

---

[9] Quoted in Adams, 1995, p. 213.

branch becomes less stable the further along it we extend ourselves. Estimates of the VaR at the 99.9% or 99.99% percentiles are, consequently, so imprecise as to be meaningless.

Yet the difficulties of fitting a distribution to the data are merely the start of our problems. In essence, most quantitative risk management is based on the paradigm of portfolio management, and this implicitly supposes that we face some relatively homogeneous set of risks, which can be approximated by some *single* multivariate statistical distribution. Our problem then, supposedly, is to fit that distribution, estimate the risks involved and thence proceed to manage them.

This works reasonably enough if you have a good sense of the risks you face *and* those risks are moderately homogeneous. For example, carefully implemented, it works reasonably well most of the time if you are dealing with equity risks and you know what you are doing. Even so, it is not easy: identifying a suitable distribution is difficult, correlations will be unsteady, and so on.

Now try extending this to incorporate other types of risks: we might want to add bonds or commodities to stocks. We then immediately realize that there is no particular reason to think that bond or commodity returns will follow the same distributions as stocks. And, in fact, they don't. All we can then do is hope that the distributions aren't too dissimilar. We put them all in the pot together and look for a distribution that "best" fits them all – or, more realistically, we are looking for a rough fit that isn't too blatantly bad.

By now the cracks should be beginning to show; the more risk factors we throw into the pot, the worse the overall fit. Equities, bonds, commodities, and the more straightforward derivatives are about as far as you can go. Don't think about putting the more complicated financial derivatives into the same pot.

Statistical purists will object that there is an alternative: copulas. The word "copula" comes from the Latin noun *copula* (a bonding together, from which we get the English word "couple") or, in its verb form, *copulare* (to copulate; by a curious coincidence, the Latin equivalent of the Anglo-Saxon that is now so widespread among derivatives practitioners).

In its statistical meaning, a copula refers to a function that binds together different distributions to take account of how the random variables involved move together. Instead of trying to fit the same distribution to different risk factors, we can let them each have their own different distribution and then model the way they move together by fitting a copula function across them, comparable to the way in which one might fit a harness to a group of horses to hold them together.[10]

We will have more to say on copulas in Chapter 8: they turn out to be one of the villains in the credit derivatives story. Suffice it for the moment to say that, even at the best of times, copulas are difficult to calibrate and still rely on estimates of correlation parameters. These are highly unreliable, as we have said many times, but in any case, even a good copula fit can only take us so far. Though in theory, a copula can accommodate any arbitrary set of inputted distributions for different risk factors, in practice, the plausibility of the copula itself is undermined if the underlying distributions are too diverse.[11] Thus, the greater flexibility of the copulas, though helpful, only takes us so far. The more diverse the distributions of underlying risk factors, the less plausible any fit becomes.

Moreover, it should be noted that the risk that can be measured best, and the one that quantitative risk managers have focused on most, market risk, is not the most important. The risks that really matter are credit, liquidity, and operational risks. Of these, the credit risk models failed spectacularly in the crisis, liquidity risks were generally ignored, with disastrous consequences, and operational risk models were, in essence, an attempt to do the impossible, but a lucrative source of revenue for self-interested risk managers and consultants.

Credit risks are those associated with the possibility of default on loans or bonds. Most of the time, a well-diversified corporate bond or

---

[10] For the purists, the distribution of each variable separately considered is known as a marginal distribution; the copula function then creates the multivariate distribution, the distribution of all variables considered together, by fitting a copula to the marginals, taking the latter as its inputs. The beauty of this approach is that the correlation structure, represented by the copula, can be separated out from the marginals. This allows for much greater modelling flexibility than is possible with traditional approaches to multivariate distributions, which jumble the correlations and marginals together.

[11] To explain further: given the copula, we can have any marginal distributions we want, but the problem is that the copula itself has to be plausible. So, for example, how do you find a copula that gives a good fit to both market and credit risks? Good luck.

loan portfolio will experience a limited number of defaults; hence losses will be low, and offset against the higher yields on bonds that might default; however in bad states, as during the recent crisis and many times before, there can be many defaults and losses can be very high.

The distribution of credit losses will almost always take a very different form from typical market risks; a very asymmetric distribution with a distinctive long right-hand tail representing those bad-state losses. Hence, you cannot fit any single distribution across both market and credit risks.

The copulas don't really help us out much here either. Except for toy examples, you can't really fit a copula across both market and credit risks: they are just too different. In any case, with credit risk, we are often concerned about a different forecast horizon, longer than the one- or ten-day horizons that market risk models are usually predicated on. The notion of the 99% combined market-cum-credit risk VaR over a one-day forecast horizon is so strained as to be laughable.

Then there is operational risk – loosely speaking, the risk of losses arising from people or systems failures. At one level, a good operational risk model has its uses. There are, indeed, certain types of operational risk that can be quantified. Fluctuations in the use of staple clips come to mind: we wouldn't want to run out of those. And there are others beyond the stock control type: frequencies of particular breakdowns, turnovers of staff, and so forth. An operational risk quantification system can be useful for run-of-the-mill operational risks like those where the frequencies and consequences of the events concerned are fairly predicable.

However, the reality is that we can only ever anticipate a limited number of possible outcomes and it is the ones we don't see that we should worry about. Some of these really matter, too: one of the biggest "operational" risks faced by modern banks is rogue trader risk. How can you estimate that?

Finally, we have liquidity risk. This is an especially difficult problem when risk managers think they have a good dynamic hedging strategy – a strategy that requires nimble market-trading footwork, such as portfolio insurance – and then seek to capitalize on it by increasing leverage. In theory, this should work fine, buy only *if* the assumptions on which it is based actually hold.

In practice, the strategy is apt to unravel in a crisis just when it is most needed – recall portfolio insurance again – in which case the bank's losses are magnified even further by its increased leverage. In many cases, the net result of this type of "risk management" is simply to smooth the smaller fluctuations at the expense of leaving banks more exposed to the very big ones.

Dynamic risk management strategies are particularly likely to unravel when there is strategic uncertainty, uncertainty that arises because the parties involved cannot predict each other's reactions to each other. Translated into risk management terms, ignoring strategic uncertainty is like assuming that you can safely get to the cinema exit in the event of a fire, without realizing that everyone else will be running for the exit as well. The problem is the assumption that you are in a "game against nature," overlooking the point that it is not dumb "nature" you are dealing but other people just like you, who think the same way.

Let's say you have come up with a VaR-based risk management strategy. When your VaR rises, you exit your more risky positions to reduce your VaR. This makes sense in a game against nature, when you are the only person implementing this strategy and everyone else carries on as before: it is as if you have noticed the fire but everyone else in the cinema is still captivated by the movie and so oblivious to it.

This of course is to reveal its weakness: the strategy is counterproductive if everyone else is doing the same thing as you are. If everyone sells in a crisis, then that collective reaction will itself exacerbate the fall in prices and create the danger of a positive feedback loop in which the crisis grows as it feeds off itself. Some initial trigger leads everyone to sell, and these sales cause prices to fall and VaRs to rise; the increased VaRs generate further sales as risk managers struggle to get their VaRs back down, and these new sales cause further price falls and even higher VaRs. The collective attempt to get individual VaRs down destabilizes the market and, paradoxically, increases everyone's VaR, destroying market liquidity in the process.

Once this problem starts, the risk management system takes over like an out-of-control robot on the rampage: even where investors had the sense to recognize that prices had fallen enough and were willing to hold or even buy rather than sell, their risk systems wouldn't allow it: their stop-loss levels were closing down their positions and credit downgrades were forcing them to sell. Investors also lose control of the composition of their portfolio: whatever they try to sell, they are likely to be able to sell only the most liquid positions, and will end up holding only the toxic waste. This is damaging in itself, needless to say, but can also create nonsensical linkages, so spreading the crisis to what would otherwise be unrelated markets.

A nice example occurred during the East Asian crisis. South Korean banks had been holding extensive dollar reserves, but the dollar interest rate was lower than the domestic one, so they sought to "enhance" the yield on their portfolio (always a recipe for trouble!) by buying various exotic derivatives – Ukrainian bonds, undeliverable forwards, Brazilian Brady bonds, and other assorted rubbish – that they stuffed into their portfolios. Once the crisis hit, the only assets among these that were liquid were the Bradys, and the South Koreans held perhaps a quarter of the market for them. The Koreans, under pressure to sell, then sold the Bradys, and both the bonds and Brazilian currency, the real, took a hit out of nowhere.

All this is perverse. From a risk management perspective, if everyone else is selling in a crisis, then the best strategy is to buy, the traditional contrarian response: you pick up bargains at basement prices and profit from everyone else's panic. This, however, requires that you have the immediate resources at hand, the courage to go against the market, and, of course, both the common sense required and the freedom to go against your own VaR model (or better, just common sense and no VaR model). Naturally, this strategy has its costs: in a bubble you miss the apparently "easy" profits while everyone else enjoys themselves. But if you do so, you will not only make a lot of money but also perform a public service in helping to mitigate the crisis by acting counter to it.

The presence of contrarian players thus helps maintain market liquidity, and so helps prevent artificial linkages to markets elsewhere that should remain unaffected: the problems of South Korean banks should not spill over into an attack on the currency of Brazil.

Naturally, when confronted with the problem of strategic uncertainty, instead of dealing with it, the risk management profession is now attempting to measure it by making assumptions about how the parties involved will react to each other in a crisis. (Note, you assume how they "will," not "might," respond: the illusion of certainty.) You then estimate your VaR (or whatever other risk measure you prefer) conditional on these assumptions and, guess what, you find that this makes a big difference to the risk estimates you would have got if you hadn't taken account of strategic interaction.

The problem is that strategic uncertainty is simply unknowable. To estimate a risk measure *conditional* on the assumed interaction misses the point. We just don't know how the parties involved would interact or second-guess each other. We can assume anything we like, but we still don't *know* and can't even guess with any degree of confidence. Come the crisis, they might interact very differently from the way we assumed. The point is that we don't know, so our risk estimates are meaningless.

This and much other "sophistication" in risk models is itself a danger. It means greater complexity (and therefore greater scope for error, unseen problems, etc.), less transparency (making errors harder to detect), greater dependence on underlying assumptions (any one of which could be wrong), and increased dangers of black-box thinking, a greater dependence on a system that is too complex to check properly but which can leave a bank exposed to all manner of hidden risks. A simple system might look primitive, but is usually transparent and risk managers can easily get a sense of its strengths and weaknesses.

In this context, it is particularly pertinent to recall that any risk management system involves an attempt to control intelligent agents who have their own interests at heart and who will respond to any control system by making the best of it and exploiting its weaknesses. If traders are remunerated by the profits they make, and if the only way to make large profits is to take large risks, then traders will take large risks. If the risks pay off, they make a nice bonus; and if they don't, it's not their own money they lost, and they can always get another job elsewhere. The trader therefore has an incentive to take more risks than the employing bank would (or at least, should) like.

Banks traditionally responded to this type of problem by imposing position limits, and one of the principal uses of VaR models was, indeed, to determine these. But from the traders' perspective, those position limits are simply a nuisance to be circumvented. The traders will therefore rapidly work out where the VaR system is weak and "game" it accordingly.

One way to do this is to stuff risk into the tails. An example is to sell very out-of-the-money options, options that are very unlikely to pay off. Precisely because they are so unlikely to pay off, many VaR systems will fail to pick up the risks involved – in effect, they occur out in the tail region and so are not detectable by the VaR. Traders can then sell them with impunity. Most of the time, the options will expire worthless and the trader will make a fairly steady income; once in a while, the position will blow up, but what the heck: it was only the bank's money.

In any case, a large loss makes them no more vulnerable to getting fired than an inadequate profit; nor can they receive less than zero from the bonus pool. A loss that is deferred for several years is even less of a problem; by that point they will have moved on at least to a different position and probably to a different institution. The wild cowboy culture of the trading floor doesn't discourage risk-taking, either.

Traders' ideal is a trading system that makes them large, fairly predictable profits. Large profits not only provide big bonuses, but increase their share of the firm's capital for the following year. Becoming a "big producer" makes them less vulnerable to the political infighting that becomes an office mania around the time that bonuses are decided. In effect, traders benefit from "martingale" risks,[12] in which there is a high probability of a moderate profit and a small probability of a large loss; they are correspondingly repelled by "anti-martingale" risks that have a high probability of small losses and a low probability of a large profit. Even if the latter risks are more lucrative, on an expected monetary value basis, it is unlikely that the trader will still be around to enjoy the bonanza when it finally eventuates.

In reality, therefore, much trading profit is simply a scam, in which traders make only illusory profits by taking hidden risks, "profits" that they will lose back one day, but not before they have walked off with fat bonuses and enriched themselves in the process. We have seen

---

[12] The term "martingale" has been so generalized by modern probabilists as to become meaningless. We refer to the eighteenth century French gambling strategy, supposedly invented by Jean le Rond d'Alembert (1717–83), by which the gambler wagering repeatedly on an even bet such as a coin-toss doubles his stake on every loss and reverts to the original stake after a win. If the bet is fair, he will have a large probability of a modest gain and a small probability of losing his entire fortune (how small depending on the size of his fortune in relation to the stake). An anti-martingale is then the contrary wager, which gives him a high probability of modest running losses and a small probability of "breaking the bank at Monte Carlo."

this again and again: Salomon Brothers in the 1980s, Barings, Orange County, and LTCM in the 1990s, and countless more post the Millennium.

To the extent that these problems can be resolved, the solution is to be found in aligning incentives: we need to change traders' remuneration so they have an incentive to take more care with their employers' money. Neither more elaborate modeling nor more technical sophistication are the solution, because they increase the danger of error, reduce comprehensibility, and fail to address this crucial underlying problem.

There is hence an inevitable limit to how much protection any system of quantitative financial risk management can ever give us.

Perhaps the biggest mistake that we can make with a quantitative model is to overestimate what we think we know, and in so doing leave ourselves exposed to dangers we are not aware of, and these are often the most dangerous of all. As the former US Defense Secretary Donald Rumsfeld famously said in a press conference in 2002, "there are known knowns; there are things we know we know. We also know there are known unknowns; that is to say we know there are some things we do not know. But there are also unknown unknowns – the ones we don't know we don't know."[13] Mr. Rumsfeld's splendid comments were widely lampooned as a model of bad English. He was, nonetheless, in his uniquely inarticulate way, spot on.

There are further problems as we move up the corporate structure. We have already discussed the problems of risk aggregation, the difficulties of adding different types of risks (such as market, credit, liquidity, and operational risks) together in a sensible way, and we never even *mentioned* the difficulties of adding *other* important risks, such as those associated with a bank's business strategy – which, after all, determines many of the risks that the bank will ultimately expose itself to. These difficulties imply that it is, in practice, impossible to produce a meaningful measure of aggregate risks across the institution as a whole, even if we think we can estimate some individual risks or groups of related risks.

A related problem is that risk managers usually lack organizational clout. There is always tension between risk managers, who want to control risk-taking, and those who directly benefit from it such as traders, who perceive risk management as a barrier to their profit-making.

---

[13] Department of Defense briefing, February 12, 2002.

The effectiveness of risk management in practice can then depend on the outcome of political infighting, in which the efforts of risk managers are frequently undermined.

This can often be quite subtle. A bank might have apparently good risk management processes, but individual risk managers will often be "encouraged" not to rock the boat and quietly look the other way. They can then start persuading themselves that things won't fall apart – at least not for a while – and succumb to the "group think" that is enveloping the bank.

It doesn't help either that the risk management and strategy functions within large banks are poorly connected. With very few exceptions, the risk people and the strategy people don't understand each other and don't communicate effectively. The risk people spend a lot of time on their risk models but often fail to grasp the broader picture; for their part, the strategy people tend to focus on profit and income, and are not particularly interested in or knowledgeable of the risks involved. Consequently, perhaps the most basic aspect of a bank's risk-taking, its core strategy, often lies beyond the ambit of effective risk management.

This is especially so for the grander strategic decisions, which are usually the pet projects of the top management. Woe betide the risk manager who questions those! And yet it is these very projects that often turn out to be fatal. As one observer later ruefully concluded, "risk management discipline rarely made it to the chief executive's office or the boardroom, or into day-to-day business decision-making. We had the appearance of risk management without the reality of risk management so when we really needed it, it wasn't there."[14]

In such an environment those few risk managers who speak out generally lose their jobs, so further encouraging the others to keep silent. A good example was Paul Moore, the head of regulatory risk at the British bank HBOS.[15] He warned his bosses, including the then CEO Sir James Crosby, that the bank was "going too fast, had a cultural indisposition to challenge, and was a serious risk to economic stability and consumer protection." His concerns were dismissed and so was he. He was later told he didn't "fit in" and clearly didn't. He subsequently

---

[14] Borge, 2001, p. 56.
[15] Quoted in *Financial Times*, February 11, 2009.

likened his experience to being "like a man in a rowing boat trying to slow down an oil tanker." Moore even raised his concerns with the UK financial regulator, the FSA, but they apparently just wanted an easy life and did nothing either.

Sir James Crosby, by contrast, went on to become an economic advisor to the British Prime Minister, Gordon Brown, advising him on how to sort out the banking mess. It's reassuring to see all that banking experience being put to good use.

There is also a perverse power pendulum at work. A bank is most vulnerable at the top of the cycle, when risk-taking is highest and easy profits appear most alluring. This is the point when it is most important to rein risks in. However, precisely because prospects seem so good, this is also the point when attempts to rein in risk-taking are likely to encounter the most opposition and are least likely to prevail. Consequently, the very time when the bank most needs effective risk management is also the time when the risk management function has the least power to deliver it.

This problem is but one aspect of a deeper and more pervasive issue dragging down not just risk management but all management: the notion that a big bank is some kind of coherent group of people all singing (more or less) from the same hymn sheet is a fiction. More often that not, especially in the modern financial behemoths, the bank consists of disparate groups with their own agendas, in some cases in a state of long-term civil war. Conflicts of interests are everywhere, and senior management has only very limited ability to manage them.

There is also abundant evidence that the senior management of many financial institutions did not know the risks their institutions were taking during the bubble. Even before the crash, Credit Suisse managed to lose $120 million in South Korea in 2006 by issuing reverse convertibles against a basket of several shares. The benefit of undertaking these arcane and artificial transactions is that dozy investors will supposedly pay too much for the conversion option. However Credit Suisse, which had a large "book" of these instruments, lost huge amounts of money when the Korean stock markets became unnaturally calm, and the volatility-based conversion premiums collapsed to a level far below that predicted by their models.[16] That may have been

---

[16] Martin discussed this transaction in detail in Hutchinson, 2006.

the most opportune $120 million loss a bank ever suffered. It made Credit Suisse adopt a more conservative approach to risk management than its main rival UBS about a year before real market trouble actually arrived, thus preserving it through 2008 in much better shape.

Another example of management lack of risk-awareness was Lehman Brothers. "Lehman has probably the best risk management and has been diversifying for years," said Mark Williams, a former Federal Reserve official who teaches finance at Boston University School of Management."[17] Lehman filed for bankruptcy six months later.

Citigroup provides a further example. As its CEO Charles "Chuck" Prince explained in July 2007, "as long as the music is playing, you've got to get up and dance. We're still dancing."[18] But not for long: shortly afterwards the financial behemoth began to spiral into collapse and Chuck was forced to resign. Citigroup's CFO later claimed that the firm was simply a victim of unforeseen events. However, as one commentator noted:

"No mention was made of the previous five years, when Citi was busily consolidating mortgage debt from people who weren't going to repay … pronouncing it 'investment grade' … mongering it to its clients … and stuffing it into its own portfolio … while paying itself billions in fees and bonuses. No, according to the masters of the universe, the downgrades were 'completely unexpected' … Like the eruption of Vesuvius; even the gods were caught off guard. Apparently, as of September 30, Citigroup's subprime portfolio was worth every penny of the $55 billion that Citi's models said it was worth. Then, whoa, in came one of those 25-sigma events. Citi was whacked by a once-in-a-blue-moon fat tail. Who could have seen that coming?[19]

The fact they were left holding so much of the toxic stuff themselves suggests that Citigroup certainly didn't.

Both these institutions were examples of a recurring problem with modern risk management: you could not afford to be notably more

---

[17] Bloomberg, March 17, 2008.
[18] Interview to *Financial Times*, July 10, 2007.
[19] Bonner, 2007.

conservative in risk management than your competitors or your market share would be devastated and you would be out on your ear.

Goldman Sachs was one of few that managed to avoid this trap, taking a substantial "short" position in securities linked to subprime mortgages, so enjoying profits from the downturn that balanced its losses in other areas. Goldman also managed to persuade the US Treasury (led at that time by its alumnus Hank Paulson) to fund payouts on AIG's toxic credit default swap book, in the process netting it a profit of $13 billion from various bankruptcies, primarily that of its competitor Lehman Brothers. Goldman's success was however a product of luck and superior connections – both undeniably useful in financial services – rather than superior risk management. It was after all Goldman's CFO David Viniar who in August 2007 uttered the immortal line about 25-standard deviation events. If nothing else, this demonstrated that Goldman's understanding of the risks it was undertaking was no better than anybody else's.

The gap between good practice and what was really going on was most aptly exposed by, of all people, Franklin Raines, longtime CEO of Fannie Mae. Fannie had already suffered a risk management crisis in 2004 (after which Raines was fired) before succumbing to bankruptcy in 2008. Before all this, he lectured an FDIC risk management symposium on the subject in July 2002. He noted that Fannie Mae's risk management practices were bolstered by seven major risk mitigants that may be instructive to other companies:

1   Continual onsite examination process by a financial regulator.
2   Annual reviews by an independent external rating agency.
3   Maintaining a minimum capital level.
4   Operating under a risk-based capital approach.
5   Maintaining liquid assets to meet unexpected demands.
6   Strengthening market discipline by issuing market-priced subordinated debt.
7   Ensuring sound financial disclosures.[20]

Glad to have your thoughts there, Franklin, but that doesn't alter the fact that your institution was an overleveraged, politically protected

---

[20] Quoted in *FDIC Bank Trends*, July 2002.

duopolist that consistently played games with its derivatives accounting and was completely unequal to handling or even understanding the crisis in its core business when it came.

Finally, a counterexample. Angelo Mozilo, CEO of Countrywide Financial, probably the single institution most responsible for creating the subprime mortgage crisis, appears to have understood pretty well the risks his institution was taking. "The bottom line is that we are flying blind on how these loans will perform in a stressed environment of higher unemployment, reduced values, and slowing home sales," he wrote in a 2006 email to Countrywide's Chief Operating Officer David Sambol about "pay-option" loans in which the borrower could choose how much of the mortgage's floating interest rate he paid. In another email to Sambol, Mozilo referred to another subprime product as "toxic" and acknowledged that the Fico credit scores of the borrowers using the product were worryingly low. "With real estate values coming down, this product will become increasingly worse," he wrote.[21] Unfortunately, those emails only came to light from the SEC indictment of Mozilo for fraud and insider trading in June 2009. Sometimes it just doesn't pay to let on that you know about your risks!

Yet the fact is that many senior managers were not so much ignorant of their institutions' excessive risk-taking but actively encouraging it. After all, their bonuses depended on it and the only horizon that really matters is the period to the next bonus. This issue was highlighted by a wonderful anecdote told by Andy Haldane, the Bank of England's Director for Financial Stability, in early 2009:

> "A few years go, ahead of the present crisis, the Bank of England and the FSA commenced a series of seminars with financial firms, exploring their stress-testing practices. The first meeting of that group sticks in my mind. We had asked firms to tell us the sorts of stress which they routinely used for their stress tests. A quick survey suggested these were very modest stresses. We asked why."[22]

---

[21] Quotations from *Investment News*, June 4, 2009.
[22] Haldane, 2009.

Various lame possibilities were discussed, but eventually the real explanation came out when one of the bankers blurted out that:

> "There was absolutely no incentive for individuals or teams to run severe stress tests and show these to management. First, because if there were such a severe shock, they would very likely lose their bonus and possibly their jobs. Second, because in that event the authorities would have to step in anyway to save a bank and others suffering a similar plight.
>
> All of the other assembled bankers began subjecting their shoes to intense scrutiny. The unspoken words had been spoken. The [Bank] officials in the room were aghast."[23]

The fact that the Bank officials were surprised is itself revealing; so, too, were their earnest attempts to persuade the commercial bankers that there *really* would be no bailout if they got themselves into trouble.

Yet the unnamed banker turned out to be spot on and, when the crisis came, the government duly rode to the rescue just as he and his colleagues had anticipated.

The point is that risk management will only ever work if those responsible have the right incentives to practice it. However good the risk managers, however good their models and risk management systems, they still report to the senior management who often pressure them to take shortcuts, turn a blind eye to the abuses they see, and produce low risk numbers in order to keep capital requirements down. The ultimate responsibility for effective risk management must therefore lie with the senior management.

In the final analysis, if it is not in the interests of senior management to contain excessive risk-taking, then no amount of "risk management" is going to contain it. And if senior management is given remuneration packages that encourage excessive risk-taking, as most do, and if they can also anticipate that their governments will bail them out should those risks turn sour, as the bankers clearly did (and were proven right after the event), then it should surprise no one if excessive risk-taking is what results: incentives are everything.

---

[23] Loc. cit.

But then again, perhaps this is simply to miss the point. Risk management can only be regarded as a "failure" if you accept it at face value. Perhaps the true purpose of all these sophisticated risk management systems was not to manage risks at all, but to allow inside parties to extract value for themselves – by making high profits from risk-taking or by "releasing" capital and using it to pay themselves bonuses – while giving the appearance of managing risks. Risk management was not so much a guardrail but a vacuum cleaner disguised as a smokescreen. From this perspective, it can only be regarded as an unqualified success.

Part Three

Interactions with the Real World

7

The Real World Becomes Modern Finance-friendly

Over the past generation, three interconnected systemic changes have revolutionized the US economy, making it more hospitable to the tenets of Modern Financial Theory, but less user-friendly for the populace as a whole, and in the long run far less stable. These are: the increasing dominance of managerial capitalism; the shift in investment focus from the long term to the short term; and the growth and metamorphosis of the financial system itself, underlying which is increased leverage throughout the entire economy.

(i) The Increasing Dominance of Managerial Capitalism

As far back as 1932, Adolph A. Berle, Jr and Gardiner C. Means[1] had identified a major problem with twentieth century capitalism: the separation of ownership from control, and the resulting conflict of interest

---

[1] Berle and Means, 1932.

between the managers who ran modern firms and the shareholders who in theory owned them.

In fact, this problem had been identified much earlier, by none other than Adam Smith in his *Wealth of Nations* in 1776. As he succinctly put it in a scathing criticism of joint-stock companies:

> "The directors of such companies ... being the managers of other people's money than their own, it cannot well be expected that they should watch over it with the same anxious vigilance ... Negligence and profusion must always prevail, more or less, in the management of such a company ..."[2]

The separation of ownership and control that Berle and Means identified boiled down, in considerable part, to the limited ability of the joint-stock form to control the conflict of interests between the managers and shareholders. The bottom line is that these are natural enemies; always were and always will be.

Before 1929, most corporations were still controlled by their founders, or by titans of finance such as J. Pierpont Morgan, so this problem was moderately well contained. For a long time even after then, many companies were still controlled by small groups of wealthy individuals, while management was modestly rewarded and allowed an existence of country-club coziness. For a top manager in such an environment it was difficult to get another job, and ripping off shareholders involved the risks of alienating people who might prove to be more powerful than him, both socially and politically. With low levels of debt on most companies' balance sheets and a relatively low-stress environment, most managers contented themselves with a reasonable remuneration and the psychic satisfaction of doing a decent job for their shareholders.

As with financial services after World War II, this was not a truly free-market system. Government was already far too big and taxation too high, particularly at the individual level. Nevertheless, in spite of being somewhat lacking in incentives compared to the small-government low-tax capitalism that had existed prior to 1929, it was an

---

[2] Smith, 1776, p. 741. "Negligence and profusion" rather sums up the modern Wall Street.

effective economic system that, over the generation after World War II, produced the highest rates of productivity growth in US history.

But the balance of power thereafter gradually shifted towards management. Institutional shareholdings, which had represented around 15% of share capital in public companies in the 1950s, rose steadily after 1960, especially as the appallingly high rates of estate duty and persistent inflation eroded and, in time, devastated the capital of the wealthy controlling families, while assets held in pension funds and mutual funds slowly built up. By 1980, institutional shareholdings in the Standard and Poor's 500 Index companies exceeded 50% of share capital, a level that has drifted upwards a little since.

Thus the typical large shareholder is no longer a powerful member of the local community, perhaps with family connections to the company, but a mid-level institutional money manager, with no long-term commitment to the company beyond its short-term share price performance, with no particular social or political power, and representing only a large group of faceless workers or small investors. Management's bad behavior at shareholder expense is no longer anything like as socially, politically, or financially dangerous as it used to be.

More shareholders with smaller holdings also creates a "free rider" problem that further weakens the incentives of individual shareholders to monitor "their" managements: the gains of shareholder monitoring are shared by all, but the costs of monitoring are borne only by those responsible few who do it. Hence, the growth of small shareholdings was accompanied by a weakening of shareholder scrutiny.

These developments took place against the emergence of new theories of corporate governance that promoted the myth of shareholder value maximization.

The financial economics textbooks and the business schools spread the myth that modern capitalism, characterized by free markets and Adam Smith's "invisible hand," ensured that the interests of managers and shareholders were carefully aligned, with managers remunerated for maximizing shareholder value and monitored by their boards of directors. Both managers and boards were supposedly monitored by, and held accountable to, their shareholders; while behind them stood the corporate takeover market, with the ever present threat of hostile takeover and of dozy managers being thrown out.

But Adam Smith had never endorsed the "invisible hand" in all possible situations and had in fact been a particularly vociferous critic of the joint-stock form. The reality was that effective corporate governance was breaking down; the conflicts of interest between managers and shareholders were getting worse and management was getting the upper hand. Over time, capitalism in the US and the UK came to be characterized by an ever more powerful and unaccountable senior management who used the language of shareholder value maximization as a smokescreen to disguise their own increasingly brazen plundering of corporate assets, and who were no longer able to see the boundary between the company's assets and their own. Executives ensured that they faced compliant boards of directors and accommodating remuneration committees who understood the need to "support" corporate policy and go along with increasingly powerful, even dictatorial, CEOs.

Together, they designed executive remuneration packages that saw executive remuneration skyrocket. Some indication of this is given by the fact that average US CEO salaries rose from 42 times that of an average worker in 1980 to 520 times that by 2008.[3] The rationale for this growth was that executives were being fairly compensated for the "value" they had "created" for their shareholders. But it is impossible to believe that the value created by management in 2008 had gone up by a factor of $520/42 = 12.38$ relative to the value created by the average worker.

In any case, the evidence does not back this up: over the period 1980–2004, when executive salaries had grown at an average rate of 8.5% a year in real terms, real profits grew at only 2.9%.[4] Of course, a moment's thought should convince one that real profits are one of those variables that can only fluctuate so much: corporate earnings' share of GDP cannot rise and rise indefinitely, any more than can the share of labor. At some point, the competitive process will push it back towards some "normal" value.

Moreover, whilst modern executives were happy to be paid extremely generously as their firms' stock prices rose, they were not partners putting their whole personal wealth on the line, and there was no question of them suffering commensurate losses when stock prices

---

[3] Bogle, 2009, p. 131.
[4] Bogle, 2005, pp. 17–18.

fell. To give just one example, James E. Cayne, the CEO of Bear Stearns, was paid $232 million over 1993–2006 as his firm's stock price rose from $12 per share to $165. Under his leadership, the firm came within an ace of bankruptcy, and was only saved when J.P. Morgan Chase rescued it in March 2008, for a price of $10 a share, considerably less in real terms than it was when he had started.[5] But Cayne was not required to pay out for the negative shareholder value he had created since 1993; nor was he even required to pay back what he had been paid by the firm.

Cases like this give the lie to the shareholder value theory. The unspoken reality was that many executives regarded themselves as entitled to massive remuneration even when they patently destroyed shareholder value. As Jack Bogle wryly comments, never has so much been paid by so many to so few for so little.[6]

To make matters worse, the breathtaking salaries paid to CEOs *massively understate* their true remuneration. There are also the executive perks, including use of company aircraft for personal travel, provision of other company "amenities" (country club dues, luxury apartments, private security, etc.); payments to terminated executives, such as the $140 million paid to Michael Ovitz for the 14 months of service he provided Walt Disney before they fired him; and generous post-retirement benefits, which often escape scrutiny. A nice example of the latter involved GE's Jack Welch, whose extramarital activities landed him in the divorce courts where his other hidden interests also came to light. Apart from nearly $1 billion compensation as CEO, his post-retirement benefits included a NYC apartment with daily deliveries of flowers and wine, the private use of a company jet, and an extra retirement stipend of nearly $750,000 a month. Welch was hardly slumming it.[7]

In addition to these perks, there are many other ways executives can boost their compensation even further, often without shareholders finding out. Leaving aside management's increasing use of compensation consultants to prove itself underpaid, executive pay is often tied to the share price, so executives can manipulate share prices upwards to

---

[5] Bogle, 2009, p. 37.
[6] Bogle, op. cit., p. 38.
[7] Bogle, 2005, pp. 19, 21.

boost their own short-term income and never mind the longer-term dangers. Among the many ways of doing this:

- Management can reduce dividends, and did: by 2000, average dividend yields in the US had been pushed down towards 1%, and have only recovered a little since.
- Management can load the company up with debt and buy back shares, thus boosting share prices at the expense of making the company more vulnerable.
- Management can indulge in creative accounting to boost earnings by writing off losses against capital as "extraordinary" without bringing them through the income statement. This raises the share price, since reported earnings are higher and can be manipulated into a smooth trend by write-backs of previous write-offs, counting on lazy Wall Street analysts not looking through past reported figures.
- Management can cut costs to boost short-term profits, particularly in areas such as research and development where the benefits are long term, and can outsource jobs to emerging markets, even if there are long-term structural dangers to doing so, such as the possibility that the outsourcees might learn enough skills to start a lower-cost competitor and later put the company out of business.

Most egregious of all is the executive stock options scam. One of the biggest falsehoods perpetrated by the corporate finance textbooks is that stock options align the interests of managers to those of shareholders.[8] In fact, the reality is that most executives sell their stock options as soon as they can and, while they still hold them, stock options often magnify the incentives of executives to take risks that boost short-term earnings at the expense of longer-term corporate financial health.[9]

---

[8] Options do not take account of dividends, so providing a perverse incentive for firms to avoid paying dividends. Also, stock options reward the absolute performance of the stock, rather than its performance relative to peers or the stock market index. This unfairly rewards dull performers in a bull market, and unfairly penalizes good performers in a bear market. And no amount of options, even short positions in which the managers write the options, will make managers look after shareholders' money as their own, unless the whole of their personal wealth is on the line and they have enough of it to pledge. But again, we go back to the merits of the old partnerships.

[9] Furthermore, stock options are a very expensive form of compensation, because their true cost often greatly exceeds their value to the CEO. The reason is that CEOs

Stock options also give rise to many new forms of chicanery, often hidden from shareholders with the connivance of accounting and SEC rules that the executives themselves have lobbied hard for.

A good example is the nefarious albeit legal practice of swapping executives' holdings of underwater options for lower-exercise-price options when the share price drops. For example, in March 2009, Google allowed its employees to swap underwater stock options exercisable at $500–600 per share for new options exercisable at $308.57, taking a charge against income of $400 million for doing so.[10] Even without a formal swap, Citigroup – bailed out with $45 billion of taxpayers' money in 2008 – was by November 2009 issuing to management and employees options over 200–300 million shares exercisable at $4 per share, thus further diluting shareholders who had seen their shares fall from more than $50 only two years earlier.

That's not even to mention the (illegal, but quite frequent, until the SEC cracked down) practice of backdating stock options issued to executives: the award of the option is recorded as having happened earlier than it did, when a lower share price typically held, thus justifying a lower option exercise price (and hence, a more valuable option), and transferring even more value from shareholders to executives.

Even the threat of hostile takeover was turned to management advantage, allowing management to entrench itself further. The best example was the "poison pill defense" by which, in theory, "shareholder rights" are triggered by an acquisition of even a large minority of shares by a single holder. In reality, this boiled down to giving management the ability to threaten, with as much credibility as possible, that it would make a hostile takeover as costly as possible for the party taking over, scorching the fields and burning everything that had to be left, and never mind the damage to shareholders' interests, while allowing the executives themselves to escape with generous "golden parachutes." Such defenses harmonize shareholder and manager interests in the same way that a marine captain's interests are harmonized with those of their

---

already have so much of their wealth invested in their firms that the further exposure represented by stock options is perhaps the least valuable form of compensation they could get: this is why they usually sell their options at the first available opportunity. On the other hand, stock option compensation does have the merit of being easier to hide from shareholders.

[10] Reuters, March 11, 2009.

passengers and crew, when he has a guaranteed private luxury lifeboat for his own personal use and they have to swim for it.

Needless to say, this environmental sea change had the usual Darwinian effect of changing the nature of those who became US corporate top managers. Intelligence is no longer a particular asset, since its benefits are primarily long term. Thus only seven of today's Fortune Top 50 CEOs went to top-tier colleges (Ivy League plus Stanford and MIT), an unimaginably small percentage a generation ago (though some followed an undistinguished undergraduate education with an elite business school, where intelligence appears to be less essential). Conversely, aggression is absolutely vital, particularly when combined with a lack of scruples. Combine those with higher stress and higher rewards, and behavior deterioration is only to be expected.

There are two archetypal CEOs of the modern era. The first is former GE Chairman Jack Welch, whom we have already met. Unusually well-educated for a modern CEO and a staunch advocate of the "shareholder value" mythology, his ruthless approach to staff-cutting earned him the nickname of "neutron Jack," after the proposed nuclear weapon that left buildings intact but destroyed everyone in them. He pushed an insanely ambitious corporate agenda: he was only interested in being number one or number two in any industry. He also instituted aggressive performance measures and would fire anyone who failed to meet them.

So every year Welch fired the bottom-performing 10% of managers and shut down factories and lackluster old-line units in droves, an approach that has since spread across corporate America. Believing in his ability to run anything, he expanded GE into other industries in which it had no expertise, such as media and investment banking; those acquisitions were either deeply mediocre performers (NBC) or outright scandals and disasters (Kidder Peabody). Welch publicly stated that he was not concerned with the discrepancy between the salaries of top-paid CEOs and those of average workers. He dismissed allegations of excessive CEO pay as "outrageous" and argued vociferously that CEO compensation should continue to be dictated by the "free market," without interference from government or other outside agencies, subject therefore only to the discipline of the "morals of the market place" – by which he presumably meant, whatever he and his ilk could get away with.

The other is Dennis Kozlowski, former CEO of Tyco, and a graduate of the academically undistinguished Seton Hall University. Kozlowski became famous for his extravagant lifestyle supported by the booming stock market of the late 1990s and early 2000s. Not content with a mere $100 million a year or so, it was alleged that he had Tyco pay for his $30 million New York apartment, which included $6,000 shower curtains and $15,000 "dog umbrella stands." But his most notorious exploit was an extravagant birthday party for his wife held on the Italian island of Sardinia, disguised as a shareholder meeting to get corporate funding and then over-billed to the company, which featured an ice replica of Michelangelo's Statue of David that tastefully doubled as a fountain exuding Stolichnaya vodka from an unmentionable part of David's anatomy. Not content with this pillage, Kozlowski went on to steal considerable amounts of further money from his company, and is now serving $8\frac{1}{3}$–25 years at the Mid State Correctional Facility in Marcy, NY.

Thus, owners' capitalism had given way to managerial capitalism, under which trillions of dollars were transferred from investors to "insiders" of one sort or another, in return for the production of profits that were no better than ordinary by past standards. Leaving aside the costs involved, such behavior undermines the public trust on which the system ultimately depends. The danger of the new system is both obvious and profound: if there are no controls on management embezzling shareholder property beyond management's self-restraint, then we are no longer in a society in which property rights are respected. Taken to its limit, this is the system of capitalism in operation in Russia, under which certain oligarchs have made themselves billionaires by fraudulent privatizations of state property, aided and abetted by the state itself, while millions of ordinary people remain impoverished.

(ii) Change in Investment Focus from Long-term to Short-term

A further major philosophical change in the last generation among providers of capital is the shift in focus from long-term investment towards short-term speculation. Traditionally, investment was for the long-term: you forecast the prospective return on an asset over its entire life; you then bought it and held onto it; and you didn't worry too much about short-term fluctuations in its value.

Even in the 1930s, John Maynard Keynes worried about the impact of speculation, in which investors attempted to make speculative profits from second-guessing the short-term movements of the market. If speculation took hold, the market would be dominated by the mass psychology of ignorant individuals and be destabilized by their fluctuations in mood and sentiment. In such circumstances, even "expert professionals, possessing judgment and knowledge beyond that of the average private investor" would become concerned "not with making superior long-term forecasts of the probable yield on an investment over its entire life, but with forecasting changes in the conventional valuation a short time ahead of the general public," and so become speculators themselves. The stock market would then become "a battle of wits to anticipate the basis of conventional valuation a few months hence rather than the prospective yield of an asset over a long term of years." As he warned, "when enterprise becomes the bubble on a whirlpool of speculation [and the] capital development of a country becomes a by-product of the activities of a casino, the job (of capitalism) is likely to be ill-done."[11]

The benefits of long-term investment over short-term trading are very apparent if one looks at stock market returns over the long term. Over the last 100 years, US stocks delivered an annual average return of 9.6%, of which 5.0% came from earnings growth and 4.5% from dividends, and only 0.1% from changes in the price/earnings ratio. Earnings growth and dividends represent the return from investing, or buying and holding; the change in the P/E ratio represents the return from speculation or trading. Over the long term, the returns from investment vastly exceed those from speculation.

Playing the market is a giant distraction that causes investors to focus on transitory and volatile investment expectations rather than on what is really important: the focus on long-term yield and the gradual accumulation of returns earned by corporate business. As the legendary investment guru Benjamin Graham used to say: "In the short run the stock market is a voting machine ... (but) in the long run, it is a weigh-

---

[11] Keynes, 1936, pp. 154, 159.

ing machine." It is the dividends and earnings growth compounding over time that really matter.

But neither Graham nor Keynes could have anticipated the vast increase in trading that came after them. In 1951, the average fund investor held shares for about 16 years; now, they hold them for only four years on average. In 1951, a mutual fund held stock for about six years; now just a year. In the 1950s and 1960s, turnover rates were less than 20%; today they are typically more than 100%. The amounts of shares traded have gone through the roof: back in 1951, only about 3 million shares were traded on the US stock exchanges each day; now, the amount traded exceeds 2.5 billion shares per day.

This shift towards the short-term inevitably erodes effective governance. Why spend money evaluating a company's performance if you are not going to hold the company's stock for more than a year? Financial research shifts from old-fashioned company valuation to trying to anticipate how the market will move in the near future. The shift to the short-term also undermines company analysis in another way. Analysts no longer had incentives to voice concerns over company management; instead, they became vulnerable to political pressure not to "rock the boat" and to avoid assigning "sell" recommendations to important or potential clients. Company analysis itself has gradually lost its integrity and has become little more than a marketing arm.

And, of course, the basic problem with trying to get rich through speculation is that speculation is a zero-sum game – the gains of one are countered by the losses of the other. Essentially, the average investor cannot expect to beat the market because the average investor *is* the market, and this would mean that they could expect to beat themselves – a logical contradiction. Those who play the market are consigned, on average, to average returns – and this is *before* costs are taken into consideration.

The essential arithmetic of returns is that investors get returns earned minus costs incurred, and these costs have soared to very high levels. For instance, the crude expense ratio of the average fund has doubled from 0.77% in 1951 to 1.54% in 2008. The direct costs (management fees, operation costs, marketing expenses) of mutual fund intermediation alone in the US in 2007 were over $100 billion a year, and on top of these are tens of billions in transactions fees to brokerage firms and other facilitators (such as lawyers), and another $10 billion to financial advisors. The total direct costs paid by investors across the whole US financial services sector (investment banking, mutual funds, retail banking, hedge funds, pension funds, etc.) are currently running at about $620 billion *per year*.[12] (Compare this to US GDP, which is a little over $14 trillion: this means 4.5% of all income earned in the US is spent on fees for financial "services"!) And this figure only refers to direct costs: it excludes such indirect but far from trivial costs such as those associated with recent bailouts of the financial system: once these are factored in, the true costs of financial "services" become very much higher.

These costs are, needless to say, a huge drag on the returns actually delivered to investors. Once you take account of these costs, beating the market becomes a seriously negative-sum game: on average, you lose big. The only consistent winner is the croupier.

Management as well as investors became more short-term-oriented during these years, focusing increasingly on quarterly results and on their reception by the Wall Street analyst community. We have already seen, for example, how Jack Welch used short-term results to determine the bottom-ranking 10% of managers each year so he could fire them. The pioneer of this mentality was Harold S. Geneen (1910–97),[13] Chief Executive of the conglomerate ITT from 1959 to 1977. Geneen, an accountant, focused laser-like on the results being produced by ITT's numerous divisions, and on building through a total of 350 acquisitions in 80 countries a business empire whose profits would always rise. His motto was: "Telephones, hotels, insurance, it's all the same. If you know the numbers inside out, you know the company inside out." He was a master manipulator of accounting data, so much so that ITT recorded 58 successive quarters of record results in 1959–74.

Needless to say, the Geneen management methodology didn't actually work all that well. His later years at ITT saw losses and were

---

[12] Bogle, 2009, p. 44
[13] See Sampson, 1973.

dogged by scandals about ITT's intervention in the installation of General Pinochet as Chilean dictator in 1973 and its financing of the 1972 US Republican Convention. His successor, Rand Araskog, broke the company up over the following decades. However, Geneen's accounting wizardry, his obsessive focus on quarterly earnings, and his total disregard for the actual businesses concerned, have inspired innumerable CEOs and private equity kings to this day.

(iii) Growth and Metamorphosis of the Financial Services Industry

At the same time as capitalism was changing shape, the financial services industry began a generation of inexorable growth. In 1981, financial corporations accounted for only about 5% of the earnings of 500 giant corporations comprising the S&P 500. This had doubled by 1991 and doubled again by 1997 to 20%, and reached 27% by 2007. But even this figure understates the true size of the sector, because it ignores the financial affiliates of giant manufacturers such as GE. Once these are taken into account, financial services account perhaps for over one-third of total earnings.

The financial sector is now by far the largest sector in the US economy, over three times as big as industrials or information technology.

Still there are vast numbers of young people queuing up to join the financial services sector, attracted no doubt by the high remuneration it offers. For example, a recent survey suggested that there are some 74,000 professional risk managers working in financial institutions – one wonders why any of them still have jobs, but that is another matter – and the number of people taking GARP and PRMIA risk manager diploma exams this year is perhaps 50,000 worldwide. From a societal point of view, having large numbers of our brightest people expending their energies in finance is a huge loss, since it deprives us all of their talents applied to more useful outlets.

Thoughtful observers are now worrying about where all this will eventually lead us. Countries like the US and the UK have overextended, indeed parasitic, financial systems, and are gloomily watching their own manufacturing sectors shrink as the search for short-term profits leads their business leaders to outsource production to India and China. We have gone from an originally agricultural economy to a manufacturing one, then to a service economy, and now, it appears, to an increasingly financial economy. We seem to be moving towards a future in which we will no longer be making anything, instead merely swapping bits of paper back and forth, while the financial system, the croupier, benefits from each such trade. At the end of the day, there is something seriously twisted with any economy whose largest sector is financial services. *They* will make their money off the rest of us, but where will *we* earn our living?

Also important has been the increase in leverage among consumers, businesses and financial institutions. Leverage is usually measured in terms of the ratio of assets to equity, where the assets exceed the equity because of borrowing. The greater the leverage, the greater the return on equity, other things being equal, but also the greater the degree of risk. So if a firm has a leverage ratio of 10 to 1, say, every 1% return to its assets translates into a 10% return on its equity; however, a fall in assets of only 10% would be sufficient to wipe out the firm's entire equity.

As touched on in Chapter 4, a major theoretical goad to the enhanced use of leverage has been the ubiquitous Modigliani-Miller Theorem. As you will remember, this implied that leverage is irrelevant to the value of a firm in a tax-free environment, but that in the current US tax system the ideal capital structure would be as much debt and as little dividend payout as possible. Finance, business, and the consumer have all spent much of the last generation trying to push toward this happy optimum.

In the crash of 2008, as we shall discuss, much of the risk came from excessive leverage in banks and investment banks. Traditionally, investment banks had had a leverage limit of about 20 to 1, and banks' assets were relatively uncomplicated and transparent: commercial paper, bonds, shares, and so on, whose values and risks were readily ascertainable. In more recent years, however, their positions became increasingly complex and risky, taking on positions in real estate, private equity funds, hedge funds, and derivatives, many of which do not appear on their balance sheets.

Yet, at the same time, they increased their leverage further, sometimes to over 30 to 1 and even higher. Leverage at this level means that a fall in asset values of a little more than 3% (and even less, if you consider all the hidden extra risks!) would wipe out the banks' capital. These leverage levels were (unwisely) deemed satisfactory in bull markets, but were to be exposed as woefully inadequate when the current crisis re-erupted in the fall of September 2008, hitting the investment banks hard and giving them the life expectancies of second lieutenants on World War I's Western Front.

The problem of excessive leverage is however not confined to the financial sector, but operates throughout the US (and UK) economies, reflecting the gradual ascendancy of the immature "now" society and its craving for instant gratification over longer term prudence – "Eat, drink, and be merry …":

- There was the two-income professional couple who thought that by buying a McMansion the size of Chatsworth, their social status would turn into that of the Duke and Duchess of Devonshire.
- There was the laid-off manufacturing worker who thought it didn't matter that he could find no job paying more than half his old union pay scale, because credit cards would allow his family to live the good life indefinitely while he waited for the "right" job to come up.
- There was the low-skill immigrant, legal or illegal, who found the wages he could earn were totally insufficient to fulfill his dreams of life in the bountiful United States, but thought that affluence might be forthcoming through a subprime mortgage.
- There was the corporate CEO, who understood that buying back stock in his unexciting company and financing the purchase by junk bonds would increase the value of his stock options, but didn't care about the damage it did to his firm's long-term corporate survival.
- There was the President of the United States, who thought he could pursue an expensive if unsuccessful foreign policy, allow his Congressional colleagues to be thoroughly sloppy on public spending, and introduce new social programs that pleased his wife, all without raising taxes.

- And, finally, there was his successor, who makes his predecessor look like a beacon of fiscal rectitude, who lectures his fellow Americans on the need for financial responsibility while presiding over trillion dollar plus deficits and costly medical care reforms, oblivious to the looming fiscal catastrophe all too rapidly approaching the still sleeping United States.

One has some sympathy with all of these hard cases, but it should be recognized that together they probably form close to a majority of the country. The idea of imposing additional taxes on the thrifty minority (or on their children through excessive budget deficits) in order to bail them out is, therefore, both morally abhorrent and fiscally impossible.

Once we recognize that attitudes to borrowing in the US economy have been pathological for the last decade or more, a key culprit for our recent troubles becomes clear. The Federal Reserve, by expanding the M3 money supply at a rate almost 5% faster than output for 13 years since 1995, and bringing interest rates to unprecedently low levels for a very long time, has made borrowing both excessively cheap and excessively easy to obtain. Not surprising, therefore, that the US savings rate dropped to less than zero and most Americans went on a credit binge. Fairly unsurprising, also, that the epidemic of loose money after 2000 spread to the globe as a whole, so that borrowers in Bangalore and Beijing are today as overleveraged and vulnerable as those in Boston.

In a period when, because of the explosive increase in international communication capability, money supply could be increased excessively without producing an immediate inflationary backlash, the Fed under Alan Greenspan succumbed to the temptation of easy popularity and admiring editorials in both the *New York Times* and the *Wall Street Journal*. President George W. Bush, not a man to adhere to Republican "sound money" dogma if he could find a more populist alternative, then chose the most dedicated soft money man he could find as Greenspan's successor, and the result was a disaster.

It is here that one can most ferociously blame Fed Chairmen Alan Greenspan and Ben Bernanke, and their decade and more of irresponsibly cheap money. By distorting price signals throughout the economy, and producing burst bubble after burst bubble without any significant improvement in living standards except at the very top, they have not only gravely damaged the economy, but enabled the Left to claim that free markets "don't work" so we must bring in government and the unfortunate taxpayer to solve our economic problems. Of course, this crisis is not a failure of free markets and not even a failure of capitalism – unless you accuse modern managerialist crony capitalism, in which case you would be right.

The combination of greater leverage and greater risk-taking made financial institutions weaker and more vulnerable than they were before. Add to this greater opacity, greater interconnectedness, and interdependence between institutions, and a tendency for them to adopt similar risk management strategies – everyone sells when prices fall, so making markets more volatile – and the result is greater systemic instability.

The problem of greater interconnectedness is especially pertinent here. We have moved from a diversified environment of relatively small banks pursuing different policies, to a more homogeneous environment in which banks are larger and doing much the same thing, and are much more interconnected. This means that the system is better at coping with day-to-day strains, but more vulnerable to a major crisis: we have fewer crises, but they are more damaging when they occur and harder to predict.

Some insights into these problems come from the newly emerging theory of networks. A network is an assemblage of nodes connected via links. Some examples would be the world's airports or an electricity grid. As networks develop, there is a natural tendency for them to organize themselves around a few key nodes that serve as central connections. This concentration makes the network more robust in the face of day-to-day strains: most problems will occur at poorly connected and therefore inconsequential spots. However, this very same architecture also makes networks more vulnerable to extreme shocks: a hit to a key node could cause systemic damage. An example was the electricity blackout experienced in the northeastern US in August 2003, which caused damage and disruption to the whole region. The same problem can occur with the modern financial system, should a key player suddenly collapse.

To put this problem into historical perspective, when the crisis of 1907 erupted, J.P. Morgan felt confident enough to allow the

Knickerbocker Trust to go bankrupt: he judged that the firm did not deserve assistance and the Knickerbocker had limited relationships with other banks. Thus, the collateral damage was limited when Morgan threw them to the wolves before orchestrating the rescue package that resolved the crisis.

Fast forward 80-odd years, to the bankruptcy of Drexel Burnham: the authorities dealt with the impending collapse of Drexel Burnham by allowing a two-stage process, whereby the expansionist Michael Milken and other top management were removed in March, 1989, while the institution continued to do business on a sharply reduced basis before its final bankruptcy in February, 1990. This was hard on Drexel's shareholders, who might well have salvaged something substantial from the wreckage if Drexel had been forced into Chapter 11 bankruptcy early enough, but it was good for Drexel's network of counterparties, who were given time to get out. The important point, for our purposes here, is the significance of the correspondent relationships: leaving aside whether the shareholders were well served, the authorities handled this problem fairly well by arranging an orderly wind-down, so limiting the broader damage.

But these problems soon became much bigger. By the time Long-Term Capital Management found itself on the brink of collapse, in the fall of 1998, the Fed judged that allowing LTCM to fail might paralyze world financial markets, and bailed it out instead. Fast forward another ten years to Bear Stearns and we have another institution with a network of counterparties many times the size and complexity of that constructed by Drexel and which also posed huge systemic risk: its network of interlocking obligations was very complex and extensive, and, again, the Fed was afraid of the consequence of letting it fail. Hence the hastily arranged shotgun marriage to J.P. Morgan Chase in March 2008; similarly with the rescue of AIG six months later.

This was not a pretty picture. The interconnected network caused by modern finance is now sufficiently fragile that the failure of any one major house, if carried out through normal bankruptcy processes, could cause major problems for the system as a whole.

It is as if the US power grid had been installed without fail-safe mechanisms, so that a local outage caused by a snowstorm in Vermont or a hurricane in Florida could cascade through the whole system and disrupt power service for the entire country.

Clearly, there is a desperate need to install fail-safe mechanisms that work.

This systemic instability is made worse by international capital regulations, which encourage similar risk management strategies through a regulatory Value-at-Risk capital adequacy standard, and by the emergence of the too-big-to-fail doctrine: the perception, generally correct, that if large important institutions get themselves into financial difficulties, then they will be bailed out. This creates a major moral hazard, as the perception of a state or central bank safety net reduces an institution's incentive to be prudent; this in turn leads to further excessive risk-taking and greater systemic instability.

And finally, to make matters much worse, there is the additional systemic damage done by credit derivatives and especially credit default swaps – the most damaging derivatives ever invented, the archetypal financial weapons of mass destruction. We will have more to say on these babies in the next chapter.

8

Modern Finance Captures Wall Street

(i) Investment Management

The first area to feel the impact of Modern Financial Theory was investment management. Before 1950, the principal instrument for institutional investment was bonds, and investment management, mostly carried out by bank trust departments, consisted primarily of simple arbitrage strategies designed to increase the portfolio's yield. Analysis consisted largely of inspecting the borrower's balance sheet and calculating its debt/equity ratio and interest cover.

With the long equity bull market of 1949–66, equities became much more important to institutional investors. The persistence through the 1950s and 1960s of economic growth caused a secular revaluation of equities, by which price–earnings ratios came close to trebling.

In these circumstances, investment management performance became highly visible and a major marketing tool. The culmination of the new "cult of performance" was Gerald Tsai's offering of the

Manhattan Fund in 1965, which attracted $247 million, then an enormous sum, by touting Tsai's record at the helm of the aggressive growth Fidelity Capital Fund. Fidelity Capital had achieved its record not by diversification but by concentrating its holdings in a few key growth companies, notably Xerox and Polaroid.

However, the obvious weaknesses of this strategy were exposed by the bear market of 1968–70. Tsai and other "go-go" fund managers found that aggressive growth stocks went down as quickly as they had gone up, and Tsai himself sold the Manhattan Fund for $27 million to CNA Financial. The cult of performance was temporarily dented.

Institutional money managers, seeking an alternative to performance that would make them appear superior to the man in the street and attract additional capital to manage, then discovered the Efficient Market Hypothesis. The notion that the market reflected all known information, and hence that superior investment performance was supposedly impossible, was rapidly achieving great success among investment academics. It was also appealing to those in the industry who had been burned by the cult of performance gunslingers; it suggested that someone like Tsai had no superior abilities, but was simply lucky, which appealed to those less gifted and wealthy than he.[1]

Institutional money managers thinking along these lines soon came to the idea of indexation, investing so as to match a broadly based index while minimizing costs. The first index funds were established more or less simultaneously by Wells Fargo and American National Bank of Chicago in 1973, and the first such fund sold to retail investors was started by John Bogle of Vanguard on December 31, 1975. Fidelity Investments' Chairman Edward Johnson mocked them by saying that he "couldn't believe the great mass of investors are going to be satisfied

---

[1] With the proceeds of the Manhattan Fund sale, Tsai took control of the life insurance company Associated Madison Companies, which he sold to American Can Company in 1982, becoming Chairman of American Can. He sold American Can's packaging operation to Nelson Peltz in 1986 for $570 million, bought the brokerage Smith Barney in 1987 for $475 million, renamed the company Primerica, and sold it to Sandy Weill's Commercial Credit in 1988 for $1.65 billion. Tsai's success was not a series of lucky random walks; he had an excellent eye as to where the global economy was going, as evidenced by his 1980s re-invention of a can company as a financial services conglomerate.

with receiving just average returns."[2] In fact investors were well satisfied by reliable mediocrity and index funds took off.

The indexed investing revolution had an unquestionable benefit for retail investors: it gave them access to the benefits of diversification that were otherwise unattainable or, at best (and even then only for very wealthy investors) only attainable at higher cost. Indeed, other than the invention of the cash machine, indexing was perhaps the *only* financial innovation in recent decades that was unambiguously positive in its impact. For this we should thank Bogle; he established Vanguard as the low-cost alternative, and by sticking to that principle forced the remainder of the industry to reduce their fee levels. Competition by index funds not only forced down annual fees in the conventionally managed fund sector, or at least that part of it that practiced passive "buy and hold" investment strategies, but also forced down the extortionate up-front fees with which brokerage salespeople rewarded themselves for putting their clients into mutual funds. Only in the most specialized investment sectors did mutual fund costs remain high.

Roughly simultaneously with the first attempts at indexation, Wall Street analysts discovered the Capital Asset Pricing Model (CAPM) and the Efficient Markets Hypothesis. As a result, detailed stock analysis and selection went largely out of fashion and "asset allocation" became the methodology of choice. Retail "financial advisors" could no longer be expected to pick individual stocks effectively, but could charge substantial fees for tailor-made investing, in which the mix of investments between domestic stocks, international stocks, bonds, and cash varied according to investors' ages, financial needs, and supposed "attitudes to risk." Investment advice had acquired a spurious coating of science.

Institutionally, these decades also saw the rise of benchmarking. Once indexed investment became feasible, institutions took to measuring their managers' performance relative to the performance of the appropriate index. Generally, benchmarking was carried out frequently, often quarterly, and managers whose performance fell short were soon eliminated. This pressured them to take a short-term view and managers increasingly became closet indexers. Since following a strategy substantially different to the index increased the probability of

---

[2] Quoted in Damato, 2001.

noticeable underperformance in some quarters and hence the chances of losing their jobs, managers couldn't afford to divert too much from the index. At the same time, the fees for active fund management – the fees for regularly moving funds around – remained high and, with few unpredictable exceptions, well above any extra "performance" they generated.

As stock investment became increasingly indexed, investment managers needed to find new ways of achieving the fees they desired. This was possible partly by investing internationally, where there was genuine value added from researching obscure markets and companies. It didn't hurt that growth prospects in emerging markets appeared better and stock prices lower. Such anomalies violated the CAPM in its strict form, but in the short term they made emerging market investments more attractive, since emerging market undervaluation could be portrayed as an "anomaly" that would profitably correct itself.

As emerging markets came more fully into the mainstream, or suffered crashes of their own – notably in Asia in 1997 – other "asset classes" were created to attract institutional investment. In the late 1990s there was a fashion for venture capital, as every dotcom idea got funded at exciting valuations in the hope of "cashing out" within eighteen months in the initial public offering market. Needless to say, while venture capital returns from 1980 had been adequate if unexciting, returns on the late 1990s flood proved abysmal.

Two notable new institutional leaders in the field were private equity funds and hedge funds. Private equity funds supposedly employed managerial and financial skill to invest in unlisted companies, and thereby produce superior returns. Hedge funds were largely unregulated short-term investment companies, typically operating from exotic "offshore" locations such as the Bahamas or the Cayman Islands, that were beyond the jurisdiction of most regulation and afforded the benefits of a luxury tropical lifestyle. Hedge funds could easily buy both long and short, used the vast flows of cheap money after 1995 to leverage to the hilt, and made extensive use of derivatives to vary their "risk profiles." All of these attributes could be marketed attractively to institutional funds providers.

Hedge funds and private equity funds have a limited role in the economy: both sectors deserve only a modest share of the investment capital pool and their managers do not deserve more than moderate remuneration. Yet the principal factor distinguishing these new market entrants was the vastly higher level of fees paid to their managers. The typical remuneration was 2% of funds under management plus 20% of any profits and 0% of any losses. This turbocharged compensation structure was spectacular by older mutual fund standards, and rendered especially reprehensible by the practice of managers marking positions to market and extracting their 20% "carry" *before* the investments had actually been sold. This allowed cash fees to be taken out based on marked-up values that were only ever notional, while leaving the fund illiquid and the investors dependent on exits that might never be achieved.

Vast amounts of funds poured into these institutions – many of them funds from other institutional investors who often failed to do elementary due diligence analysis – and yet returns on both hedge funds and private equity funds remained poor. And, since then, the downturn has delivered very heavy blows to both sectors – blows that were richly deserved.

Again, there was nothing irrational in Wall Street selling these new funds; the irrationality lay in institutional investors buying them. Pension funds in particular have an exceptionally long horizon, so their investing in short term oriented hedge funds was especially inappropriate. Indeed, once it has become obvious what devastation has been wreaked on beneficiary pensions from these investments, it will become clear that any of these institutions that invested heavily as fiduciaries deserve to be sued by their beneficiaries. Doubtless some of the more enthusiastic fiduciary participants will find themselves in class action court, if not in jail.

In the 2005–07 bull market, marketers of such funds increasingly focused not on median returns of a particular category, but on top quartile returns, or even top decile returns – so collectively pretending, as in Garrison Keillor's Lake Wobegon, that all funds are above average. Needless to say these provided more interesting numbers, but were entirely unrepresentative of the asset class as a whole and gave investors no indication of the returns that they could expect. Other tricks were also tried, such as the old classic of starting several tiny funds at the beginning of a year and then marketing only the most successful to money sources in the following year. Many of the same tricks had been used by investment trusts in the 1920s and by mutual funds in the

1960s; it is remarkable that they were as successful among supposedly sophisticated institutional investors in 1995–2008 as they had been among patently unsophisticated retail investors decades earlier.

Then there were the big long-term institutional funds, whose fund management was exemplified in the "Yale Model" pioneered by David Swenson, investment manager of the Yale endowment from 1985. Under this type of model, investment is diversified among five or six expensively managed asset classes. In the Yale version, these included domestic stocks, international stocks, private equity, hedge funds, real estate, and timberlands, but not cash, bonds or commodities, thought to provide inferior returns. By such diversification, long-term returns were supposed to be maximized and volatility of returns reduced. The Yale Model then came spectacularly unstuck in the year to June 2009, when the Yale endowment lost 24.6% of its principal value and the similarly managed Harvard endowment 27.3%. In that period the Standard and Poor's 500 index lost 28% of its value but the Lehman 20-year bond index returned 6.7%, so a traditional portfolio mix of bonds and stocks would have substantially outperformed the expensively managed endowments. In practice, while traditional investment management would also have recommended asset diversification, the Yale Model (and others of the same ilk) mostly represented diversification into paying vastly higher fees for mediocre returns.

(ii) Trading/insider Trading

A second key theme of modern Wall Street is extensive extremely profitable trading; more particularly, insider trading – the use of privileged information to earn above market profits, and most of it legal, too.

Financial institutions had always traded for their own account and used insider information, broadly defined, to do so. Both merchant bankers and senior corporate management naturally had access to inside information, and it was equally natural that they should trade on it: it was regarded as one of the perks of the job, like good lunches. Large brokers were also privy to the details of new issues and had knowledge of funds flows and of particular institutions' intentions with respect to the market: jobbers and specialists, for instance, needed to know who might be interested in a particular line of stock, so they could square their positions when necessary. All parties involved made money for themselves from this knowledge and little distinction was drawn between inside knowledge of corporate activities and that of funds flows: both were equally useful inside information.

The main factor restraining market participants in traditional financial markets from trading extensively on insider information was the importance of client relationships and reputation. If it was known that a participant traded extensively on insider information, thereby damaging the interests of its clients, corporate or institutional, its reputation would suffer and its clients would desert. For major houses, insider trading was therefore only a peripheral operation, carried out in modest quantities, primarily for personal account.

Nonetheless, the term "insider trading" is an evocative and misunderstood one. It is defined by Random House as "the illegal buying and selling of securities by persons acting on privileged information."[3] That definition rather prompts the question; if nobody makes insider trading illegal, then according to Random House it doesn't exist! It also raises the question of what information is "privileged." In the original Securities Exchange Act of 1934, insider trading was forbidden only if carried out by Directors or 10% owners of a company. However, SEC activity since 1934 broadened the definition greatly to include such people as printers and newspaper columnists, and in some cases taking it to a ridiculous extent. One such case was that of the analyst Ray Dirks, who was taken all the way to the US Supreme Court for telling his clients about the fraudulent accounting at the Equity Funding insurance company; another involved Thomas S. Lamont, a senior partner at Morgan Stanley, who was prosecuted for trading half an hour *after* the public announcement of a minerals find had gone out across the wires.

But even before its statutory prohibition (in 1934 in the US, in 1980 in the UK), insider trading was frowned upon by common law. In 1909, the US Supreme Court declared that a director who bought a company's shares on favorable information immediately before their price jumped was committing fraud against the other shareholders. In

---

[3] *Random House Unabridged Dictionary,* Copyright © 1997, by Random House, Inc., on Infoplease.

1912, the British Marconi scandal nearly brought down the Liberal government when it was revealed that three Cabinet ministers, one of them the future Prime Minister David Lloyd George, had profited from advance knowledge of contracts being negotiated with the Marconi company. They got off on the technicality that they had bought the shares of the US Marconi subsidiary, not itself a party to the contracts.

The US prohibition on insider trading arose in the 1930s from revulsion at the practices of the 1920s bull market, and a mistaken belief that they had in some way been responsible for the subsequent economic misery. In Britain in the 1970s, on the other hand, there was a general trend towards greater regulation and a revulsion against the "old boy network" of the traditional City and its cozy practices. In political circles it was felt that moving to an SEC-type approach to insider trading would somehow magically improve the quality of London's markets.

When insider trading was prohibited, in both the US and Britain, the definition of insider information was restricted to knowledge of pending corporate activities. It was felt that knowledge of market funds flows was part of the stock in trade of brokers, jobbers (in Britain), and specialists (in the US), so it would be both unfair and impracticable to prosecute trading based on this knowledge. Of their activities, only the practice of "front running" was prohibited.

"Front running" remained, however, a frequent source of trader profits – even after it was made illegal. And there were always those who pushed their luck by illegal insider trading in other ways, too. This was especially noticeable in the 1980s. One of the most notorious was Ivan Boesky. He epitomized his own catchphrase, "greed is good," and made a large fortune by acquiring information on merger deals from informants in investment banks, whom he rewarded in cash or through participations in his own deals. His insider treading was often brazen – such as massive purchases only days before takeover announcements – and he was easily caught even by the SEC and sent to jail. Boesky was linked with the Drexel Burnham junk bond operation run by Michael Milken, who cut a few insider trading corners himself.

Legal insider trading flourished as well. A defining feature of the 1980s and the decades since has been the growth of the importance of trading as a whole. This was formalized by the establishment in the major Wall Street houses of separate proprietary trading desks, seeking to make profits using the firm's own capital. Among the most important of these were at Salomon Brothers, where the bond proprietary desk was established by John Meriwether, the future CEO of Long-Term Capital Management, and at Goldman Sachs, where it was built up by the future Treasury Secretary Robert Rubin.

The new proprietary trading desks were not investment management operations in the conventional sense. Instead, the purpose of proprietary trading desks was to make money through superior knowledge of the markets and to some extent to innovate in trading and hedging.

An early example of proprietary trading desk activity was the purchase of the French gold-linked bond Emprunt Giscard by the "hero" Sherman McCoy in Tom Wolfe's 1987 novel, *Bonfire of the Vanities*. McCoy attempted to buy $600 million of the Emprunt Giscard, about 15% of the total issue, hedging the purchase in the gold futures market. McCoy's trade fell apart, but one of us (Martin) can testify that with a less greedy protagonist it worked fine, buying about $5 million and making a perfectly hedged $200,000 for his employer. This trade was carried out about a year before the book appeared, roughly the same time as "McCoy" was attempting it.

The Emprunt Giscard trade was proprietary trading at its most benign; it involved no insider information – well, maybe McCoy would have had to know who the major holders were to buy so much – and rested on a large balance sheet and a certain amount of hedging sophistication, rarer then than today.

Since the mid-1980s, proprietary trading desks have developed into major profit earners at all substantial investment banking operations. Some of this is achieved through legitimately exploiting their balance sheet to carry out arbitrage operations that would be impossible for smaller houses or houses less well connected to the market's ebb and flow.

Program trading, for example – defined by the New York Stock Exchange as the purchase or sale of 15 stocks with a value of $1 million or more – requires a large balance sheet and a fast computer. One form of it, "index arbitrage" between futures on stock indices such as the Standard and Poor's 500 Index and the stocks that comprise that index, performs a desirable function in keeping the futures and cash markets in line with each other.

Like the derivatives market as a whole, program trading is an example of the proliferation of instruments having hugely increased the income potential of trading operations. Nevertheless, program trading can take abusive forms, such as where program traders buy large numbers of stocks at the same time to fool institutional computers into triggering large orders, thereby triggering large market moves.

Nevertheless, since earning superior returns (net of costs) by superior investment skill is either impossible (if you believe the Efficient Market Hypothesis) or at least extremely difficult, proprietary trading desks have necessarily earned much of their superior returns and stellar bonuses for their participants through insider trading (broadly defined) or crony capitalism – or, very often, deals that represented both.

With the proliferation of markets and the spread of computer-based trading after 1980, the advantages of inside information about funds flows have multiplied. Computers are able to react in milliseconds and take advantage almost instantaneously of new information about funds flows. Trading with such inside information, repeated in thousands of transactions daily, is a major advantage for houses that control a substantial percentage of the order volume. Through insider trading, it is more than twice as profitable to know 20% of a market's order flow than to know 10%.

In recent years, much of the share volume on the New York Stock Exchange has been generated by high-frequency traders (HFT) – computers that trade stocks instantaneously based on algorithms and information about money flows and are located physically inside the Exchange building to minimize communication times. The financial consultancy TABB Group has estimated that high frequency trading represents 70% of the New York Stock Exchange trading volume and that the total revenues from such trading amount to $21 billion annually.[4] Although there are around 100 high-frequency trading houses, one institution, Goldman Sachs, has been estimated to have a 20% market share, and so presumably derives about $4 billion in annual revenues from this business. Most of that revenue must drop to Goldman's bottom line as net income, since the trading is done by computers, with no human traders involved.

---

[4] "US Equity High Frequency Trading: Strategies, Size, and Market Structure," TABB Group 2009.

HFT takes a number of forms:[5]

- Liquidity-rebate traders take advantage of volume rebates of about 0.25 cents per share offered by exchanges to brokers who post orders. When they spot a large order, they fill parts of it, and then reoffer the shares at the same price, collecting the exchange fee in return for providing liquidity to the market.
- Predatory algorithmic traders that take advantage of institutional computers that chop up large orders into many small ones. They make the institutional trader that wants to buy bid up the price by fooling its computer, placing small buy orders that they withdraw. When the price has then risen, the "predatory algo" shorts the stock to the institutional trader, and the price will typically fall back, so locking in a profit after having goaded the institutional algo to pay a higher price.
- Automated market makers "ping" stocks to identify large reserve book orders by issuing an order very quickly, then withdrawing it. By doing this, they obtain information on a large buyer's limits; they then use this to buy shares elsewhere and on-sell them to the institution.

Such trading has caused volume to explode, especially in NYSE listed stocks. The number of quote changes has also exploded and short-term volatility has shot up. NYSE specialists now account for only around 25% of trading volume, instead of 80% as previously.

The examples of HFT listed above, all perfectly legal, constitute insider trading, in the sense of taking advantage of privileged information not available to the market as a whole. The HFT computers are located in a privileged position (for which the NYSE is said to charge $300,000 annually) so they get order information before outsiders. They use simple but proprietary programs to trade at superior prices, making money in the same way as the old illegal "front runners."

At the other extreme are returns achieved through privileged contacts with government, the essence of crony capitalism. We would argue that Goldman Sachs' $13 billion payoff from AIG credit default

---

[5] Arnuk and Saluzzi, 2008.

swaps, at the same time as receiving payoffs on CDS written *on* AIG is a classic example. (The Treasury Secretary responsible for the $85 billion of public money initially devoted to the bailout, Hank Paulson, was the immediate past chairman of Goldman Sachs.) Another such example was the more than $6 billion profit it realized through investing in the Industrial and Commercial Bank of China six months *before* its initial public offering, at a much higher price, which was led by Goldman Sachs.

It should not however be imagined that Goldman Sachs' practices differ significantly from those of other top investment banks, although it has unquestionably been more successful in carrying them out over the last decade. In all these cases, insider knowledge of a deal, order flow in particular sectors, or access to top politicians can prove exceptionally profitable.

Indeed, so profitable have insider trading and crony capitalism proved on Wall Street that an entire new industry of hedge funds and private equity funds has been created to carry them out beyond the investment banking community. Consequently, returns in these sectors are exceptionally skewed; a few top operators such as the Carlyle Group, Blackstone, and Kohlberg Kravis and Roberts private equity funds, with exceptional political access, can generate very superior returns (at least for their partners), but the great majority of money in these sectors is achieving at best merely average market returns and, on average, by the laws of arithmetic, less.

One additional problem from the inexorable growth in trading is the inherent conflict of interest in major financial advisors or arrangers of deals being themselves large participants in the market. Buying a few shares in a successful new issue is a traditional practice and probably does little harm: it tilts the playing field, but only modestly. However, ramping up the firm's capital until it is as large as the major banks, and then leveraging that capital 30 to 1 to invest in illiquid speculations, is not just a recipe for disaster, but also inserts the advisor, quintessentially an intermediary, into the market as principal. This distorts its advice and provides a gigantic source of "insider trading" profit, since the advisor has inside information, not necessarily on the issuer, but certainly on the market.

Goldman Sachs' 2006 investment in the Industrial and Commercial Bank of China is a perfect example. Goldman not only ignored, but positively took advantage of a massive conflict of interest between its duties as advisor to ICBC and arranger of its financing, and its huge speculative shareholding in the bank. To make matters worse, two-thirds of the investment was taken not by Goldman itself but by funds controlled by Goldman partners, so providing a further conflict of interest between the partners and the corporation.

As we have said before, the private partnership is by far the most appropriate vehicle for what is essentially a team-based and reputation-based advisory business. Experience has now shown that control of a public company, particularly a public company with resources that are a multiple of their own wealth, provides temptations to Wall Street bankers that those fallible souls are unable to resist. In London, the disappearance of traditional merchant banks, whose capital had been provided primarily by their top management, and their replacement by Wall Street or other investment banking operations controlled by financial behemoths produced the same effect: greater conflict of interest as the capital involved in the business simply became mere "dumb money" that could be manipulated to enrich those who controlled its disposition.

(iii) Derivatives

Modern Financial Theory had major effects on most of Wall Street, but it more or less created the modern derivatives business. Traditional finance has long included a modest place for derivatives: the Chicago Board of Trade, established to trade commodity futures and options, was founded in 1848; the London Stock Exchange included options trading, both before and after World War II, albeit with a 19-year gap from 1939 to 1958; and forward contracts of one sort or another have been traded since at least Roman times.

A number of new organized markets that traded derivatives were then founded from the early 1970s on. These included the Chicago Board Options Exchange established in 1973, trading initially in call options on sixteen common stocks. The American, Philadelphia, and

Pacific Stock Exchanges also began trading calls on common stocks in 1975–76, then put options in 1977. Treasury bond futures were first traded in Chicago in 1977, options on those futures in 1982, foreign currency options in Philadelphia in 1982, and the first stock index options, on the Standard and Poor's 500 Index, were traded in Chicago in 1983. The establishment of these exchanges helped make for greater price transparency and, in time, greatly increased trading volume and a reasonable degree of market liquidity.

Trading does however require some means of valuation. For the simple "linear" instruments, forwards and futures, this was easy: you could value these using simple formulas and knowledge of the values of the underlying asset and the yield curve (or, more correctly, the spot interest rate term structure). The same was the case with swaps and some of the more straightforward interest rate derivatives (such as some of the simpler structured notes) when they got going.

Options posed more of a problem. Until the early 1970s, options trading was constrained by the lack of generally accepted valuation formulas. However, the publication of the Black-Scholes-Merton model for the valuation of European options in 1973 was a major breakthrough. This model also had the advantage of being satisfyingly incomprehensible; there was no chance of inquisitive minds among top management questioning its validity. Another attraction, for a number of years, in all but the most disturbed markets, was the fact that all major participants used the model to make the model work better – since the model was used by all the major players to price options, options had a gratifying tendency to trade at prices predicted by the model.

This model was soon followed by others applying much the same approach to other options (currency options, exchange options, barrier options, etc.), by alternate models based on alternations to the Black-Scholes-Merton assumptions (allowing the stock price to jump, volatility to change, etc.) and, over time, by more complicated models applied to more difficult-to-value positions, such as interest-sensitive options, which were complicated by the need to handle the term structure.

Options were not the only new development of the 1970s; interest rate and currency swaps were developing on a parallel track. Currency swaps came first; they developed out of parallel loans, by which British institutions, in the days before 1979 when exchange controls were still in force, would lend US multinationals sterling for their UK operations in return for dollars that could be invested on Wall Street – so avoiding the hideously expensive "switch and surrender" mechanisms imposed by the exchange control authorities.[6] When British exchange controls were abolished in October 1979, the parallel loan market was expected to disappear. Instead, the parallel loan structure was streamlined and found a new use in the nascent market for currency swaps, by which obligations in two different currencies were exchanged.

It was quickly discovered that the most interesting opportunity for these transactions was arbitrage between different capital markets. The landmark event occurred in 1981 when a swap was agreed between the World Bank and IBM. The World Bank wanted finance in Swiss and German bond markets, but had borrowed extensively in those markets and was now looking at paying a premium for further borrowing there; it could however borrow in US markets on a triple A basis. On the other hand, IBM was looking to borrow in US bond markets, but did not enjoy the World Bank's rating in those markets; however, it could raise funds more cheaply than the World Bank in the Swiss and German markets. And so each organization could borrow more cheaply than the other in the market in which the other wanted finance. The solution was for each to borrow, as it were, on behalf of the other, and then to swap the resulting debt payments.

Interest rate and currency swaps then took off in spectacular fashion. Typically, interest rate swaps would involve swaps in the same currency (such as the swap of a fixed rate payment for a floating one); and currency swaps as they developed would involve swaps across currencies, say, fixed in one currency for floating in another. These were very versatile and useful financial instruments, and were often much cheaper than alternatives, especially as the profit on them for the arranger quickly fell to less than 0.1% per annum.

---

[6] You bought "premium dollars" in a special closed market to invest in US shares; then when you sold the shares you had to switch the dollars back into sterling, surrendering 25% of the premium as you did so. The entire system was a Third World disgrace, invented by Maynard Keynes, and had gone on for more than 30 years after the war had ended.

In retrospect, it is surprising that such a simple idea took so long to catch on. Martin spent most of 1982 marketing the interest rate swap concept in the US, without huge success: this suggests that the unfamiliarity of the idea was an initial barrier to its adoption; alternatively, it might say something about Martin's marketing skills!

Nonetheless, the first few deals, when profits of more than 1% per annum were possible, were bonanzas for their arrangers.

The search was now on for new trades and new securities that would replicate the exquisite profitability of the first options and swaps. The mathematicians were key to this, and quickly discovered that their new-found affluence depended on getting their priorities right. You got nothing (or even thrown out on the street) by finding the flaw in some brilliant new scheme to provide attractive-looking but in reality inferior returns to investors, and convert them into cheap funding for clients. Instead, their job was to design new, superficially attractive but increasingly complicated and ever more opaque securities, often with large hidden costs, and sometimes large hidden risks too, and help the traders and corporate financiers sell them a few profitable times, at least.

One consequence was a proliferation of dubious financially engineered investments offered to investors. A good example was Japanese warrant bonds,[7] issued in profusion in the late 1980s as the Japanese stock market mania approached its height: very few investors were aware of the risks involved, and very few of these bonds provided investors with a reasonable return, particularly after the Japanese market went into long-term decline after 1990 – the value of Japanese warrants outstanding declined from $65 billion to $3 billion between December 1990 and August 1992.

Another such innovation was auction-rate preferred stock, first issued in 1984, among others by Citigroup. Under this structure, Citi issued medium-term preferred stock[8] with a maturity long enough to count as capital. Instead of paying a fixed dividend, however, the divi-

---

[7] Bonds with medium-term warrants attached to invest in the issuer's shares at a fixed price.
[8] An equity security ranking senior to common stock, with a fixed par value and paying a dividend that was either fixed or depended on interest rates, not on the bank's profitability.

dend rate was reset every 30 or 90 days by an auction process, in which the major dealers would bid for stock, and the lowest-dividend bids would be accepted. A higher penalty interest rate was to be set in case auctions failed, but that was not expected to come into effect. Because the dividend rate was reset every 30 or 90 days at short-term rates, investors were told that these were similar to short-term money market investments, since they would always trade near par and could be resold in a liquid market, but would in general produce higher yields. Auction-rate preferred, auction-rate bonds, and auction-rate municipal bonds were sold primarily to institutional investors, although after 2000 an increasing individual investor market also grew up in them.

Once the market became turbulent, in the first months of 2008, buying interest in the auctions dried up, with insufficient bids being received for one auction after another. By this point, with around $330 billion in auction-rate securities outstanding, the securities reverted to paying their penalty interest rates, and began trading if at all at heavy discounts to par (or were hurriedly redeemed if the penalty rate was too high).

Essentially the entire market collapsed, inflicting heavy losses on holders and causing major funding problems for issuers, aggravated further by their buying back many retail-owned auction rate securities in a desperate attempt to avoid the even greater expenses of class action suits from injured investors. Instruments that had been treated as short-term obligations with little credit or price risk now revealed their true character as long-term obligations with both price risk and (because of their junior position in the issuer's capital structure) substantial credit risk.

The game had lasted 24 years, largely because of the decreasing interest rates and increasingly easy money throughout that period, and numerous traders, corporate financiers, and bank mathematicians had retired rich from the profits of these issues. They were based on the lie that the *same* instrument could be both a short-term investment for the investor and a long-term finance instrument for the issuer. But eventually market reality caught up.

In general, banks would sell clients anything that they would buy, regardless of whether the products met the client's needs (such as the structured notes sold to P&G, Gibson Greetings, and Orange County in the early 1990s, of which more later) or, in some cases, regardless of whether the product had any natural use at all (such as CDO squareds, Collateralized Debt Obligations (CDOs) based on underlying assets that were also CDOs: more later on those too).

As an aside, one of the biggest scams in the finance industry, and one of the key pitches exploited by unscrupulous derivatives salesmen, is the promise of high yield for investors (or its equivalent for borrowers, lower financing costs). Many products were designed explicitly to give clients higher yield and marketed on that basis, so appealing to one of humanity's baser instincts: its eternal quest to get something for nothing. High yield sounds good, until you know what it really means. "Yield" is *not* the actual return received, but a measure of the prospective return assuming (a big if!) that default does not occur, a distinction usually lost on naive investors and business school students. One does not get higher yields for nothing; higher yield entails higher risk, often the more dangerous precisely because it is hidden. Indeed, high yield is just another name for junk: the yields are high precisely because the risks are high, but whether you are aware of this extra risk is your problem. A good half of the derivatives and mis-selling problems since the 1980s would have been avoided had clients understood this simple but profound truth.

In many respects the ideal financially engineered products were those driven by the end-user's desire to circumvent accounting, regulatory, or tax rules. These were ideal because of their value to clients, enabling niche financial institutions to make large profits, again and again, without returns diminishing rapidly towards zero. Unlike the plain vanilla swaps of earlier years, these also allowed their designers to put in all sorts of hidden bells and whistles, so boosting their profits even further. A perfect example was the tobashi trades in Japan post-1990 – here clients were desperate to avoid having losses revealed in their firms' end-year accounts, so they were willing to pay Morgan Stanley and other American investment banks almost anything for innovative ways of hiding their losses for a while. And then there were the many billions in lucrative tax avoidance trades, in which companies like Enron and Global Crossing were highly active.

But perhaps the most astonishing feature of the derivatives market is its breathtaking size. In 1957, the market value of the stocks in the S&P 500 was $220 billion, and futures and options markets on that index, indeed, the index itself, did not exist. By the end of 2008, the

S&P 500 was worth $9 trillion. However, there were $39.3 trillion of currency swaps outstanding and $41.9 trillion in credit default swaps (having come down from a peak of $62 trillion the year before). For its part, the total volume of derivatives outstanding was $514 trillion (!), or about *ten times* the Gross Global Product.[9]

The intellectually curious must wonder what these numbers signify. The knee-jerk reaction of the finance establishment is to point out that these notional principals are to some extent "scare numbers," because in many cases, such as swaps, the net exposure is a small fraction of the outstanding amount. This is true, but the flipside is that the vast amounts involved indicate very large hidden interdependencies, with obvious potential implications for systemic stability. These cannot be ignored – a small fraction of $62 trillion is still a lot of money.

Then there is the related question of what purpose this activity serves. The stock response is to trot out a standard litany of risk management purposes that financial instruments provide: hedging, liquidity, and diversification. Let's consider each of these in turn:

- The hedging argument can only account, at best, for a very small fraction of the total volume of derivatives outstanding. For example, the credit obligations subject to credit default swaps were only around $2 trillion or so by 2007,[10] at best, so leaving some $60 trillion (at their peak) of CDS positions that must have served some other purpose. Similarly, with a gross global product of around $50 trillion or so, only a modest fraction of the $514 trillion in outstanding derivatives can possibly serve a hedging purpose.

- The second argument is that these derivatives help provide liquidity to the market. This is true, but how much? The market only needs so much liquidity, and the amounts needed are presumably some fraction of the amounts used for hedging. So this doesn't take us very far either.

- The third argument is perhaps the most elusive, but one thing is very clear: in crisis after crisis, and especially in the recent crisis, we have seen diversification disappear like a will-o'-the-wisp: investors might have thought they were diversifying, but one suspects

---

[9] Bank for International Settlements Quarterly Report, September 2009.
[10] Jones, 2009.

that much alleged portfolio diversification is more a matter of mis-applied theory than fact.

If we dismiss these three arguments as explaining only a fraction of the amounts outstanding, then there must be some other explanation. No doubt some of these positions are speculative, but there has to be more to it than just that: most of ten times Gross World Product cannot be merely speculation. The only remaining possibility is rent-seeking: the extraction by the industry of value from the economy without providing any economically meaningful service in return. The explosion in derivatives and trading volume serves the interests of Wall Street rather than its clients. It is a combination of a gigantic vacuum cleaner and a smokescreen that has enabled Wall Street to extract truly enormous rents from the remainder of the economy.

(iv) Securitization

The other major capital markets innovation of these decades was securitization. Under a securitization transaction, a number of assets are placed in a pool and claims against those assets are sold to investors, secured against the assets in that pool. The technique remained confined to the home mortgage market until 1985, when the first securitization was carried out for a pool of automobile loans. Once that transaction had been proved successful, the technique spread to credit card loans, home equity loans, commercial loans, insurance obligations, student loans, equipment leases, and aircraft loans. The volumes involved grew enormously: by the second quarter of 2008, the total outstanding securitized debt was estimated at $10.25 trillion in the United States and $2.24 trillion in Europe.

Securitization transactions generally involve some kind of credit enhancement, so that investors are not simply buying interests in the home loans, credit card receivables, etc. but benefit from the enhanced credit on those underlying assets. At its simplest, the credit enhancement may consist of Fannie Mae, Freddie Mac, or Ginnie Mae guarantees of home mortgages; for other assets, there may be a guarantee by an insurance company (often a "monoline" insurer that specializes in credit guarantees of this kind) or by the bank arranging the securitization.

The credit enhancement helps make the new security attractive to potential investors, who are often constrained to invest in securities of a minimum credit rating such as triple A or investment grade (triple B or above).

Most securitizations are channeled through special purpose vehicles: new companies set up in favorable regulation environments (such as the Bahamas) that would purchase the securitized assets and be responsible for the liabilities involved, and which would ensure that the transaction is taken off the balance sheet of the financial institution doing the securitization.

The claims against the pool of underlying assets can be straightforward homogeneous bonds or, alternatively, heterogeneous tranches of bonds, differentiated by the seniority of their claims. In the latter case, low-rated tranches would bear the first losses and higher-rated tranches would only suffer losses once the lower rated tranches had been wiped out. To provide information to investors about what they're buying, the bonds issued are rated by the rating agencies, who (theoretically) satisfy themselves as to the likely level of loss in the underlying assets and (where there are tranches) their likely exposure to those losses. Hence, different bonds issued against the same pool of assets might have very different credit ratings, and the most secure top-rated bonds would often be rated AAA, making them eligible investments, in theory, for the most conservative investors.

For securitizers, the principal advantages of securitization are twofold. First, it reduces the capital that needs to be held against a portfolio of assets; and second, it can provide an up-front profit if (as is usually the case) the assets are sold to the special purpose vehicle at a higher value than they had been acquired for. Consequently, securitization benefits the balance sheet, the income statement, and the bonus pool; and the value of these benefits often greatly exceeds the very considerable legal and transactions costs involved.

For investors, the principal advantage of securitized bonds was that they usually carried a yield somewhat higher than ordinary corporate bonds with the same credit rating, an advantage that readers should by now recognize as a red flag! A second advantage, at least in theory, was diversification: the benefits of a low beta and a more diversified portfolio.

Securitization was often presented as a useful addition to the financial toolbox, allowing the benefits of greater risk-sharing and access to capital. In practice, it created a separation of credit origination from credit risk, allowing unscrupulous salesmen with high-pressure techniques to wreak havoc, while greatly enriching themselves in the process.

A good example of this is the Collateralized Debt Obligation (CDO). For example, home loan securitizations begin when some hyped up mortgage broker/salesperson finds mortgage borrowers and takes a commission of maybe 2–4% from a bank for his pains. The bank packages up these mortgages into a CDO, takes a commission itself, has the CDOs rated by a rating agency, which charges a fee of maybe $400,000 for the service and then gets the loans rapidly off its books. The stockbroker then takes a commission when he sells the security to customers. Everyone along the chain takes their cut, however deeply hidden, paid for by some combination of the people at both ends of the chain: the individual who takes out the mortgage and the investor who buys the CDO.

There is nonetheless a basic economic problem with loan securitizations. In the old days, loans were made with the intention that the lender would keep them on its books. In this lend-and-hold model, any bad loans made by the lender came straight back to him in the form of default losses and lower profit. This gave the lender a strong incentive to be careful with his loans. Indeed, judicious lending and credit management was the key to a commercial bank's (or savings and loan/ building society's) long-term profitability, and involved the cultivation of longer-term relationships with borrowers to the mutual benefit of all: the lender and the borrower understood each other and the lender bank was better informed about individual borrowers than other possible lenders. This was, indeed, the very essence of a credit relationship: the word "credit" comes from the Latin verb "credere," meaning "to believe" and, implicitly, "to trust."

Once we get into securitization, the lend-and-hold model gives way to originate-to-distribute: the lender originates loans with the explicit intent of selling them on; indeed, in some cases selling all of them – without keeping any "skin in the game" at all. Under this model, the old incentives – to be careful, to screen prospective borrowers, manage their longer-term credit, and cultivate long-term relationships with them for mutual benefit – all vanish, and loans are made for the quick sale only. Thus, many of the benefits of the old system were thrown away, and the quality of loans (and underlying that the integrity of the credit management process) sharply deteriorated. All things considered, the new system was much inferior to the old.

In essence, credit risk moved from the banks, who knew how to assess it, to other investors, who did not. In comparison to manufacturing, where "the market price is set by the smartest guy with the best, cheapest production process," in securitized markets, the price is "set by the dumbest guy with the most money to lose."[11]

The process involved is also distinctly alchemical. The original loans, the lead, might have fairly poor credit quality. However, thanks to the wonders of modern financial engineering, all this lead is mysteriously converted into a CDO with most of its bonds rated AAA, that is, gold, making them (supposedly) respectable for investors. The easiest (and usual) way to achieve this magic is by assuming that defaults are independent of each other – in other words, that default on one says nothing about the probabilities of default on the remainder. This convenient assumption not only allows default and loss probabilities to be calculated using straightforward binomial probability theory, but also (as discussed in Chapter 5) produces reassuringly low estimates of default probabilities. This means that the majority of the bonds on even a subprime CDO can be rated as having triple A default rates, even though the underlying assets might be rubbish.

In reality, defaults on mortgages are not independent events. A mortgage bubble such as that of 2004–06 causes a simultaneous slackening of underwriting standards, with even minimal control procedures being abandoned throughout the entire asset class, so leaving investors highly exposed, while a nationwide house price decline or interest rate rise causes the mortgage holders to get into simultaneous difficulty. In a general housing downturn, such as we saw in 2008, even prime loans will exhibit a high degree of default correlation. As for subprime loans, to the extent that these consist of "liar loans" or "no-dox" loans, their chance of default in a housing downturn is very high indeed, as the decline in house prices would make default economically attractive for almost all subprime borrowers; hence, large numbers of subprime

---

[11] Quoted in Hansell and Muehring, 1992.

mortgages would default simultaneously. Even without a general housing downturn, the correlations between housing defaults may still be quite high, because they depend also on common economic, monetary policy and other factors (such as irrational exuberance and lax underwriting standards).

CDOs are a classic example of innovation benefiting the financial system rather than the clients. The borrowers are sold products with no regard for their suitability, and investors, all too often are sold lead disguised as gold. Investors in Germany, Japan, and elsewhere naively assumed that a Moody's or Standard and Poor's AAA credit rating would magically transform the credit risk of a blind pool of US home mortgages that were known to be in some way "subprime." In such an environment, the concept of a "sophisticated" investor becomes laughable.

Nor were the end investors the only suckers involved. When they produced their first CDOs, then known as "bistros," in the late 1990s, the credit derivatives team at J.P. Morgan persuaded themselves that they were even safer than AAA: they were "super-senior." In its initial deal in 1997, worth $9.7 billion, they calculated that they would need only $700 million in capital cover. The ratings agencies agreed, but the regulators initially insisted that they insure their exposure; the J.P. Morgan team then found a counterparty, AIG, who was willing to insure it for just 0.02 cents per dollar insured. Multiply that by a few billion here and there, and it seemed to AIG that it was onto a real money spinner. This fateful deal however set AIG on the road to ruin: insuring vast amounts of credit exposure for a pittance, only to be ruined in spectacular fashion in 2008 when super-prime had turned to super-toxic and AIG was revealed to be unable to honor its commitments.

These instruments also illustrate another aspect of Modern Finance: it does not matter whether Modern Finance rests on true assumptions or not. Instead, a huge amount of money has been made (and lost) by betting that those assumptions are true. The belief that the market can assess and price risks more or less automatically means that even the doziest mortgage broker can originate subprime mortgages for even the least worthy customers. The fact that the borrowers are incapable of making payments on the mortgage will magically be priced into the mortgage by the securitization process, which will bundle the mortgage with other mortgages originated by a similarly lax process and sell the lot to an unsuspecting German Landesbank unwisely attracted by the high initial yield. Everybody will make fees on the deal and the Landesbank and the homeowner will have nobody legally to blame when the homeowner is unable to make payments and the Landesbank finds a shortfall in its investment income.

We have so far discussed securitizations of mortgage loans, where the assumption of independence was widely made in part because of lack of data and in part by the fact that the US housing market hadn't undergone a major correction since the 1930s (and, of course, in part because no one wanted to upset the applecart!). In the corporate CDO market, however, things were a little different. Datasets were better, albeit very limited; those who knew the field knew that corporate defaults were correlated and rose when the economy went down. Consequently, in the corporate CDO market, trading was held back, to some extent, by the absence of a suitable model that could accommodate correlated defaults: what traders needed was an equivalent to Black-Scholes-Merton that would handle default correlations.

Their dreams came true in 2000 when a J.P. Morgan statistician, David Li, published a paper "On Default Correlation: A Copula Function Approach" in the *Journal of Fixed Income*. In this paper, Dr. Li showed a model, known as a Gaussian copula, that could handle the probabilities and losses associated with multiple defaults, taking account of the correlations between corporate defaults. A copula was an ingenious solution to this problem because it allowed the user to use existing models of the default probabilities of firms individually considered; the copula itself would then give the probabilities and losses associated with multiple defaults. The particular copula used, the Gaussian copula, was especially attractive because it was tractable and made use of standard Pearson correlation estimates.

The model had its limitations: among other problems, it was sensitive to correlation estimates and took no account of how correlations might change with the business cycle. Li himself had warned of its limitations, but as far as CDO traders were concerned, the Li model gave them the valuation model they were looking for, and they were not interested in the technical small print. An additional problem was that its near universal adoption created a new form of correlation risk: if the model went wrong, then everyone would experience catastrophic losses at the same time.

The model then paved the way for new products of greater profitability to their issuers. An example was synthetic CDOs. These are equivalent to conventional CDOs with their bonds replaced by credit default swaps; these had the attractions that they tied up less capital (because there were no bonds to buy), provided opportunities for increased leverage, and generated up-front fees for little initial outlay. Another, more pathological, example was the CDO squared: a CDO based not on the tranched payments of bonds or even swaps, but on the payments of CDOs themselves. The risk management purposes of these and much more risky instruments are impossible to discern and presumably do not exist; they did however have great leverage potential and generated large fees for their issuers.

Yet, ironically, the Li copula model did relatively little in practice to solve the underlying problems it solved in theory: it took account of correlations, but, since the correlations in the data were low, it made only a small difference, and this was so whether it was used for corporate or mortgage defaults; moreover, the default models used almost always ignored the impact of business cycle and other common factors, and so missed the key vulnerability to which all these markets were exposed.

One nice little postscript on the subject of CDOs: these vehicles not only caused havoc in the recent crisis, but gave some of their issuers a richly deserved bite in the derrière as well. In order to sell securitizations, many issuers had committed themselves to buying them back at face value, issuing so-called liquidity puts, but giving little thought to what these might entail. And so, when the music stopped, Citi found itself holding not only $55 billion in toxic CDOs that it still had on its books – which itself says a lot about the quality of Citi's own risk management – but also had to buy back an additional $25 billion of CDOs on which it had written liquidity puts. Amazingly, Citi's chair, Robert Rubin, later admitted that until the summer of 2007, he had never even heard of a liquidity put: Citi had issued $25 billion of them and its chair never even knew what they were!

(v) Housing Finance

Notoriously, the most intensive field for use of the new securitization technology was the housing market. Traditionally, in both the United States and Britain, local financial institutions made home loans, funded from their own resources. In Britain the institutions making the loans were generally mutual "building societies," funded by homeowners themselves; in the US they were generally (but not always) profit-seeking institutions. In practice there was little difference; the ethos of Jimmy Stewart as owner of the "Bailey Building and Loan" in the 1946 Frank Capra classic *It's a Wonderful Life* differs little from that of the management of a traditional British building society. Both wanted to increase the prosperity and stability of their local community by fostering home-ownership on a conservatively financed basis.

In Britain, the traditional system of housing finance could have continued forever, in part because home loans were traditionally made on a floating rate basis, which made them less vulnerable to inflation risk, in part because building societies were allowed to amalgamate and better diversify their risks, and, most importantly, because they were not subjected to anything like the same degree of misguided government meddling.

In the US this began just after World War I. Energized by statistics that showed the US rate of home ownership had sharply fallen from 45.9% in 1910 to 45.6% in 1920, Commerce Secretary Herbert Hoover, always irresistibly inclined to meddle with the market, forecast dire consequences of "increased tenancy and landlordism," and responded with the "Own your own home" campaign that produced a 45% increase in mortgage loan volume at national banks between 1927 and 1929.[12]

Following the inevitable housing crash (itself a major trigger of the epidemic of bank failures in 1930–33), the Feds increased their involvement rather than stepping back, forming the Home Owners Loan Corporation, the Federal Housing Agency, and then, in 1938, Fannie Mae, so providing an effective federal guarantee on a high proportion of home mortgages and also generating government subsidized

---

[12] Malanga, 2009.

competition to the S&Ls. By 1949, more than 40% of home loans were government-subsidized.

The 1968 "privatization" of Fannie Mae made little difference, and was in any case offset by the creation of her siblings Freddie Mac, intended to promote a secondary mortgage market, and Ginnie Mae, to provide a direct federal government guarantee of mortgages for low-income homeowners, both continuations of the bizarre US policy of having government-related entities guarantee home loans. These Government-Sponsored Enterprises (GSEs) were to have a disastrous impact on the US housing finance market in later years.

By guaranteeing home loans, directly or later indirectly through one of the GSEs, the government changed a heterogeneous asset class into a homogeneous one. That weakened Jimmy Stewart's grip over his mortgage portfolio, making it ripe for securitization. The government itself carried out the first securitization, selling a pool of Ginnie Mae-backed mortgages in February 1970, and opening the doors for Wall Street later.

As we discussed in Chapter 3, the 1970s were not a kind decade for the US savings and loan business, and by 1982 most S&Ls were insolvent. They turned in desperation to Congress for help, who responded by giving them a tax break to help them: they could sell mortgages at a loss and offset those losses against taxes paid over the previous ten years. The S&Ls became desperate to sell on almost any terms so they had the required losses to show the IRS.

As it happened, the only investment bank with a fully functioning mortgage department was Salomon Brothers, who now enjoyed a temporary monopoly that netted them a fortune. They would often give the S&Ls 65 cents on the dollar for securities that would be sold off at par under a Freddie or Fannie guarantee, and then recycle them to other S&Ls. In one case, a thrift sold assets at 65 cents on the dollar and bought similar assets at 75 cents on the dollar. The Salomon sales pitch was crude but effective: "it's not a very good deal, but if you don't do it, you're out of a job."

Having recycled their mortgage portfolios, the newly deregulated S&Ls added credit losses in the real estate market to their previous interest rate losses and went hopelessly bust in the late 1980s, causing the crisis described in Chapter 3. The securitized home loan market was now the only game in town: the originate-to-distribute model had driven out lend-and-hold in the housing finance market.

None of this brought much benefit to homeowners. The average yield on conventional prime 30-year home mortgages in 1972–78, the earliest years for which Fed data is available, before securitization really got going, was 8.71%, or 108 basis points (1.08%) over the yield on 20-year US Treasury bonds over those years. The average yield on conventional home mortgages in 2000–06 (before credit worries became a big issue) was 6.50%, 122 basis points above the average yield on 20-year Treasury bonds in 2000–06.[13] Thus, the mortgage spread increased by 0.14% between the earlier and later periods.

Since the overall yield structure was lower and more stable in 2000–06 (and so the perceived mortgage refinancing risk was lower) and the market appetite for risk was generally greater, one would have expected the 'spread' between mortgage yields and Treasuries to be lower; instead it was higher. This strongly indicates that the entire Wall Street mechanism of securitized mortgages was a rip-off, whereby the homeowner paid more for their money than under the Jimmy Stewart system, and the excess went to Wall Street and mortgage broker intermediaries. The 0.14% differential between the 1972–78 spread and the 2000–06 spread may not sound like much, but on $11 trillion of home mortgages it represents $15.4 billion per annum, and is clear evidence of the rent (profit without providing any additional service) that Wall Street was extracting from this market.

And this is without considering the marked deterioration in the quality of the service their customers received: many householders were given loans they couldn't pay, only to be turfed out of their homes later, and whole neighborhoods in American cities are now blighted by the consequences of subprime mortgages. The securitization of their mortgages also deprived many mortgage holders in difficulties of any chances they might have had under the old system of the lender allowing them to defer or reduce payments to avert default.

Alert readers will at this point ask: if the new system is so much less efficient in delivering value to the ultimate customer, how did it drive out the old?

---

[13] Federal Reserve Board table H.15; annual averages. The Fed did not collect mortgage yield data before April 1971.

The answer is the system of twisted incentives and, most of all, the twisted incentives of salesmanship. Anybody who has lived in a US suburb with an economically attractive zipcode and no butler will recognize that excessive salesmanship is the bane of American life. This is even more true in the mortgage business. Homeowners today don't go into their local S&L, save for half a decade, and request a mortgage from Jimmy Stewart. Instead they are sold a mortgage product, either directly or over the Internet, by an aggressive salesman. That product is then securitized by an investment bank trader who in good years is paid a *large* multiple of what Jimmy Stewart earned. With others it is sold to a securitization vehicle of immense complexity that has been set up by Wall Street lawyers who are paid a *very large* multiple of what Jimmy Stewart earned. Costs have been increased at every point in the process, but aggressive salesmanship and twisted incentives had driven Jimmy Stewart out of business.

These problems were especially apparent in the subprime mortgage market, where a blatantly undesirable outcome arose from a process in which participants' activities at each stage were economically rational:

- Low-income consumers took on mortgages they had no prospect of affording because they believed from the experience of others that house prices would rise sufficiently to bail them out. In any case, being often near bankruptcy, the potential profit from successful speculation often appeared to them greater than the potential loss from default.
- The encyclopedia salesmen and used car dealers who functioned as mortgage brokers sold subprime mortgages because they got a generous commission for selling them (better than for the technologically obsolescent encyclopedias or even used cars) and were not responsible for the credit risk.
- Investment banks packaged the subprime mortgages into multiple-tranche mortgage-backed securities because they received fat fees for doing so and, again, had no responsibility for the credit risk.
- Rating agencies gave the upper tranches of mortgage debt favorable ratings because they made a great deal of money from providing ratings for asset-backed securities, needed to keep in the favor of the investment banks who brought them this attractive business,

and had mathematical models (either their own or the investment banks') "proving" that the default rates of the securitized mortgages would be low.

- Investment bank and rating agency mathematicians produced models "proving" that default rates would be low, ignoring the real-world correlations between defaults on low quality consumer debt, because they had succumbed to the group-think affecting everyone else – and because they were well paid and the alternative was to return to a miserable low-paid existence in academia.

- Finally, the investors bought asset-backed securities because they could achieve a higher return on them in the short term than their borrowing costs, and could tell their funding sources (in the case of hedge funds) or bosses (in the case of foreign banks) that they were taking very little risk because of the securities' high rating.

Each step of the process was rational (albeit operating on imperfect information), yet because incentives were hopelessly misaligned, the final result was an irrational, twisted market in which loans that would not be repaid were securitized and sold to investors seeking an above-market return at below market risk, a combination that in the long run cannot exist.

Looked at in this way, the subprime mortgage was simply a scam, and the market a giant Ponzi scheme that could survive only as long as more people entered into subprime mortgage contracts, keeping house prices high and mortgage brokers active. Once interest rates began to rise, the demise of the market became inevitable, and it will remain open only through the activities of Fannie Mae, Freddie Mac, and the government propping up an economically damaging product.

The role of the government and its agencies was central in all this. It was the government agencies that kick-started the process of mortgage securitization: it is likely that the mortgage bond market would never have achieved sufficient investor acceptance without these government guarantees – investors would have been rightly suspicious of a package of mortgages to unknown homeowners scattered around the country, and would have demanded a yield high enough to have made the transaction impossible. The government and its agencies then meddled repeatedly, especially in the late 1970s and early 1980s and then again post the Millennium, in pushing for greater homeownership.

In particular the Community Reinvestment Act of 1977, reinforced by much legislative and regulatory activity thereafter, mandated that bank regulators assess banks' mortgage lending in low income areas and to minorities, in the process undermining traditional lending standards.[14] Needless to say, the worst victims of this activity were low-income mortgage borrowers themselves; pushed into subprime mortgages they had no hope of affording. The ultimate result was the NINJA (no income, no job or assets) mortgage, and no-deposit no-questions asked loans to, among others, a Mexican strawberry picker who could speak no English and with an income of $14,000 who got a loan of $720,000, and a 24-year-old web designer who bought seven houses in five months and in the process ran up a debt of $2.2 million.[15]

In a normal market, subprime loans would have been a self-liquidating problem, because lenders who made them would quickly have gone bust. In the US subprime market, however, lenders who made them were effectively guaranteed by Fannie Mae and Freddie Mac, who themselves were guaranteed by the taxpayer. These institutions leveraged more than would have been possible without the government's quasi-guarantee, used taxpayers' money to lobby like crazy to ensure they were not properly regulated and collapsed thankfully into the arms of the taxpayer as soon as the consequences of their own ineptitude became clear. It is indeed astonishing to consider how they managed to turn the soundest product in financial markets, the home mortgage, into a speculative casino, causing collateral damage of many times their own losses.

(vi) Credit default swaps

Of all the financial innovations since the 1970s, the most spectacularly spurious has been the credit default swap. During the explosion of the derivatives market in the early 1980s, in which Martin was an active

---

[14] This very complicated story has been well covered by other writers. See e.g. Kling, 2008 or Liebowitz, 2008.

[15] See Lewis, 2008 and Das, 2009.

albeit minor participant,[16] he looked extensively at the possibility of designing credit derivatives. The need, after all, was obvious: there were banks excessively exposed to particular borrowers and equally other banks and insurance companies with appetite for credit and no exposure to those borrowers. Credit derivatives could allow participants to buy and sell credit risks, aligning their exposures with their beliefs about the market.

We have already considered credit derivatives of the CDO type; in this section, we look at credit default swaps, swaps in which one payment leg depends on a defined "credit event," typically the default (somehow defined!) of a specified party or specified debt obligation. CDS were first developed in 1997 and marketed, with enormous success, as instruments to manage credit exposures. The CDS market then grew at a truly staggering rate: surpassing $100 billion in size by 2000, $6.4 trillion by 2004, and peaking at a little more than $62 trillion in late 2007. Come the recent crisis, they then revealed their true nature as the archetypal financial weapon of mass destruction.

As Martin spotted a generation ago, there were always three fundamental problems with CDS, some of which also apply to other credit derivatives, and none of which was ever properly sorted out:

- There was the difficulty of nailing down the credit event with sufficient clarity. What is and what is not a default is a much more difficult problem than it might first appear to be: an inadequately defined "default" merely leads to arguments later and undermines the enforceability of the contract; and, at the same time, if the default event in the contract is not specified carefully, then there is a serious danger that it will not occur at the same time as the default event that brings about the loss that the CDS are meant to hedge, which will undermine the effectiveness of the hedge. This is the old problem of basis risk, the slippage between what happens to the position being hedged and what happens to the hedge instrument itself.

---

[16] Martin ran derivatives desks at Enskilda Securities and Creditanstalt-Bankverein from 1982-87, enjoying the initial product-creating phase of the market, but growing uncomfortable (and bored) as it degenerated into a trading circus. It has to be said however that he was always concerned with the economic pointlessness of much derivatives activity.

- The second and worse problem is how to assess the size of the de-fault-contingent payment, which is meant to represent the market value of the defaulted obligation. The solution the market found was to determine this amount by a post-default auction of a very limited amount of the obligation concerned. In some cases, this auction amounts to sales of a few million dollars of paper to settle CDS with a face value worth many billions, an auction involving assets worth perhaps one-thousandth of the amounts whose value they sought to establish. In such cases the auction becomes highly "gameable," with enormous scope for manipulation by interested parties.

- The third problem is that payouts are very highly lopsided between one side and the other – one side is at risk of not receiving a modest annual premium, but the other is at risk of not receiving the entire principal amount of the swap. The side that buys the swap there-fore has a potentially huge credit exposure to the party that writes it: CDS entail potentially massive credit risks of their own.

The recent crisis also revealed another fundamental problem: CDS provide the ideal instrument to carry out highly levered "bear raids," driving firms into insolvency, particularly highly levered financial in-stitutions whose debt is a large multiple of their equity.

For one thing, look at the economics involved. An equity short seller wishing to drive a company into bankruptcy has to take the risk that the stock will rebound, forcing it to cover its position at a loss that is theoretically unlimited; it has little leverage available, so it must put up an amount of money that is comparable to its potential winnings. An alternative is to buy put options; these do not have infinite potential loss, but on the other hand their premium is substantial and the time decay of option premiums is rapid, so that it has only a few months to carry out any nefarious schemes it may have.

Conversely, a CDS holder, like an option buyer, need pay only a modest annual premium, so its potential gain can be many times its investment. Moreover, CDS are typically outstanding for several years, so it can wait until market conditions are propitious before striking.

But perhaps the greatest attraction of CDS as a vehicle for bear raids is their outstanding volume. In July 2009, for example there were $1.4

billion nominal of Citigroup and $2.1 billion of J.P. Morgan Chase outstanding in the traded equity options market, while the short interest on both banks was of the order of $1 billion. Yet the outstanding CDS volume was over $60 billion for each bank. For a hedge fund wishing to make an extraordinary return through promoting bankruptcy, the CDS market offers far greater buying power, lower prices and lower risk than any alternative. The choice is a no-brainer.

A related perversity is that CDS allow bond-holders the opportunity to "game" the bankruptcy process itself. In essence, CDS holders, who if they are also bondholders can vote in the bankruptcy process, have an obvious and massive conflict of interest. In debt negotiations surrounding a potential bankruptcy, they act like spectators at a suicide, yelling "Jump, jump" and giving their victim a helpful nudge over the edge, pushing companies into default in order to reap bonanza profits from their CDS positions.

These sorts of problems seem to have figured prominently in the Lehmans bankruptcy, where CDS holders relentlessly shorted the stock to destroy confidence in the firm and so destroy the firm itself. They also manifested themselves in negotiations between debt-holders, some of whom had nil or even negative economic exposure because of their CDS hedges, in a number of corporate bankruptcies in 2009. General Motors was the most notable of these but they also included the Canadian paper company Abitibi-Bowater and the shopping center developer General Growth Properties. Such problems also arose in the case of other institutions that got themselves into major difficulties, including AIG, Citigroup, Fannie Mae, and Freddie Mac. Short sellers got much of the blame in the media, but the reality is that CDS were the real culprit.

As an entertaining aside, in 2009, a small house, Amherst Holdings, beat the Wall Street titans at their own horrid game. It found a pool of $29 million of particularly repulsive California subprime mortgages, then sold $130 million notional of CDS on them, pocketing around $100 million in premiums, since this waste was so toxic the big houses were prepared to pay up to 80% to insure against it, so between them selling insurance for 4½ times the maximum possible loss. Amherst then quietly went round and paid all the debts of the lucky homeowners owing the $29 million. At that point, since there were no defaults, it was able to keep the $101 million in premiums (net of the loan repayments, a $71 million profit). The Wall Street firms were furious, but in fact Amherst's coup was a perfectly legitimate use of this foolish structure, far more so than many of the shenanigans undertaken some of the big players – after all, Amherst's operation *prevented* a number of defaults and foreclosures.

CDS were often touted as a form of insurance, and there is, indeed, a natural historical analogy: the life insurance market. Like credit derivatives, life insurance provides cash flow in the form of premiums in its early years, while losses in the form of deaths occur only later, often decades later. Like credit derivatives, the proper reserving for such losses was initially poorly understood, so life insurance companies with aggressive salesmen and low premiums could record excellent profits, and raise additional capital on the basis of those profits.

The tsunami of new business and apparent surge in profitability enabled rewards to be paid to such companies' proprietors, who were acting economically rationally in the same way as today's credit derivatives traders. More ominously, since it was possible in the early days of the London market to buy a life insurance policy on a complete stranger, insurance companies began to notice the high incidence of unexpected homicides among their lives assured, a fairly obvious form of moral hazard akin to that which we see in the modern CDS market! The solution, though it took time to develop, was the concept of insurable interest, codified by the Life Assurance Act of 1774. Today you can't buy a life insurance policy unless you can demonstrate some loss by the assured party's death.

The analogy between the credit derivatives market and eighteenth century life insurance is a close one, even if it is difficult to imagine credit derivatives traders taking to periwigs and snuff, and decamping to Antwerp rather than Brazil when things go wrong. It also suggests a possible solution to the problem: failing other means of discouraging corporate homicides, insurable interest may well be the solution for CDS too.

Another worrying problem with CDS is that, despite their (in retrospect, all too obvious) pathology, the risks they entailed failed to show up in institutions' risk models. This was, in part, due to indefensible but common assumption that defaults were uncorrelated, which was in and of itself sufficient to hide their risks completely. It was not however helped by the use of the VaR risk measure: the value of a CDS on a major name varies very little during periods of market stability; consequently its 99% VaR will be low in such periods and indicate nothing of the risks involved. So even if a risk manager had believed VaR's estimate of CDS risk grossly underestimated potential market volatility, until 2008 they would have had no data on which to base this suspicion. Hence banks and brokers were able to load up on CDS without their risk management systems waving any red flags.

Moreover, since the market had only been in existence in its current form since 1997, CDS were untested in a real credit crunch until 2008. A major innovation thus grew to a staggering size without having gone through the revealing crucible of having survived a major downturn in good shape. The only protection left to market participants was therefore their intuition and whatever integrity they had:

- Towards one extreme, Bill Demchak, a key member of the J.P. Morgan team that helped create CDS in the first place, felt uncomfortable very early on with the size of the amounts involved, and J.P. Morgan began to back off from the market. Later, as senior vice chairman of the Pittsburgh bank PNC, he started to reduce his bank's credit exposure in 2006, alarmed at the way the corporate bond market was going. In both cases, these contrarian decisions meant forgoing the lure of apparently easy profits and were no doubt difficult to make in the circumstances of the time.
- At the other extreme, there were institutions like Citi and, worst of all, AIG, that were out to make every penny they could. AIG sold CDS like there was no tomorrow, and for AIG eventually, there wasn't: in September 2008 it was bankrupted to the tune of $180 billion of taxpayer dollars by a unit based in London with 100 employees, which as a subsidiary of AIG came to be a problem for the US rather than British authorities, much to the later embarrassment of the former. AIG was not uniquely stupid, though it was always known as a house that pushed the limits. It was, however, extremely unwise, reaping short-term gains while ultimately destroying its own long-term viability.

A key concern here relates to the staggering size of the market. The size of this market – more than $62 trillion at its peak, relative to US corporate debt of about $5 trillion and about $12 trillion of home mortgages

– exposes the Big Lie that CDS represent hedging transactions, and undermines the argument that risk is transferred to institutions better able to bear it.

Proponents of the market will indignantly point out that the $62 trillion figure for the total principal amount of credit derivatives outstanding is a "scare" number, in the sense that the aggregate exposure in the credit derivatives market is far smaller than this, because for every contract there is a winner and a loser. This is true, but misses two points: first, we don't know what the net value is; a small fraction of that amount is still a lot of money. Second, $62 trillion is itself a very large number that represents a huge set of highly opaque criss-crossing obligations and, hence, potential systemic vulnerability.

Moreover, the gains and losses are not confined to the "banking system" however that amorphous entity is defined, but are spread among insurance companies, hedge funds, investment institutions, and well connected riff-raff. Although the modest hiccups of normal years can easily be absorbed, in a major credit crunch such losses will be bunched in a context where the credit system is already under serious strain. If a sufficient number of underlying companies fail, financial institutions will be placed in a precarious position at a time when funding is hard to come by, and a cascade effect will take over, with each default making other defaults more likely. So, even if the financial institutions don't initially fail, their counterparties may fail in large numbers, plunging the system into disaster.

There is also the more worrying concern that some institutions became so pivotal in the credit derivatives market – Bear Stearns and AIG come to mind – that the prospect of their failure became so threatening that the Fed felt (rightly or wrongly is another matter) it had little practical choice but to rescue them and worry about the moral hazard and other side-effects later. By this point, the system has truly become systemically unstable.

In reality the CDS market moved beyond simple hedging and risk transfer many years ago. It creates many times as much risk as it hedges or transfers. Selling a credit risk more than once is not hedging, and it is hard to make out a case that it is good diversification. Instead, it is mainly a form of speculation that sharply increases the overall risk in the financial system. Add to this the interdependencies CDS create, in which the failure of one firm can trigger off the failures of many others that would otherwise have been largely unaffected, and the fact that these interdependencies are "known unknowns" – we know they are there, but don't know how bad they might be – and we have a recipe for systemic disaster. CDS represent a huge and (because they were traded OTC) largely hidden iceberg that could strike the shoddily designed financial system Titanic at any time.

9

And Wall Street Metamorphoses

The last chapter described the new product innovations deriving from Modern Financial Theory, and how and why Wall Street eagerly adopted them. This chapter discusses the structural changes on Wall Street that coincided with these product innovations and that were in most cases at least partly caused by them.

We need to see institutional changes in Wall Street and the City of London within the context of increasingly entrenched crony capitalism on the one hand, and against the backdrop of increasingly out-of-control managerial capitalism on the other. It helps if we now summarize the main institutional changes before going on to explain some of them in a little more detail. We have:

- a vast increase in the size of the major houses, with a move away from what was left of the old partnership form;
- a move towards towards a trading culture (discussed in Chapter 8), a corresponding shift in power towards trading from traditional investment banking, and the spread of a short-termist bonus culture;

- the degradation of investor analysis and ratings, themselves symptoms of the broader deterioration in Wall Street standards; and, last but not least,
- the rise of mark-to-market accounting.

Each of these involved less effective corporate governance and more uncontrolled moral hazard.

Taken together, what we see is the transformation of finance and "high finance" especially, into a huge rent-extraction machine: the industry became expert in extracting value for itself, privatizing the gains. As we shall see when we come to discuss the financial crisis, it was to be equally adept at socializing the losses. The implicit social contract: "heads I win, tails you lose."

Before the "big bangs" of 1975 in New York and 1986 in London, brokerage commissions were fixed; consequently the brokerage business acted as a cozy club, in which client service and research were paid for by commissions on large orders. Trading volume was moderate and fairly inelastic, since complex trading strategies by institutions were ruled out by the high level of brokerage commissions and, in London, by stamp duty as well.

The "big bang" deregulations of commissions made life much tougher for brokers. In New York, the 1970s saw a plethora of bankruptcies and forced mergers of once famous names, as the previously solid base of brokerage income shrank. Corporate finance-oriented houses found life very difficult, and the only houses that survived were those that had either already or soon embraced an aggressive trading orientation. However, even by the early 1980s it had become obvious that for the largest trading-oriented houses, like Salomon Brothers, previous standards of income, both firm-wide and individual, were being revised sharply upwards.

In London, the senior partners at major brokers saw the Big Bang as a heaven-sent opportunity to sell out and retire at 40, a typically British reaction to unexpected change. The resistance to bureaucratization and invasion by foreign houses was therefore far less intensive than one might have expected. The merchant banks, the major eventual losers from change, foolishly welcomed it, wrongly believing that they could scale up their operations sufficiently to survive in a trading dominated world, and that their remuneration would escalate in London as it was already doing in the United States. Instead, the period after the London Big Bang saw mass takeovers of London merchant banks by larger institutions and an epidemic of unexpectedly early retirements by the flower of London merchant banking.

One advantage gained by the larger houses after the Big Bangs was increased barriers to entry into their ranks.

In the 1960s Donaldson, Lufkin, and Jenrette in New York had built itself into a "major bracket" house in a decade through superior stock research; but after 1975, the economies of scale through knowledge of the order flow in trading soon proved insurmountable to outsiders, and there were no major new entrants to New York after then.

In supposedly stuffy London before its Big Bang, Warburgs and Hill Samuel had moved from insignificant presences to positions at the top of the league tables in the generation after World War II. Their success was not repeatable after 1986. In London, this was also due, in part, to the appalling levels of bureaucracy produced by the 1986 Financial Services Act, which not only led to a significant deterioration of business integrity, but also made it impossible for new entrants to compete because of the gigantic overheads the Act imposed.

The high entry barriers for anything more than a "boutique" advisory firm in post-Big Bang London were aptly illustrated by the pathetic fate of Caspian Securities, formed in 1995 with $250 million in capital and the finest brains from the now defunct Baring Brothers. Caspian specialized in emerging markets. "Caspian has never been in better shape to take advantage of market conditions in the whole of its [by then almost three year] history," [1] said its chairman Christopher Heath bullishly in March 1998. Four months later it was gone, swept away by the Asian crisis.

Naturally, this shift involved a move away from the old partnership structure. From the perspective of Modern Finance, the problems with the partnership structure were that it discouraged risk-taking and focused on the long-term. The former was a barrier to profit-making and the latter prevented those in charge getting their hands on the accumulated value built up over decades, if not centuries.

---

[1] *Euromoney*, 1998. We shall meet Heath again in his earlier Barings incarnation in the next chapter.

An egregious instance of this, and an ominous foretaste of things to come, was the decision by Salomon Brothers CEO John Gutfruend, the "King of Wall Street," to turn his firm from a private partnership into a public corporation.[2] He had been made CEO only after promising his predecessor, William Salomon, that he would keep the partnership form. He still professed to support Salomon's view that the partnership form was the key to the firm's success: it was, he believed, the only way to ensure the loyalty of key employees, since they were obliged to keep a substantial portion of their wealth tied up in the firm, which they would forfeit if they left. But having become CEO, he and other partners could not resist the temptation to "unlock" the firm's accumulated value and siphon it into their own pockets. (This materialism disgusted him, said Salomon afterwards.) In 1981, they sold the firm to the commodities broker Philips Brothers for $554 million, making Gutfreund himself an immediate personal killing of about $40 million, an amount that might seem piddling by today's standards but was a huge amount in those days.

The change led to a marked deterioration in employee loyalty: traders increasingly demanded (and obtained) rapidly rising remuneration by threatening to move to rival firms, so feeding the bonus frenzy and leading to a situation where the traders would ultimately become the best paid people in Wall Street.

The sale of Salomon Brothers also implied a marked shift in risk-bearing, transferring risks from themselves to their shareholders. There was however no corresponding transfer of profits; on the contrary, the values of their shares fell markedly over the next two decades or so.[3]

The heads of other Wall Street firms all tut-tutted and said what a bad thing Gutfreund had done, but they too soon gave in to the same temptation.

The last to go was Goldman Sachs, which was forced to postpone its Initial Public Offering because of the Long-Term Capital Management debacle, but finally in March 1999 sold a mere 12.6% of its equity in an IPO notable for the fact that the 12 co-managers in the deal were paid fees but not allotted any of the stock to sell. While the

---

[2] See Lewis 1989, pp. 149–50, 268–9; 2008.
[3] A Salomons share was worth $42 in 1986, and its equivalent, 2.26 shares in Citi, was worth only $27 in December 2008 and $9 in December 2009.

continued ownership after the IPO by Goldman partners of 48% of the stock might be thought to preserve much of the traditional incentive structure, this preservation was only temporary. By January 2010, 76% of Goldman Sachs shares were held by institutions and mutual funds, the ultimate dumb money, while only 5% were held by insiders.[4]

As Gutfreund freely admitted many years later, "When things go wrong, it's their [the shareholders'] problem," he said. He failed to mention that it can also become the taxpayers' problem, but what he really meant was that it wasn't *his*. As he explained, "It's laissez-faire until you get in deep shit."[5] The beauty of the system was that you get to keep the profits, but share the losses.

★★★

The shift towards a trading focus by the banks brought with it a shift in the balance of power towards traders and away from traditional investment bankers. A good example was Lehmans in the early 1980s. There the tensions between traders and investment bankers reached the point where the CEO, Pete Peterson, a very well-connected corporate financier and former Commerce Secretary, felt obliged to make the head of trading, Lew Glucksman, his co-CEO – by this point, the traders were making more than corporate finance, and seeking commensurate power. Eight weeks later, Glucksman walked into Peterson's office and told him he was taking over *now*. Peterson slinked away, leaving the traders in charge. Glucksman hated the bankers and liked to intimidate them with his crude physicality and fits of rage, in one of which he ripped the shirt off his own back. His successor, Dick Fuld, another trader, was of the same mould. The bankers called him the "gorilla" because he seemed to grunt rather than speak in full sentences. Fuld made the aggressive image his own, and put a life-size toy gorilla in his office.

By the late 1990s, trading revenues were able to dominate not merely a medium sized investment bank like Lehman but the giant commercial banks such as J.P. Morgan Chase and Citigroup. The result was a sharp change in focus, even among top management, from building a business over the long term to making the next quarter's

---

[4] Yahoo Finance, 2010.
[5] Lewis, 2008.

bonus. Even the largest financial institutions acquired the aggression, intensity, instability, and paranoia of Lehman's top managers. For the financial system as a whole, it was not an improvement.

The increased emphasis on trading also intensified the short-term bonus culture. It has been obvious since at least the 1980s that Wall Street's compensation structure was cuckoo: remuneration was approaching stratospheric levels that bore no conceivable relationship to actual performance or value-added.

Part of the problem was also that bonuses were massively top heavy relative to basic salary: bonuses could be 10, 20, or even 100 times salary. It's one thing when bonuses earned represent 10–25% of one's income; it's quite another when they represent almost all of it. The sheer amounts involved inevitably distort incentives. Wall Street bankers became fixated on playing games with year-end valuations in order to maximize their bonus payout: lobbying to protect your bonus became the only activity that mattered. This was not only a major distraction from what should have been the bankers' core business – serving customers – but became the core business itself. This led to all sorts of unpleasant and unproductive office politics and a major deterioration in ethical standards, as well as the inevitable accounting shenanigans.

For their part, unscrupulous managers often played political games of their own, manipulating bonuses to minimize payouts to those who were disfavored and maximize the amounts available for the in-crowd. Needless to say, banking became highly politicized. Common tricks included moving the disfavored to a different department in November, deciding unilaterally that no bonuses would be given at all that year, and firing the disfavored on Christmas Eve, relenting only in the New Year.[6]

★★★

As well as leading to domination by trading, Modern Finance, inspired by the "efficient market" nonsense of Modern Financial Theory, also resulted in the corruption of Wall Street analysis. (Were the Efficient

---

[6] All three of these happened to Martin in the 1980s. There must have been innumerable other tricks; it is impossible that Martin's modest career encompassed the entire gamut of Wall Street bonus game-playing.

Market Hypothesis true in its strong form, analysis would be entirely useless in any case.)

Traditional analysis was a respected profession: investors valued the quality of analysts' work and the independence of their opinions. For the investment banks, good analysis was good public relations.

This began to change in the 1980s, as the investment banks became more short-termist and more focused on trading. The more serious analysis came to be private and was used to inform proprietary trading. Publicly released analysis deteriorated into puffery designed to encourage business, and analysts began to complain that their function had degenerated into marketing. Or, as Satyajit Das put it in his inimitable way, "research evolved into entertainment" and analysts "became a species of trained performing animal."[7]

Analysis deteriorated further in the 1990s, as investment banks began to link analysts' pay to the amount of business their recommendations brought in, despite the all too obvious conflict of interest this created. This practice was however kept secret until after the dotcom crash in 2000, when the market collapsed and the industry's dirty secrets started to come out.

Bankers and clients pressured analysts not to make negative or controversial claims. "Buy" recommendations predominated – over 90% of recommendations during the dotcom bubble – and "sell" recommendations became infrequent. The catchphrase was "pump and dump": analysts at investment banks would pump up stocks with over-optimistic reports, especially those relating to recent IPOs; insiders would then dump them as soon as they were able to, when lockup periods expired, leaving investors holding overvalued stocks.

Work pressure also increased. Analysts no longer had the time to digest company reports properly; it was often easiest, and created few problems for the analysts themselves, if they just accepted a company's claims at face value and labeled it a "buy." Analysts also became cozy with the firms they covered, and company officials often rewarded friendly analysts by giving them advance information; the analysts could then use this information to improve their "predictions," so bolstering their own credibility while in reality serving merely as the mouthpieces of the firms they were meant to scrutinize.

---

[7] Das, 2006, p. 62.

The debasement of analysis reached its nadir with the hi-tech boom in the late 1990s, when analysts shamelessly promoted all manner of dubious IPOs – Pets.com and similar rubbish. The most prominent analysts, such as Mary Meeker and Henry Blodget, became very well paid stars with large numbers of internet readers. Their heavy promotion of hi-tech investments contributed greatly to the dotcom craze, pushing prices higher and keeping them high for longer than would otherwise have been possible. Instead of rapidly correcting, the market then kept rising, so rewarding momentum traders who kept getting richer and penalizing those few sober-minded bears who knew that the boom was unsustainable. Towards the end, there were very few bears left and almost everyone had persuaded themselves that the "new economy" was genuinely different, and that a new paradigm had dawned with different ground rules. Then the market crashed and people came to their senses again.

After the collapse, New York Attorney General Eliot Spitzer took a healthy interest in what had been going on and a lot of the dirt came out. In some institutions, Merrill Lynch being apparently the worst example, the practice of analysis was revealed to be rotten to the core. Many analysts had been issuing high public ratings whilst privately ridiculing the same stocks as "dogs" and "crap."

Perhaps the most disgraceful example was Merrill's coverage of the internet search company GoTo.com. Merrill's executives were chasing investment banking business from GoTo and dangled before it the prospect of a favorable rating. The company seemed to go for the bait and helpfully wrote parts of the draft report. A junior analyst at Merrill, Kirsten Campbell, did not share GoTo's management's bullish opinions of its own prospects, however, but her inconvenient objections were overruled. Merrill's star analyst, the unscrupulous Henry Blodget, then waded in and gave GoTo the puff its management wanted, while secretly having one of his assistants prepare a less flattering report in case GoTo went to another investment bank. And then, when GoTo did, indeed, go to CS First Boston, Blodget published the less favorable report and its new recommendation a few hours later.[8]

Merrill Lynch ended up with a $200 million fine for issuing fraudulent research and a string of suits from disgruntled investors. For his

---

[8] Partnoy, 2003, pp. 286–91.

part, Blodget was fined $4 million and banned from the securities industry for life.

There were some improvements in the years that followed and some of the more obvious bad practices were banned, such as linking analysts' remuneration to the profits from investment banking work. Nevertheless analysts remained far from reliable sources of information. In the housing bubble, a notable example was David Lereah, Chief Economist of the National Association of Homebuilders, who in August 2005 distributed "Anti-Bubble Reports" to "respond to the irresponsible bubble accusations made by your local media and local academics," asserting that "there is virtually no risk of a national housing price bubble based on the fundamental demand for housing and predictable economic factors."[9]

However, not all pre-crash analysis was poor. An honorable exception to the run of the mill was Meredith Whitney, an analyst from Oppenheimer Securities who had seen through the subprime bubble and called it for what it was. She was ignored at first as a Cassandra, but as the storm clouds gathered people began increasingly to listen to her. Her pitch was simple: if you want to know what the Wall Street firms are really worth, take a look at their crappy assets and ask what they would fetch in a distress sale. (Answer: zilch.) Her defining moment came on October 31, 2007 when she predicted that Citigroup had got itself into such a mess that it would either have to slash its dividend or go bust. Financial firms instantly fell $369 billion in value; four days later, Citigroup chairman "Chuck" Prince resigned.[10]

Another sound analyst was Vincent Daniel, an analyst at the hedge fund FrontPoint Partners. He knew there was something wrong from his earlier work at Arthur Anderson, where he had audited Salomon Brothers. "It was shocking," he said afterwards. "No one could explain to me what they were doing." He went on to specialize in subprime in its early days. "I was the only guy I knew covering companies that were all going to go bust. I saw how the sausage was made … and it was really freaky," he said. His firm then shorted the market as the subprime boom approached its peak. Its head trader, Steve Eisman, went public on July 19, 2007; the same day that Ben Bernanke told the US Senate

---

[9] *E-Finance Directory*, 2007.

[10] The material in the rest of this sub-section is based on Lewis, 2008.

that he expected as much as $100 billion in subprime losses, Eisman announced that he expected losses of $300 billion from CDOs alone, for good measure telling his audience that they should throw their models in the garbage can.

These were among the very few people who anticipated the total collapse of the investment banking industry. "The investment-banking industry is f****d," Eisman told Michael Lewis in late 2008. Within a few weeks it was virtually extinct.

★★★

Analysis failed not only in the investment banks, but in the rating agencies, whose purpose is to guide investors by giving ratings of the credit-worthiness of the debt issues of particular firms and, more recently, of securitizations. Traditionally, a large investor would pay one of the rating agencies to rate a particular debt issue, and the rating would have credibility because of the agency's concern to maintain its own reputation. A rating agency that provided poor ratings would soon lose credibility and its business would dry up. What kept the system honest was investor demand for good ratings and the agencies' self-interest in maintaining their reputation, on which their long-term business depended.

From the 1970s, however, the practice of issuers paying for ratings began to spread and, ultimately, became dominant. Over time, the agencies' activities grew enormously and, post-Millennium, they were making very large fees from rating hundreds of thousands of individual securities and their various tranches. By the mid-1990s, there was already evidence that ratings were being inflated and, post-Millennium, the evidence of ratings inflation and sometimes downright poor ratings was overwhelming. The inflation of ratings was especially pronounced for new products such as CDOs, where the absence of a long track record gave plausible deniability to agencies willing to inflate their ratings.[11]

Despite the rating agencies' much vaunted modeling expertise in the securitization area, their models were actually very poor. Standard and Poor's, for example, had been using a model that assumed that real estate prices could not go down, a model that was therefore blind to the most important risk involved.[12]

---

[11] See Calomiris, 2009.
[12] Lewis, 2008.

There is also evidence that the ratings agencies were aware of the looming subprime crisis in 2006, but did not react to it, continuing to offer ratings based on models they must have known to be faulty and only making changes to their modeling assumptions (and even then only inadequate ones) in the middle of 2007.

And, as we write, the accusations are flying: the former head of compliance in Moody's, the most reputable and conservative of the ratings agencies, alleges he was pushed out because he objected to the firm's policy of inflating ratings; another former Moody's insider alleges that the firm knowingly gave inflated ratings on complex sub-prime-related securities even into 2009. Moody's of course denies the allegations.[13]

Part of the problem was, naturally, the fact that ratings agencies were being paid by the issuers of the securities being rated. Issuers will always want generously high ratings, because the higher the rating, the better the price they get. Further, many investors were constrained to buy ratings of at least a minimum standard, so the rating also affected the size of the potential investment pool into which issuers could tap.

This creates an obvious conflict of interest. When the issuer pays for a rating, the incentive is to keep the issuer happy and give them the rating they prefer. At the same time, if the agency is too accommodating to its clients, its ratings will lose credibility with investors and, pushed to the limit, become no more than a sophisticated form of marketing that sensible investors would ignore.

Associated with this was the increasingly common practice of ratings shopping. Issuers would shop around for the highest rating, putting competitive pressure on the agencies to be accommodating: an agency that was too conservative or honest would lose business to rivals with fewer scruples. A related practice in the securitization area was for issuers to tell the agencies the ratings they wanted and the agencies would suggest the "right" asset mix to achieve the desired rating. There was also the practice of ratings arbitrage, in which issuers would visit the agencies' websites where details of their models were published, and then work out how to tweak their securitizations to achieve the rating they wanted.

---

[13] "Moody's Says Review Sees No Wrongdoing", *Wall Street Journal*, October 1, 2009, C4.

We also need to consider the investor side of the market. If the big investors really did want sound, impeccable ratings, then they would have demanded and got them, even if they had to revert to the old practice of paying for them themselves. The ratings could therefore only deteriorate if the institutional investors had some reason to go along with that process.

Two such reasons come to mind. The first is that their managers were getting rich from managing other people's money and therefore had a strong incentive to go along with the pretense that these were reasonable investments. The fact that the ratings were high and everyone else was doing the same also gave them plausible deniability. The alternative was to forgo good business and tell their clients to invest elsewhere. This line of reasoning suggests that the big investors have some serious due diligence questions to answer and should anticipate class-action suits from disaffected clients.

A second reason is provided by the regulatory system, which used ratings to determine capital requirements: the higher the rating, the lower the capital requirement; thus leveraged investors had an incentive to go along with inflated ratings to obtain the benefits of reduced capital requirements. The ratings agencies themselves were also sanctified by the regulatory system, which gave them its blessing as Nationally Recognized Statistical Rating Organizations (NRSROs). This created a cozy cartel with the usual effects of stultifying innovation and, no doubt, higher fees.

As with the banks, by late 2009 the ratings agencies were back to their old tricks, profiting from the crisis they helped create and taking financial engineering to new lows. They are now helping to design and rate new products known as re-remics ("re-securitizations of real estate mortgage investment conduits"), in which poorly performing portfolios are broken down into new securitizations, leading to better ratings, lower capital requirements, and of course fat fees for the agencies.[14]

---

[14] "Wall Street Wizardry Reworks Mortgages," *Wall Street Journal*, October 1, 2009, C1, C3. We note but gloss over one other modern development in the ratings space: the growth of corporate governance rating agencies after the scandals of the early Millennium. These rate the quality of corporate governance, but are subject to similar problems as credit rating agencies, and their ratings appear to be of little or no value. It would appear that their clients buy their ratings merely to cover themselves against fiduciary duty legal claims by dissatisfied customers. See Calomiris and Mason, 2009.

★★★

The financial services industry was also very successful in achieving self-serving changes to the accounting standards. Fair value accounting, by which items on a company's balance sheet are "marked to market" – written up or down to their market price – has been hyped by accountants and regulators as the epitome of modern financial reporting, enabling investors to gain a completely true and up-to-date picture of their investment's financial position. As with so much else in Modern Finance, fair value accounting is self-evidently desirable in theory, but failed to work in practice.[15]

Mark-to-market accounting is best understood in comparison to traditional book value accounting, the key principle of which was that the value of an asset or liability was recorded at the lower of cost or realizable value. Typically, everything was dumped on the balance sheet at cost price, occasionally marked up or down if the position had a clear realizable value that had changed, and generally stayed there for decades while the world turned. No one worried about occasional wobbles in value and everyone understood that most assets and liabilities were to be held to maturity, making interim valuations unimportant. The only exception was where shares or bonds had declined sharply in value, in which case their value would be written down, and any bonds concerned would be reclassified as "impaired." The fun for analysts was in finding companies whose downtown real estate was still held on the books at its value of 1926, when it had been bought, since there just could be a little teensy-weensy asset profit that might be unlocked from the company if one could figure out how.

Traditional British merchant banks did not use mark-to-market, even though they held substantial amounts of tradable securities. Most of their assets were held on a "back book" investment account and valued at cost. This allowed merchant banks to manage earnings very effectively; generally they built up large "hidden reserves" in good

---

[15] The beancounters were quite effective self-interested lobbyists themselves. Their most notable achievement, post Enron and the associated demise of Arthur Anderson, was for limited liability partnerships to insulate partners' personal wealth from the consequence of any future mistakes, thus creating more moral hazard and driving a further wedge between their interests and those of their clients.

years that were amortized into earnings in years of unexpected dearth, so that the overall picture was smoothed. The result was to increase the confidence of the market in each merchant bank; people assumed that 200-odd-year-old institutions had accumulated enough "hidden reserves," and undervalued real estate to smooth out any problems that might arise.

The mark-to-market approach was first used in the 1940s by US investment banks, who used it to value their large holdings of tradable securities, under pressure from their regulators to show that their capital was adequate. Mark-to-market accounting then spread beyond the traditional investment banks around the late 1980s, and seemed to be the ideal solution to the increasingly pressing problem of valuing tradable securities in an environment of rapidly growing trading activity. Conventional book value accounting was derided as old-fashioned and the original acquisition cost of a position scorned as hopelessly irrelevant to an up-to-the-minute valuation.

Mark-to-market also had a major attraction to executives who were for the first time paid a large portion of their remuneration based on profit-related bonuses: no longer did you have to sell that illiquid investment in order to realize a profit on it and be paid a bonus; you could now recognize its increase in value by marking it to market, without having to sell it.

The next stage in its development was Financial Accounting Standard (FAS) 133 in 1998, which attempted to establish fair value for derivatives positions. The result was an utter disaster. Despite its ostensible aim of establishing transparency, the new standard was anything but, and even the best accountants struggled to understand it. It was a muddled mess, completely alien to the way most firms did their business, and was aptly described by one contemporary headline as the "accounting standard from outer space" being "incomprehensible, unpredictable, unmanageable, and downright frightening – FAS133 is threatening the financial world like an alien life form."[16]

One of the biggest problems of mark-to-market accounting is that by forcing firms to mark positions to market, it injected considerable volatility into their earnings, serving to confuse even the most sophisticated investors. At the same time, its bizarre and cumbersome

---

[16] Hunter, 1999, p. 16.

rules governing hedge accounting combined with the spurious earnings volatility created by marking to market hedge positions often led firms to forgo economically worthwhile hedges. Thus, whatever its rarified theoretical merits, mark-to-market in practice made for incomprehensibility and, from a risk management point of view, meant that many companies that reduced their risks intelligently saw their reported earnings fluctuate wildly for no underlying economic reason. FAS133 was simply not up to the job.

One skeptic at the time wondered whether FAS133 would make people so miserable that they would welcome mark-to-market for everything.[17] How right he was! The mark-to-market juggernaut rolled on like the Golem of Eastern European Jewish folklore, wreaking increasing havoc, reaching its most recent manifestation in the new accounting standard FAS157, propounded in September 2006 and coming into effect for fiscal years beginning after Novermber 15, 2007, the essence of which is to apply mark-to-market to everything, regardless even of whether a market actually exists. This standard divides financial assets into three "levels" according to their degree of marketability. Level 1 assets are those for which a ready market exists, Level 2 assets are those for which a market exists for comparable securities, and Level 3 assets are those for which no market exists, which are to be valued by use of mathematical models as a substitute. In this latter case, Fair Value really means mark-to-model.

There were major problems with each of these levels. At Level 1, where mark-to-market is strongest, the new standard did little or nothing to alleviate the problems of lack of transparency, artificial earnings volatility, and the discouragement to hedge that were already apparent with FAS133. There were also other fairly intractable problems:

- Even large markets can often be only partially liquid, and in such circumstances even the market price can give a false indicator of realizable value. An example occurred in October 2008, when Porsche revealed it had secretly increased its stake in Volkswagen from 35% to 74%; given that the state of Lower Saxony already had 20%, this meant that the free float in VW stock had fallen from a healthy 45% to only 6%. A number of hedge funds had sold VW

---

[17] Cited in Hunter, 1999, p. 23.

short, however, and their rush to cover their commitments led the VW stock price to rise more than fivefold, making VW briefly the largest company in the word by market capitalization. In the process, the funds took mark-to-market losses of some $20 billion. However, these losses were based on an artificial stock price that was temporarily driven up by lack of liquidity and a very tight market squeeze on the funds.[18]

• A second problem is that Fair Value is not required for all assets, with the upshot being that superficially comparable financial statements might not be comparable at all. For example, at the end of 2007, more than 75% of Goldman Sachs' assets were carried at fair value, but less than 50% of Morgan Stanley's and little more than 25% of Bank of America's. The institutions also have considerable discretion over the valuation approaches they use and the numbers they obtain.[19]

The problems with mark-to-market increase as positions become less marketable. Level 2 deals with positions that are valued using "comparable" securities and, by implication, market valuation in which markets are always thin. Such valuations are therefore unreliable and open to gaming. So for example, traders using mark-to-market have an incentive to create and acquire "benchmark" assets in thinly traded markets whose values can be manipulated upwards to boost the mark-to-market profits on "comparable" securities.

The consequences of such dubious valuations can be very serious: a bank might have positions that it intends to hold to maturity and that it expects will pay out in full at maturity, and yet suffer interim mark-to-market paper losses that are fundamentally irrelevant, but that might affect its credit rating and access to credit. Bad as that is, the real danger is that it will then be pressured to offload its allegedly loss-making positions in a distress sale, so converting paper losses into very real losses, which then lead to further mark-to-market losses as prices fall further, creating a vicious circle that not only threatens to bring it down, but also threatens other institutions exposed to similar positions as well.

---

[18] *FT*, October 29, 2009.
[19] "All's Fair," *The Economist*, September 18, 2008.

As for Level 3; inevitably, being free from the loosest constraints of market value, the "Level 3" designation has given rise to all kinds of model-building creativity, resulting in large bonuses paid to executives in actual cash based on model-based but entirely imaginary increases in value.

This problem was thrown into sharp spotlight by the unluckily timed implementation of FAS 157. If Level 3 assets can be valued only by reference to an internal valuation model, and have been allowed to accrue supposed value in banks' financial statements for a decade or more, then how do we know they are really worth anything close to what the model says, and how do we go about realizing them, in a market where confidence has vanished?

To ask those questions is surely to answer them. Since every incentive led bank mathematicians to devise models that maximized the reported value of the bank's holdings, and since little or no market existed by which those values could be checked, it is likely that those assets' book values were highly overstated. Moreover, even in banks where the mathematicians and their bosses were scrupulously (even impossibly) disinterested and intelligent, there still remained the problem that those assets are worth far less in a downturn because their illiquidity made them intrinsically unattractive in a market where liquidity had become once more important. Anyone who has attempted to sell venture capital positions in a bear market can attest to how rapidly and completely the value of such assets can disappear. It is thus perfectly possible that the true realizable value of "Level 3" holdings in a bear market is only a very small fraction of their book value, and is best conservatively valued at a big fat zero.

There is also a related problem. While providing for some form of market valuation, "Level 2" valuation techniques allow an institution to ignore prices received in a "distress sale." However, in a bear market almost all sales are distress sales; the asset holder is distressed that their asset has declined in value and is only selling it because he needs the cash. Come the crisis, it is then hardly surprising that many institutions take the convenient route of ignoring distress sale prices and reclassifying assets as "Level 3" so they can give them higher than market valuations.

A notable case in point is Goldman Sachs in the last quarter of 2008, when their Level 3 assets increased from $54.7 billion to $82.3

billion. Since it seems most unlikely that Goldman, a smart operator if ever there was one, had deliberately loaded up on $27.6 billion worth of illiquid rubbish the previous quarter, the change must result largely from strategic reclassification from Level 2 to Level 3. However, since its capital was only about $36 billion, it was then immediately apparent that the institution was in very deep trouble. Unlike Nomura, for example, which sold everything possible and wrote the remainder down to zero, Goldman Sachs could not do this because it did not have the capital to withstand a loss of anything like $80 billion, and this is without considering its Level 2 or any other valuation problems. It could then only survive by pleading for a federal guarantee to keep it on life support, before thumbing its noses at the taxpayers who had saved it and resuming the bonus game in late 2009, adding insult to injury by claiming that it was doing God's work and that the public should be happy to see normal practices return.[20]

From the mid-1980s in the United States and from about 1990 in Britain the trading-oriented behemoths that had won the battle for survival were very much in charge. Given their size and sensitivity to regulation, lobbying both regulators and politicians directly became increasingly important to them. Most of the major houses increased their political influence, buying up whatever influence and politicians that money could buy; but by far the most successful in this effort was Goldman Sachs, which within the last two decades produced: two US Treasury Secretaries, one from each party (Robert Rubin and Hank Paulson) and, directly or indirectly, four out of the last six holders of that office;[21] a US Senator and Governor of New Jersey (Jon Corzine); a White House Chief of Staff (Josh Bolten); a Deputy Secretary of State and President of the World Bank (Robert Zoellick); a Chairman of the US Eximbank (Kenneth Brody); a Director of the National Economic Council (Stephen Friedman); and an Undersecretary of State (Robert Hormats). Also John Patterson, chief of staff to Treasury Secretary Tim Geithner, was formerly a Goldman Sachs lobbyist. It's an impressive list.

---

[20] Watts, 2009.

[21] This was hardly the norm: of the previous six Treasury Secretaries, only one even had a finance background.

Goldman Sachs was also the top corporate giver in the 2008 election cycle, focusing primarily on Democrat candidates, and giving more than $1 million to President Obama's campaign.[22]

With this amount of lobbying power deployed, it's not surprising that the trading behemoths achieved a number of major successes in manipulating the regulatory and political systems, or more broadly, the rules of the game, in their favor. Their lobbying was a classic case of public choice theory in action, in which a focused, well-organized and extremely wealthy special interest group was able to prevail over the broader but more diffuse general interest.

Their earlier successes included the hugely successful lobbying campaigns of the 1980s and 1990s, in which the industry fought off threats of new regulation, despite evidence, even then, that their preferred "solution" of industry self-regulation was not working.[23] They had already formed ISDA in 1985 to lobby (successfully) against the regulation of swaps; in the early 1990s, they formed another lobby group, the Group of 30. Their 1993 report, *Derivatives: Practices and*

---

[22] In the last twenty years, the industry has made more than $2.2 billion in US political contributions, more than any other industry; it also tops the lobbying list too, having spent $3.5 billion in lobbying over the last ten years alone. From their perspective, this is taxpayers' money very well spent. See Zingales, 2009.

[23] This is a long story. A number of observers had been warning about the dangers of derivatives. They included the president of the New York Fed, E. Gerald Corrigan, who gave a strident speech about the dangers of derivatives and off-balance sheet activities in January 1992. "If this sounds like a warning, that is because it is," he said with characteristic bluntness. Another prominent warning came from a comprehensive reported issued by the House Banking Committee in November 1993 under the direction of Jim Leach, one of very few members of Congress of unquestioned integrity and who was beyond the reach of the industry's lobbying, because he refused to accept contributions from it. Leach sounded the alarm, calling derivatives both "the new wild card in international finance" and a "house of cards". In May 1995, the GAO then issued a report that was also highly critical of derivatives practices, criticizing uncontrolled risk management among other problems, and recommending a sweeping overhaul of derivatives regulation in the US. The industry launched a sustained counter-attack, and the GAO Report was met with particular ferocity: ISDA's point-by-point counter-attack shrugged off the GAO's concerns. ISDA not only managed to squash proposals for regulation, but its lobbyists even managed to persuade many journalists to stop using the word "derivatives" in discussing the current scandals, because of its negative connotations; they were to use the more reassuring term "securities" instead.

Principles, argued that the industry was best left to regulate itself: derivatives, wisely used, were a major benefit to society, and regulation could be counterproductive and costly. The report also set out some of the basic motherhood and apple pie principles of derivatives risk management and became the core text of the new discipline of financial risk management. These principles, in turn, were rapidly incorporated into bank regulations.

Other industry lobbying successes included:

- The Riegel-Neal Interstate Banking and Branching Efficiency Act of 1994 abolished the 1927 McFadden Act and earlier restrictions against interstate banking, allowing the largest banks to expand unchecked across the United States, absorbing regional banks by acquisition using their high stock prices of the late 1990s. This created a small cadre of full service behemoths and a tight oligopoly at the top, with a huge gap (currently between $300 billion and $1 trillion in total assets) between them and the remaining independent regional banks.
- The 1999 Gramm-Leach-Bliley Act abolished the Glass-Steagall division between commercial and investment banking. This allowed the largest commercial banks to enter the investment banking businesses and pay their top management accordingly. A side-effect was to leave the investment banks at a competitive disadvantage, because they lacked the commercial banks' large resources of low-cost government-guaranteed deposits, suggesting that the days of the big independent US investment banks were now numbered.
- The abolition in April 2004 of the net capital rule, under which brokerages had been limited in their maximum leverage. This allowed investment banks to set their own leverage using their risk management models and resulted in the average leverage of the five large investment banks increasing by December 2007 to around 30 to 1.
- The abolition in July 2007 of the "uptick rule" under which short selling of US equities was allowed only after a price uptick. This allowed the brokers to undertake profitable "bear raids" on companies in which they held credit default swaps, and which were

to precipitate the bankruptcy of Lehman Brothers in September 2008.

All these measures, even before the lobbying surrounding the events of September–October 2008, to which we shall come later, were motivated by the self-interest of the most powerful financial institutions.

The banks' influence over public policy goes beyond mere crass self-interest. Inevitably, the bankers see the world through the eyes of bankers. So, for example, when Henry Paulson told Congress in the fall of 2008 that the world would end if it did not approve the $700 billion bailout, it *could* be argued that he was acting in good faith. His world might indeed have ended: Goldman Sachs and others like it would have been bankrupted, and many of his banking buddies would have been down to their last ten or fifty million, although hardly ruined. The bailout was therefore good for Wall Street, but this prompts the question of whether the bailout was good for the economy as a whole. To make matters worse, when the financiers are so influential, it is hard for the elected policy makers, such as the President, to get good advice from people other than financiers. The politicians are then bombarded by the same advice – bail out the banks, buy the toxic assets, you have to go along with the bonus system, and so on.

In the UK, the industry's lobbying was equally successful. Its biggest success was to persuade the UK authorities of the benefits of a "light-touch" regulatory regime, policed by one of the most toothless bulldogs of all time, the Financial Services Authority: this would keep London competitive, attract foreign capital, and so on; it would also give London the edge over its arch-rival, New York. In fact, the British system was not light-touch in the sense of regulation-free, as it was bogged down by the onerous restrictions of the Financial Services Act of 1986. It was however light-touch in the sense that it allowed the giants of the industry to get away with almost anything, providing its victims with little more than paper protection.

The lobbying power of the industry in the UK was also highlighted by its successful campaign to achieve "nondom" status – non-domiciled status for tax purposes – for more than 100,000 of its best paid workers: this allowed them to work in London while pretending to live elsewhere for a yearly payment of £30,000 or so all-in, no questions asked. The political and tax authorities bought the self-serving line that this was necessary to keep London competitive, and never mind the punitive high tax rates under which the plebs had to live.

A final and telling example in both countries has been the successful campaign by the industry to protect the bankers' bonus racket in the crisis. Even after having been bailed out by the taxpayer and with most banks effectively in public ownership, the bankers continued to argue brazenly for their precious bonus system, and successfully fought off (and one suspects, effectively bought up) the politicians and others who called for an end to its abuses. Both governments rode roughshod over the public anger on this issue; one UK academic spoke for many when he wondered aloud about the possibility of a future in which the bankers would be lynched in the streets. He was suspended from his position and put under police investigation: so much for freedom of speech.

Another example of regulators doing the finance industry's bidding came in the design of the Basel capital adequacy standards, discussed in more detail in Chapter 12. They established a regulatory capital standard based around the highly perverse VaR risk measure – a measure that, nonetheless, was also highly convenient because it could be used to generate satisfyingly low-risk measures and hence low regulatory capital requirements. These rules grew out of an extraordinarily cozy atmosphere of excessive trust between the regulators and the largest banks, but one in which the banks had the overwhelming firepower.

★★★

Most of the changes discussed in this and the last few chapters – the rise of managerial capitalism, the move towards a short-term bonus-oriented trading culture, the growth of derivatives, the move away from the old partnerships, the degradation of ratings and analysis, the move towards mark-to-market, and even the rise of "financial risk management," which effectively operated as a figleaf to cover the naked plundering that was endemic to Wall Street – are symptomatic of the transformation of Modern Finance into a vast rent-extraction machine.

This transformation was closely associated with rise of the "greed is good" mentality, immortalized in the December 1987 film *Wall Street*, which soon came to epitomize the new Wall Street. Bankers have always been interested in acquiring wealth, but from the mid-

1980s their thirst for wealth acquisition became increasingly overt and immoderate, and their activities went well beyond highly remunerated wealth creation to brazen rent seeking.

Perhaps the most obvious evidence of rent seeking can be found in the breathtaking levels of remuneration. For example, in 2007 alone, the 50 highest-paid hedge fund managers between them made $29 billion, ranging from a cool $3.7 billion for the top ranking manager, to a mere $360 million made by the poor man ranked 50th.[24] It simply beggars belief that these levels of personal remuneration can possibly reflect the value of their activities to society at large. The true economic value of hedge fund and trading activities is, at best, fairly marginal.

There is also other abundant evidence, such as the rise in the financial sector's share of US corporate profits from 5% in 1981 to about a third of corporate profits on the eve of the crisis. Very little of this growth represented products and services that provided true value to the economy as a whole. Consider the possibilities:

- It certainly did not represent greater efficiency – major financial transactions such as share issues and acquisitions took far more man-hours in 2007 than they had thirty years earlier, because of their additional legal and documentation complexity.
- Securitization was mostly a complex and expensive means of getting assets off banks' balance sheets, and was often highly damaging to the other parties involved, adding cost in the home mortgage market, for example.
- Derivatives helped manage risks, but only a tiny percentage of the vast outstandings in the derivatives markets represented risk amelioration.
- Hedge funds and private equity funds were mostly a means of excessively multiplying the fees charged for investment management; they almost drove out of business the true venture capital funds, which had a genuine economic value.
- Principal trading, the most exciting activity of all in the glory years for greedy investment bank partners, was simply a means of using large amounts of outside shareholders' capital to trade on insider information about the market's deal flow.

---

[24] Bogle, 2009, p. 38.

All of these activities were legal; none of them added much value to anybody but their immediate practitioners, while they represented additional costs and lower returns for everybody else. In other words, they fulfilled the dictionary definition of rent seeking.

So what purpose does all this outstanding value serve? As we discussed in Chapter 8, it is very hard to make out a case that any more than a small percentage of this volume serves any purpose to the wider community. If the economic value of hedging and liquidity are modest compared to the galactic amounts of contracts outstanding, or even to the enormous sums earned by trading, then it follows that some pretty large percentage of trading revenues represents nothing more or less than pure rent seeking.

This makes sense. Investment bankers and traders are intelligent, capable people, but (going by the latest figures as of end 2009) an average remuneration of $527,000 in nine months, or $703,000 per annum, for the entire staff of Goldman Sachs including janitors and interns suggests that some mysterious force is preventing those returns from being driven down to a level for which all but the most senior of Wall Street veterans would happily work. It's not a question of the "social value" of trading, a dubious concept at the best of times. It's a question of what barriers to entry prevent every corporation in the US from setting up a derivatives trading department in order to extract some of these extraordinary returns for themselves.

The same applies to "proprietary trading," by which modern investment banks deploy large amounts of capital to achieve very high returns. The Efficient Market Hypothesis postulates such excess returns to be impossible, since capital would rush to the nexuses where they existed, and drive returns down to an equilibrium level. One need not be a believer in this Hypothesis to agree with its conclusions in this respect; Warren Buffett, the greatest investor in the US, has achieved returns only barely above 20% annually in his 50-year investment career. It is simply not reasonable to suppose that ever greater amounts of capital could be deployed into achieving returns considerably greater than that, year after year, unless some artificial barrier to competitor entry were involved.

There are two barriers to entry that appear to prevent capital from arbitraging away investment banks' trading returns. The first is insider information, not generally the illegal kind about corporate activities but the entirely legal kind about money flows, equally valuable in a trading environment. If you are one of a handful of major dealers in a particular type of derivative contract, or you have a computer set up at the New York Stock Exchange that sees the order flow before competitors, you have insider information that is not available to third parties, just as surely as if you knew the secrets of next quarter's earnings.

The second and most important barrier to entry is that of crony capitalism. In the private sector, having the right connections is the way business has always been done; a company's CEO is a close friend of one investment banker rather than another, so gives them preference when there is a transaction to be done. The position becomes much more doubtful when the public sector is involved, as is increasingly the case. If the Treasury Secretary is an alumnus of Goldman Sachs, as was Hank Paulson, for example, there must be some suspicion that he would throw the odd bone or two to his old chums at Goldman Sachs; there must therefore be some suspicion that, when bailouts were being arranged, this connection might have had something to do with Goldman receiving a $13 billion payoff at public expense on credit default swaps issued by AIG, among the various other handouts it received. To put it bluntly: such largesse had not been available to Lehman Brothers. But then Lehmans didn't have the same connections.

Similarly, large government-directed contracts that are awarded without full competitive bidding, advisory work where the investment bank's government contacts are themselves leveraged, or investment opportunities not available to the general public, are all instances where crony capitalism must at least be suspected. With the immensely greater amounts of capital now available to the major Wall Street houses and the death of the "it's not cricket" gentlemanly prohibitions against brazen plunder, it is hardly surprising that financial institutions made such huge profits for so long, which no one else was able to emulate.

10

Derivatives and Other Disasters

Over the past generation, Modern Finance techniques and risk management based on Modern Financial Theory have caused an extraordinary number and variety of disasters.

The predominant sectors for these disasters have been derivatives and, more recently, securitization. That's not surprising: those are the sectors that allow participants to take on the most leverage in their activities. They are also the sectors in which there is least historical experience about what the levels of risk actually are. Credit default swaps, for example, were celebrated as a great success in the derivatives area going into the 2007–08 crisis; the reality was that the CDS market had not existed at the time of the 1990–91 downturn and was in its infancy in 2000.

Both derivatives and securitization structures were also dominated by traders differing from traditional merchant/investment bankers in their short-term time horizons and laser-like focus on the next bonus, and often operating under weak control. Mistakes that would have been caught in a traditional banking organization, if not by the perpetrators then by their superiors, were then allowed in the modern trading culture to grow to monstrous size and wreak destruction.

The first major derivatives scandal occurred in the late 1980s, when the markets had already grown far beyond their initial modest aspirations and had morphed into a trading-dominated culture. In 1986, Bankers Trust (BT) hired a young currency trader from Salomon Brothers called Andy Krieger. Krieger was a daring trader who specialized in using options to leverage up his risk, enabling him to control positions that were many times bigger than his own, and was a master at finding options that were undervalued because other traders' computer models understated volatilities. He was also a master of the feint attack, taking on multiple offsetting positions that other traders could only partially assess, so disguising his real intentions and often catching other traders off guard. Krieger's misdirection plays grew in size and he was soon controlling positions worth billions that sometimes dwarfed Bankers Trust's other business.

Bankers Trust, a New York commercial bank, had been a pioneer in the derivatives market, realizing early that dominance in derivatives would enable it to rise up the financial institutions' pecking order, in which it was barred from much investment banking activity by Glass-Steagall and limited in commercial banking by local competition from the much larger Chase Manhattan, Morgan Guaranty, and Citicorp. Bankers Trust was noted in the mid-1980s for its aggression and (by the primitive standards of those times) what was thought to be the sophistication of its risk management. As subsequent events were to show, the latter was path-breaking mostly in its predatory attitude towards its clients and in the latitude it allowed to over-aggressive traders.[1]

Krieger's most celebrated exploit involved trading on the New Zealand dollar (or kiwi), in which he took a position that exceeded the entire New Zealand money supply, mounting a one-man speculative attack. In a matter of hours, the kiwi "fell like a wounded pigeon" and lost 5% of its value, creating a currency crisis that seriously damaged the country and, naturally enough, drew an angry response from New Zealand's Chancellor of the Exchequer. Charles Sanford, BT's

---

[1] BT pioneered the new practice of scorched earth banking and traders delighted in a bloodlust culture where the main sport was to 'rip the faces off' clients regarded as too stupid to deserve any better: you 'smoke' the client by taking him out in one big trade. As one BT insider laconically put it: "Lure people into that calm and then totally f*** 'em." (Quoted from Partnoy, 1998, back cover.) A derivatives salesman hadn't made it till he had blown up a few of the clients who had trusted him.

chairman, commented that Krieger's positions had not been too big for BT, but they had been for the kiwi market: it was New Zealand's fault for being small.[2] You see what we mean about Bankers Trust's risk management …

Krieger resigned the next year in disgust at the paltry $3 million that BT paid him in return for the $300 million or so he made for the bank. It wasn't the money, he said; it was the principle. Of course if his trades had gone wrong, Bankers Trust could have headed down the Suwannee; one can thus see management's point – $3 million wasn't then the pocket change on Wall Street that it has since become!

The Krieger affair was an ominous foretaste of things to come: a trader operating on his own, betting huge amounts of his bank's capital, and subject to only the loosest controls; who took complex positions that even his own bank failed to understand; and who was unconcerned by the damage that his activities caused to innocent third parties.

The next example is one we have met before, portfolio insurance. The idea behind portfolio insurance was to mimic the payoff of a put option, giving the investor the prospect of upside return if the market went up, but downside protection, if the market went down. The idea was dreamt up by Hayne Leland, and his firm, Leland O'Brien Rubinstein, started selling portfolio insurance strategies in 1980. Portfolio insurance was easily programmed, but instead of selling individual stocks, which would then have been more cumbersome and costly, portfolio insurance was implemented by switching into and out of market index futures. By October 1987, around $50 billion of assets was being managed by portfolio insurance strategies.

When the stock market started turning down on October 19, 1987, the portfolio insurers were forced to start selling en masse. The stock index futures price then fell rapidly, well below the level of the New York Stock Exchange index. Normally, arbitragers from the stock market would have moved to cash in, but the large volume of futures sell orders hitting the market caused stock traders to hold back, in part because they wondered what was going on, and in part because of their natural reaction to distressed sellers: they smelt the blood in the water and positioned themselves to make a killing. Stock prices then fell,

---

[2] Thomson, 1998.

triggering further sell orders from the portfolio insurers, and creating a cascade effect in which the price falls fed off themselves to produce the biggest daily percentage stock price fall in US history.

There were a number of problems with portfolio insurance: it depended on a string of assumptions that didn't hold (perfect market liquidity, the ability to trade quickly at low cost, etc.) and it was a strange strategy, in the sense that it called for investors to sell when the price had fallen, and buy back when the price had risen, whereas you usually make profits by the opposite strategy: buy-low, sell-high. But perhaps most of all, portfolio insurance requires that traders using it be price takers unable to affect the market price. Once too many people use it, they affect the price itself and the strategy no longer works, even in theory.

The role of portfolio insurance in the 1987 crash highlights some further problems of Modern Finance: the dependence of risk management strategies on unrealistic assumptions; their tendency to break down when really needed and when too many traders use the same strategy; and their role in making markets more volatile. These problems, already apparent in 1987, were to recur repeatedly in later years.

★★★

The mid-1990s witnessed a string of trading disasters, so many that we are spoilt for choice. But our favorites are these:

Procter & Gamble

In 1993, Procter & Gamble was looking to raise finance. In normal circumstances, a company like Procter & Gamble would be able to raise money at commercial paper rates – but now blessed by a finance department operating as a profit center, it foolishly hoped to do better than that. It approached Bankers Trust for assistance, and Bankers Trust were only too happy to oblige, designing financial products that appeared at face value to reduce Procter & Gamble's financing costs. These "structured notes" were made to look like bonds, superficially, but, apparently unbeknown to Procter & Gamble, what they were in fact was highly leveraged "plays" on interest rates. They would do exactly what Procter & Gamble wanted, but only if interest rates remained low. If interest rates should rise, Procter & Gamble would suffer swingeing losses.

It was said that in one of the sales meetings, the Bankers Trust sales team had offered Procter & Gamble various versions of a transaction with alternative degrees of leverage. Then, as a joke, one of the Bankers Trust team drew an outrageously leveraged structure as an additional alternative. The Bankers Trust people were then astonished when Procter & Gamble chose this structure; it was obvious that Procter & Gamble had no idea what it was doing: it was a perfect customer for the predatory Bankers Trust.

Interest rates then rose in 1994, and Procter & Gamble ended up with a $157 million loss. Procter & Gamble then sued, and the resulting court case was noted for the taped evidence of Bankers Trust's sharp practice and Procter & Gamble's cluelessness. When he heard that Procter & Gamble had just signed the highly leveraged deal just mentioned, making Bankers Trust a cool $7.6 million from the trade, the head of Bankers Trust's leveraged policy group, couldn't conceal his delight: "I think my ... just fell off," he said.[3] Kevin Hudson, the Bankers Trust's salesman covering Procter & Gamble, was caught bragging to his fiancée that Procter & Gamble did not understand the leverage of the deal or how much Bankers Trust was making on it: "That's the beauty of BT," he concluded.[4]

This case, and the broadly similar case of Gibson Greetings, another Bankers Trust victim, did great damage to Bankers Trust's reputation and business, so much so that in 1998 it was forced to sell out to Deutsche Bank.

This said, not everyone was so sympathetic to Procter & Gamble. The former chair of the Chicago Mercantile Exchange, Leo Melamed, summarized it differently: "I'd say that Procter & Gamble did what their name says, they proctored and gambled. And now they're complaining."[5] He had a point.

The resulting public outcry led to Congressional hearings about the dangers of derivatives. Defenders of derivatives complained that if Procter & Gamble had lost the same amount of money on a new brand

[3] Quoted in Partnoy, 2003, p. 57.
[4] Loc. cit.
[5] *Futures*, December 1994, p. 14.

of Pampers that had tanked, then Congress wouldn't have batted an eyelid. Maybe, but then diapers are not such a threat to the financial system.

Daiwa

The story of Daiwa Bank's Toshihide Iguchi is a rogue trading classic, albeit in bonds rather than derivatives. In 1984, Iguchi lost $200,000 trading US Treasury bonds in New York. He tried to cover his losses by unauthorized trading and deception, and over the next 11 years he racked up $1.1 billion in losses, about $400,000 a trading day. Mr. Iguchi was clearly not cut out for trading, but Daiwa was something of an "orphan stepchild" among Japanese banks also, having alienated Japanese authorities in the 1950s by refusing to spin off its trust bank (investment management) operations as the other big Japanese banks had done.

Iguchi hid his losses by the simple expedient of not booking his loss-making trades. Nobody realized when bonds had been sold because Iguchi did the back office booking of trades, helped by the fact that the bonds were held by Bankers Trust and Iguchi used stolen letterhead to forge statements from Bankers Trust. It is astonishing that no one noticed the yawning hole in Daiwa Bank's balance sheet. For their part, US regulators didn't notice either, despite "red flags" that suggested there might be a problem.

One can only speculate how long this might have continued had Mr. Iguchi not had the decency to turn himself in. His bosses in Tokyo responded by trying to cover up the losses themselves. By the time the US regulators discovered the scandal, months later, they were incandescent with rage, and pursued Daiwa and Iguchi with a vengeance: Daiwa got an unprecedented fine of $340 million and lost its US license to trade, and Iguchi got four years in jail: on average, one day in jail for each three-quarters of a million dollars lost.

Orange County

Orange County, the Nirvana of Southern California, was in 1994 the richest county in the United States. Its treasurer, Bob Citron, had delivered the highest investment returns for any county in the country throughout the 1980s and early 1990s, by which time he was managing an investment portfolio worth $7.4 billion. Instead of investing in Treasury bonds, as most other counties did, Citron was investing in structured notes. Like Procter & Gamble's, his structured notes were a big bet on interest rates remaining low, and his success was largely caused by the generally declining interest rate environment of the late 1980s and early 1990s. Not content with this success, he then levered up, borrowing about $13 billion. By early 1994, Citron had made a $20 billion bet on interest rates remaining low.

The Federal Funds rate target then doubled from 3% to 6% over 1994 (the last time Fed Chairman Alan Greenspan seriously attempted to tighten money) and things went horribly wrong. Losses escalated and, by December, Orange County was forced to file for bankruptcy.

The Orange County case highlighted the dangers of relatively unsophisticated Treasury types putting their trust in derivatives dealers. Citron had worked in the County Treasurer's office all his life and might have been presumed to be an expert on Treasury matters. He had angrily dismissed those who questioned what he was doing: in July 1993, when asked how he knew US interest rates would not go up, he modestly replied, "I [sic] am one of the largest investors in America. I know these things."[6] But he soon changed his tune after the county's bankruptcy, claiming to be an "inexperienced investor" who didn't actually know what he was doing. It also came out that he had been consulting psychics and astrologers for advice. In April 1995, Citron pled guilty to state securities fraud, but managed to escape prison time on the grounds that he had been suffering from dementia.

Barings

The collapse of the once great House of Baring Brothers is another wonderful tale of rogue trading, in which a 28-year old trader, allegedly operating on his own, brought down the oldest merchant bank in the UK. The trader, Nick Leeson, was working in the bank's Singapore office, where he both traded and settled the bank's apparently

---

[6] Quoted in Partnoy, 2003, p. 119.

profitable operation, arbitraging between the prices of Nikkei 225 futures contracts trading in Singapore and Osaka.

Barings' failure makes for interesting sociology. The old London merchant banks varied considerably in their social exclusivity. Martin's first employer, Hill Samuel, was pretty open – as an aristocratic friend, who worked at the much posher Lazard's described it: "Frightfully middle class bank – all the directors live in Kingston."[7] Hill Samuel thus had plenty of room for middle class math nerds like Martin, who had no social connections or contacts whatever, but were useful because of their IQ and decent education.

Barings was at the other end of the merchant bank spectrum, still a family-run bank, more than 200 years old, wholly owned from 1985 by the Baring Foundation, whose directors mostly went to Eton but now depended on bonuses rather than dividends for their income. Barings hired the working classes for the back office and the trading desks, but was very short on middle class math nerds. When Barings expanded into international trading, its recruitment practices were described by its trading head Christopher Heath, in 1989 Britain's highest paid employee, as follows: "If he spends money on parties and racehorses I say 'Fine' because he will want more. I want a guy who lives well and is hungry."[8]

The head of Barings' Investment Division Peter Norris came from a traditional Barings background (and as an Oxford history graduate was no math nerd), while Barings' CEO (from 1988) Andrew Tuckey and its Head of Derivatives Ron Baker (Leeson's immediate boss) were born in Rhodesia and Australia respectively, neither of which were traditional Barings catchment areas. Thus Barings never had the math-nerd analytical capability that might have kept its risk management under control, though its Head of Futures and Options Settlements Brenda Granger, with solid well-grounded common sense, queried Leeson's activities a month before the collapse. Peter Baring, on the other hand, the bank's ineffectual Chairman, famously commented

---

[7] Sorry, non-UK readers! Kingston is a wealthy suburb of London, but the aristocracy traditionally lives in Mayfair, Chelsea, or on their country estates.

[8] Quoted Kynaston, 2002, p. 650. Heath was to meet disaster a decade later as Chairman of Caspian Securities.

to the Bank of England's Brian Quinn in 1993 that "the recovery in profitability has been amazing following the reorganization, leaving us to conclude that it was not actually terribly difficult to make money in the securities markets."[9]

Leeson's unofficial activities began when a clerical error on a trade led to a small £30,000 loss. Rather than own up to it, he gambled to make it back and got away with it. When no one at Barings questioned his activities, he then got into the speculative habit; he was not however a good trader and his speculative trades generally lost money. He compensated by expanding the size of his operations and by the highly risky strategy of selling options: you make a small premium if you are right, but the downside loss is unlimited if you are wrong.

All those losses had to go somewhere, so Leeson hid them in his error account, which would normally be no more than a minor housekeeping pocket, where no one noticed the losses piling up. He also hid his losses by using his control of the back office, regularly sending head office fraudulent reports that showed mounting paper profits, resulting in bonuses all round. Head office was delighted and Leeson was soon the bank's star trader: over 1994, he turned in paper profits of over $30 million, 20% of the bank's total profits.

Virtually no one questioned the source of his profits – arbitrage trades give a steady but low return, and have aptly been described as picking up sixpences from in front of a steamroller. But no one wanted to know either. Barings' top management was just happy to have the profits. At the height of his fame, Leeson was the hero of the bank's year end conference. There he explained "how he did it," but apparently without mentioning his secret ingredient, rogue trading; one can only suppose that his audience must have found his explanation a little puzzling.

Meanwhile, as Leeson's paper profits mounted, so too did his all too real losses. By the end of 1994, Leeson's positions were underwater to the tune of $285 million. Leeson responded to this looming disaster as he had always done, with another, bigger, gamble: he was so far underwater that he no longer had anything to lose. In early 1995, Leeson sold billions of dollars of options on Japanese stocks, betting that if the market stayed where it was, the premiums he was getting would pull

---

[9] Quoted in Leeson, 1996, p. 72.

him out of the hole. Then on January 17, 1995, a major earthquake hit Kobe, Japanese stocks crashed, and Leeson's positions nosedived.

He responded by one last very big roll of the dice. He greatly increased his bets, betting that the Japanese market would recover. It nearly worked, too: Japanese stocks did briefly recover, but in mid-February, Leeson's luck ran out: Japanese stocks fell and his losses were catastrophic. By this point, the game was up and Leeson knew it. He faxed a brief note to his boss – "Apologies, Nick" – and quickly fled the country.

On February 23, Barings' Board of Directors was astonished to find that Leeson had lost $1.4 billion, more than the bank's entire capital: Barings was bust. After a last-ditch appeal for a bailout, which the Bank of England refused, Barings went into receivership and was sold to the Dutch bank ING for the princely sum of £1.

Such was the inglorious end of the great House of Baring Brothers: once rated as the sixth great power of Europe, Barings had been ruined by a wide boy from Watford and sold off to a foreign bank for a measly quid.

Ironically, just two days before the dreadful news of their ruin arrived from Singapore, Leeson's managers in London received a Value-at-Risk report for Leeson's positions: Leeson's VaR was zero; no risk there, then.

Leeson was extradited to Singapore and sentenced to six and a half years for fraud. He now exploits his ill-gotten fame on the after-dinner circuit; he is, by all accounts, a very good speaker.

The Barings case provides a perfect illustration of a dangerous moral hazard unique to trading: once a trader gets underwater, he has no incentive to come clean, because he will be fired if he does so. Instead, his only way out is to gamble; and if his gamble fails, then his only way out is to keep gambling until he gets above the waterline again, gets caught, or brings down his bank. In this way, an initial minor loss can grow into a major disaster.

★★★

In terms of size and effect on the global economy, Procter & Gamble, Orange County, Daiwa, and Barings paled before the next derivatives disaster, the 1998 collapse of the hedge fund Long-Term Capital Management.

Long-Term Capital Management (LTCM) grew out of the proprietary trading desk at Salomon Brothers. It was founded in March 1994 and led by John Meriwether, who had left Salomons in 1991 under a cloud, tainted by the Treasury securities auction rigging scandal that had nearly put Salomons out of business. He quickly signed up Robert Merton and Myron Scholes as partners. The firm's fees were high even by hedge fund standards – investors paid a 2% annual management fee and gave up 25% of their earnings beyond a certain threshold. Some investors complained that this was excessive, but any reluctance soon disappeared as the LTCM bandwagon got going. LTCM's investors and strategic partners included many banks and other financial institutions, various governments, and even the Bank of Italy.

The firm operated with obsessive secrecy: it vaguely talked the language of arbitrage trading and Scholes liked to characterize the firm as a giant vacuum cleaner, sucking up nickels from all around the world. However, by the mid-1990s, there were lots of hedge funds making similar trades; returns were low and the only way to ramp them up was to increase leverage. This is exactly what LTCM did; indeed, it massively expanded the scale of its operations to the point where it came to dwarf any competitors.

LTCM cultivated the image of a superior institution with the best talent around, implementing the best strategies. Its principals bristled if anyone dared to suggest that the firm was anything as common as a hedge fund: LTCM was in a class of its own, and later events were to prove them right. Its prestige rose further in 1997, when Merton and Scholes were awarded the economics Nobel.

For its first four years or so everything went LTCM's way and the firm delivered impressive returns: 20% for the period it operated in 1994, 43% in 1995, 41% in 1996, and 17% in 1997. This track record and the prestige of its associates made LTCM the darling of Wall Street.

Its glamour was such that the banks that invested in LTCM and acted as its counterparties took LTCM's propaganda at face value and failed to exercise proper scrutiny. After its subsequent collapse, the head of Goldman Sachs' risk management looked at LTCM's books and said that he was struck by two things: the first was that LTCM had been making the same bets as Goldman's in-house traders. This meant that Goldman had been paying LTCM over-the-odds remuneration to do exactly what it was doing itself, which was not especially clever. The other point he noticed that LTCM's positions were ten times larger than Goldman's.

LTCM's high returns were due not just to its leverage but to the fact that, over time, the fund's activities became more and more speculative, often on a very large scale and often using OTC derivatives, which could be highly levered themselves. LTCM dabbled amateurishly in merger risk arbitrage, short equity volatility positions (gambling that the stock market would become more stable), and unhedged currency positions, in none of which had its principals any particular expertise, or even authorization from their investors to venture.

LTCM's biggest mistake was its convergence trades, betting that bond spreads would fall. These had initially worked well, in 1995, when LTCM had made a great deal of money betting on Italy's convergence towards the future eurozone. However they were very dangerous in emerging markets, and especially in Russia, on which the firm increasingly focused: only the most self-deluded could have thought in 1997–98 that Russia was converging westwards in any but the most geological of time frames.

By December 1997, the fund's assets had grown to about $120 billion and the fund's capital to about $7.3 billion. However, despite this high leverage – the fund was operating on a leverage ratio of more than 16 to 1 – the management of LTCM concluded that its capital base was too high to earn their target rate of return – that is to say, their greed got the better of them. Consequently, they returned $2.7 billion of capital to shareholders, increasing its leverage ratio to around 26 to 1. (Some shareholders complained about this, feeling deprived of their share of the profits everyone still expected LTCM to make: in retrospect, they were the lucky ones.) The reality was that the management of LTCM had taken a major gamble, making the firm much riskier, in the hope of bolstering the returns to remaining shareholders.

LTCM's luck ran out not long afterwards. Most markets were edgy during the first part of 1998, but market conditions deteriorated sharply in the summer and led to major losses in July. Disaster then struck the next month, when the Russian government defaulted. These events led to a major deterioration in the credit-worthiness of emerging markets and to large increases in the spreads between the prices of Western government and emerging market bonds. The fund's convergence trades had backfired disastrously.

The problem was not just that LTCM got hit because it had bet big and got it wrong. Part of the problem was that LTCM had failed to allow for the similar strategies of other firms; it even had the brass neck to complain that it was disadvantaged because others, unbeknown to it, were doing the same thing as it was![10] An even bigger part of the problem was that LTCM was way too large to be even remotely a price-taker; LTCM's own actions were pushing prices against it.

As an aside, LTCM had a sophisticated Value-at-Risk system that tells an interesting story. By the beginning of August, its 99% VaR over a daily horizon was about $35 million; thus, according to its VaR system, there was only a 1 in a 100 chance of a daily loss exceeding $35 million. Average daily losses in August were, by contrast, about $135 million. Using a model like this to manage risks was rather like bolting the stable doors, while overlooking the fact that a hurricane had flattened the rest of the stable, horses and all.

By the end of August, LTCM's capital was down to $2.3 billion and its leverage ratio had climbed to more than 45 to 1 – a very high ratio by any standards, but especially in this environment. Information soon leaked out about the fund's difficulties and the vultures started to circulate, knowing that LTCM would have to sell at almost any price. Having traded on a huge scale, LTCM was now like a hunted elephant trying to hide in knee-high grass.[11]

As LTCM's situation continued to deteriorate, the fund's management spent the next three weeks looking for assistance in a frantic effort to keep afloat. However, no help was forthcoming, and by September 19 the fund's capital was down to its last $600 million and its leverage ratio was now approaching stratospheric levels.

Wall Street and the Fed had watched LTCM's deterioration with mounting concern. A delegation from the New York Fed and the US Treasury duly visited the fund on Sunday, September 20, to assess the situation. At this meeting, fund partners persuaded the delegation that LTCM's situation was not only bad, but potentially much worse than

---

[10] This prompted the perceptive journalist Martin Mayer to comment shortly afterwards, "If you don't know what other people are doing, how can you have the slightest notion of what risks you are running?" To ask the question is to answer it. See Martin Mayer, *Derivatives Strategy*, August 1999, p. 35.

[11] Bookstaber, 2007, p. 104.

market participants imagined. The Fed concluded that some form of support operation should be prepared – rapidly – to prevent LTCM failing, in order to forestall what it feared might be major adverse effects on financial markets. LTCM had succeeded in spooking the Fed.

Accordingly, the New York Fed invited a number of the creditor firms most involved to discuss a rescue package, and it was soon agreed that this Fed-led consortium would mount a rescue if no one else took over the fund in the meantime. However, when representatives of this group met on the early morning of Wednesday, September 23, they learned that another group had just made an offer for the fund, and that this offer would expire at lunchtime that day.

This alternative offer was made by a group led by Warren Buffett's firm, Berkshire Hathaway. They offered to buy out the shareholders for $250 million and put $3.75 billion into the fund as new capital. However, the existing shareholders would have lost everything except for the $250 million take-over payment and the fund's managers would be fired.

The management of LTCM rejected the offer, perhaps hardly surprising when by this point they could anticipate that the Fed would not let them fail. The hapless Fed then re-convened discussions to hammer out a rescue package, which was agreed by the end of the day. Under the terms of this deal, 14 prominent banks and brokerage houses agreed to invest $3.65 billion of equity capital in LTCM in exchange for 90% of the firm's equity. Existing shareholders would retain a 10% holding, valued at about $400 million. This offer was clearly better for the existing shareholders than the Berkshire Hathaway offer.

The story of LTCM reads like a Greek play: a classic case of hubris followed by humiliating nemesis. As one observer commented, "The ultimate error is to put a ton of money on geniuses who 'never lose money.' When all hell breaks loose, those guys lose everything."[12] LTCM could have survived one Nobelist, but with two they were doomed.[13]

It turned out later that there was nothing sophisticated about what LTCM was doing. It was doing the same things as many others, but on a bigger scale. LTCM's managers had learnt nothing from the experi-

---

[12] Parker, J. (1998), *Wall Street Journal*, October 29, p. C1.
[13] Cited in *Futures*, December 2000, p. 75.

ence of portfolio insurance a decade earlier: failing to take account of other firms following similar strategies, failing to take account of the impact of its own size on the markets in which it operated. LTCM also defied the old Copybook Heading telling us to beware the perils of leverage: its high returns in the good years were no different in kind from those of Orange County's Bob Citron, using the tools of psychics and astrologers rather than the latest in high-tech Modern Finance; and its ultra-high returns soon turned into ultra-high losses when the markets turned against it. LTCM also defied another old Copybook Heading: if it looks too good to be true, then it probably *is* too good to be true. The gods of both Copybook Headings took ample revenge.

The LTCM debacle also had important ramifications for public policy. Though the Fed's rescue of LTCM was widely welcomed with relief, we would suggest it was a major blunder. Had the Fed washed its hands of LTCM even as late as the morning of September 23, the management of LTCM would have faced a very different set of alternatives from those they actually faced. Instead of choosing between the Buffett offer and the likelihood of a better offer later, they would have had to choose between the Buffett offer and certain failure. The Buffett offer was not a generous one, but it was much better than nothing, and we must suppose that LTCM's management would have accepted it had it been their only choice.

LTCM had provided the Fed with an ideal opportunity to make an example *pour encourager les autres* and send out a clear message that no firm, however prominent, could expect to be rescued from the consequences of its own mistakes, even if that had meant that LTCM would have failed. There would have been some temporary adjustment problems in some financial markets, and some possibly severe repercussions on LTCM counterparties and hedge funds with similar portfolios, but the world financial system was still sound enough to have absorbed these effects and recovered. Other firms would have strengthened themselves and financial markets would have been more stable in the years that followed. Instead, the Fed opted for the weak, easy solution, thus confirming too-big-to-fail and leaving it and the whole financial system exposed to the moral hazard problems that followed. The Fed's rescue of LTCM was also immensely damaging to the moral authority of US policymakers:

"For 15 months, as financial markets in country after country collapsed like straw huts in a typhoon, the United States lectured the rest of the world about the evils of crony capitalism – of bailing out rich, connected insiders while letting everyone else suffer. … Thai peasants, Korean steelworkers and Moscow pensioners may suffer horribly as their local economies and currencies collapse – but we solemnly told them that was a cost they had to pay for the greater good. … Cronyism bad. Capitalism good."[14]

Then came the imminent collapse of Long-Term Capital Management, the quintessential "member of The Club, with rich fat-cat investors and rich hotshot well-connected managers. Faster than you can say 'bailout,' crony capitalism US style raised its ugly head." The reality was that the US was already well into crony capitalism by this point; nonetheless, the damage to the moral authority of US policymakers was incalculable.

★★★

And so we come to Enron, the biggest corporate disaster of the 2000–02 downturn, a $100 billion company with 22,000 employees that simply vaporized within two months between September and November 2001.

There are a number of common misconceptions about Enron. First, it was not primarily a scam, although there was criminality involved. Second, it was not solely a trading disaster; Enron's non-trading operations were at least as responsible for the company's failure as Jeff Skilling's derivatives desks, although the counterparty requirements of the trading operations precipitated the collapse. Third, contrary to popular belief, its trading innovations were generally economically valuable and its notorious "rip-off" of California's electric power system was largely due to fatuous regulation in California and elsewhere.

Enron originated through a 1985 acquisition of Houston Natural Gas by the well-run Omaha gas pipeline company InterNorth, in which HNG's young CEO Kenneth Lay took control six months after the merger. Lay moved the headquarters to Houston and built the nat-

---

[14] Sloan, A. (1998) "What Goes Around," *Newsweek*, October 12.

ural gas pipeline business nationwide through acquisitions, leveraging heavily to do so and declaring rapid profits growth through aggressive accounting.

After 1991, Enron began to diversify internationally, in an effort led by Rebecca Mark, head of Enron International from 1996, who extraordinarily escaped much criticism after the Enron collapse. Under Mark's aggressive leadership Enron bought power plants, pipelines, pulp and paper companies, gas distribution companies, and electric utilities all over the world.

Two purchases were particularly noteworthy. Enron was granted concessions to build the Dabhol power station, in Maharashtra, India, by bribing local Congress Party politicians. When Congress lost power in Maharashtra in 1995, the new BJP government refused to recognize the Enron concessions, claiming correctly that they would allow Enron to sell power from the plant at prices far above the market rate. Construction costs of the plant soared to more than $3 billion and at the time of Enron's bankruptcy it had still to begin operation.

Mark's second major mistake came in 1998, when Enron decided to devote $1 billion to creating a new water company, Azurix Corporation, and put Mark in charge. In spite of a 1999 IPO that raised $695 million, Azurix "chewed up a lot of capital," in Kenneth Lay's words, and in August 2000 Mark resigned.[15]

Jeff Skilling, Lay's successor (for six months in 2001), took the opposite strategic view from Lay and Mark: that Enron did not need a heavy asset base to succeed. Instead, he built trading operations, initially in natural gas, then in electric power and communications "bandwidth." His thesis was that vertically integrated producers were competitive in only some of their operations. Thus traders like Enron could "mix and match" between operations of different producers, cutting out a great deal of overhead and reducing the cost of production and distribution of the product concerned. Enron was named "Most Innovative in America" by *Fortune* magazine for six consecutive years from 1996–2001; it was Skilling's trading operation that deserved this accolade.

---

[15] "Rebecca Mark's Exit Leaves Azurix Treading Deep Water," *Wall Street Journal*, August 28, 2000.

Enron was blamed, at the time and especially later, for California's energy crisis in the winter of 2000–01, when power prices spiked and shortages ensued. In the Congressional hearings a year later, tapes were played of Enron traders rejoicing at their success in gouging California energy consumers – the episode was held up as an example of why market deregulation did not work. However, California's energy deregulation of 1996 had been highly politicized, with far too much input from existing monopoly producers. In particular it had forbidden Californians from entering into energy derivatives transactions, locking in cost over a prolonged period, and leaving the state's entire power consumption exposed to the vagaries of the spot market. In addition, the Mexican electricity generator CFE, which at that time had ample spare capacity, was not permitted to sell power across the border.

Some of Skilling's innovations, notably bandwidth trading, were disasters; communications capacity overproduction in 1996–2000 caused bandwidth prices to collapse, producing large losses. Another, the trading of carbon emission credits, has proved irresistibly attractive to foolish and dirigiste environmentalist politicians in the EU and elsewhere. However, Skilling's overall thesis of increased flexibility and lower cost through de-integrating production in an asset-light operation had some merit. His mistake lay in pushing asset-light too far, implementing that thesis in a company that already had vast quantities of assets of questionable quality, and excessive leverage attached. Once Skilling had set up the world's largest energy derivatives trading platform in a company with dodgy finances and a BBB credit rating, when things started to go wrong the whole edifice collapsed remarkably rapidly.

Another major mistake was Enron's total opacity: its managers, lawyers, and accountants conspired to set up a pattern of inter-company trading activities that that was so complex and hidden that no one had a clue how it worked. But the rot really set in with the over-aggressive and in some cases fraudulent accounting undertaken by, among others, Enron's CFO Andrew Fastow, including hiding assets in off-balance sheet vehicles with illicit multi-million-dollar commissions to Fastow's personal bank account. Enron's collapse was not directly caused by the gossamer constructions of Modern Financial Theory, but shows how fragile those can be in the context of the ethical failings of Modern Financiers.

★★★

Finally, we come to the most recent disaster, that of the reprehensible Bernard Madoff. Madoff was arrested in December 2008, at which time he was alleged to have embezzled about $50 billion in a gigantic Ponzi scheme. In reality, the amount directly embezzled was only $18 billion; the $50 billion figure (actually $65 billion) included the fictitious gains Madoff had declared and in many cases paid to clients.

Madoff took the Modern Finance scam one stage further, by pretending to employ sophisticated arbitrage strategies while in fact simply embezzling the money. Madoff was a top notch conman – a pillar of the finance industry (and a former chairman of the Nasdaq, no less) and a noted philanthropist who could obviously charm the hind legs off a donkey. He operated on a breathtaking scale and was highly secretive about his methods, expelling the occasional client who asked awkward questions and further bolstering the Madoff mystique by doing so. His secrecy was reinforced by his practice of clearing his own trades – or, rather, those he claimed to be making – and by the fact that he was audited by a tiny audit firm, consisting of one auditor, a secretary, and an 80-year-old in Florida. The combination of his obsessive secrecy and his suspiciously steady returns through thick and thin, making hardly a ripple on the markets, should have altered investors. But they were mesmerized.

Yet not everyone was fooled. A good citizen, Harry Markopolos, had pointed out to the SEC as far back as 1999 that Madoff could not be making the returns he claimed to be making using bona fide methods. He then spent years trying to persuade the SEC that Madoff was a crook, but they dismissed him, and Madoff was only found out when his sons eventually turned him in.

The list of those he fooled included many prominent individuals, some of whom were ruined by him, as well as some of the biggest and most prestigious financial institutions, and of course the SEC.

Does Madoff count as another Modern Financial Theory disaster? Certainly his sales pitch involved heavy use of the relevant jargon, and the possibility of achieving superior returns by a sophisticated "black box" was devoutly believed in by almost everybody on and off Wall Street. But we would not wish to push the point too far: doubtless, if some other theory had dominated investment thinking, Madoff would no doubt equally have constructed a sales pitch around that instead. He was however representative of Modern Finance in his hard sell, his total lack of scruple, his use of political connections, his secrecy, and his dodgy accounting. At the end of the day, the Madoff scandal confirms yet again the old saying that there will always be sheep to be shorn and those willing to fleece them.

Even before the collapse of 2007–08, which dwarfed all previous Modern Finance disasters, the new Millennium had continued to produce unexpected Modern Finance-related collapses – one thinks of Allied Irish Bank, the Amaranth hedge fund, the unexpected Credit Suisse losses in South Korea, sinking the ship in a flat calm, the $4.7 billion Société Générale losses from the rogue trader Jerome Kerviel, etc. We can without question be sure that, since Modern Financial Theory and its risk management offspring continues to dominate Wall Street, since over-leverage remains so prevalent worldwide and since money creation has become even more excessive in recent years, there will be many more spectacular disasters to look forward to in the future.

Part Four

Policy Accommodates Modern Finance

11

Loose Money

Federal Reserve Chairman (1951–70) William McChesney Martin, Jr encapsulated the central goal of a fiat currency monetary policy when he said in a frequently misquoted speech: "The Federal Reserve, as one writer put it, after the recent increase in the discount rate, is in the position of the chaperone who has ordered the punch bowl removed just as the party was really warming up."[1] Regrettably, he demonstrated in his own career that fiat currency monetary policy was just about impossible to manage, given the political pressures on the Fed chairman. A decade after his famous bon mot he allowed inflation to take off through his inability to resist the uncouth badgerings of President Lyndon Johnson. Less famous, but more appropriate to his career, is his valedictory speech in January 1970: "I wish I could turn the bank over to Arthur Burns as I would have liked. But we are in very deep trouble. We are in the wildest inflation since the Civil War."[2]

Actually, Martin did not quite do himself justice. The 12-month inflation rate in the year to December 1969 was 5.9%, lower than the 6.0% of 1951, the year he was appointed, and considerably lower than in several wartime and immediate post-war years. Nonetheless, Martin was right to be worried: the main difference between 1951 and 1969

---

[1] Address before the New York Group of the Investment Bankers Association of America, Waldorf-Astoria Hotel, October 19, 1955. FRASER St. Louis Fed., historical documents.

[2] Bremner, 2004, p. 276. Said at a dinner on January 17, 1970.

was that inflation was going down in the early 1950s and up in the late 1960s (and destined to go up much further). Johnson's budget deficits and forced monetary sloppiness led to renewed inflation, but the real problems were to emerge after August 1971, when President Richard Nixon "went off gold," ending the post-war Bretton Woods system of exchange rate management.

The Bretton Woods system, established by the eponymous conference in 1944, had been a Gold Standard in theory rather than in fact. While the gold price was fixed, only governments were allowed to deal at that price; trading in gold was heavily limited by legal restrictions and, outside the US, the system was propped up by a complex and oppressive system of exchange controls.

Then in the 1960s Martin lost control of US monetary policy and the Kennedy and Johnson administrations felt free to pursue dreams of welfare state combined with expensive foreign policies, including in particular the Vietnam War; faced with the choice between guns or butter, they opted for the archetypal 1960s response: both.

In the late 1960s, the cracks in the Bretton Woods system were becoming ever more apparent, and various new expedients – such as expanded Special Drawings Rights by the IMF – were suggested to expand global liquidity while hanging on to what was left of the Bretton Woods system, spurred on by Keynesian economists who never liked the discipline it imposed on their spending plans.

The heroes of the story were the Chicago monetarists, led by the soft-spoken gentlemanly New Yorker, the great Milton Friedman, and the legendarily hard-drinking Canadian (and now sadly almost forgotten) Harry G. Johnson, who repeatedly warned that countries such as the US and the UK were allowing money supplies to grow at rates faster than was consistent with the constraints of even the emasculated Bretton Woods Gold Standard. Their warnings were ignored.

The situation in the late 1960s was similar to what it had been much earlier, in the sixteenth century, when Spanish gold was slowly flooding the European economies with money, causing prices to rise in its wake. When King Philip II of Spain sat in his gloomy Escorial, counting his gold coming in from the Americas, he doubtless pulled at his beard in puzzlement and wondered where all the inflation was coming from. Then, as in the 1960s, the problem was simple: the money supply was growing too fast.

The result was a drain of gold out of the United States and a steadily rising price of the metal on the free market in Paris, a sure sign of monetary excess. President Nixon proved unequal to the challenge: rather than bite the bullet and rein in monetary growth, on August 15, 1971 he announced that the US government would no longer attempt to peg the price of gold, so consigning the last remnant of the Gold Standard to the dustbin of history. For the first time ever, the economies of the world were on an inconvertible fiat standard (or rather, set of standards: every man for himself) without any intention to revert back to the discipline of a commodity standard.

It was a fateful decision: the genie of easy money was out of the lamp and out of control. Keynesian economists told the governments they advised that they were now free to do whatever they wanted: like adolescents discovering the pleasures of alcohol, they could drink themselves stupid with no one to take the booze away. The results were entirely predictable. The rate of growth of money supply accelerated and inflation mounted. By late 1971, the United States was in the grip of an inflation crisis, and the only response Nixon's Keynesian advisors could think of was to impose wage and price controls – a "solution" that did nothing to address the underlying causes of the problem and was also deeply unpopular.

Arthur Burns, the new Fed Chairman, was nominally an inflation hawk: he was a student of Wesley Clarke Mitchell, whose *History of the Greenbacks* (1903) was a classic on the evils of expansionary monetary policy. Yet in practice he was first and foremost a Republican party loyalist who lacked the strength to resist the political pressure to stoke the inflationary fire, expanding money supply at an increasing rate. The M2 broad monetary aggregate had grown by 3.7% in 1969, the year before Burns took over, but grew by 5.0% in 1970, 6.6% in 1971, 13.4% in 1972 and 13.0% in 1973. The corresponding figures for the broader M3 aggregate were for the most part even higher. It was no wonder that the inflationary pressure in the system was growing.

This mounting pressure blew the lid off Nixon's controls in early 1973 and inflation then took off, eventually peaking at 12.2% in November 1974, just as the economy was falling into a sharp recession; welcome stagflation.

As inflation rose, the new President, Gerald Ford, declared inflation to be "public enemy number one" and introduced a "Whip Inflation

Now" (WIN) campaign whose most notable feature was to encourage people to wear WIN buttons, a peacetime evocation of the solidarity symbolized by the V-campaign during World War II. The buttons were widely ridiculed; skeptics took to wearing them upside down, explaining that "NIM" stood for "Nonstop Inflation Merry-go-round." The Chairman of Ford's own Council of Economic Advisers, Alan Greenspan, later recalled thinking that this policy was "unbelievably stupid." Needless to say, the WIN gimmick didn't win the inflation battle and was soon abandoned as an embarrassment. However Ford's subsequent major economic activity – preventing Congress by a record exercise of the veto pen from engaging in an orgy of anti-recession "stimulus" – was wholly beneficial and very important.

It's not surprising that inflation soared during the 1970s. Over the course of the decade to October 1979, M2 grew by an annual rate of 9.6% and M3 by an annual rate of 11.4%. The inflation problem was only to be resolved when the underlying cause – loose money – was properly addressed.

Another damaging feature of the inflationary 1970s was very low real interest rates, another aspect of loose money, which were often negative: these were a major disincentive to save. The monetary chaos of the 1970s was also associated with the end of the high-wage, high-productivity performance that the US economy had enjoyed for a quarter of a century in 1948–73. US productivity growth fell off a cliff after 1973 and was never to recover fully; for low-skilled US workers, real wages fell thereafter, and still haven't returned to their 1973 level.

But US policymakers were not yet ready to swallow Friedman's unpleasant medicine. Inflation had come down somewhat in mid-1970s in a response to a modest tightening of monetary growth and a sharp recession. However, the new President, Jimmy Carter, embarked on yet another attempt to "boost" the economy, and Arthur Burns resumed his underlying policy of rapid monetary growth. Burns was succeeded as Fed Chairman in January 1978 by G. William Miller, the Chairman and CEO of Textron, a successful conglomerate – he is so far the only Fed chairman from a corporate background. Despite ongoing high inflation, Miller was committed to expansionary policies and it was said afterwards that if Burns had lit the inflationary fire, it was Miller who poured the gasoline on it. The result was to send the dollar into a nosedive, leading to a crisis that prompted the Carter administration to launch a panic dollar rescue package, including emergency sales of US Government gold holdings and borrowing from the IMF. But these policies didn't work either: unemployment rose along with inflation and the US subsided again into stagflation.

By this point, the inflation hawks were becoming more influential – it was increasingly obvious that Keynesian policies had failed – and in August 1979 President Carter responded with a major Cabinet reshuffle, making Miller Treasury Secretary and appointing the arch-monetarist Paul Volcker as the new Chairman of the Fed.

Volcker was very different from his predecessor. Six foot seven inches tall, Volcker was a devoted disciple of Milton Friedman: people joked that they saw eye to eye when he sat down and Friedman stood up. With a decade at Chase Manhattan, five years as Under Secretary of the Treasury under Nixon and four years as President of the New York Fed, Volcker had a perfect background for the job and high credibility with the markets.

Volcker pondered his options for six weeks; then, in the weekend of October 7–8, 1979 he acted decisively and hoisted the discount rate by an unprecedented 2%, to 12%, and making it clear that interest rates would rise as far as needed and for as long as it took to conquer inflation. He also announced a new policy by which the Fed would no longer target interest rates, but would now target monetary growth rates along textbook monetarist lines.

Volcker continued tightening interest rates through the winter of 1979–80 and the Fed Funds rate rose to over 19% by April 1980. At that point, Carter imposed credit controls and the economy shrank sharply. In response, Volcker eased up on the pressure and interest rates more than halved in just three months. Monthly inflation, which had peaked at 1.5% in March, hit zero in July, and the economy began to expand again in the last two quarters of the year. A cynic might have thought that Volcker, a Democrat, was trying to help Carter get re-elected.

But Carter lost to Ronald Reagan, and in the weeks after the election Volcker tightened policy mercilessly, presumably because he saw the interregnum as a politically opportune time to do so. The Federal Funds rate, which had rebounded to 13% by election time, soared to the unprecedented level of more than 20% in the first week of January 1981; the nascent economic recovery then stalled, and unemployment started to rise again.

The 12-month rate of inflation peaked at 14.7% in April 1981, but remained around 10% throughout 1981 before falling down to 3.8% over the course of 1982. President Reagan himself supported Volcker's tight money policy far more wholeheartedly than had Carter, but Congressional Republicans, up for re-election in 1982, were less supportive, as the deep recession that hit in late 1981 made them highly unpopular. The Fed Funds rate slowly declined to 8.5% in May 1983, before climbing again to peak at 11.8% in August 1984. With inflation down to under 5%, real interest rates were extraordinarily high, and economic recovery was slow. Having helped Carter's electoral prospects in 1980 through his spring relaxation in monetary policy, Volcker did no favors for Reagan in 1984.

Reagan won anyway, but it was not entirely surprising that when Volcker's own term of office came up in 1987 the Reagan team were not especially enthusiastic. They had supported Volcker for a second four-year term in 1983, when the victory over inflation was still fragile, but by 1987 that battle had been won. Moreover, Reagan's economic team had ambitions for banking de-regulation that Volcker did not share. Consequently he was replaced in 1987 with the apparently solidly conservative, even libertarian figure of Alan Greenspan, a former devotee of the radical free market philosopher Ayn Rand and a supporter of the Gold Standard.

Volcker achieved spectacular success against inflation. When examined in detail, however, his record was not perfect and quite political. In retrospect, it is likely that victory over inflation could have been achieved more quickly, with only a "single dip" rather than a "double dip" recession and less severe unemployment, if Volcker had ignored the electoral cycle and held firmly to his anti-inflationary policies in spring 1980. But perhaps that is too much to hope for from the holder of such a politically charged office.

Greenspan gained market credibility by his reaction to the stock market crash of 1987, when he swiftly cut interest rates and saw the market recover without renewed inflation. It was nonetheless a dangerous lesson, because it reinforced the tendency of politicians and politically oriented central bankers to react to each little market hiccup with a rate cut, while being much slower to tighten in periods of market euphoria. Greenspan's later mis-reaction to the Long-Term

Capital Management debacle in 1998, organizing a bailout and cutting rates, derived in part from this success in 1987.

Greenspan's monetary policy was in essence one of gradually easing from Volcker's austerities and on July 22, 1993 Greenspan formally abandoned monetarism in his biannual testimony to the Senate Banking Committee. As he explained:

> "The historical relationships between money and income and between money supply and the price level have largely broken down, depriving the aggregates of much of their usefulness as guides to policy. At least for the time being, M2 has been downgraded as a reliable indicator of financial conditions in the economy, and no single variable has been found to take its place."[3]

By early 1994, the Federal Funds yield had fallen to around 3%, a level not seen since the early 1960s. This was little higher than the inflation rate itself and monetary conditions were now clearly too lax. Greenspan responded with an appropriate tightening and US interest rates doubled by the end of 1994. The rise in interest rates was modest by earlier standards, but was enough to trigger some high-profile derivatives losses on the part of those who had bet on low interest rates – most notably the staggering $1.6 billion loss suffered by California's Orange County, which defaulted on its debts in December 1994 – and to prompt a lot of squealing from Wall Street. By this stage the Street was far more leveraged than it had been a decade earlier, both directly and indirectly through its exposure to derivatives contracts. These large unexpected losses should have been an indication to Greenspan that Wall Street's practices needed to be reined in. Instead they led him to open the monetary spigots further than at any time since the 1970s, and then to keep them open.

One explanation for Greenspan's remarkable switch in policy in 1993–95 is left unmentioned by sober monetary observers, but deserves examination. Greenspan had been a close friend and philosophical

---

[3] Testimony before the Committee on Banking, Housing and Urban Affairs, United States Senate, July 22, 1993, pp. 9–10. St. Louis Fed, FRASER.

partner of Ayn Rand, who died in 1982, but had enjoyed only a brief first marriage in the 1950s. The conservatism he had acquired with Rand in the 1950s and 1960s was strong and heartfelt; it was not, however, entirely compatible with his social status as an eligible bachelor moving in fashionably liberal circles. From 1985, when he was already 58, he began dating the much younger TV journalist Andrea Mitchell, whose politics were conventionally liberal Democrat.

Mitchell moved in with Greenspan around 1990 and they married in April 1997. After 1993 she doubtless was politically useful to the nominally Republican Fed Chairman through her closeness to Hillary Clinton and other senior Clinton administration figures. "Cherchez la femme" may be the simplest explanation for Greenspan's conversion – from the early 1990s until Greenspan's retirement US monetary policy appears to have been at least partially influenced by Andrea Mitchell. By 2008, when Greenspan admitted to House Banking Committee Chairman Henry Waxman that he was shocked because his free market ideology hadn't worked,[4] he was in deep denial; by that stage he hadn't been a true free marketer for the best part of two decades.

Greenspan's definitive monetary policy shift occurred in February 1995. In his biannual Humphrey-Hawkins testimony to Congress on February 22–23, he indicated that his program of rate rises, the last to a 6% Federal Funds rate on February 1 that year, had ended. Elliptical as ever, Greenspan's hint of easing was veiled: "There may come a time when we hold our policy stance unchanged, or even ease, despite adverse price data, should we see that underlying forces are acting ultimately to reduce price pressures."[5] Those obscure words set off a bond and stock market rally that sent the Dow through 4,000 for the first time the following day; that same month, the broader monetary aggregates, M3 and St. Louis Fed Money of Zero Maturity (MZM), began to expand at a notably faster rate.

The following table examines US money supply growth, nominal and real GDP growth, and the real federal funds rate for several periods, as follows:

---

[4] Testimony to the House Banking Committee, October 23, 2008.
[5] Testimony to the House Banking Committee, February 22, 1995.

- October 1959 – October 1969: a decade in retrospect of halcyon post-war stability, though with gradual inflation towards the end.
- October 1969 – October 1979: the decade of high inflation, ended by Paul Volcker's sharp change of monetary policy in October 1979.
- October 1979 – February 1995: the period of disinflation and monetary stringency in which inflation was reduced from double digits to a state of quiescence, ending with Alan Greenspan's monetary policy change of February 1995.
- February 1995 – February 2006: the eleven remaining years of Alan Greenspan's tenure, during which monetary policy differed considerably from his early years, and asset bubbles occurred in stocks and housing.[6]

Table 1: Macroeconomic Indicators, 1959–2006

Growth rates	1959–69	1969–79	1979–95	1995–2006
M2	7.0%	9.6%	5.9%	6.2%
MZM	5.1%	6.3%	8.2%	8.3%
M3	7.4%	11.4%	6.0%	8.1%
Average	6.5%	9.1%	6.7%	7.9%
Nominal GDP growth (annual)	6.9%	10.2%	6.9%	5.5%
Real GDP growth (annual)	4.3%	3.3%	2.8%	3.3%
Inflation rate (annual)	2.4%	7.1%	4.9%	2.6%
Real Fed. Funds rate (average)	1.8%	0.0%	3.4%	1.5%

1959–69: October 1959 – October 1969
1969–79: October 1969 – October 1979
1979–95: October 1979 – February 1995
1995–2006: February 1995 – February 2006
(GDP for quarters containing October and February, respectively)

A number of things become clear from Table 1, which takes account of the variations in money supply data, so that MZM (the St. Louis Fed's Money of Zero Maturity) grew significantly more slowly than other aggregates in 1969–79, while M2 grew more slowly than other aggregates in 1995–2006. Real GDP growth was fastest in the first period, before the productivity slowdown of 1973, and slightly slower

---

[6] February 2006 is also the last month in which the Fed released M3 statistics.

in the 1980s while inflation was being brought under control. The real Federal Funds rate was lowest in the 1970s, as interest rates failed to keep up with accelerating inflation, and highest in 1979–95, when the reverse process applied.

However, the most interesting analysis from a monetary policy point of view is derived by taking the average of the three monetary aggregates (thus washing out definitional peculiarities between them) and comparing it to the inflation rate. In 1995–2006, the money supply growth, measured by the average of the three data, was 5.3% above inflation, thus much more expansionary than was appropriate in a mature economy over so long a period. Indeed, money supply growth ran 2.4% faster than nominal GDP during that period, whereas in all three of the other periods it ran slower than nominal GDP, as you would expect with a gradual increase in monetary velocity through technological advance.[7]

The relaxation of monetary policy since February 1995 has been greater than the figures given above, however, because of the Boskinization of US price statistics. The Boskin Commission, headed by Stanford economist Michael Boskin, was appointed by the US Senate in 1995 to study US price statistics, with a view to reducing the indexation of social security payments and income tax brackets. Unsurprisingly, it reported in December 1996 that the consumer price index overstated inflation by about 1.1% per annum, and proposed adjustments to the CPI to "correct" for this bias. This conclusion was politically convenient, because it enabled the federal government to save billions on indexed payments. The acceptance of this conclusion was also comforting, as it suggested that economic and real wage growth had actually been considerably higher than had previously been thought, and so helped defuse criticism of the US economy's lackluster performance. It also made late 1990s growth look *really* exciting![8]

The essence of the Commission's findings was the alleged presence of "sample selection bias" in the construction of the CPI: the CPI "basket" of goods and services over-samples prices that are rising

---

[7] The Fed's own Taylor rule, invented by John B. Taylor in 1993, shows Fed policy as having been grossly over-expansionary from 2002, and so a major cause of the housing bubble. However, growth in the US monetary aggregates accelerated from 1995, not 2002. We would regard that as a better indicator than the somewhat artificial and indeed Keynesian Taylor calculation.

[8] For more on the Boskin Commission see, e.g., Palley, 1997.

relatively rapidly, and under-samples prices that are rising more slowly or even falling. There is a nice irony here, as the Commission itself was a perfect example of sample selection bias: all its members were already of the view that the CPI was overstated and the Commission not only failed to include prominent economists who felt that there was no such bias, but it even failed to take evidence from them. Its conclusions were therefore hardly surprising.

The Commission proposed a methodology of "hedonic [or quality adjusted] pricing," to "correct" the bias believed to be present in the CPI. This attempts to take account of quality improvements in products and services, such as those arising through the greater power of computer chips.

The problem with this hedonic pricing methodology is that greater processing power does not always translate into product improvement. Anybody who suffered through using Microsoft Windows Vista knows the problem; it was considerably less capable than its simpler predecessors Windows XP and Windows 2000. Furthermore, Boskin did not take proper account of the additional costs imposed on consumers by such innovations as automated telephone answering systems; hedonics works both ways.

The Bureau of Labor Statistics introduced the new "Boskinized" index in 1997. If we grant that there was in fact little or no bias in the original CPI, then the new Boskinized CPI has been understating inflation since then by about 1% per year. Such a conclusion is also supported by the widespread suspicion among many that there has been "hidden" inflation, and also by other evidence. You can get a rough idea of the market's view of the bias by comparing US Treasury Inflation Protected Securities, introduced in 1997 using the Boskinized index, with the British index-linked gilts, introduced in 1980 using an un-fudged index.[9] Until the recent difficulties cast a shadow of doubt over both countries' credit quality, US TIPS yielded around 0.8% more than British index-linked gilts – the "fudge" in US inflation figures would therefore appear to be in the range 0.8–1.0%.

Boskinization means not only that "true" inflation has been underestimated, but that real GDP growth has been overestimated: instead

---

[9] Britain now also has a fudged price index, but the government can't legally change the index used for index-linked gilts already in existence.

of being about 3.3% over 1995–2006, it would have been closer to 2.3%, masking the reality of the US economy's poor performance in the bubble years.

The stock market went on a bender in 1995–96, rising more than two-thirds. By the middle of 1996 it was already obvious that increased asset wealth might be causing the economy to overheat – except at the Fed, which at that stage and for a few years afterwards was operating under a bizarre theory that increases in wealth had no effect on consumption.[10] To his credit, Greenspan was aware of the problem and, in a speech that became famous, on December 5, 1996, he warned about the dangers of "irrational exuberance" leading to "unduly escalated asset values, which then become subject to unexpected and prolonged contractions" as they had done a little earlier in Japan, for all to see.[11]

The Dow Jones Industrial Index promptly dropped 3% during the following day, and the investment banking community howled, fearing that Greenspan had stolen their lunch bucket.

Yet Greenspan failed to follow up his brave words with action. Instead, the following July, he came up with an explanation of why the high stock market might not be so excessive after all. In his usual Delphic manner, he remarked that "important pieces of information, while just suggestive at this point, could be read as indicating basic improvements in the longer-term efficiency of our economy."[12]

Greenspan's cautious utterances were seized by the media as a "productivity miracle." This "theory" was made more plausible by the huge technological change of the Internet, then expanding rapidly through the US economy, but also by the fact that productivity growth figures reported at that time for 1995–97 were unexpectedly high. These figures were however revised down afterwards, and later figures suggested that labor productivity grew by an average of only 1.5% an-

---

[10] Martin put the point to William McDonough, president of the New York Fed, at a Harvard Club meeting in May 1996, and was slapped down for his pains. At the Fed in the late 1990s, exuberance was truly irrational. The Fed later disowned the theory, but too late for those who had invested in the dotcom bubble.

[11] Speech at the American Enterprise Institute for Public Policy Research dinner, Washington DC, December 5, 1996, p14. St. Louis Fed, FRASER.

[12] Testimony before the Senate Banking Committee, July 23, 1997, p. 2. St. Louis Fed., FRASER

nually in 1995–97, below the annual average of 1.6% in the previous decade.[13] There was no US productivity miracle, then or later.

The Internet and modern telecommunications did indeed produce a productivity miracle, but it occurred primarily in the giant Asian economies of China and India. From about 1996, outsourcing of products and services across the globe suddenly became much easier than ever before, and much US manufacturing and service industry was thus outsourced. The result was a secular decline in costs, similar to that that had been effected by railroads and refrigeration in the 1880s. As in the 1880s, this should have resulted in a substantial decline in prices in Western economies. However, the rapid rise in money supply counterbalanced this effect in consumer price data while producing a huge increase in asset prices.

By about 2007–08, there were signs that this effect was beginning to play itself out. Inflation in China and India was running at double digit rates that, combined with appreciating currencies, caused Chinese and Indian costs to appreciate. The economic downturn of 2007–09 has masked this change, but it is likely that in 2010 and thereafter the artificial suppression of prices in Western economies will no longer hold, and monetary laxity will feed through more directly to inflation, as it did in the 1960s and 1970s.

In the interim, it fed through into bubbles: first the dotcom bubble of 1997–2000, then the housing bubble of 2002–06, and, since mid-2009, apparently a commodities bubble too. The increase in dollar availability around the world also stimulated investment in the emerging markets, making them more competitive with Western producers, while allowing the surplus countries of Asia and the Middle East to pile up foreign exchange at an astonishing rate.

The trigger for the huge increases in global foreign exchange reserves was the 1997 Asian crisis and the collapse of Russian credit a year later. The east Asian economies had over-extended themselves by borrowing heavily in the flood of global liquidity of 1995–97, and they paid a heavy price. In its aftermath, local political leaders resolved to build up national foreign exchange reserves to prevent any possibility of a future repetition of the crisis. Thus with Asia after 1998 and the

---

[13] Bureau of Labor Statistics, Major Sector Productivity, and Costs Index, 1947–2009.

Middle East (after oil prices began to rise around 2002) both accumulating reserves, the annual increase in global foreign exchange reserves from the end of 1998 was 15.0% for the next decade, from $1.60 trillion in 1998 to $6.49 trillion ten years later.[14] Effectively this too was an increase in money supply; it produced global asset price inflation in the short term and in the long term will undoubtedly cause a major outbreak of global consumer price inflation.

The Long-Term Capital Management crisis of 1998 demonstrated how completely the Fed had bought into the new banking paradigm.

But instead of using LTCM's collapse and the consequent losses as a useful wake-up call for the more aggressive denizens of Wall Street, Greenspan organized both a bailout of LTCM and three subsequent interest rate cuts to overcome any trauma the market might be feeling. Since both the US economy and the stock market, far from being traumatized, were at that stage in a phase of manic boom, the interest rate cuts fuelled a still greater orgy of speculation, causing the bull market to reignite and continue for an additional 18 months.

On Wall Street, speculation fed into ever more hyperbolic prices for internet-related tech stocks, with stock valuations becoming far more over-extended than in 1929. There was also an outbreak of witless "day trading" by the over-stimulated general public. Greenspan further fed the mania by buying into the highly dubious "Y2K" hysteria, which postulated that the global banking system's computers would crash since they could not cope with the change to a new Millennium.[15]

Greenspan began tightening cautiously in July 1999; by May 2000 he had tightened the Federal Funds rate three times, raising it by 1.5% to 6.5%. These increases met with considerable criticism after the stock market bubble finally burst in March 2000, particularly from supply-side economists oblivious to the market's obvious excess. Greenspan

---

[14] IMF "Currency Composition of Official Foreign Exchange Reserves (COFER)," 3rd quarter, 2009.

[15] Martin worked as a Pensions Valuation Clerk at the Eagle Star Insurance Company in 1968. Eagle Star's pension clientele at that time included many young scheme members, whose expected retirement dates (on which actuarial calculations were based) were after 2000; the company's primitive computer software coped perfectly well with this.

defended himself later by saying that "live" bubbles were hard to identify and difficult to treat even when identified. As he put it:

> "As events evolved we recognized that, despite our suspicions, it was very difficult to definitively identify a bubble until after the fact – that is, when its bursting confirmed its existence. Moreover, it was far from obvious that bubbles, even if identified early, could be pre-empted short of the central bank inducing a substantial contraction in economic activity – the very outcome we would be seeking to avoid."[16]

Yet Greenspan's first sentence is wrong – he *had* correctly identified the bubble, in December 1996. His second sentence identifies the key problem with giving a central bank a mandate to promote economic stability: the central banker, unless they are a Paul Volcker of exceptional strength of character, never wants to get the blame for a downturn, but would rather wait until it happens independently – more economically painful than if the central bank had forestalled it, but without central bank fingerprints on it. The Greenspan policy in effect boiled down to fuelling the market and hence contributing to its excess, while seeking to avoid the "correction" that that excess would inevitably require. Greenspan had made "irrational exuberance" rational.

The disputed election of George W. Bush as president in November 2000 brought a sharp stock market drop, and by December it was clear that the economy was entering recession.

At the beginning of 2001, Greenspan decided to fight the embryonic recession and the deflationary effect of declining stocks by monetary means (so demonstrating his easy-money policy to be asymmetric, not fully balanced by tight money in a bubble). In a series of cuts stretching over two years he brought the Federal Funds rate down from 6.5% all the way to 1%, a rate that had not been seen since 1961. The result was a bottoming out of the stock market in late 2002, well above the level (relative to nominal GDP) at which it had stood in early 1995; the bubble had been only half-deflated.

---

[16] Opening remarks at the Fed's Jackson Hole symposium, August 30, 2002, p5. St. Louis Fed. Fraser.

It's not entirely clear why Greenspan felt that aggressive monetary loosening was more desirable in this very mild downturn than in previous downturns. While the 9/11 attacks certainly increased uncertainty, fiscal policy was already becoming highly expansionary through the Bush tax cuts, the build-up in military spending, the spending effects of the "No Child Left Behind" education act and the Medicare prescription drugs program passed in December 2003. The effect of the policy, even more than of the 1998–99 easing, was therefore to confirm the existence of a "Greenspan put" (or downside guarantee) in the market, giving speculators an assurance that the Fed would not tighten significantly as the market went into overdrive, but would loosen policy aggressively to fend off any downturn.

Greenspan's eventual successor Ben Bernanke made his first major appearance on the national stage at a National Economists' Club meeting in November 2002, at which he propounded the theory that the US economy was in danger of heading into deflation and that the Fed could rectify this problem by printing money and dropping it from helicopters.[17] The "helicopter money" idea was in fact a parable first used by Milton Friedman many years earlier to illustrate the workings of the Quantity Theory of Money. Bernanke took Friedman's innocent parable and offered it as serious policy; transformed later into "Quantitative Easing," it was to play a very significant (and highly damaging) role when the next big crisis erupted and "Helicopter Ben" was running the Fed.

Bernanke's fears of deflation were far-fetched, however. Even when he made his speech, the latest 12-month rise in the CPI was a robust 2.0%, so it was clear even then that Bernanke's deflation fear was merely another rationale for looser monetary policy. Thereafter, the deflation bogeyman was repeatedly wheeled out whenever necessary to justify loose money; it too was to play a major role when the crisis came. From this point on, Bernanke's influence grew and the Greenspan (and now increasingly Greenspan/Bernanke) put was becoming increasingly turbocharged.

---

[17] Fed Governor Ben S. Bernanke, Remarks to the National Economists Club, November 21, 2002. Martin was present at the Chinese restaurant where this historic event took place (Chinatown Garden, 618 H Street NW, Washington DC, good dim sum), and (inevitably) asked a snotty question.

A second phrase that has governed recent monetary policy is the "Great Moderation," a phrase coined in a 2002 paper by Harvard economist James H. Stock and Princeton's Mark Watson.[18] It was picked up by Bernanke in February 2004,[19] using economic data over the relatively short period since 1990 to "prove" that the volatility of economic growth and inflation had declined. Be that as it may, the Great Moderation phenomenon turned to be as ephemeral as the old Philips curve – yet another example of economists' eternal ability to believe in convenient relationships that they imagine speak to them in the data but that never existed in the first place.

As we now know, the reality was that sloppy monetary policy and the good luck of the Internet's invention and dissemination had combined to produce a lengthy period of moderate growth, modest inflation, and spiraling leverage and asset prices, which was to come to a sticky end in the 2007–09 recession, the least "moderate" since World War II. Nonetheless, while it appeared to exist, it was used by the Fed to justify a monetary policy that was increasingly out of touch with reality and to gloss over the looming excesses of a housing market in which reality played no discernible role at all.

Nor was this hubris confined to the United States. The British were at least as bad. By mid-decade the Chancellor of the Exchequer, Gordon Brown, was boasting that his policies (and those of his overseas colleagues) had effectively ended the vagaries of the business cycle. Cheers, Gordon.

The god of that Copybook Heading took an especially splendid revenge. Brown had long nursed the grievance that he should have been Prime Minister instead of Tony Blair, complaining privately that Blair had cheated him of his birthright. Someone linked to the Prime Minister's office responded by leaking to the press the Prime Minister's opinion that Brown was "psychologically flawed," unsuited to the responsibilities involved, perhaps the only time when either of us has agreed with anything that that unprincipled politician ever said. A very entertaining low-level civil war ensued for years at the very heart of the British government, tearing it apart. For all sorts of good

---

[18] Stock and Watson, 2002.

[19] Remarks by Fed Governor Ben S. Bernanke at the Eastern Economic Association, February 20, 2004.

reasons, the government's popularity ratings collapsed. Just before the crisis erupted, Tony turned around and gave Gordon exactly what he had been hankering for: "You can take over now, Gordon," said Tony in June 2007, as he scarpered off to the lucrative US after-dinner speaking circuit. Brown took over just as the crisis was about to explode.

But we digress.

2002–06 were the years of the great housing bubble and of Wall Street's definitive self-indulgent wallow in the joys of leverage and excess. The Fed kept rates down at 1% for a year, from July 2003 to July 2004, setting off what Steve Hanke memorably described as "the mother of all liquidity cycles and yet another massive demand boom."[20] Interest rates remained below the true inflation rate of around 3% for almost four years, from 2001–05, and the increase from 1% after 2004 was at the glacial pace of 0.25% at each of the eight annual Federal Open Market Committee Meetings. Thus, real interest rates were negative for a sustained period, a classic sign of impending trouble.

Whereas in 1995–2000 Europe and most of Asia had been monetarily cautious, this time the move to monetary profligacy was worldwide. The European Central Bank had come into existence at the beginning of 1999 with a strong hard-money influence from the Deutsche Bundesbank, notably through its German Board member Otmar Issing,[21] but after 2003 its cautious Dutch President Wim Duisenberg was replaced by the more expansionary Frenchman Jean-Claude Trichet. By mid-decade, Euro M3 money supply was also increasing by 10% annually. In Asia, China was enjoying an extraordinary economic boom fuelled by rapid monetary expansion and no-questions-asked lending by its state-owned banks (which got huge new chunks of capital through international share issues in 2006–07). The bubble was now global, though a few countries, notably Germany and Japan, did not fully share in it and the full glory of housing mania was confined to a few countries, notably the US, Britain, Spain, and Ireland.

Greenspan retired at the end of January 2006 after an 18½-year term. The housing market was still fully inflated and Greenspan left office to almost universal acclaim. The obvious successor – given his

---

[20] Hanke, 2008.
[21] Issing, 2008.

soft-money proclivities and the George W. Bush White House's pen-chant for the economic soft option – was Bernanke.

Loose monetary policy after 1995 combined with modern financial theories that had taken over Wall Street since the 1970s to revolutionize Wall Street's operations and the financial services business in general.

There is no question, first, that loose money and low interest rates increased Wall Street's leverage. Both absolute levels of interest rates and spreads for risk declined to record low levels, so it became espe-cially profitable to borrow at prevailing rates, below zero in real terms, and invest in higher-yielding assets. In particular, leveraging very heav-ily and investing in assets with only a modest perceived degree of risk (such as mortgage-backed securities) was thought to give potential returns that were both higher than could be achieved through con-ventional stock investing, and (supposedly) "uncorrelated" with the stock market. In 2002–06, Wall Street houses became laboratories for this thesis, which gave theoretical justification for levels of leverage that in previous decades would have been thought (rightly) as highly irresponsible.

Effective or true leverage was also much greater than the (itself very high) leverage reflected in balance sheets, because of the miracles of securitization and other forms of hidden risk-taking.

As well as encouraging leverage, sloppy monetary policy encour-aged excess risk-taking and raw speculation. It made it much easier to raise money, as pools of investment capital were seeking new higher-return uses, the ever-treacherous search for higher yield. By doing so, it also brought pressure on established investment managers from new entrants to the market. In 1995–99 conventional investment funds did well and, indeed, the most speculative flourished most. Then reality temporarily reasserted itself after 2000 when the stock market declined and the dotcom bubble burst.

The Fed then started throwing gasoline on the fire again: con-ventional investment funds fell out of favor and hedge funds, charging much higher fees and investing in ever more exotic securitization in-struments (assisted by greater leverage) became increasingly popular. Private equity also was able to raise large amounts of money, as investors supposed that through "financial engineering" (more leverage) compa-nies that had been lackluster in public form could be transformed into high-return investments. Most of these exotic investment alternatives achieved little for investors, but were sources of exorbitantly high fees for the managers of hedge and equity funds.

In the process, most investors forgot what leverage really entailed: leverage magnifies the gains on the upside, but also magnifies losses on the downside. Leverage only "works" when the market is going up. The search for higher returns using greater leverage eventually boils down to more sheep for the slaughter. The perils of leverage are another one of those inconvenient Copybook Headings, and its god is still gorging himself on the blood of his victims. When will investors realize that leverage is not a free lunch?

A further consequence of low interest rates and the asset price bubble was the decline and eventual disappearance of the US savings rate. Naturally, with savings disappearing and the government running budget deficits, the US began to run increasingly unsustainable balance of payments deficits. In the late 1990s, while the government still ran surpluses and the dollar was strong, these were justified by the supposition that returns in the high-tech US were better than elsewhere. After 2000, that hypothesis became unsustainable and it became increasingly clear that the US as a country was eating the seed corn that would sustain its own future growth. The ephemeral prosperity of the 2000s was sustained only by increasingly heavy borrowing, the costs of which were bearable while interest rates remained artificially low, but would increase unsustainably once rates were forced to rise. Meanwhile, the global excess of capital made it almost as cheap to finance investment in the most exotic emerging market as in the United States.

Coming out of the downturn, it seems likely that the US will in the long run no longer be a particularly wealthy country. The increased ease of international communications was in any case likely to reduce somewhat the relative wage levels of advanced economies, by making outsourcing much cheaper and easier. The US no longer has the advantage of possessing a large fraction of the world's capital pool. As capital costs finally increase again, it will discover the costs of this decline, which will be measured in lower real wages for its inhabitants as living standards between the West and Asia slowly level out: there is no longer any particular reason for westerners to expect more than modestly higher living standards than their counterparts in mainland Asia.

The loose monetary policy of the post-1995 period has been highly enjoyable for Wall Street, combined as it has been with the changes wrought by Modern Finance. It seems likely to have imposed very heavy long-term costs on the rest of the US population, however. For emerging markets, particularly China and India, loose US monetary policy greatly sped their emergence to economic power and it remains to be seen whether the political backlash from their exceptionally rapid emergence will not impose further costs on the greatly weakened Western powers. The record of history suggests that it will: China and India too will want their place in the sun.

12

Government Meddling in the Financial System

One of the recurrent themes in this book is that there are certain Copybook Headings, eternal verities that we often reject and whose gods then come back to haunt us for having disbelieved in them. But these also have their ugly cousins, self-evident "truths" that we readily believe but that are not true. These false beliefs have demons rather than gods that guide us into foolish actions and then come back to punish us for our foolishness in having believed in them. Nowhere are these dangers more beguiling or more damaging than in the area of economic policy and government intervention. All too often, state intervention into the economy and regulation of its workings is predicated on falsehoods masquerading as self-evident truths and the results are disastrous.

★★★

This is especially so in the financial system: so much so, in fact, that this is the defining theme of the history of government intervention in this sector. Naturally, the demons of error were given a huge boost by the Great Depression, a truly frightening economic event, particularly in the United States, that was completely misunderstood at the time, to such an extent that full elucidation of the policy errors and adverse conditions that caused it took over half a century. To accuse US policymakers of the 1930s, both in the Hoover and Roosevelt administrations, of economic illiteracy is fair, if only because their opposite numbers in Britain avoided most of their errors. However it has to be said in mitigation that the situation with which they were working was truly extreme, so it is not surprising that a number of error-demons took control of their attempts to change the US economic system.

The first such error, instituted with the Banking Act of 1933, was that of deposit insurance. For the demon, this is beneficial, even necessary. The argument for deposit insurance is seductively simple: banks operate on a fractional reserve, issuing deposits that greatly exceed both their reserves and their capital; consequently, they are always vulnerable to a run by depositors, which would drive them out of business. Thus fractional reserve banks are inherently unstable. Fortunately, this problem can be solved by reassuring depositors that their money is safe, and this is exactly what deposit insurance does.

This argument had won almost universal acceptance in the United States by the 1960s, and was accepted by almost all free market economists as well as those more disposed to government intervention. For instance, in their landmark *Monetary History of the United States* in 1963, Friedman and Schwartz noted how the numbers of bank failures in the 1930s fell from an average of 1,500 in 1930–32 and 4,000 in 1933 to a handful in 1934. They attributed this to the introduction of Federal deposit insurance in 1934: it was, they said, one of the few beneficial reforms of the 1930s.

This belief ruled unchallenged until a small group of radical economists began to dispute it in the early 1980s.[1] Kevin first heard of this when he was a junior policy analyst at the Ontario Economic Council in Toronto. The OEC was holding a conference on financial reform and the star speaker, Ed Kane from Ohio State University, stunned everyone with a brilliant speech in which he turned the conventional wisdom about deposit insurance on its head; deposit insurance was actually *very bad* for the banking system. Kevin's initial reaction was

---

[1] See, e.g,. Kane, 1985 or Kaufman, 1988.

that Kane must be mad, but he was soon won over once he digested what Kane was saying.[2]

A new and very different picture now came to emerge. Contrary to what most people had assumed, banking in the United States had been highly stable in the decades before deposit insurance. Of course, depositors were concerned about their safety, but this made them cautious in whom they banked with. They demanded reassurance from their banks, and the banks gave it to them. Pressure from depositors forced the banks to be conservative, to lend carefully, to keep their leverage ratios low, and to disclose their broad positions. The bankers themselves were conservative even in their dress, but this was itself reassuring, and the solid architecture of the banks' offices reinforced the notion that they were pillars of the community with solid roots in it. The key to banking was maintaining the confidence of depositors and not taking that confidence for granted.

Before deposit insurance, a bank that took too many risks would eventually undo itself. It would do well for a while, increasing market share and generating better shareholder returns than the fuddy-duddy banks, which would feel the pressure. However, come the inevitable downturn, the cowboy bank would experience heavy losses on its questionable lending, liquidity would tighten, and a point would come where the frightened depositors would run for their money: the cowboy would be literally run out of business. These occasional crises were unpleasant, but good for the long-term health and even stability of the system: the runs would expel the cowboys from the system and give a salutary reminder to those who survived. The system itself was

---

[2] At the same time as Kane and his colleagues were alerting us to the dangers of deposit insurance, other financial economists were building models to explain why we still needed it. The seminal paper was "Bank Runs, Deposit Insurance, and Liquidity" by Douglas W. Diamond and Philip H. Dybvig, published in the *Journal of Political Economy* in 1983, which built a model purporting to show how deposit insurance could solve the inherent instability of banking. The Diamond-Dybvig model was however irrelevant to real-world banking – the banks in their model have no equity capital (!) and the 'need' for deposit insurance disappears when you introduce such capital. The Diamond-Dybvig model is also inconsistent in that the 'solution' of deposit insurance is not feasible in the model environment that supposedly justifies it! Yet articles on deposit insurance still regularly cite Diamond and Dybvig as showing why we need deposit insurance, oblivious to the study's flaws. See Dowd, 1992 or 1996.

rarely seriously at threat, because the depositors would redeposit their funds with the safe banks. There would typically be a flight to quality, a transferring of funds within the system, rather than a run on or threat to the system as a whole. Thus, it was the threat of a run that kept the bankers in line.

Once you introduce deposit insurance the situation changes profoundly. Deposit insurance allows the bankers to take their depositors' confidence for granted. This takes the pressure off the bankers, who can now safely increase both their lending risks and their leverage ratios, thereby increasing returns to their shareholders (or, in modern Wall Street, to themselves). For their part, the depositors are no longer concerned with the risks their banks are taking, but only with the rates they get on their deposits. Consequently, deposit insurance subsidizes risk-taking, so leading to excess risk-taking with the deposit insurance agency and, ultimately, the taxpayer, picking up the tab.

Nor does the damage end there. With deposit insurance, there is no longer any run to fear and even the most insolvent banks following the most unsound "shoot to the moon" investments can now remain in business indefinitely, attracting more funds and staying in business by merely raising deposit interest rates. The process of competition then becomes utterly subverted: instead of allowing the conservative banks to drive out the cowboys, even if it takes a little time, the process of competition now rewards the cowboys and penalizes the good banks. It therefore pays to become a cowboy and, eventually, all banks do.

This is more or less what happened to US banks between the 1930s and 1980s. Bank leverage ratios rose sharply after deposit insurance was introduced and, over time, banks' risk-taking increased. Perhaps the most telling example was in Texas in the late 1980s: every single bank was insolvent, but they were kept alive by brokered deposits that by this point were paying hundreds of basis points above the national average. All the banks had become zombies and without the threat of runs from worried depositors, there was no longer any market mechanism to put them out of business. The only way to get rid of them was then for the regulators to close them down, but there were too many of them and the regulators didn't have the staff. As Gerald O'Driscoll, then a Vice President at the Dallas Fed, told Kevin at the time: the Dallas Fed only had the resources for two half-day site visits a year, on average. If you couldn't fool the visitors for two afternoons a year, then you really did deserve to be put out of business.

It turned out that these damaging effects had been anticipated: the American Bankers Association had bitterly opposed the introduction of deposit insurance in the 1930s for exactly these reasons. But decades later, American bankers had become an altogether flashier lot, much more prone to risk-taking and hooked on the artificial support of deposit insurance: deposit insurance had become a crutch they could not live without.

Nor was this the country's first experience with deposit insurance. It had been tried out in Texas in the 1920s and earlier still in some of the northern states in the early nineteenth centuries. In each case, the results were disastrous, leading to increased bank risk taking and eventually the failures not only of the banks concerned but also of the state deposit insurance agencies that had subsidized their gambling. To quote one assessment of the Texas experience:

> "The plan made too many banks and too few bankers. All kinds of incapable people tried to start a bank under the protection of the fund. The system gave a false sense of security – people looked to the fund for protection and paid no attention to the soundness of the banks themselves, nor to the ability of the managers. Prosecution of bank wreckers and crooks was made impossible. The depositors got their money from the fund, so they were not particularly interested in prosecuting the unscrupulous or incompetent men who caused the banks to fail. Such an unsound system of banking weakened the financial structure of the entire state."[3]

So the pattern was established even then. United States policymakers had failed to learn from their own experience, but no one else was learning either, as one country after another set up deposit insurance schemes of their own: India in 1962, Canada in 1967, the UK in 1983, the EU generally in 1994, and Japan in 1996 (just in time!).

You can nevertheless see why deposit insurance appeared attractive in 1933 – one third of the banks in the United States had just failed,

---

[3] Harr and Harris, 1936, p. 141.

and it was only thirty years later that the role of the Fed in causing their failure came to be understood. The introduction of the Fed's unaccountable and error-prone bureaucracy to the US financial system had itself caused the disaster it was meant to avert, and this in turn helped pave the way for deposit insurance. However, where deposit insurance has to be lived with, it should be much more modest in amount than the $100,000 established in 1982, let alone the $250,000 imposed temporarily in 2008, and should provide cover for 80% or 90% rather than 100% of the deposits insured.[4] By limiting the scope of deposit insurance, at least some of the benefits of an insurance-free regime would be retained.

The Europeans were particularly receptive to deposit insurance, dovetailing as it did with the European penchant for paternalism: policies that ostensibly protect the little people, but often end up fleecing them, so that they pay double in their other capacity as taxpayer. By the late 1980s, Kevin, by then back in the UK, was on a hiding to nothing lecturing on the evils of deposit insurance. "You are surely not promoting the dreadful American line that banks should be allowed to *fail*, old boy?" as a crusty old banking professor rebuked him after one seminar. But that was *exactly* what he was saying, not that it made the slightest difference.

★★★

Another demon that has damaged the global financial system is the principle of investor protection, or, more precisely, the establishment of regulatory systems to provide such protection. This, together with buyer remorse from those who had seen their 1929 stock values reduced by nine tenths, led to the establishment of the US Securities and Exchange Commission in 1934 and to comparable bodies in other countries.

---

[4] Martin as US Treasury Advisor was involved in the introduction of deposit insurance to Croatia in the 1990s. Martin and the very able Adolf Matejka of the Croatian National Bank wanted to introduce a system with 90% coverage and a maximum of only 100,000 kuna (then $15,000.) We took the view that the local mafia was quite capable of buying one of the decrepit local small banks, injecting deposits into it, lending the money to their shadowy empire where it was lost forever and then claiming it back from the insurance fund. Alas, we won only a partial victory; the Croatian deposit insurance maximum is only 100,000 kuna, but with 100% coverage.

At first, the principle of investor protection seems self-evident. After all, who doesn't want investors to be protected? But this misses the point, which is not *whether* investors should be protected, but *how*.

At its root, the problem with investor protection is the same as the problem with deposit insurance. In both cases, the responsibility for protecting the individual involved, be it the depositor or the investor, was taken away from the person best placed to bear it: the individual concerned.

Traditionally, investors knew that there were a lot of potential conmen around and their money was at risk. So you had to be careful: you didn't deal with people whom you didn't trust and you didn't trust anyone who just came in off the street. Investment firms understood this, and had to provide clients with credible reassurance. Firms did so by building up good reputations and putting down roots in the community – they built up their "name" and protected it jealously – and the investor would rely on that. A firm that lost its name, for example, through a scandal, was unlikely to retain the business to survive. Everyone also knew that if you cut corners and invested with the cheaper outfit that just opened down the road, then you had only yourself to blame if you woke up one morning to find that it had disappeared overnight with your money. Of course, such things did happen now and then, but you were brought up to know better: it was no one else's responsibility but yours to look after your money. The system worked well and the occasional scandal merely reinforced the need for investors to take responsibility for themselves.

But once the SEC was established, firms could now argue that they were safe to do business with because the SEC had licensed them and because SEC rules gave the investor the protection they had hitherto lacked: the SEC license became a substitute for a good "name." Unfortunately, it was a poor substitute and provided little assurance of good service. Furthermore, in licensing firms, the SEC had now taken implicit responsibility for ensuring that firms were "fit" to operate. The investor was no longer responsible in the way he had been before, and firms no longer faced the same market pressure to look after the investor in order to protect their "names." Thus, the SEC undermined the mechanism that had made the old system work and standards deteriorated. As Jonathan R. Macey put it, we moved from a reputational paradigm to a parasitic one, in which investors rely on other people for their protection.[5]

The SEC was also prone, like any other government agency, to a tendency to expand both its size and its remit. Initially, it was not taken entirely seriously by the Roosevelt administration, which appointed the well-known bootlegger and insider trader Joseph P. Kennedy to head it. However under its second Chairman, the activist future Supreme Court justice William O. Douglas, it expanded its remit beyond its initial fairly narrow focus on investor protection. It then grew to an estimated 3,800 in 2010:

- It took a more holistic approach to the stock market, increasingly seeing itself as having a mandate to maintain market confidence, even if that confidence had a false foundation. This made it increasingly loath to take actions that might be seen as potentially damaging market confidence.
- The SEC started to regulate the ratings agencies. In 1973 the SEC revised capital rules for broker-dealers, allowing for markdowns to be based on credit ratings provided by ratings agencies. Later, the SEC and bank regulators were to extend the practice of outsourcing their supervision of credit risk to the ratings agencies under the Basel capital regulatory system, of which more below. The SEC was now concerned about the quality of those ratings, so it began to regulate the rating agencies themselves, requiring that they conform to the standards of Nationally Recognized Statistical Ratings Agencies. This however created an entrenched oligopoly in the ratings industry, stifling innovation and, by creating a captive market, inadvertently helping to promote the very deterioration in ratings quality that had prompted them to regulate the ratings agencies in the first place![6]

Especially after the 2000 dotcom bust the SEC increasingly took on responsibility for the prudential supervision of the entire operations of

---

[5] Macey, 2008. Note that this same argument also affects the quality of ratings and audits as well: the problem is systemic.
[6] Calabria, 2009, p. 2.

the securities firms, including not just small investment firms but the big investment banks and their holding companies. This took place in the context of the run up to Basel II and the international "harmonization" of regulatory standards across investment firms, banks and insurance companies. Notoriously, however, it failed to regulate their leverage properly, freeing investment banks in 2004 from restrictions that had kept at least some feeble rein upon their reckless expansion.

A second, related, objective of the SEC regime was to help investors by promoting transparency. As the Securities Bill that would create the SEC was being considered by Congress, President Roosevelt had taken to heart the admirable words of the eminent jurist Louis Brandeis: "Sunlight is said to be the best of disinfectants. Electric lights the most efficient policeman."[7] The proposed Act would require companies to file detailed accounts of their finances and activities, and bankers would have to report fees and commissions.

Reporting requirements have increased enormously since then, with the computer systems audit requirement mandated by Section 404 of the 2002 Sarbanes-Oxley Act being especially onerous. In the ten years to 2005 alone, the SEC issued more than 30 major rules requiring new disclosure protocols, and vast amounts of data poured in. The SEC's public database, Edgar, now catalogs some 15 million pages of text, a near-sixfold increase in just ten years. To quote one dismayed commentator:

> "... the volume of data obscures more than it reveals; financial reporting has become so transparent as to be invisible. Answering what should be simple questions – how secure is my cash account? How much of my bank's debt is tied up in risky debt obligations? – often seems to require a legal degree, as well as countless hours to dig through thousands of documents. Undoubtedly, the warning signs of our current crisis – and the next one! – lie somewhere in all those filings, but good luck finding them."[8]

---

[7] Quoted in Roth, 2009.
[8] Op. cit.

So vast is this deluge of data that even the regulators can't keep up with it. A Senate study of 2002 revealed that SEC officials had managed to review fully only 16% of the 15,000 annual company reports submitted in the previous fiscal year, and they hadn't reviewed Enron in a decade. SEC officials were overworked, underpaid and undermanned, and were hopelessly unable to keep up with the pace of innovation. By the time the SEC had a grip on a new product class, others of even more devilish complexity had already been created; Wall Street was always at least one step ahead of it.

Every now and then the SEC struck a modest blow for small investors, such as 2000's Regulation FD, which prevented companies from releasing corporate insider information only to Wall Street and the institutions. However, in general, regulatory capture was close to total – the SEC has for example made no attempt whatever to control Wall Street's privileged access to insider trading-flow information, from which through "fast trading" it makes tens of billions annually.

But without doubt, the SEC's finest moment was Madoff, a Ponzi scheme of unprecedented size that operated for many years right under their noses without them noticing. The good citizen Harry Markopolos warned them repeatedly over a nine year period. To the extent they bothered to look into Markopolos's claims at all, even though they were not that difficult to verify, they still didn't spot any problem. Indeed the scheme might still be going strong had Madoff's own sons not done the decent thing and turned him in themselves.

It is trite and no doubt true to blame these failures, especially the Madoff case, on incompetence. No doubt, too, SEC staff were overwhelmed by the work that their own rule books created for them. But the root problems go much deeper. Part of it is politics: any challenge to serious corporate malfeasance could backlash, bringing uncomfortable political pressure or a disturbance to the market for which the SEC would get the blame. Instead, as the recent crisis showed, it was easier for the agency to focus its energies on softer targets, such as thinly capitalized short selling speculators, who were less able to fight back.

Most important of all, the SEC, like any other regulatory system, was captured by the very people it was meant to regulate – in effect, outgunned – and manipulated to serve their ends. This capture manifested itself in a number of ways:

- Wall Street had powerful political friends who could (and often did) bring pressure to bear to achieve self-serving changes in policies and rules, and intimidate individual officials who stood in their way.
- The huge salary differential between Wall Street and the regulators meant that Wall Street generally got the best talent, and could hold carrots in front of the regulators themselves. Regulators were often reluctant to challenge the industry for fear of jeopardizing their future chances of lucrative jobs, and a steady stream of gamekeepers turned poachers gave the industry inside information about the regulatory system and knowledge of how best to game it. Conversely the SEC regulatory apparatus was always losing staff, sometimes leaving key positions unfilled for long periods.
- The SEC, like regulators elsewhere, lacked the financial resources of the Wall Street behemoths who were able to hire better lawyers and, more often than not, to get their way merely by threatening legal firepower that the regulators could not easily match.
- Though the regulators had some very good people, they lacked the technical resources such as top notch legal and quants teams available to the big financial institutions. This gave Wall Street the edge in the technical discussions involving the precise framing of rules and calibration of models.

The bottom line was that instead of protecting the investor, the SEC ended up primarily protecting the big firms that it was designed to protect the investor *against*: so much for investor protection.

★★★

A third demon that has intensified the moral hazards of Modern Finance was the de-stigmatization of bankruptcy, carried out by the Bankruptcy Reform Act of 1978. This greatly increased the items that could be excluded from personal bankruptcy, including notoriously McMansions, and put strict limitations on the time a personal bankruptcy remained on the record. This, together with the invention of the unsolicited credit card offer by Citicorp's John Reed in 1978 (a hugely unsuccessful effort initially), made excessive borrowing an American sport, to the great detriment of the US savings rate, ethical standards, and consumer welfare in general. (Credit card debt, like casinos, tobacco, and chocolate cake, is a product that the weaker brethren consume too much of for their own good.) The result was a tsunami of additional consumer bankruptcies, from the then alarming average of 200,000 per annum in the 1960s to a peak of 2.05 million in 2005. The Bankruptcy Abuse Prevention and Consumer Protection Act of 2005, passed at the request of the credit card industry, tightened bankruptcy conditions considerably – just in time for the biggest recession since World War II.

On the corporate side, the 1978 Act had a similar effect, with even more damaging results. Whereas corporate bankruptcy had previously been considerably stigmatized and controlled primarily by creditors, under the 1978 Act's Chapter 11, control passed largely to the management who had driven the company into the ditch. As a result, asset-heavy companies such as airlines found it attractive to engage in repeated bankruptcies, the same executives remaining in control throughout. One particularly battle-hardened case, Frank Lorenzo, managed to go through three separate bankruptcies in twelve years – Continental Airlines in 1983, Eastern Airlines in 1990, and Continental again in December 1990. As of 2006, more than 60% of US airline capacity was controlled by companies in bankruptcy.

With bankruptcy so painless, and companies controlled primarily by management rather than their shareholders, looting of corporate assets became too easy. Not only was there limited liability for all those involved in controlling the companies, but their lavish remuneration packages continued through bankruptcy filings as if nothing had occurred. Hence the atmosphere of "heads I win, tails you lose" became prevalent. With management further "incentivized" by generous stock option packages, their motivations became those of a Wall Street trader, seeking short term "pop" in the share price without regard to the long-term consequences to the organization, its business, or its employees.

★★★

Moving over the Atlantic, we come to the British experiments in financial regulation. These derived from a false-idea demon of overpowering strength, first spotted in the 1970s, that continues to wrack the British financial system: the idea that a system of state regulation and equal access for foreign behemoths would in some mysterious way work better than the self-regulated City of London that had operated successfully for nearly 300 years.

For many years, as we described in Chapter 2, the British financial regulatory system consisted of a set of informal cartels such as the Accepting Houses Committee. The regulatory process, such as it was, was one of negotiation and compromise between the supervisory bodies and the firms they supervised. However, the principal enforcer of good behavior was not the regulators, who focused on only the worst abusers, but the cartels themselves, which ensured that "fringe" operators were kept out, left to compete for scraps of business, and avoided by all careful market participants.

Inevitably, in the atmosphere of meddling that began in the 1970s and persisted through the Thatcher years, as ministers who failed to understand the City were guided by interventionist civil servants, some sensitive scandals were manipulated to provoke a major outcry, leading to the predictable criticisms that the regulatory system wasn't working and calls for something to be done. The Thatcher government would have preferred to do nothing, but it was getting a lot of political flak for being soft on its "friends" in the City and was certain to get more when the next institution failed. Most notable amongst these was the failure in 1981 of the minor investment management firm Norton Warburg, with losses of a mere £12 million, which was inflated in the media to a public that did not know the difference between the spivvy fringe operator Norton Warburg and the premier merchant bank S.G. Warburg. [9]

The Government in the time-honored way commissioned a report, asking the distinguished company lawyer, Professor L.C.B. ("Jim") Gower, to review the existing framework of statutory protection for small investors and recommend how that protection might be improved. Gower was conscientious and engagingly frank, but he was a lawyer's lawyer who saw the problem of investor protection in narrowly legal terms and had no interest in the economics of regulation or even the costs involved. He appears not to have understood the virtues of the traditional City, which could have been explained to him by (for example) the 1960s Bank of England Governor and former Barings Chairman Lord Cromer, then still very much with us.

---

[9] Apparently that ignorance extended to the Bank of England, which had sacked some employees but advised them to invest their redundancy money with Norton Warburg.

Gower completed his report in October 1983 and a long and difficult series of debates ensued. Special interest groups – particularly within the industry – immediately pounced on Gower to argue for all manner of self-serving changes. The "consultation exercise" that followed involved a vast amount of behind-the-scenes negotiation and horse-trading, and the eventual upshot was the Financial Services Bill presented to Parliament in late 1985. The Bill then went through a particularly tortuous process of Parliamentary scrutiny as the various interest groups continued to fight over it, and more than a thousand amendments were tabled to it – a Parliamentary record. Not surprisingly, debates were very wearing and participants often lost all perspective: at one point, the House of Lords was debating whether the Act was going to catch the chap who had a chat to another chap at the golf club and said "I've got some promising Far Eastern Units;"[10] at another point, Parliament debated whether the Act should apply to collectible stamps and coins. But the Bill eventually emerged in much-modified form as the Financial Services Act – a kind of financial Frankenstein's monster, and a very overweight one at that – receiving Royal Assent in November 1986.

The new Act set up a highly convoluted regime with, on paper, iron-clad protection for investors. There were strict codes of conduct on the industry, including a "best advice" requirement, an extension of common-law fiduciary duties, breach of which was a criminal offence; the Act also provided for elaborate and detailed paperwork to show that sellers were aware of their customers' needs, including lengthy FactFinds that detailed both the circumstances of the customer and the advice supposedly given.

This Act was passed in the context of the other changes of the time, most notably, the creation of the personal pension scheme in 1988, which encouraged people to start their own pension schemes. This scheme was a good idea in principle, but in practice it opened up a new and vast (not to mention, tax-subsidized) market and the industry lost little time taking advantage of it. With potentially enormous profits, and commissions at stake, the less savory elements in the industry mounted a huge sales drive and, over the next seven years, persuaded

---

[10] These and other quotes on the Financial Services Act fiasco are taken from Dowd and Hinchliffe, 2000, which also discusses this story in much more detail.

some eight million people to take out personal pensions, while many millions of others, sometimes the same people, were persuaded to take out endowment mortgages and various insurance policies.

The atmosphere in some firms "could best be best described as Wild West mixed with eastern bazaar." Bad practice abounded, much of it illegal: many firms operated with breathtaking disregard for ethical or even legal considerations, telling their staff to focus on the sales and not worry about the paperwork. Stories abounded of salespeople misrepresenting the options put to clients, doctoring paperwork to misrepresent their discussions with clients, and blatantly ignoring the legal requirement to provide "best advice."[11] Compliance with regulatory requirements was a joke and the regulatory response was minimal. One industry executive admitted afterwards:

> "I'd never seen so many sleazy backrooms in my life – it was grievous. I remember one guy, saying to me a few months before the FSA was due to come into force. 'What Financial Services Act?' and so I briefly explained to him about the Act and about compliance. He said, 'Oh yes. *You* can do all that stuff. I can tell you that once my salesmen are in the front room with the punter, they will say anything to get them to sign. And it doesn't matter what the law says!' This attitude was … not unusual."

Not surprisingly, the industry was soon facing some well-deserved very bad publicity. As the *Economist* observed in December 1993, "The British have come to regard life-insurance salesmen with the deepest disdain. They may be too generous …"[12]

The salespeople were easy to blame and richly deserved it, but they operated with the connivance of the senior management. As one

---

[11] Other practices included hiring new sales staff, encouraging them to sign up their family and friends and then firing them when the contracts were in. Then there was the "television policy," by which salespeople would target the elderly, get them to cash in existing policies to buy a new TV, and then get them to sign a new policy for which they would earn a nice commission. Such practices were not so much merely bad as reprehensible.

[12] *The Economist*, "Disillusioned with life: Mis-selling British pensions," December 1993.

industry bigwig admitted privately to a colleague of Kevin's, who made
a point of interviewing boozed-up executives after their liquid Friday
lunches, armed with a tape recorder:

> "Everybody knew what was going on in the late 1980s. I came
> across it myself. We all knew that life assurance salesmen were
> bloody awful people, who were to be avoided at all costs."

Another cheerfully told Kevin's friend:

> "I've got at least a meter and a half of files in my office on
> pensions mis-selling … The industry always had a crap
> reputation; now it's just crappier than it was… Have you seen
> *Groundhog Day?*"

The bottom line was that management knew what was happening, but
did not ask; in any case, they didn't give a damn and weren't scared of
the regulators either.

The new regulatory system established by the Financial Services Act
was a dismal failure. It was established to provide very high standards of
protection and competence for small investors with immaculate, albeit
expensive, guarantees for the people it was meant to protect. But this
cast iron "protection" turned out to be worthless, in effect, a license for
the industry to exploit the public with impunity, and the list of victims
ran into many millions, many of whom were never compensated. All
this while the government and regulators stood by and wrung their
hands.

★★★

Shortly after it came to power in May 1997, the new Labour government of Tony Blair replaced the byzantine UK financial regulatory
structure with the big monolithic regulatory body, the new Financial
Services Authority (FSA), for which his party had always been hankering. This took place in the context of a re-division of responsibility and
the establishment of a new tripartite system, with responsibility divided
between the Bank of England, the Treasury, and the new FSA. Britain
now had a nicely coordinated system with each of these three parties
assigned its own purpose role, working together in perfect harmony

with each other. Or so we were told: the author of the new system, the new Chancellor of the Exchequer, Gordon Brown, rarely missed an opportunity to crow about the system *he* had created.

As one insider later acknowledged privately, however: "Basically, the tripartite banking supervisory model doesn't work – each party has a pathological loathing of the others and ... everyone knows this."

Beneath the glossy facade of a modern financial regulator, the FSA was fur coat and no knickers. It had got off to a bad start when the Bank of England kept most of the better people. Funded by a levy on the industry, it had limited resources, high turnover and low morale. The main concerns of individual officials were petty office politics, their own career advancement, and, most of all, the mouthwatering prospect of jobs in the City, when they could cash in on their FSA experience. Everyone knew that the FSA was a springboard to the City: you got in, got some experience, made useful contacts and moved on. There was no sense of a shared commitment to their collective task.

One of its principal activities – and one at which the FSA excelled – was the production of rulebooks, long and impenetrable rulebooks that no one could digest. One of the few people with the intestinal fortitude to try was the Institute of Economic Affairs' Philip Booth, and even he only got so far. "Its not easy to navigate the FSA's rulebook," he wrote with measured understatement, but the main handbook for banks contains ten sections, and he then explains how one could drill down to get relevant information giving the following example:

> "The section entitled 'Prudential standards' is divided into eleven subsections. The subsection 'Prudential sourcebook for banks, building societies and investment firms' is made up of fourteen sub-subsections. The sub-subsection 'Market risk' is divided up into eleven sub-sub-subsections. The sub-sub-subsection 'Interest rate PRA' had 66 paragraphs. This is known as 'principles-based regulation by the FSA.' As far as I could see, based on this example, there could be over 1,100,000 paragraphs: it is not feasible to count all the paragraphs and nor is it possible to download the whole book. Remarkably, I could find nothing on liquidity risk, the main failing of Northern Rock, though I am sure it must be addressed somewhere."[13]

---

[13] Booth, 2009, pp. 159–160.

We suppose we can be thankful that FSA regulators had, as they interminably claimed, avoided the mindlessly complicated rule-based regulations of their SEC counterparts!

When it audited the FSA in 2006, the UK National Audit Office praised the FSA as "a well-established regulator with an impressive set of processes and structures to help tackle high-risk organizations and markets." Then along came Northern Rock.

This was an institution that had grown very rapidly over a few years (a traditional red flag), one that had an extreme business model (another red flag!) and that relied more heavily than any other major UK bank on access to wholesale funding and securitization for its financing (yet another red flag: anyone remember Overend & Gurney?).

How did the FSA handle Northern Rock? For much of the period, it had the bank supervised by *insurance* regulators (huh?) who knew little about how a mortgage bank operated: apparently the FSA wanted to give them some work experience on a safe bank where nothing much could go wrong. Only eight supervisory meetings were held between 2005 and August 9, 2007, and most of those involved low-level FSA staff. Of these meetings, five were held over just one day and two were by telephone; then, when the internal auditors looked for a paper trail, it turned out that the supervisors hadn't even taken notes.

From February 2007, Northern Rock's share price started to deteriorate (red flag #4) and, as the year progressed, concerns about mortgage defaults started to rise (possible red flag #5?). Did it occur to the FSA that Northern Rock might be in any danger or that it might be a good idea for the FSA to suggest that the bank stress-test its liquidity exposure?

Not at all. Instead the FSA's response was to approve a dividend payment and fast-track the approval process for its models. Northern Rock then hit the rocks shortly afterwards and all hell broke loose.

The FSA's own (and, to be fair, refreshingly honest) internal investigation published in March 2008 reads like a farce, and the subsequent report into the fiasco by the Treasury Select Committee was scathing in its criticism of the FSA's handling of the case – "asleep at the wheel" being the gist of it. The FSA was guilty of "a systematic failure of duty," said the chairman, MP John McFall.

The FSA's chief executive Hector Sants gave an apology of sorts: "We're sorry that our supervision didn't achieve all it could have done," he said. Damned right it didn't.

In the meantime, there was some reshuffling at the FSA: a few heads rolled, others moved on, and by the end of the year the FSA had a new chairman, Lord Turner of Ecchinswell, an experienced City insider. Turner acknowledged the need for a major overhaul, and was soon reassuring the public that FSA would hire better regulators in future. He also argued that their pay should be increased – this did not go down well in the media, but we can see his point: better pay might attract better people – and that the agency should get a major increase in staff.

Needless to say, this latter argument did not go down well at all, and on this issue we side with the critics. The FSA had already almost doubled its staff in the previous ten years. And what did they do? They busied themselves with writing rulebooks and ticking boxes, setting up websites advising us how to plan for our funerals, warning us not to borrow too much, and sundry other activities, some worthy enough, others completely useless. It also sent out the occasional warning to the industry to behave itself, to which the industry responded like naughty schoolboys, politely listening to Headmaster while knowing that they still hadn't been found out. However, it completely missed the impending disaster that it was there to protect us against. The FSA's main problem was not so much lack of resources, but its failure to do the right things with the resources it already had. You could double the agency's staff, and then double it again and again, and we still would be no safer than we were.

As for the industry, Lord Turner was soon warning them to "be afraid, be very afraid" of the FSA in future. Sorry my Lord, but you'll have to do better than that: huff and puff didn't work before, and isn't likely to work in the future either.

With all due respect, we would suggest that a more promising approach would be to go after those most responsible and obtain some serious criminal convictions: only the prospect of personal bankruptcy and jail time will frighten these people. But it's probably best for the FSA to give itself a good housecleaning first.

Yet the most astonishing after-effects of the crisis were still to come out. Having just presided over the collapse of much of the UK financial system, in April 2009 the FSA paid *bonuses* to most of its staff, with one top "performer" getting £90,000. Turner defended the payments, saying with an apparently straight face that otherwise the FSA would struggle to attract the best people. In any case, an FSA whistleblower soon revealed that "The targets were not exactly challenging. You had to be incompetent not to get an award." This good citizen also revealed something truly egregious, that banks had fed the FSA information on which to allocate the bonus payments: thus, the FSA was *incentivizing* its staff to curry favor with the institutions they were meant to scrutinize. "You give us a hard time, sonny boy," you can imagine the banker hinting to the young man from the FSA, "and I will make sure you don't get your pathetic little bonus."

The Liberal Democrat frontbench MP Don Foster spoke for many when he found it "utterly bizarre that the FSA is actually paying anyone bonuses this year." We agree, but would go further. In the days of the old Roman republic, an army that had disgraced itself in battle was literally decimated: every tenth man was killed and the unit itself was dishonored, and there was certainly no question of rewards for anyone involved. We are not suggesting, of course, that every tenth or even every twentieth person in the FSA should walk the plank from the top floor of the agency's offices in Canary Wharf. Surely, common decency, if nothing else, should suggest that the Authority had shamed itself and should bear collective as well as individual responsibility: it happened on their watch, after all. These disgraceful bonuses show that the regulators are just as arrogant and unaccountable as the people they allegedly regulate.

Then in May 2009 came the stunning revelation that the Bank and the FSA had actually anticipated the Northern Rock disaster three years earlier. They had conducted a war games scenario analysis in which they had anticipated a scenario chillingly close to what later happened: an initial crisis leading to the withdrawal of wholesale deposits from Northern Rock, a resulting liquidity crisis, leaving the authorities an awkward choice between bail out and chaotic failure, and the crisis then going systemic and engulfing HBOS. What they missed was the trigger (they had considered a hypothetical European court ruling rather than subprime) and the fact that HBOS got into difficulties only after a while, and only then after the Lehman failure.

This shows that the authorities were well aware of the dangers of a small trigger event leading to a major crisis, and contradicts Sants' late 2007 claim that the crisis could not have been foreseen. This prompts the question: if it *could not be* foreseen, please explain how it actually *was* foreseen?

It gets even worse: in the aftermath of the war game, the authorities concluded that they needed authority to instigate a special bankruptcy procedure to deal with such a crisis, but they did nothing about it. As the Treasury permanent secretary acknowledged to a House of Lords Committee in March 2009: "in retrospect, we should have treated this more urgently," before helpfully reminding their noble Lordships that others were "dragging their heels" too, then pointedly referring (and so implicitly shifting the blame) to the Bank of England and deflecting it all with the "explanation" that there "was a general perception that this was not the highest priority." So that's all right then?

And what about the alternative of using their existing regulatory powers to do something to rein in Northern Rock and HBOS? As one insider revealed: they couldn't do that or the banks concerned would have protested. That's right, *protested*.

Who exactly is being accountable for this, we wonder?

★★★

For a long time now, many central banks and regulators have imposed minimum requirements, formal or otherwise, on banks' capital. These capital adequacy ratios were designed to protect the solvency of individual banks and, more importantly, the financial health of the banking system as a whole. The ratios usually took the "building block" form: assets would be divided into classes of riskiness, and for each asset in each risk class, a bank would have to maintain a minimum level of capital.

Meanwhile, in 1974, in the aftermath of the Herstatt case, the Bank for International Settlements had set up a Committee on Banking Regulations and Supervisory Practices, the so-called Basel Committee, with the intention of closing gaps in international bank supervision. However, in 1988 the Committee massively expanded its remit by adopting the Basel Capital Accord, a minimum capital adequacy standard to be applied to banks in all member countries, with capital requirements built on the "building block" principle.

The Accord, later to be known as Basel I, was then amended in 1996. A key feature of this amendment was to allow banks, subject to certain conditions, to use their own market risk management models to determine their regulatory capital requirements using the VaR risk measure. Thus, the models and the VaR were now built into the regulatory system. The Basel system was revised further, after much tortuous debate, in the form of Basel II, which took effect in 2008. A notable feature of Basel II is that it allows for the capital requirements against credit and operational risk to be determined for "sophisticated" banks using banks' own internal risk models, while retaining the principle that the capital requirements against market risk positions can be assessed using VaR models. Thus, Basel II expanded the regulatory use of banks' risk models.

The principal purpose of this system is to ensure the stability of our financial system and it is pretty clear that it hasn't worked (or is it just us?). But we would suggest that there was never any good reason to think it would. Consider the process that produced it:

Regulations emanated from a highly politicized committee process, and were the product of innumerable arbitrary decisions, irrational compromises, and political horse-trades – not to mention the personalities and prejudices of the main participants involved. This necessarily led to inconsistent treatment, regulatory arbitrage opportunities, an artificial and arbitrary "regulatory standard," and a compliance culture, while imposing large implementation costs on regulated firms. It also led to ever longer rulebooks that attempted to standardize practice in an area where practice is always changing and where the development of best practice requires competition in risk management practice – not an ossified rulebook that is out of date before it comes out.

Riccardo Rebonato tells a nice anecdote from a big risk management conference in 2005. He quotes an unnamed "very senior official of one of the international regulatory bodies" who, in "looking over the hundreds of pages of the brand new, highly quantitative, bank regulatory regime (Basel II) … sighed: 'It does read a bit as if it has been written without adult supervision.'"[14]

It is naive to expect that such a process of politicized committee group-thinking would produce a set of regulations that could work

---

[14] Rebonato, 2007, p. xxiii.

or, indeed, that there is any point "having another go," as our masters are now proposing, in an effort to get the regulations "right" the next time. Basel I, II, or III doesn't matter: the process itself is irredeemably flawed.

But there are also other problems with the Basel system, many of which we have encountered already, all of which serve to destabilize the financial system in one way or another:

- It bases capital requirements on the discredited VaR risk measure, which virtually guarantees that risks will be underestimated.
- It pressures all banks to follow similar risk management strategies, ignoring systemic interactions and aggravating systemic stability.
- It allows top-tier banks to determine their own risk management methodologies, while smaller banks have to use a standardized system. This penalizes smaller banks against their behemoth brethren, precisely the reverse of what sound systemic risk management would advise.
- It creates pro-cyclical capital requirements: as the business cycle approaches its peak, risk assessments will fall, leading risk-based capital requirements to fall and lending to rise, just at the point where the danger of a systemic downturn is greatest. Thus, risk-based capital regulation (such as Basel II) not only makes crises more likely but also more severe.[15] Proponents of capital regulation have suggested that the solution is to make capital requirements countercyclical instead, but it is difficult to see how that could be done in practice, not least since the downturn usually takes everyone by surprise.
- It allows for capital requirements to be based on ratings and these are unreliable, especially toward the peak of the cycle.
- It is open to gaming in all manner of ways, of which more presently.
- Last, but not least, there is the ultimate, decisive argument: it didn't work, and allowed the whole financial system to sleepwalk into a catastrophe.

Some of these problems – such as the use of VaR – could be patched up (although it is notable that the regulators are still not proposing to

---

[15] Danielsson, 2002.

do so!), but most of the others are fundamental problems that, taken together, call into question the very principle of "risk-based regulation": modern capital regulation might simply be attempting the impossible.

It is also important to appreciate that the "true" risks to which capital adequacy requirements should be directed are irrelevant: all that matters in practice are the regulatory requirements themselves and the banks' incentives to get these as low as possible.

This is in stark contrast to a rational system – such as that prevailing under the old partnership banks – in which key decision makers such as the partners bore the consequences of the risks they were taking; this gave them an incentive to assess their risks carefully so they could take on risks prudently. And, of course, in such a system there was never any need for capital regulation: the banks could be counted on to be prudent, because prudence was in their own self-interest.

In the modern irrational system, by comparison, the key decision makers have no such incentive, since they are shielded from the harsher consequences of their decisions: their main concern is to get profitable products out almost regardless of their true riskiness, and then maximize profitability by getting the lowest possible capital requirements for them. Unlike the old system, this one *is* prone to excess risk-taking and systemic instability, but capital adequacy regulation is not the answer and only makes the problem worse. Instead, real risk management is replaced by a compliance culture – the critical question being: what can we get away with? – and all manner of dangerous products then come out backed with what would later turn out to have been woefully inadequate capital.

An example is the now infamous J.P. Morgan "Bistro" ("Broad Index Secured Trust Offering," for those who want to know) deal back in 1997, which we mentioned in Chapter 8. The team that put this together argued that these securities were "super-safe," safer than US Treasuries, and accordingly lobbied for "easy" regulatory treatment. They argued that a $700 million capital cushion was more than adequate to cover the $9.7 billion notionally at stake, and the ratings agencies agreed, apparently on the basis of much the same flawed models that assumed defaults were independent. The regulators' initial response was to suggest that they insure the "missing" $9 billion and the investment bank did so, insuring them with AIG Financial Products and, in the process, inadvertently setting AIG on the path to ruin.

The regulators then changed their minds and said that the bank did not need to insure the remaining risk after all, but could keep the risk on the books provided they post capital reserves against it of one-fifth of the usual 8% capital requirement – the capital requirement was cut from 8 cents on the dollar to 1.6 cents on the dollar. This meant that what would later turn out to have been a very risky $9.7 billion dollar exposure could be "covered," for regulatory purposes, by a paltry $160 million. The only conditions were that the banks could "prove" the risk was truly negligible and get a triple A credit rating, and both conditions were easy to meet given the crappy models everyone was using. Bankers were now joking that "Bistro" referred to BIS Total RipOff.

Then there was the practice of regulatory arbitrage – in essence, financial engineering to reduce regulatory capital requirements. This occurred with the early collateralized debt obligations in the late 1980s. In fact, CDOs were invented by Fred Carr, the head of the insurance company First Executive Corp., and a good buddy of Mike Milken. The principal attraction of CDOs was the same as that of junk bonds: the lower rated securities outperformed the less risky ones on average, in part because legal rules made the lower rated securities less attractive and, hence cheaper. The game then began by which a portfolio of junk bonds would be securitized – the top tranche would be rated triple A, the second tier some lower investment grade, and then there was only the bottom tranche to worry about, as it still merited junk status – and the creators of these securities and the rating agencies were soon making a fortune. This fortune fed, in effect, off the fact that while the original pool all had junk status, the upper tranches of the CDO based on that pool were now investment grade.

Carr then used this logic to pull off a particularly cheeky coup in 1989. When regulators insisted that First Executive's junk bond portfolio be backed by the usual full capital requirements, he securitized the lot, kept them all on his books and managed to persuade the regulators that only the bottom tier needed the full capital requirement. He was in effect arguing that by re-labeling his positions, keeping exactly the same exposures as before, First Executive now merited lower capital requirements. Amazingly, the regulators bought the argument and Carr saved his firm $110 million in capital. As Partnoy put it, it was as if the owner of a three-storey house had claimed that it was really three separate pieces with only the ground floor subject to property tax. One has to admire Mr Carr's style.

Part Five

Götterdämmerung

13

Bubble, Bust, and Panic

After the dotcom bubble burst, the major US share price indices bottomed for the second time on March 11, 2003, just before the United States invaded Iraq. That bottoming was followed by a sharp upward move, while it had already become evident that the short, mild recession of 2001 was well over. Market participants breathed a sigh of relief; the immense stock market bubble of 1999–2000 has been deflated, apparently, without either a plunge to the depths that had seemed likely or a major recession. As in 1987, the stock market crash had not led to a depression; only for Enron and a few other companies had 2001–02 proved fatal. It appeared that, fuelled by two tax cuts in 2001 and 2003, financial markets and the US economy generally could look forward to a prolonged, well-balanced boom.

It was not to be. As discussed in Chapter 11, the Fed had engineered the stock market's apparently healthy "soft landing" by an unprecedented monetary expansion, and by 2003 real short-term interest rates were sharply negative and were to remain so for the next two years. The result was the notorious housing bubble. The S&P Case-Shiller 20-cities home price index, which had increased 7.9% in 2001 and 12.2% in 2002, increased by 11.3% in 2003, 16.2% in 2004, and 15.5% in 2005.[1] (It should be noted, incidentally, that if housing costs were included in the consumer price index with any reasonable percentage weighting, as they had been before 1980, even the future

---

[1] Standard and Poor's website.

Fed Chairman Ben Bernanke could not have fantasized about imminent deflation by November 2002, when he made his "helicopter"
speech.)

The housing bubble had a number of drivers on both the supply
and demand sides. On the demand side, the principal factor leading to
an exponential increase in demand for housing loans was the growth in
the shadow banking system. Whereas the conventional banking system
– with total assets of around $10 trillion in 2007, of which $6 trillion
was in the top five bank holding companies[2] – is subject to capital
requirements, bank supervision, and deposit insurance premiums, the
shadow banking system (consisting of investment banks, asset-backed
commercial paper conduits, securitization vehicles, hedge funds, money market funds, and monoline insurance companies) is not subject to
the same disciplines and capital requirements.

This was described in a speech by Tim Geithner, then President of
the Federal Reserve Bank of New York, in a speech on June 9, 2008:

> "The structure of the financial system changed fundamentally
> during the boom, with dramatic growth in the share of
> assets outside the traditional banking system. This non-bank
> financial system grew to be very large, particularly in money
> and funding markets. In early 2007, asset-backed commercial
> paper conduits, in structured investment vehicles, in auction-
> rate preferred securities, tender option bonds and variable
> rate demand notes, had a combined asset size of roughly $2.2
> trillion. Assets financed overnight in tri-party repo grew to
> $2.5 trillion. Assets held in hedge funds grew to roughly $1.8
> trillion. The combined balance sheets of the then five major
> investment banks totaled $4 trillion."[3]

Thus the "shadow banking system" was as large by 2007 as the conventional banking system, having grown from maybe one quarter the

---

[2] At that time, Citigroup, J.P. Morgan Chase, Bank of America, Wells Fargo, and
Wachovia. Wachovia merged with Wells Fargo in September 2008.

[3] Timothy F. Geithner, President, Federal Reserve Bank of New York, "Reducing
Systemic Risk in a Dynamic Financial System," Economic Club of New York, June
9, 2008.

size in 2000. Its growth was exacerbated by the 2004 SEC decision to remove leverage restrictions on investment banks – the average leverage of the five top investment banks soared from less than 20 to 1 in 2003 to around 30 to 1 in 2007, although Goldman Sachs was more cautious, its leverage topping out at 25 to 1. This growth artificially increased the supply of lendable funds, raising the velocity of money and making even more egregious the expansion of money supply that the Greenspan/Bernanke team was then pursuing.

As the denouement was to prove, many of these off-balance-sheet vehicles were not truly independent of their sponsoring banks. Their creation had been caused by the drive for short-term profit (particularly in fee income) by the endless supply of cheap money, and by the flawed Modern Finance risk management models that led banks, rating agencies, and investors alike to imagine that the risk of such vehicles was modest, and that their extraordinary leverage was appropriate.

A second demand-side factor was the growth of the government-sponsored enterprises Fannie Mae and Freddie Mac, in particular their drive to build balance sheet size by increasing their leverage and buying mortgage-backed securities. They were by statute exempt from the normal financial institution capital requirements, so were able to build up vast portfolios of mortgages and mortgage-backed securities – $760 billion in Fannie Mae and $710 billion in Freddie Mac in 2007.

Both institutions were major users of the derivatives market, and of the risk management techniques of Modern Finance. Indeed, as investigations later showed, Fannie Mae took those techniques further. They would enter into an interest rate swap, hold it for several weeks before deciding whether to close the position, and then book its profit as income or hold the swap until maturity, burying its loss against future years' income – the income so created inflated top management's bonuses. In total, Fannie Mae mis-stated earnings by $10.6 billion between 1998 and 2004. There's little question that, had these accounting frauds been discovered in a private sector bank, the top executives would have faced substantial jail time, but Fannie Mae in particular and Freddie Mac were protected by an Iron Curtain of political connections. When the inevitable bankruptcy occurred, the federal government was then available to bail them out.

The political connections of the home mortgage market undoubtedly benefited Fannie Mae, Freddie Mac, and the major mortgage originators such as Countrywide Financial. The trail of political contributions and mortgage favors to the major players such as Senator Christopher Dodd (Democrat, Connecticut) and Representative Barney Frank (Democrat, Massachusetts), the Chairmen from January 2007 of the relevant congressional committees, is sufficient evidence of this. The 1977 Community Reinvestment Act mandating loans to low-income housing, and its extension by the Clinton administration in 1999, also played a substantial and damaging role in the growth of the subprime mortgage market. Nevertheless, politically inspired claims that the political nexus between the housing market and the leading Democrats caused the entire problem are false; it merely worsened the mud at the bottom of the mortgage pool. The pool itself, its excessive growth, and its deterioration in quality, were the work primarily of the Fed, Wall Street, and Modern Finance.

On the supply side, the principal forces driving home-mortgage creation were soaring house prices, caused by the Fed's excessively stimulative monetary policy, and the changed incentives resulting from mortgage origination's move from a lender-originated to a broker-originated process.

Soaring house prices drove mortgage origination in two ways. They led to a wave of refinancing to extract home equity and they pushed marginal borrowers to join the speculative bandwagon. Free cash from home equity extraction doubled from $627 billion in 2001 to $1.43 trillion in 2005; a total of $5 trillion for the whole period, or more than 7% of GDP annually.[4] Naturally, this had a huge economic effect in boosting consumption and destabilizing the balance of payments through excessive imports, but it also had a mortgage market effect in extracting $5 trillion of equity from total home assets of $20 trillion.

Subprime mortgages were encouraged by three trends:

• the push by the Community Reinvestment Act to lend to minority group members with imperfect credit;
• soaring house prices, which had an important "push" effect; and
• the new importance of mortgage brokers, which had an important "pull" effect.

---

[4] Greenspan and Kennedy, 2007.

Subprime mortgage originations remained well below 10% of the total until 2004, but escalated thereafter to more than 20% of total originations in 2004–06, so that by March 2007 more than 7.5 million subprime mortgages were outstanding, with a total value of $1.3 trillion or 12.5% of the total mortgage pool – up from $130 billion in 2000. Most subprime mortgages were packaged into subprime mortgage bonds, which were sliced and sold to investors, the top tranches being rated AAA. Even prime mortgages were made on a less conservative basis; by 2005 the median home mortgage down payment was 2%, and 43% of mortgage borrowers had no down payment at all.

Beyond the subprime growth itself, there was a considerable element of mortgage fraud in the process. Lenders such as Countrywide and Ameriquest pushed loans with low "teaser" rates of 1–2%, whose interest rate soared to an above-market level after a few years. Borrowers and mortgage brokers indulged in an epidemic of "liar loans" in which no documentation of income was required or given – hence the stories of strawberry pickers with incomes of $14,000 buying $720,000 houses in California with no money down.[5]

As if there were not enough subprime or fraudulent mortgage loans to invest in, the derivatives market created extra ones. Led by AIG Financial Products, the credit default swap market created artificial subprime mortgage bonds, multiplying the default risk many times over on both AAA-rated and lower-rated subprime mortgage bonds. Hedge funds and other sharpies eagerly bought the CDS, thus giving the subprime mortgage market an artificial additional source of rotten paper to sell to gullible investors.

Selling subprime-backed rubbish on domestic and international bond markets required it to get a credit rating. Here Standard and Poor's, Moody's, and Fitch must bear a substantial share of the blame. They took portfolios of subprime mortgages, ignored the correlations between them, and rated the top 50–60% of the risk profile AAA. Their computer models, even where they did not ignore altogether the possibility of a house price decline, treated it as an extremely unlikely risk. Not only did the rating agencies ignore risk correlation in subprime mortgages themselves, they also made the assumption of independence

---

[5] See, e.g., Lewis, 2008 – as always with Lewis, amusingly written and well researched, if not always financially sound.

on BBB-rated subprime mortgage bonds (which themselves bore the mortgages' risks down to about the 85th or 90th percentile). The rating agencies would thus rate as AAA even "CDO-squared," in which the underlying credit represented lower-tranche returns on subprime mortgages.

It wasn't just bond buyers who went mad at the top of this boom; acquisition deals were done that the buyers subsequently regretted. Deutsche Bank was relatively modest in its purchase of the subprime mortgage originator Mortgage IT in August 2006, for only $438 million, but the losses caused by Mortgage IT's portfolio of business were several times its purchase price. Merrill Lynch's purchase of the mortgage originator First Franklin Mortgage for $1.3 billion was more damaging, both because of First Franklin's stronger market position and because Merrill Lynch put its origination muscle behind its acquisition in the months before the bust, increasing its leverage from 21 to 31 times in the following year.

However, the mother of all mistimed acquisitions was Wachovia's purchase of the California mortgage lender Golden West Financial for $25.5 billion in 2006. This deal was not only to bankrupt Wachovia in 2008, but it also gave Golden West's owners Herb and Marion Sandler $2.4 billion in cash with which they have subsequently proceeded to attack the capitalist system through tax-exempt foundations.

★★★

The housing market slowed sharply in 2006; the S&P Case-Shiller 20-cities index peaked in July 2006 and at the end of the year was only 1% up on the previous year-end. However the first tremors in the subprime mortgage market came with the bankruptcy of American Freedom Mortgage, one of the leading subprime and Alt-A mortgage brokers, on January 30. Instead of the normal gentlemanly Chapter 11 filing, AFM filed a voluntary no-asset Chapter 7 bankruptcy, indicating that it had essentially been operating as an empty shell.

This spooked the market, which was troubled throughout February, as various small mortgage brokers and subprime lenders got into difficulties, and New Century, the second largest subprime lender, was rumored to be in trouble. On February 22, HSBC Bank wrote down its holdings of subprime mortgage-backed securities by no less than $10.5 billion and fired the head of US mortgage lending, which got the market's attention. On February 27, Freddie Mac announced that it would no longer buy subprime mortgages that did not qualify for its criteria at their full interest rate, not just at the low "teaser" rate.

Then on March 9, New Century, which had had 7,200 employees at the beginning of the year, disclosed that it was under criminal investigation. On March 12 the New York Stock Exchange de-listed New Century, which filed for Chapter 11 bankruptcy on April 2. In May, Ameriquest, another large subprime lender that had settled a $325 million predatory lending suit with various states attorneys general in August 2006, announced it was closing all its branches, and ceased business in September.

Still at this stage although many still thought that the problem was localized, the market was taking the problem seriously; asset-backed securities values declined steadily over the spring and early summer, with even AAA-rated tranches trading at levels previously thought impossible.

Nevertheless even as late as July 19, Bernanke, by then Fed Chairman, informed the Senate in his biannual Humphrey-Hawkins testimony that the likely losses on subprime loans would be no more than $100 billion. Since that represented less than an 8% loss rate on the $1.3 trillion of subprime loans outstanding, it was by this stage a hopelessly optimistic calculation. As early as March 12, Martin had by careful analysis estimated the likely losses on subprime and Alt-A mortgages at $1 trillion – still too low, but a damn sight closer than Bernanke![6]

The first clue that mainstream Wall Street might have been clueless, rather than just the obscure and gamey third-tier mortgage brokers and banks, came on June 7, when Bear Stearns suspended redemptions on its High-Grade Structured Credit Enhanced Leverage Fund. Then on June 22, 2007, Bear Stearns announced a $3.2 billion collateralized loan to bail out its High-Grade Structured Credit Fund. These actions sparked a run on subprime mortgage CDOs, as other investors worried that Bear Stearns might have to liquidate these hedge funds. On July 16, Bear Stearns announced that both funds had lost essentially all of their value, and on July 31 it announced their liquidation. The funds had invested in subprime CDOs, and had sold at heavy discounts to meet redemptions.

---

[6] "The Bear's Lair: The Main Street Crash," *Prudent Bear*, March 12, 2007.

The managers of the funds, Matthew Tannin and Ralph Cioffi, were to be indicted a year later on the grounds that they had known about the plummeting value of the funds earlier than others and had therefore misled investors. Fortunately in November 2009 they were acquitted; a conviction would have made risk management impossible, since any red flags over a portfolio would have to be immediately disclosed publicly, thus causing mass sales by other investors and, in an illiquid market, the very collapse risk managers were attempting to prevent.

★★★

The slide quickened pace in August 2007. On August 7 American Home Mortgage, another major mortgage lender, filed for bankruptcy. A day later, IKB Deutsche Industriebank announced it had received a $5 billion bailout because it could not obtain financing for its securitized investments vehicle (SIV). On August 9, the French bank BNP Paribas halted redemptions on three investment funds that it managed, about a third of which were in subprime mortgage securities – their net asset values had declined 20% in three days. On August 17, Landesbank Sachsen Girozentrale announced it had received $24 billion in emergency funding from other German landesbanks because it could no longer obtain commercial paper financing for its SIV; by the end of August it was being sold to Landesbank Baden-Württemberg.

The two German banks, IKB and Sachsen LB, had both made the mistake of expanding too far into a market they did not understand. Domestically, both were squeezed by larger competitors and by the tight lending conditions in the German market. For prestige reasons, they found it attractive to expand internationally; then their international staff needed something to do, so found the slick salesmen of Wall Street only too ready to set them up with SIVs. They would fund these through commercial paper and invest in subprime mortgage CDOs and other high-rated junk, the profits from which would flow through to the bottom line. Needless to say, they did not understand the risks involved; no doubt the debt ratings on the securitized paper (mostly AA in the case of Sachsen LB) and the comforting theses of Modern Finance, by this stage penetrating even the German banking system, made it all sound irresistibly attractive.

In bull markets, local banks over-expand into foreign businesses that they do not understand and in which they have no comparative advantage. Modern Finance and modern Wall Street have only exacerbated this tendency. The US subprime mortgage market was particularly tempting. Even Nomura Securities, the largest brokerage house in Japan, was active in the market – it announced in August that it was closing its subprime mortgage SIV and in October that it was exiting the mortgage business altogether, taking a loss that eventually became more than $1 billion. Whether banks had poor domestic positions and market, like Sachsen LB, or a magnificent domestic position and market, like Nomura, the allure of US subprime mortgages and other high-yield securitized rubbish, based on a complete misappraisal of their risks, was the same. Indeed, the allure of making foreign losses was so great for Nomura that as others got in trouble over the next couple of years, it beefed up in both London and New York, buying the Asian operations of the bankrupt Lehman Brothers.

The next shoe to drop was the announcement on September 14 that the British housing bank Northern Rock plc was to get public liquidity support of up to £35 billion. This was a much bigger shoe than those previously dropped; while it didn't show the crisis extending to the finest names, it demonstrated that solving it was going to prove very expensive indeed.

The traditional British method of financing housing was even sounder than the traditional Jimmy Stewart mechanism in the US, because it did not leave housing finance institutions with interest rate risk. Beginning in Birmingham in 1774, local homebuyers banded together and created a building society organized on a mutual basis that made home mortgages at floating rates of interest, the rate set by a central cartel. These building societies had grown over the years on a regional basis with few problems. The system had worked well in the 1970s, when British inflation became much higher than in the US and interest rates had correspondingly increased. Building society management was modestly paid and conservative, but that was fine. Entrepreneurial aggression is entirely superfluous, indeed economically counterproductive in the mortgage lending business, which should be kept as simple as possible to avoid scamming the public.

The system fell apart after the misguided Thatcher-led banking "deregulation" of the 1980s. New legislation allowed building societies to demutualize and become shareholder-owned, paying the profits from the inevitable IPO to their savers. Human nature being what it is, building society managers saw a chance to become paid like bankers rather than like public servants, while their savers were bribed by the short-term gains to vote for demutualization.

Once demutualized, building societies, as large institutions with fairly dozy managements, were prey to the temptations of banking in a similar fashion to the US savings and loans in the 1980s. No longer having their solid base of relatively cheap funding and being forced to compete aggressively, they were natural victims of every get-rich-quick scheme Modern Finance merchants could devise. They became far more aggressive both in making mortgages and in engaging in dodgy securitization deals to clear their balance sheets for more mortgages. Needless to say, traditional standards of prudence in terms of down payments and income coverage were scattered to the winds, while all kinds of "low-start" and "flexible" mortgages lured unwary borrowers to their financial doom.

To be fair, traditional income coverage standards would have made home purchase practically impossible in south-east England because of the ludicrous over-inflation of property prices. (The median house price to median household income ratio, which in the US never on average got above 4.5 times even at the peak of the bubble, topped 6 times in Britain.) An excessively loose monetary policy (though less so than in the US) and an even sloppier fiscal policy, combined with over-tight building controls dating from the 1940s and the influx of foreign City of London wide-boys and the Russian mafia, began to drive the British housing market to unimagined excesses. Maybe Tokyo real estate in 1989 was more overpriced than London's in 2007, but not by much.

Northern Rock, formed in Newcastle in 1850, had undergone the typical building society transformation in the 1990s, being floated in 1997. It then expanded aggressively (its home base of the industrial north-east being unattractive), using securitization techniques through a £45 billion vehicle called Granite to build its balance sheet. (The Granite name was presumably chosen to suggest solidity; in retrospect it should have warned lenders that its contents were financially radioactive!) It also partnered with Lehman Brothers to originate sub-prime mortgages – presumably neither partner in this venture dreamed for one moment that it might cause Lehman to go bankrupt while

Northern Rock survived. The Northern Rock/Lehman venture was particularly active in the "buy-to-let" business, in which speculators would buy multiple homes and attempt to let them out. This activity was characteristic of all US housing booms but was relatively novel in the UK, where the rental market had been almost completely smothered until 1988 by rent controls and expansive public sector house building.

Northern Rock's distinctive business model involved rapid growth, large-scale reliance on the capital markets for finance, and an innovative and very accommodating mortgage: the racy "Together loan," in which customers could borrow 125% of their property value and up to six times their annual income. The boring days when customers could only borrow 80% of their property value and a maximum of three times their income were over. This aggressive business model worked well in the good times and the bank grew to be the fifth-largest mortgage provider in the UK, but soon came unstuck as the subprime crisis broke in the summer of 2007. The bank then lost the confidence of its depositors and experienced a run in September 2007 – the first run on an English bank since Overend, Gurney & Co. in 1866 – before being bailed out at great cost and subsequently nationalized.

Amazingly, having just obtained a bailout at public expense, Northern Rock cheerily announced that it still intended to go ahead with a planned dividend payment, presumably to protect its executives' bonuses: it took a public outcry to get the dividend payment cancelled.

After the bailout, the bank's senior executives still insisted that the bank's business model was a good one because it had worked well until August that year. They also maintained that they had done nothing wrong, while admitting that they hadn't stress-tested their exposure to a market dry-up. This has the same credibility as the captain of the *Titanic* saying that everything was OK until the iceberg turned up. The resulting public uproar forced them to resign, but even then the chief executive Adam Applegarth was able to retire comfortably to his mansion. While the Northern Rock workforce could anticipate major job losses, Applegarth was able to retire on a generous settlement package, and it transpired that he had been quietly cashing in his own Northern Rock shares – a nice vote of confidence in his own leadership – getting £2 million for his shares while other shareholders lost everything.

The fact that so obscure an institution could be deemed "too big to fail" and thereby leech so much off taxpayers should not have come as a surprise to those who remembered the 1970s secondary banking crisis; it was a harsh comment on the unsoundness of the British banking system that so few of the people involved, as regulators or leading bankers, had been around that long.

★★★

British prime minister Gordon Brown's reaction to the Northern Rock debacle was a panicky bailout. Bernanke's immediate reaction to the US subprime mortgage problems was to cut interest rates at the Federal Open Market Committee meeting on September 18. (Those who may suppose that this is Bernanke's reaction to all situations are almost certainly unkind. There must be situations to which Bernanke would react differently – we just haven't found them yet!) Having, with his predecessor Alan Greenspan, painfully brought the Federal Funds rate up from 1% to the still accommodative 5.25% over a period of more than two years at the stomach-churning pace of a 0.25% rate increase at each of the eight annual Federal Open Market Committee meetings, Bernanke seized the opportunity to push them down again, initially by 0.50% to 4.75%, but eventually in stages all the way to a 0–0.25% range target by December 2008.

The Fed's rationale for the rate cut was to prevent the housing decline from impacting the wider economy. However, since the economy as a whole was still growing fairly rapidly and global liquidity had been pushing up commodity prices, its immediate effect was an astonishing boom in commodity and energy prices that was to double the oil price from its September level of around $70 or so to $147 per barrel by the following July. Apart from providing cash and encouragement to various of the world's bad guys – possibly, for example, stimulating Russia's August 2008 invasion of Georgia – this huge increase in commodity prices produced consumer price inflation higher than the initial interest rate level, making real interest rates strongly negative.

In retrospect it's pretty clear that even by his stated objective of avoiding recession in the short term, Bernanke would have done much better to leave interest rates where they were, or preferably raise them a little further to counteract the effect of the tidal wave of liquidity he was to provide the banking system over the months to come.

These liquidity injections were primarily necessary because of the decline in the asset-backed commercial paper market (the principal funding source for all the securitization vehicles) whose outstandings peaked at $1.2 trillion on August 8, 2007, then ran down by $447 billion over the next five months before bottoming out temporarily in January 2008. The first injection attempted was a private sector affair, an announcement on October 15 by Citigroup, Bank of America, and J.P. Morgan Chase of an $80 billion Master Liquidity Enhancement Conduit, through which the asset-backed commercial paper market would be supported. However, that didn't work; there were no buyers and the facility was abandoned two months later.

By that time, Bernanke had announced the first Fed liquidity injection, the Term Auction Facility (TAF) by which term funds would be auctioned to financial institutions against various forms of collateral. The first auction of $20 billion took place on December 17, 2007; regular auctions were held until March, at which point the auction size was enlarged to $50 billion.

The market took a further lurch downwards on October 31 when the respected Oppenheimer analyst Meredith Whitney predicted that Citigroup would either have to slash its dividend or go bust. Financial stocks immediately plunged and, four days later, Citigroup chairman "Chuck" Prince was forced to resign.

During the last months of 2007, a new source of uncertainty appeared, in the Financial Accounting Standards Board's implementation of FAS157 on fair value accounting, adopted in December 2006 and to come into effect for fiscal years beginning after November 15, 2007 (thus catching Goldman Sachs, then with a November year-end, but initially missing a host of mutual funds with October year-ends). Wall Street houses had welcomed this standard, because it would allow them to take holdings of private equity and exotic securitizations, and mark them up in value, using their Modern Finance mathematical models, without the tiresome bother of actually having to find buyers for the things.

In the event, FAS157's timing was terrible. It was quickly revealed that even Goldman Sachs had "Level 3" assets – those for which no discernable market existed – of twice its capital. It didn't take a financial genius to see that in a real bear market, institutions that had loaded up with illiquid rubbish to that extent were in deep trouble. FAS157 raised further doubts about the investment banks' solidity and was blamed ferociously in 2008 by Merrill Lynch, Lehman Brothers, and other troubled houses for forcing them to take massive writedowns. However, in reality, FAS157 was just bringing into the open the reality that Wall Street had taken exorbitant risks based on Modern Finance risk management and valuation models that were pure fantasy.

★★★

There was a certain amount of optimism at the beginning of 2008 that the worst might be over, and that the world could escape from the subprime mortgage collapse with no more than a minor downturn, if any. The Asset-Backed Commercial Paper market bottomed out temporarily in January, while the Fed's interest rate cuts and liquidity injections appeared to be allowing the US to benefit from what was still a rapidly expanding world economy. On January 18, Bank of America gave tangible evidence of its commitment to this optimistic view of the world by buying Countrywide Financial, the US's largest mortgage lender.

Countrywide had been founded in 1969; in 1997 it spun off its mortgage lending arm, which became known as IndyMac – one of 2008's larger bankruptcies. From 1982 to 2003, Countrywide stock returned investors 23,000%. However, even in 2006, 19% of its subprime loans had gone bad. Thus Bank of America's $4 billion purchase was an optimistic decision, to say the least. Given Countrywide founder Angelo Mozilo's subsequent indictment, and the revelations of the "Friends of Angelo" program to reward many of the dodgier politicians, Bank of America can hardly be said to have been purchasing much goodwill either!

Between Bank of America chairman Ken Lewis's two big deals in 2008 (the other being Merrill Lynch), this was definitely the stupider. The value added of Countrywide to Bank of America is wholly unclear: the bank already had 6,100 branches at December 2007 – how many more dozy home mortgage sourcing outlets did it need? Many poor decisions were made in the lead-up to the 2008 crash, but Bank of America's Countrywide acquisition has to be up there among the dumbest.

The optimism of January 2008 turned to pessimism the following month with the collapse of the auction-rate securities market, discussed in Chapter 6. When examined closely, the remarkable thing about this market was that it took so long to collapse – a full 24 years from its first financing in 1984 for a structure that was very obviously built on flim-flam rather than reality. Nevertheless the markets, full of people who had been in grade school in 1984, took the collapse rather badly.

With things looking grimmer, it was time for the politicians to steam to the rescue. On February 13, President George W. Bush signed the first fiscal stimulus: a flat-rate tax rebate costing $150 billion, with checks being mailed out in May. For the politicians, this was a great success. Since the rebate checks pushed second quarter GDP to a tiny gain, it made the 2008–09 recession statistically only a four-quarter recession from a peak in the second quarter of 2008 rather than a post-war record six-quarter recession from the peak in the fourth quarter of 2007. The reality was that it was just another $150 billion that US taxpayers will have to pay back sometime.

The Fed tried to help again too. On March 11 it launched the Term Securities Lending Facility, to lend up to $200 billion of Treasuries against agency debt and mortgage-backed securities, allowing banks to improve the quality of their balance sheets at the Fed's expense. There was by this time an increasing recognition that much of the securitized paper in the market was truly noxious. The following weekend, as well as rescuing Bear Stearns, the Fed established the Primary Dealer Credit Facility, allowing brokers as well as banks to borrow from the discount window. [7]

The game then changed fundamentally with the collapse of Bear Stearns, rescued by J.P. Morgan Chase on March 14 at a price of $2 (later revised to $10) per share, plus a $29 billion non-recourse loan

---

[7] Primary dealers are those houses (18 in July 2009) that deal directly with the Fed in the government securities market. The "Big Five" investment banks were members, as are Citigroup, J.P. Morgan Chase, and Bank of America (but not Wells Fargo, Wachovia, or any regional banks), eleven foreign banks/brokers, and, extraordinarily, until July 15, 2008, Countrywide.

from the Fed. Bear Stearns had always been the weakest of the "Big Five" investment banks, as well as the most trading-oriented. Unlike the other four majors, it had no great base of mergers or capital markets issuance fees with which it could hope to recoup trading losses. It had been a pioneer in the securitization business, but that was now a hindrance to survival rather than a help. In addition, it had suffered substantially both financially and in reputation from the collapse of its funds the previous summer. The advent of mark-to-market accounting also did not help; it was revealed that Bear Stearns had $28 billion of illiquid "Level 3" assets at November 2007, versus a net equity position of only $11.1 billion, which backed a total of $395 billion in assets – a leverage ratio of 35.5 to 1. Naked short selling in the stock market and in the credit default swap market undoubtedly worsened Bear Stearns' credibility.

The motivation for the authorities in organizing the Bear Stearns rescue was clear – the firm had a derivatives book totaling $13.4 trillion, so its collapse would have destabilized the global derivatives market. J.P. Morgan Chase's motivation for buying it was much less clear, although it was a leader in the global clearing business in which J.P. Morgan Chase was also an important player. It was a better "buy" than Countrywide, especially at a price of minus $25 billion or so – but as events were to show, there were better bargains to come.

With only $395 billion in assets (many of them highly dubious), doubtful management quality, and excessive leverage, Bear Stearns should not have been regarded as too big to fail – its assets were only a fifth of Citigroup's, for example. In addition, Bear Stearns' excessive trading orientation, aggressive reputation, and major businesses in securitization and derivatives would have emphasized to other players the dangers in those businesses at a time when the Dow Jones index was at 11,951 and the US economy was only marginally in recession. At the same time, without the Fed's $29 billion subsidy, it is unlikely Bear Stearns would have been rescued by JPMC or anyone else.

Had Bear Stearns been allowed to fail, Lehman Brothers, a much more important house both in terms of size and reputation, would have taken its own plight (at that stage, not critical) more seriously and so might have avoided its later collapse. Other investment banks, such as Merrill Lynch, would have deleveraged on an emergency basis. More important, severe losses would have been incurred in the derivatives markets and particularly in the credit default swap markets, causing a massive re-pricing in those bloated sectors. Finally, the market would have been forced into contraction six months earlier than it was, lessening that contraction's economic impact. Thus, by allowing a moderate banking crisis in March, it's likely that the Feds would have been able to avoid a much more severe one in September.

The next few months were quiet ones; the general assumption was that Bear Stearns was as far as the rot spread. However, a further nail was knocked into the coffin of the asset-backed securities market on June 5 when Standard and Poor's downgraded the monoline insurance companies (which had provided guarantees to mortgage pools) from AAA to AA, so undermining another prop to the securitization markets. The market had however already effectively discounted this.

The next downward lurch occurred in July. On July 11, IndyMac, the 28th largest bank in the United States, which had started life as Countrywide's mortgage-lending arm, was placed into conservatorship by FDIC. Then, two days later, the inevitable happened: the Fed announced an increase in the credit lines for the housing finance agencies Fannie Mae and Freddie Mac, and announced that the Treasury was authorized to inject capital into them if necessary. Though short of a formal bankruptcy (which was not to happen until September 7), this marked a further escalation in the crisis; the two agencies were each more than twice the size of Bear Stearns, and it was obvious that if capital was needed, the cost of such capital was likely to exceed $100 billion. Serious taxpayer risk was becoming involved.

The collapse of Fannie Mae and Freddie Mac had been inevitable since soon after the crisis began. Both agencies had used political pull to wangle themselves exceptionally favorable deals on such matters as capital and supervision, while the accounting scandals earlier in the decade had made it quite clear to impartial observers that neither agency was competently or even honestly run. The pretence by which both were private sector entities, able to reward their staff at lavish private sector rates while benefiting from a Treasury guarantee on their obligations that was only implicit and would never be called, was highly unstable and wholly unsound. As in Britain, entrepreneurship should have been kept out of the home mortgage market; although in the agencies' case, only management's rewards were truly entrepreneurial.

Like Bear Stearns, Fannie and Freddie should never have been rescued. They had no confidence-inspiring "name" or reputation as separate entities; the only reason anyone trusted them with a bent nickel was the implicit federal guarantee. Nevertheless, reneging on the implicit federal guarantee on existing "conforming" home mortgages would have been highly damaging to the market and the US economy, however salutary a lesson it would have been for Wall Street. Thus the mortgage guarantees should have been picked up by the federal government, with only direct obligations of the two agencies allowed to go into default. (In practice, losses on those would have been minor, since the agencies' principal assets were home mortgages that would now benefit from a full federal guarantee.) Because of the appalling underwriting standards at Fannie Mae and Freddie Mac, the losses to the taxpayer would still have been substantial, but they would have stopped growing further once no further guarantees were written.

The most beneficial action that could then have been taken would have been to put both Fannie Mae and Freddie Mac immediately into liquidation, ending the system of government guarantees of mortgage debt once and for all. The home mortgage market should then have been allowed to find its own level. The market for "jumbo" loans at this point remained active if sticky, at about 1.5% higher yield than "conforming" Fannie/Freddie loans; so essentially, from this point on, all loans would have become jumbo. Had the George W. Bush administration consisted by this stage of anything more than inept timeservers and former Goldman Sachs honchos, this would have been done. The bankruptcy could have been used to fulfill a long-standing and often-stated Republican goal of returning the housing market fully to the private sector and closing down the Fannie/Freddie/Democrat slush fund operations.

The other event of July was the Securities and Exchange Commission's emergency order of July 15 that banned short selling in the stocks of Fannie Mae, Freddie Mac, and the "primary dealers." By the Commodity Futures Modernization Act of 2000, however, neither the SEC nor the Commodity Futures Trading Corporation had any authority over the credit default swap markets, so huge amounts of speculation against the debt of Lehman Brothers and AIG (the latter not covered by the SEC order against short stock sales) occurred in these markets, precipitating but probably not causing the next stage of the crisis.

★★★

The pivotal week of the entire crisis occurred in mid-September, with the bankruptcy of Lehman Brothers, the sale of Merrill Lynch to Bank of America, and the rescue of AIG. The final federal takeover of Fannie Mae and Freddie Mac had occurred the previous weekend, so the market was unsettled, although the Dow Junes Industrial Index closed on September 12 at 11,422, still far above its fair value by any standards save those of the post-1995 bubble.[8]

Lehman had been active in subprime mortgage bonds, and had kept an excessive inventory of unsold bonds from its securitizations; in the second quarter of 2008, it was forced to write down its holdings by $2.8 billion and, as the summer wore on, pressure on Lehman through the CDS market and the stock market intensified. In growing desperation, Lehman attempted to reach a deal with Korea Development Bank, which wanted to expand into international investment banking. However, this was rightly vetoed by the South Korean authorities, who had spent considerable public money rehabilitating KDB and didn't want it to wreck its balance sheet once again by a merger with the much larger and overleveraged Lehman. Lehman then held discussions with Barclays and Bank of America, which went nowhere. On September 11 the bank announced that it would report a further loss of $3.9 billion in the third quarter, and that it intended to sell its fund management arm Neuberger Berman. Since this third-quarter loss represented close to 20% of Lehman's capital, this announcement caused a further loss of confidence, and Lehman was forced to file for bankruptcy at 1 a.m. on Monday, September 15, with assets of $639 billion and bank debts of $613 billion.

Lehman had a better (albeit still weak) case for state rescue than Bear Stearns, Fannie Mae, Freddie Mac, or AIG. It was a historic name on Wall Street, and unlike AIG or Bear Stearns had few questions over

---

[8] Martin had published a piece for BreakingViews.com on June 9, 2008, when the Dow Jones Industrial Average was above 12,000, demonstrating that, based on its February 1995 value of 4,000 inflated by the subsequent rise in nominal GDP, an equilibrium value for the Dow at that time was 7,800. Since nominal GDP has increased little since then (late 2009), that is still approximately the case.

its business practices. Had Bear Stearns been allowed to go the previous March, Lehman could almost certainly have been saved because its crisis would have occurred six months earlier, when both Lehman and the markets were in better shape. Allowing Lehman to go bankrupt would have made sense if the authorities had decided to pursue an austere but economically correct policy of non-rescue of the financial sector. However, since the authorities rescued AIG the same weekend, had already rescued Fannie Mae and Freddie Mac, and were prepared to waste hundreds of billions in taxpayer money propping up other houses, allowing Lehman to go merely increased the level of uncertainty over the whole system. As a minor side-benefit, rescuing Lehman would have increased the competitiveness of investment banking during the artificial cheap money bubble of 2009–10, so reducing the "problem" of Goldman Sachs' 2009 bonuses.

The same weekend as Lehman failed, AIG teetered towards collapse. AIG was a major international insurance company that in 1986 had decided to goose its earnings through derivatives trading. Naturally, to make the largest profits available for bonuses, this division – AIG Financial Products, whose credit rating rested on the insurance operations of the rest of AIG – aggressively took advantage of Modern Finance theories of risk and valuation. Its accounting was also aggressive – one of the factors reducing confidence in AIG in September was that it was found to have valued securitized subprime debt at 1.7 to 2 times that debt's valuation in the books of the bankrupt Lehman Brothers.

AIG Financial Products had also gone heavily into credit default swaps, insuring $441 billion of AAA rated securities, of which $58 billion were structured securities backed by subprime loans. When in September the credit rating agencies announced they were considering downgrading AIG below a AA rating, the amounts of collateral it had to put up against these CDS short positions was sharply increased. On September 14, New York regulators allowed AIG Financial Products to borrow $20 billion from other AIG subsidiaries. Then, two days later, the Fed provided a credit line of $85 billion to back up AIG's CDS in exchange for warrants for a 79.9% equity stake.

The $85 billion eventually grew to $182.5 billion in equity investment and credit lines while a snail's pace piecemeal sale of AIG's insurance affiliates was undertaken. AIG was to record a fourth-quarter loss of $61.7 billion for a total 2008 loss of $99.3 billion, and pay out $53.5 billion to CDS counterparties, including Goldman Sachs ($13 billion) and several major European banks.

Whatever the case for propping up Lehman, that for propping up AIG was much weaker. AIG Financial Products had a gamey reputation throughout its existence, so its "name" was mediocre, and it was in no way central to the operations of US financial markets in the way that Lehman was. The effect of its bankruptcy on AIG's mainstream insurance operations should have been limited, since they would as far as possible have been ring-fenced by the liquidator. Policyholders might have lost out partially but they were protected by various state and foreign government insurance protection schemes. AIG's bankruptcy would probably have destroyed the CDS market, but to thoughtful regulators that should have been one of its benefits – even in September 2008 it should have been obvious that CDS's dangers far outweighed the advantages. However, outside the CDS market, the market effect of an AIG bankruptcy in any but the shortest term would have been minimal.

A far better principle for bailouts was propounded by Martin in a column "The Bear's Lair: The Wrong Rescues,"[9] published less than a week after the AIG bailout:

> "The principles of sound bailout policy are clear. Bailouts should be very rare. They should be confined to institutions that are important to the market as a whole, that have a long and eminent track record, and the great majority of whose business is sound. Fly-by-night operations, or those with fraudulent or excessively aggressive business models, should be allowed to go to the wall, in order to discourage the piranha community."

By that standard, in the five bailout decisions the Fed and the Treasury had to make in 2008, they went 0 for 5.

★★★

---

[9] "The Bear's Lair: The Wrong Rescues," September 22, 2008. © Prudent Bear, 2008.

Later that week two further rescue takeovers were arranged: one in the US, one in Britain, both pushed hard by the respective governments, both of which had the effect of turning the rescuers into basket-cases. They were the takeovers of Merrill Lynch by Bank of America and of HBOS plc by Lloyds Banking Group.

Merrill Lynch was a major and very important name in investment banking that had acquired a habit of making mistakes in businesses that others managed better. It had been the defendant and forced to pay out $400 million in the Orange County, California derivatives case in 1994, in which the county's bankruptcy was blamed on inappropriate derivatives sold to it. Then it bought a subprime mortgage issuer at the top of the market, reported an $8.4 billion loss as early as November 2007, and paid the chairman who had engineered the deal, Stanley O'Neal, $161 million in stock option and termination benefits. It was accident-prone, in other words.

However, even more accident-prone was Bank of America's Ken Lewis, who on September 14 offered 0.85 shares of Bank of America for each share in Merrill stock, valuing the company at 1.4 times net asset value. Given Merrill's ongoing losses and the fact that its closest competitor Lehman Brothers filed for bankruptcy at 1 a.m. the following morning, this was a remarkably generous offer that Merrill shareholders and management gratefully accepted. When he found another $20 billion in Merrill losses during the "due diligence" process, Lewis tried to back out of the deal, but Treasury Secretary Hank Paulson and Fed Chairman Ben Bernanke bullied him into going ahead, threatening to fire him and the entire Board (under what legal authority?) if he pulled out of the deal, as he was legally entitled to.

Lewis was over-generous in his offer for Merrill Lynch. The correct price for it in the circumstances was zero, especially given its undisclosed losses. However, the acquisition that pushed Bank of America into the arms of the Feds was not Merrill Lynch but Countrywide; without that, the Merrill acquisition would have made good strategic sense, even if painful in the short run. It essentially gave Bank of America an investment banking franchise competitive with those of Citigroup and J.P. Morgan Chase, which an overgrown Charlotte-based regional bank like Bank of America could never have grown organically. However, with Lewis forced out and the Pay Czar determining what his successor can be paid, it must be doubtful whether so convoluted and extensive an operation can be held together for very long.

Meanwhile, on the other side of the Atlantic, Lloyds Banking Group thought it had spotted an opportunity and on September 17 made an offer of 0.83 Lloyds shares for each share of HBOS plc, itself the result of a half-baked 2001 merger between the Halifax Building Society and the Bank of Scotland. This was an acquisition that made no strategic sense whatever; it gave the combined group 28% of the UK market, thus drawing the unwelcome attention of the EU Commission and very probably forcing the sale or closure of Lloyds' crown jewel, the Cheltenham and Gloucester Building Society – a much higher-quality operation than the Halifax.

Even without the EU's heavy hand, HBOS gave Lloyds no additional business lines and could only work if followed by massive redundancies. Since HBOS was in serious trouble at the time of the Lloyds deal, and was large enough to endanger Lloyds and push it into eventual public ownership (while Lloyds shareholders were to get only 56% of the combined group), the upside of the deal was minimal and the downside vast. The deal ranks with Bank of America's acquisition of Countrywide for sheer stupidity. It can only have enraged the largely Tory customers and shareholders of Lloyds and the Cheltenham and Gloucester further to know that the deal had been personally urged by prime minister Gordon Brown, a man whose previous financial coup was to sell half Britain's gold reserves at the bottom of the market in 1999.

For the authorities, both the Merrill and HBOS deals must be regarded as bad mistakes. They took two fairly large (but probably, in that market, doomed) institutions, and semi-forced their merger into two even larger (but probably, even in that market, viable) institutions, thus condemning the acquirers to failure also. Not a recipe for maximizing the health of the financial market or minimizing its calls on the public purse; certainly not a recipe for minimizing moral hazard or maintaining proper shareholder control of the banking system.

The week of September 15 must have seemed endless for the authorities on both sides of the Atlantic, but two further events of that momentous week bear mention. On Tuesday, September 16, the Reserve Primary Fund, a money market fund that had held substantial Lehman Brothers debt, "broke the buck" – which had only happened once before in money market funds' 34 years of existence – and allowed its net asset value to fall to 97 cents.

The following day saw massive redemptions from institutional money market fund shareholders, but net investments by retail shareholders who doubtless rightly saw money market funds as sounder investments than the major banks. Nevertheless, on Friday 19, the US Treasury Department announced an optional program to guarantee up to $50 billion in assets of money market funds in return for a fee. By this stage the Treasury, on the brink of proposing the infamous $700 billion Troubled Assets Relief Program, had gone intervention-crazy; the support of retail investors for money market funds that week shows that there was no need for such a heavy-handed measure. It would have been much better if the Fed had raised interest rates to a level where money market funds did not have to stretch so far to achieve an acceptable yield.

The other major regulatory action that week was a complete ban on short selling of shares by the SEC. This was a market-damaging and crisis-irrelevant measure, since the stock market was overvalued, non-financial companies showed no signs of being in danger, and in any case the ban did not extend to credit default swaps, the true nexus of the short-selling "problem".

The following couple of weeks saw further reverberations of the banking crisis. On September 21, Goldman Sachs and Morgan Stanley, the remaining investment banks, announced that they had agreed to obtain banking licenses, making them subject to the tighter leverage requirements of the Fed and the Comptroller of the Currency, but also giving them access to the benefits of deposit insurance. This stabilized their position at the cost of introducing yet more risks into the banking system and adding to the obligations of the Federal Deposit Insurance Corporation – though since neither house at that point had significant retail deposits, the FDIC's liability was initially modest.

Two further major banks were sold in the following days. The largest savings and loan institution remaining in the US, Washington Mutual, with $328 billion of assets in 2007, was seized on September 25 by the Office of Thrift Supervision and the banking subsidiaries (minus unsecured debt and equity claims) were sold for $1.9 billion, unquestionably a knock-down price, to J.P. Morgan Chase. The Washington Mutual holding company filed for Chapter 11 bankruptcy the following day. This was an almost-classic 1907-style operation (except for the public sector involvement), with Morgan possibly getting a bargain and the OTS getting a problem off its hands. It helped that Washington Mutual was small enough not to be considered "too big to fail" or to endanger J.P. Morgan Chase significantly.

The failure of Washington Mutual destabilized the position of Wachovia Corporation, forcing its stock price down 26% on September 26 and draining it of $5 billion in deposits on that day. Wachovia was basically a sound bank, the fourth largest in the US, formed by a 2001 merger between Wachovia Bank (historically the best of the North Carolina banks) and First Union (another North Carolina bank). However, it had made one huge mistake: the top-of-the-market purchase of Golden West Financial in August 2006, and in this market that was enough to put it in danger – it had made an $8.9 billion loss on mortgage write-downs in the second quarter of 2008. On September 27, the FDIC declared that Wachovia was "systemically important" to the economy and so could not be allowed to fail – the first time this determination had been made since the passage of a 1991 law allowing the FDIC to handle large bank failures.[10]

Wachovia had been in merger negotiations with Wells Fargo, the fifth largest US bank, but Wells had backed out owing to concerns about Wachovia's commercial real estate loans. Accordingly, the FDIC decided to sell Wachovia to Citigroup for stock worth $1 per Wachovia share, a quite extraordinary decision since Citigroup was obviously far worse run and in far more widespread and deeper trouble than Wachovia. The FDIC agreed to absorb Citigroup's losses above $42 billion in return for $12 billion in stock and warrants.

Wachovia's management and shareholders both hated the Citigroup deal, which more or less wiped out shareholders and would result in the destruction of Wachovia's franchise. Consequently, management re-opened negotiations with Wells Fargo and on October 3 announced an all-stock merger with no FDIC involvement valuing Wachovia at $15.1 billion, far more than the Citigroup deal although still very cheap. The FDIC consented, since its liability had been removed. Citigroup sued – inevitably – but seems unlikely to get far. The

---

[10] The same determination had been made for Continental Illinois Corporation in 1984, before the 1991 law.

Wells-Wachovia merger appears to be working well. The combined bank is large enough and has enough California experience through Wells to absorb the inevitable losses from the remains of the ineffable Golden West. Certainly the bank's position as one of the four largest US banks, with a nationwide consumer franchise and fewer problems than all its big competitors except J.P. Morgan Chase, is an enviable one. A private sector success was thus rescued from what would have been a public sector disaster.

On September 29, the Fed authorized an extension to $330 billion of swap lines with foreign central banks, to prevent liquidity shortages internationally – so ensuring that liquidity excesses would be spread throughout the global financial system.

Inevitably, these bailouts led to huge public anger directed mainly at the vastly overpaid senior executives who had led their companies to destruction. The saturnine Dick Fuld, the former Lehman CEO, soon became the focus of this anger. "I take it as a personal failing to lose money," he used to say, before his "Mother Ship" hit the rocks. In a Congressional hearing on October 6, 2008, Congressman John Mica (Republican, Florida) bluntly told Fuld that he was the villain and should play the part; he did so magnificently, and looked the part too. Congressman Waxman said to him, "You made all this money by taking risks with other people's money. The system worked for you, but it didn't seem to work for the rest of the country and the taxpayers, who now have to pay $700 billion to bail out our economy."

Fuld's response was extraordinary: "I take full responsibility for the decisions that I made and the actions that I took," he said, but quite what he meant by that is hard to fathom as he then denied that he had made any errors or misjudgments in the period leading up to the firm's bankruptcy. When the touchy subject of his remuneration then came up, he went on to defend the compensation system that had paid him about $350 million between 2000 and 2007. As he explained, "we had a compensation committee that spent a tremendous amount of time making sure that the interests of the executives were aligned with shareholders," as if that explained anything. Fuld's "acceptance" of responsibility was merely notional and no one was fooled: having been grilled by the Congressional Committee, Fuld then had to run the gauntlet of an angry mob outside. Far from accepting any real responsibility, Fuld painted himself as the victim: Lehman should have been bailed out too. It also came out that senior Lehman executives had been working on their golden parachutes at the same time as they were pleading for a federal rescue, and that three departing executives had been paid bonuses just days before the company collapsed.

It would be wrong to blame Fuld alone; his Wall Street defenders would point out that he had also lost a lot of money himself, allegedly nearly a billion dollars in Lehman stock that became worthless. But it should be pointed out that he had made an immense fortune out of Lehman and was still a very wealthy man after the firm collapsed – no nineteenth century bankruptcy here!

★★★

Undoubtedly panicked by the signs of meltdown in the US banking system, Treasury Secretary Hank Paulson announced on September 20 the Troubled Assets Relief Program, under which up to $700 billion of taxpayer's money would be spent to buy troubled mortgage-backed securities debt from US banks. Legislation was immediately introduced in Congress to this effect. Republican presidential candidate John Mc-Cain promptly suspended his campaign to help get TARP through Congress; Democrat presidential candidate Barack Obama was more circumspect, although he too supported the program.

TARP in its original form would have been almost a pure handout to the big trading houses, as sharpies in the trading community would have manipulated the prices of dubious mortgage backed securities to offload the most toxic rubbish on taxpayers at inflated prices. $700 billion would have been spent and very little achieved. The probability of waste became even more obvious when Bernanke proposed to the Senate Finance Committee on September 23 that TARP should buy assets at above market prices in order to prop the banks up further.

That's not to say an asset purchase program of some sort couldn't work, although it would involve pouring more capital into an economic sector that had shown itself unproductive, so starving better uses of funding. As remarked in Chapter 3, Treasury Secretary Andrew Mellon suggested a somewhat better program in 1931. Mellon's proposed program had several crucial advantages over Paulson's. First, it was entirely private sector and involved no public money. Second, because of this, the major banks would operate it, so purchases would have been made at true market prices. There would have been no question of sellers pulling the wool over the eyes of buyers, who would generally have been savvier than the selling regional banks. Finally, it involved only loan assets, which were not at that time traded. Hence the precise content of each asset was known and there was no universe of traders throwing sand in the eyes of buyers and sellers alike.

Thus it is a great pity Mellon's plan was not tried in 1931; while it would have mitigated the 1931–33 disaster only somewhat, it would have been an excellent precedent for Paulson on which Bernanke, as the resident scholar on the Great Depression, could have enlightened him.

The House of Representatives, recognizing the taxpayer rip-offs likely in Paulson's original TARP, especially as administered with the help of Bernanke, rejected it on September 29 by 228–205. However, with several Senate sweeteners – mostly even more unproductive uses of money – it was resubmitted, passed by both houses, and signed by President Bush on October 3.

For the next ten days, the authorities sucked their thumbs wondering how to spend the money. Then, on October 14, the US Treasury announced that it would buy preferred stock and warrants in the nine largest US banks, and would allow other banks to apply for similar bailouts. Whether or not a bailout was justified, this seemed the form of bailout most likely to provide some value for money for US taxpayers. Indeed it has proved so; $84 billion of the money was repaid within a year, plus modest profits for taxpayers on the warrants.

It also had the advantage of being much cheaper than any attempt to buy out the mortgage bond market would have been. At November 2009, $210 billion remained in the $700 billion TARP fund, even though more than $100 billion has been used as a government slush fund to bail out AIG and the automobile manufacturers. What's more, only about $150 billion or so of the government's capital investments in banks has been irretrievably lost, so the total cost to taxpayers is probably only about $250 billion – which could have been reduced still further had a good auditor prevented the government from diverting the money to improper uses. However, the TARP money did nothing to stimulate bank lending, its stated objective, which dropped by $600 billion over the following year.

The first bank to use TARP money properly was PNC Corporation, which received $7.6 billion and used it on October 24 to buy National City Corporation, a Cleveland bank that had run into difficulties. The acquisition seems to have worked well and, if successful, will vault PNC to the largest regional bank below the Big Four. PNC has announced that it will repay TARP by January 2011, but through building up its reserves rather than issuing equity at discounted prices. However, against this success must be placed a number of failures, including several banks, such as US Bancorp and BB&T Corp, that in spite of being healthy were in 2009 compelled to slash dividends to shareholders in order to repay TARP.

A few banks got extra goodies as well as TARP money. On November 17, Citigroup was granted an additional $20 billion in TARP money, beyond its initial $25 billion, plus a guarantee of $306 billion in Citigroup's loans and securities. This bailout – the fourth that Citigroup has received from the federal government[11] – stabilized its situation in the short term, but was to be followed by conversions of the TARP injections into TARP equity during 2009. Bank of America also got an additional $20 billion and a guarantee of $118 billion in debt and securities on January 16, 2009 when it was learned how bad its losses on Merrill Lynch and Countrywide had become. These asset guarantees greatly escalated the risk of the bailouts to taxpayers and strongly suggest that Citigroup and Bank of America should have been allowed to fail, rather than emerging from the recession with their operations intact, albeit at considerable expense to their shareholders.

For the remainder of 2008, as the US and global economies fell into recession caused partly by a tight credit squeeze, the Fed's principal priority was providing liquidity, which it did to the extent of doubling the monetary base, trebling the size of its own balance sheet, and eventually creating more than $1 trillion of excess reserves. Several Fed announcements followed:

- October 6: announced that it would pay interest on bank reserves held with it;
- October 7: announced firstly a commercial paper funding facility to provide a backstop to US issuers of commercial paper through a

---

[11] The previous three being in 1931, through the Reconstruction Finance Corporation; in 1982, when the Latin American market went sour; and in 1991, when Prince Al-Waleed bin Talal bought a strategic stake.

special purpose vehicle, and secondly in increase in deposit insurance to $250,000 per depositor;

- October 14: introduced the Temporary Liquidity Guarantee Program to guarantee the senior debt of all FDIC-registered institutions and their holding companies;
- October 21: announced the Money Market Investor Funding Facility to buy assets off money market funds; and
- November 25: announced the creation of the Term Asset-Backed Securities Lending Facility, under which it would lend up to $200 billion on a non-recourse basis to holders of AAA-rated asset-backed securities – the same day, it announced that it would buy up to $500 billion in obligations of Fannie Mae and Freddie Mac.

By these actions, the Fed increased its balance sheet from $946 billion on January 1, 2008 and $959 billion on September 17, 2008 to $2,301 billion at December 31, 2008. In other words, it created $1.34 trillion of liquidity in less than four months. By any standards, it had avoided the mistake of its sorry predecessor in 1931–32.

Walter Bagehot said in his classic *Lombard Street*:

> "Very large loans at very high rates are the best remedy for the worst malady of the Money Market when a foreign drain is added to a domestic drain. Any notion that money is not to be had, or that it may not be had at any price, only raises alarm to panic, and enhances panic to madness." [12]

Bagehot's remedy of very large loans at very high interest rates is still valid. But he also said these loans should be to solvent institutions and be backed by top quality assets. The Fed, by contrast, had built up a huge $1 trillion-plus of excess reserves on bank balance sheets – a major inflationary danger – while also exposing itself to massive credit risk. In fact, the Fed now had a balance more appropriate to an extremely large, highly leveraged hedge fund.

★★★

---

[12] Bagehot, 1873, pp. 56–7.

By December 2008 a global economic downturn was in full swing, the most severe since World War II. Attention was beginning to move from monetary excess to fiscal excess. On December 17, the outgoing Bush administration granted $17 billion in loans to GM and Chrysler under TARP, so demonstrating that program's usefulness as a general slush fund for politicians. On December 21, as we now know, Bernanke and Paulson strong-armed the hapless Ken Lewis into going through with the Merrill Lynch acquisition.

The new Obama administration focused on fiscal rather than monetary means to help the economy. (In any case, it is difficult to imagine how monetary policy could have become even more stimulative other than, in Bernanke's famous phrase, by dropping $100 bills from helicopters, preferably on the populace as a whole rather than only onto Wall Street.) The $787 billion stimulus that passed on February 17, 2009 without any Republican support gave enormous pleasure to traditional Democrat constituencies, but very little direct uplift to the economy, while bringing the federal deficit (which was to exceed 10% of GDP in both the fiscal years 2009 and 2010) to the forefront of national concerns for the first time.

Needless to say, Bernanke was ready to help out, announcing on 16 March a program to buy up to $300 billion in federal debt, thus embarking the US on the same perilous course of monetizing government spending trodden by the Weimar Republic in 1919–23. However, he was only following the Bank of England, which had announced a £150 billion gilts-buying program on March 5. In terms of the overall size of the economy, the Bank of England's program is roughly four times that of the US, and the UK deficit is also larger, so adverse inflation effects are likely to be more severe in Britain.

In the banking sector, the market nadir was reached in late February when the Obama administration was forced to announce that the government stood behind the US banking system, and that "stress tests" would be conducted, based on a predicted economic outcome and a "worst case" outcome that was in fact somewhat less severe in terms of unemployment than the future trajectory of the recession. These announcements produced an up-tick in bank stock prices, which merged with an astonishing stock market rebound, taking it back almost to summer 2008 levels, which began on March 10. In consequence, when the stress test results were announced May 7, most of the participating banks were easily able to raise additional capital from the private markets, some of them using the opportunity to demonstrate their strength by repaying TARP.

Two substantial bankruptcies occurred in spring 2009, both of them negatively "assisted" by the presence of substantial credit default swap holders among the creditors. The pulp and paper company Abitibi-Bowater filed for Chapter 11 protection on April 16, with $5 billion of debt, after a debt reorganization had failed because around $2 billion of the debt was covered by CDS, giving holders an incentive to push the company into bankruptcy. The same day, the shopping mall developer General Growth Properties filed for Chapter 11 after its bondholders, many holding CDS, refused to accept a restructuring; at the subsequent "auction," the CDS were settled for 71% of par – a nice return for pushing a company over the edge! Similar CDS shenanigans were to play out in the General Motors and Chrysler bankruptcies in June.

Finally, on April 2, the Financial Accounting Standards Board caved in to the financial services industry, allowing for "fair market" valuation to revert to a mathematical model valuation if the market has become "disorderly." This allowed traders and managers to game the accounting system even more than they already had, making mark ups freely available in good times, but abandoning the fair market principle in bad times if it gave answers that were too unpleasant.

By the second quarter of 2009, the global recession was clearly bottoming out, and later in the year a slow recovery began. Commentators suggested however that full recovery might be delayed in the US and Britain, since the collapse of the financial system would not be overcome so quickly. More likely – since monetary and fiscal stimulus remains in place and is running in both cases at unprecedented levels – a further asset and inflation bubble will ensue, to be followed by a second downward leg once the economic imbalances created in 2008 begin to be seriously addressed.

Our detailed analysis of the events surrounding the 2007–09 financial meltdown ends here, with the stress test results announced in May 2009. It does not consider the liquidity-fueled bubble that has occurred since then, nor the extraordinary profitability of Wall Street trading operations that excessive liquidity has caused; nor do we dwell on the arrogant "happy days are here again" response of the bankers, thumbing their noses at the taxpayer and resuming large-scale bonus payments while still being on state support. Those events, while highly significant in themselves, are not part of the story of the financial crash and will have their own consequences in the future. We can, however, say without hesitation that the flaws in the financial and political systems that caused the crash have not so far been remedied and in many cases have been made very much worse.

14

The Slope Down Which We're Heading

Chapter 13 looked in detail at the recent past, the collapse and bailout of the US and British banking systems, ending in May 2009 – by which point the patients had been declared, prematurely, to be out of immediate danger. This chapter looks at the future, assessing where the US financial system and economy is likely to go if present trends continue – and the future does not look too good.

★★★

President Obama's admirers have sometimes compared him to his distant predecessor Franklin D. Roosevelt. This is a very apt comparison. Both presidents inherited economic emergencies created, or at least exacerbated, by the incompetent meddling of their immediate predecessors, and both responded to those emergencies by huge expansions of federal government activities. In Roosevelt's case, those policies left the US economy in a very poor state all the way up to Pearl Harbor in December 1941.

Obama's policies promise to be no more effective and for much the same reasons. Then, as now, none of those in power, political or financial, wanted the economy properly reformed in a free-market

direction. On the contrary, the Obama administration's hallmark policies of massive bailout and profligate spending on an unprecedented
scale have been wasteful and ineffective and did virtually nothing to
address the underlying problems that caused the crisis. In the long term
they will turn out to have been highly counterproductive, leaving the
economy debilitated and exposed to even more severe problems down
the road.

Monetary policy, the principal institutional cause of the crisis, has
been neither improved nor reformed, and the highly dangerous policy
of loose money has continued with a vengeance. This has been aggravated further still by the Federal Reserve endangering its own financial
health through highly dubious asset purchases motivated by the irresponsible policy of quantitative easing, which threatens to bankrupt
the Fed itself. If the history of the low interest rate policies since 1995
tells us anything, it suggests that recent policies of sustained, almost
zero interest rates are already creating a new asset price bubble on a
scale that will dwarf any of its predecessors.

Getting the economy on its feet requires fixing its financial engine
and this, in turn, requires eliminating unsound institutions and rebuilding the balance sheets of remaining ones, restoring them to financial
health. Very little has been accomplished on either front:

- Almost all the bad actors of 2002–07 are still in business thanks to
  state bailouts. Countrywide and Merrill Lynch have been absorbed
  by Bank of America, but Fannie Mae, Freddie Mac, Citigroup,
  RBS, and even AIG continue on their merry way, their style little
  altered by the enormous amounts of public money that have been
  poured into them.
- The government completely botched the rebuilding of the banks'
  balance sheets. The best approach would have been to (1) push
  them into emergency Chapter 11-type reorganization, ruthless-
  ly writing down their assets, wiping out the shareholders, firing
  much of the management, and imposing any remaining losses on
  depositors; and (2) rebuild the banks' capital bases with compul-
  sory debt-for-equity swaps. Instead, the government guaranteed
  deposits and threw vast amounts of taxpayers' money into a bot-
  tomless pit of bailouts, guarantees, and asset purchases, in a vain
  attempt to prop up the banks' assets. In so doing, it left the banks

still crippled and most of the management not only still in charge, but also bailed out courtesy of the taxpayer and lavishly rewarded for their own incompetence.

To say the least, this is not the way to restructure the financial system.

Nor have there been any significant reforms of banks' risk management practices. This, however, should come as no surprise. The purpose of "risk management" was not to manage risks, but merely to pretend to do so: real risk management would have meant severely dented profitability, and who wants that? In any case, now that risks have become socialized, there is even less incentive to control risk-taking than there was before and neither governments nor regulators have shown themselves able to do anything about it. No wonder bankers are defiantly rejoicing that happy days are here again.

Finally, matters have been made much worse by truly astonishing fiscal laxity, including the global nonsense of "stimulus." This has been immensely costly and almost completely ineffective, and crowds out a great amount of economically worthwhile activity. It also poses grave threats to the solvency of governments across the world and is certain to lead to government defaults as the crisis enters its next stages.

★★★

Looking forward, let's begin with the macroeconomic prognosis. The year-on-year CPI inflation rate, having been at a low of −2.1% in August 2009, is bouncing back (latest figure: 2.7% for January 2010) and clearly on the rise. Evidence of this is also provided by the soaring prices of gold and other commodities, the former especially being a traditional leading indicator of inflation.

As the economy recovers, however hesitantly, we can also expect recent rapid monetary growth to feed through to prices: inflation will therefore rise further. How much will depend on how quickly and how successfully the Fed manages to claw back that monetary growth, and especially the extraordinary expansion of the monetary base (which rose from a fairly steady value of under $900 billion before the second half of 2008 to double by the end of that year, and has risen further to more than $2 trillion currently).

The reappointment of "Helicopter Ben" Bernanke for another four-year term as Fed chairman does not reassure us that the Fed will be able to handle this problem effectively; nor are we reassured by recent rumors that other senior Fed officials are now openly admitting that they can't see the end game: having taken us up the creek, they are now saying that they don't have a paddle to get us back. Thanks, guys. Putting all this together, we would therefore expect inflation to return with a vengeance.

For the past fifteen years, US inflation as reported has been suppressed by globalization. With money so cheap, the process of outsourcing manufacturing and many services to countries in which labor is much cheaper has been accelerated, although the process itself was inevitable anyway. That process has now achieved an unstoppable momentum, since the high savings rates and dedication to education in poorer Asian countries have enabled them to build domestic pools of capital and skilled labor that make them fully competitive with the US and Europe, whatever happens to global interest rates.

Another factor that will help re-ignite US inflation is an outbreak of inflation worldwide. Global foreign exchange reserves quadrupled in the decade to 2008, a rate of increase far in excess of world growth plus inflation. These new gigantic liquidity pools are themselves inflationary; they also explain the continuing imbalances such as the perpetual US balance of payments deficit. At some point, they will not merely push up the gold price, but cause resurgent worldwide inflation that will inevitably affect the US.

When that inflation appears it will be virulent, because of the magnitude of the effects causing it. It will also be very hard to eradicate, because of rising emerging market wage rates finally limiting the inflation-suppressing effect of rapid globalization.

As inflation comes back, we must expect pressure on market interest rates to rise. The Fed can only resist this pressure temporarily, and only then by pumping more money into the system: such a policy would only stoke inflationary pressures further and should certainly be avoided. If the Fed tries to keep interest rates down, it will only create higher inflation a year or so down the road. A really determined effort on the Fed's part to keep interest rates down would be truly catastrophic, as it would lay the foundations for a potential hyperinflation that would destroy the value of the currency entirely and of course wreck the economy. To quote a memorable passage from Keynes's

1920 *Economic Consequences of the Peace*, when Keynes still believed in the Quantity Theory of Money:

> "Lenin is said to have declared that the best way to destroy the Capitalist System was to debauch the currency. By a continuing process of inflation, governments can confiscate, secretly and unobserved, an important part of the wealth of their citizens …
>
> Lenin was certainly right. There is no subtler, no surer means of over-turning the existing basis of society than to debauch the currency. The process engages all the hidden forces of economic law on the side of destruction, and does it in a manner which not one man in a million is able to diagnose."[1]

We can only pray that the US will be spared such horrors. But whatever the Fed does, interest rates will rise, we hope sooner rather than later. With so much hot money flowing into it, the Treasury bond market shows all the signs of being in a major bubble itself. A comparatively small event – a small rise in inflation, for example, or a default in some minor European, Asian, or Latin American country – could then trigger a bond market crash as speculators realize that prices can only go down and race to the exit. This could be very unpleasant indeed.

A bond market collapse could then trigger collapses in stock and real estate markets, and put the nascent economic recovery into reverse. The combination of economic downturn and higher inflation would take us back to the dubious pleasures of stagflation, which those of us of a certain age can remember only too well.

As foreign holders flee the US Treasuries market, it would also likely trigger another dollar crisis, and a falling dollar would mean higher import prices feeding through to increase inflation further.

Any meltdown in the Treasury bond market would also trigger a major fiscal crisis, possibly even a solvency crisis, for the US federal government. Higher interest rates would put huge additional pressure on the government's already overstrained finances by increasing the government's borrowing costs. At the same time, a renewed economic downturn would raise its deficit further as tax income goes down and

---

[1] Keynes, 1920, pp. 235, 236.

spending on unemployment benefits and similar outlays goes up. To make matters even worse, there is also the danger that the government would respond as it has done with yet more unstimulating stimulus packages, crippling the economy even more and risking its own bankruptcy in the process.

With the monetary, fiscal, and structural problems that the US economy has now developed, a decline in living standards is inevitable. Continued high immigration, both legal and illegal, undertaken to appease the interest groups – among them, bankers wanting cheap, readily available maids and gardeners – will immiserate the domestic workforce further, especially at the low-skill end. Fiscal problems and populist legislation will make taxes on legitimate businesses and the wealthy higher still, increasing their tendency to leave the country. After-tax wages will decline rapidly as export sectors find themselves competing with Chinese manufacturing, and domestic service sectors find themselves competing with Mexican labor. Then, in a vicious circle, declining real wages will erode the US tax base further, exacerbating the fiscal problem.

Even before the crisis, informed observers had been warning of a looming fiscal disaster in the United States and other developed countries. They had been warning of the longer-term fiscal gap – the extra tax burden that would have to be imposed on current and future taxpayers, relative to current policy, for the federal government to meet existing longer spending commitments: the impact of an ageing population, longer life expectancies, rising medical costs, and greater entitlements on the government's finance.

Even before the crisis, this burden was estimated to be approaching $100 trillion dollars and rising, an unfunded debt obligation of well over $1 million for each family of four. A leading authority on this subject, Boston University economist Laurence J. Kotlikoff, was already asking "Is the United States bankrupt?" and envisaging a possible scenario in which future generations of educated Americans emigrated abroad in very large numbers to flee the burdens currently being built up for them, in some cases before they were even born.[2] To quote another authority, Richard W. Fisher, the president of the Dallas Fed:

---

[2] Kotlikoff, 2006

"I see a frightful storm brewing in the form of untethered government debt. ... Unless we take steps to deal with it, the long-term fiscal situation of the federal government will be unimaginably more devastating to our economic prosperity than the subprime debacle and the recent debauching of credit markets."[3]

And remember that all this was in the pipeline *before* the current crisis hit and government spending and borrowing went through the roof, bringing national bankruptcy forward at a truly alarming rate – while most US citizens from the President down are (or at least pretend to be) blissfully unaware of the problem. The situation for many other Western economies is not that much better – in some cases, worse.

★★★

On Wall Street, banks that have been deemed "too big to fail" will get bigger: in part because it pays to be too big to fail, and in part because of the huge advantages of scale in trading businesses. On this latter point, dominance in a particular product line (and especially knowledge of the funds flows by investors within that product line) vastly increases an operation's profitability. In truly competitive markets, such as foreign exchange, this does not matter; the relatively small merchant bank Hill Samuel remained a market leader in foreign exchange through the 1970s, even against competition from British and international commercial banks many times its size. However, since the derivatives and securitization markets are neither truly competitive nor transparent, the opportunities to fleece participants through superior knowledge of money flows are everywhere.

In the private sector, global leverage is recovering as though nothing had happened. Hedge fund capital soared back beyond $2 trillion in late 2009, and while the leverage available on that amount is not what it was in 2007, it still represents a huge pool of hot trader-dominated money seeking markets to destabilize.

The level of trading-based rent seeking increased in 2009, after the crash, and seems likely to increase further. "Fast trading" in which computers are stationed at the Stock Exchange to instantaneously pick

---

[3] Fisher, 2008

up the pattern of trading activity, then trade on that insider knowledge, is becoming more sophisticated and more profitable all the time. Other factors adding to trading profitability are continuing sloppy monetary policy and the fact that asset bases can be expanded without concerns about stability, because of the implied bailout guarantee created by "too big to fail."

As a corollary to the growth of "too big to fail", moral hazard will get worse. Now that bailouts appear to be available almost on demand, traders will look for new ways to shove the "tails" of risk distributions onto taxpayers and further socialize risk, making the best possible use of new mathematical models and ever more exotic derivatives and securitization techniques. Regulatory arbitrage will become even more profitable.

Nothing has been done to rein in accounting and rating agency abuses, and we can therefore confidently expect these to continue. The only major change to mark-to-market accounting has been to make it even more agreeable to Wall Street, by allowing banks to eliminate write-downs in illiquid securities if the result is too unpleasant. This covers up the continuing weakness in banks' balance sheets with potentially fatal consequences for the future, while doing nothing to prohibit the fictitious mark-ups that did so much damage in the run-up to the crisis.

The problem of the rating agencies remains unsolved, despite interminable discussion. In any case, these marginally competent entities were probably incapable of keeping up with the risks incurred by securitization, but their total dependence on issuer fees meant they didn't try very hard and, indeed, had no incentive to.

On the investment management side, there still remains the problem of fiduciaries investing in fee scams such as hedge funds and private equity funds. The evidence that these operations provide superior returns is underwhelming, not to say non-existent, yet major pension funds and other fiduciaries continue to devote large portions of their assets to them, certain only that the management fees involved will be enormous. Since investment returns are likely to be low for a decade or so, the net returns after expenses to investors will be minimal. This problem is likely to be exacerbated by the further growth of high-fee instruments whose pricing is not transparent to investors, so that entrusting your assets to an investment manager will become even more expensive than it has been. Of course, these problems will just encourage investors, the silly creatures, to seek out ever more exotic and expensive ways of losing their money.

Derivatives will remain a major source of Wall Street's profitability and are therefore, given the chance, likely to continue their long-term expansion. It was particularly unfortunate that the government protected Wall Street from the pain it should have experienced at the time of the AIG rescue. Consequently, while Wall Street houses pay lip service to the need to cut the market back, they still haven't learned the necessary lessons. They will continue to trade credit default swaps irresponsibly, keep trades opaque and risk-manage CDS positions using models that could have been designed to hide their risks. There will be no solution to the misuse of CDS in bear raids or the problem of "empty creditors" in bankruptcy negotiations, in which creditors holding CDS are motivated to destroy a tottering company against creditors' natural interests to the contrary.

For the same reason, as markets appear to stabilize, new exotic securitizations will appear, and are already doing so: re-remics and the like. Like CDS, they will have pathological risk profiles, so score well on conventional risk management models while in reality involving a high degree of hidden risk. Even if the financial engineers move out of subprime mortgages because of their notoriety, there are plenty of other areas such as credit card loans and real estate lending in which an almost infinite volume of plausible seeming and profitable junk can be produced.

Derivatives will remain the largest single threat to the global financial system: their volumes are so enormous in relation to the system overall that any problem in their management quickly overwhelms the system's limited capital base. Without proper reform, it's likely that the financial system will blow up every five to seven years, each time on a bigger scale, and each time dragooning ever more unhappy taxpayers to bail it out, until the whole system – and with it, probably the world economy too – eventually collapses.[4]

---

[4] Propaganda that the Troubled Assets Relief Program was not particularly costly fails to focus on the reality that it was by no means the only bailout in the autumn of 2008. The bailouts of AIG, Fannie Mae, Freddie Mac, and Citigroup have already cost taxpayers many hundreds of billions of dollars, and if those entities are allowed to continue in business long term, the cost will escalate further.

Risk management is likely to continue as a fig leaf to justify higher leverage and keep the regulators happy, rather than a serious or even meaningful attempt to manage risk. Although most quantitative risk management practices have shown themselves to be virtually useless, banks have done nothing to replace them – and since banks need a function labeled "risk management," life carries on as if nothing has happened. This is because ineffective risk management serves the interests of Wall Street. Even before the crisis, excess risk-taking served the interests – that is to say, the short-term interests – of traders and the senior managers who lived off them: they got the profits if the risks came off and other people took the losses if they didn't.

This most egregious of moral hazards has been made even worse since the crisis, as "too big to fail" has become enshrined as a key pillar of public policy. The downside cost of risk management going wrong has been laid off not on the shareholder or even the creditor, who had at least chosen to be contractually involved, but on the taxpayer – the ultimate innocent victim, who got no profit from the transaction, never agreed to it and was never consulted, who was least able to protect himself from Wall Street predators, and was let down by those he elected to represent his interests.

The US housing sector has become even more of a morass of subsidies than before 2008. Housing loans are effectively government-guaranteed because the housing behemoths Fannie Mae and Freddie Mac have been granted a blank check by the US Treasury. The FHA program will continue allowing those of modest means to borrow for home purchase with only a 3% down payment, or close to it, thus short-circuiting the credit process in the conventional mortgage sector and virtually guaranteeing high default rates in the future.

By this means, local housing lenders will be suppressed by government-subsidized competition – their principal value added, the benefit of knowing their local credit risks, will be negated by government guarantees and securitization. Hence the housing finance market will remain securitized with default rates that are high by historic standards and subject to periodic crises at a nationwide rather than a local level.

The inevitable rise in interest rates will then trigger yet another crisis in the housing markets. Add to this a likely decline in US wage levels due to competition from emerging markets, and the potential exists for another housing meltdown similar to that of 2007–09 but starting from a lower level of house prices. At present, house prices remain somewhat above their historical average in terms of earnings – not surprising, with all the subsidies – but that position is untenable and will eventually correct itself.

The one function that the ever enlarging behemoths do not perform well is that of corporate finance, the original raison d'etre for the investment banking business: arranging financings and merger transactions for clients. The trading behemoths not only provide inferior service, because of their cumbersome size, but also suffer innumerable conflicts of interest for any but the most isolated client. If you are asking an investment bank to arrange your tricky new financing, you don't want that house to have a proprietary trading desk that takes a position in direct opposition to your needs. So, for example, although it was very clever of Goldman Sachs to be shorting the mortgage market at the same time they were arranging mortgage deals, both issuer and investor clients (to the extent they are still in business) can reasonably feel somewhat miffed, and future clients might prefer to deal with institutions that have no such conflicts of interest.

For these sorts of reasons, the corporate finance business has been migrating to "boutique" houses over the last several years. Greenhill & Co., founded in 1996, is now a publicly traded company with capital of $250 million, comparable in real terms to the merchant or investment banks of the early 1970s – most of whose services it now offers. Evercore Partners, founded the same year, is of approximately the same size. These institutions are only one hundredth of the size of Goldman Sachs in terms of capital, yet they are perfectly capable of competing with it in most traditional investment/merchant banking areas of business. Even underwriting, traditionally held to be a business requiring a large capital base, can very well be undertaken by these houses using the underwriting capacity of the big investment institutions, as was done in London in the 1970s. In a truly free market, the trading behemoths would wither on the vine.

Unfortunately, this won't happen quickly until the behemoths' rent seeking is reined in. They are so much bigger than Greenhill and Evercore that they can, if necessary, cross-subsidize their corporate finance activities by profits from their rent-seeking trading. Only when the profitability of trading has diminished, therefore, can we expect the majority of corporate finance business to migrate away from the trading behemoths to its natural home in the boutiques.

We can also expect to see deteriorating standards of services to small and medium-sized business, with attendant deleterious effect on financial innovation.

Part of the problem with small business is that it tends to fall into the "too difficult" file. Private equity companies no longer invest much in venture capital, having lost their shirts after the tech bubble collapsed in 2000 – buying established companies and playing financial and asset-stripping games brings much quicker returns. Goldman Sachs and its ilk pay such enormous hourly wages that nobody there can afford to take the time to focus on the sector. Banks would rather lend to hedge funds – the amounts are greater and the monitoring difficulties fewer. Moreover, the huge borrowing requirements of the federal government and the steep yield curve have given the financial sector a much easier way to make money than messing around with the prospects of obscure companies.

The commercial banking system, traditionally the main source of finance for small business, is not doing its job: it has too many opportunities for high leveraged returns by borrowing short at the Fed's ultra-low rates and investing in Treasury bonds or, even better, in government-guaranteed mortgage bonds and home mortgages. Commercial and industrial credit, already in December 2008 only 17% of bank balance sheets, has shrunk in volume by 20% since then while bank balance sheets as a whole have shrunk by only 4%.[5] The Federal Reserve Board's quarterly Survey of Senior Loan Officers reports little demand for loans from small business, and a higher failure rate among small businesses than their larger brethren. That's not surprising, because banks have tightened their lending standards drastically for small business. Naturally, small businesspeople have more sense than beg for loans they won't get. The Senior Loan Officers therefore sit in their plush office suites playing with the paper clips and reporting that loan demand is poor, while outside in the snow small businesses, unable to get the funding they need, expire in droves.

---

[5] Federal Reserve Board: Assets and Liabilities of Commercial Banks in the United States (H8), February 5, 2010, and Senior Loan Officer Opinion Survey, January 2010.

To make matters worse, the US's appallingly low savings rate and high levels of estate duty mean there are few pools of private capital available for start-ups and early stage ventures. (By and large, wealthy traders aren't good at spotting such opportunities and mix in different social circles from entrepreneurs.) With venture capital also more or less out of the game, it is going to be damn difficult to get a start-up financed over the next decade, particularly if it is not in some currently fashionable business sector.

Within the big companies, on the other hand, the laser-like focus on quarterly returns will make top management reluctant to invest in research and development, or in enterprises likely to have a long-term risky payoff. After all, the benefit of the new enterprise is probably not enough to affect the parent company bottom line much, whereas its cost can knock a point or two off *this* quarter's earnings. There are no equivalents of Bell Laboratories, the Xerox Corporation's PARC, or Lockheed's Skunk Works in the Modern Finance economy.

With neither large private fortunes nor venture capital nor large corporations interested in funding innovation, the bottom line is that there won't be much of it. The main funder of innovation will be the government, and with government-funded innovation the political games and grant-gaming strategies will quickly ease out any truly innovative ideas. Thus the United States, however much its politicians and business may delude themselves to the contrary, will become a low-innovation economy, as well as, increasingly over time, a low capital economy too.

The total internationalization of finance means that assets, operations, and people will be shuffled between centers to an even greater extent than currently. Whereas the relatively impoverished non-financial residents of New York and London could once console themselves with the thought that at least the billionaires were adding substantially to the tax base, this will become increasingly less true. As the trader class becomes increasingly cut off from the rest of humanity, it is ever more able to relocate itself to tax havens, thus appropriating value to itself without the tedious business of paying tax on that appropriation. An example was the Tullett Prebon move to shift their brokers out of Britain temporarily in response to the 2009 bonus tax.[6]

---

[6] *Wall Street Journal*, December 14, 2009.

Another reason for this will be to avoid the auditors: it is so much easier to "wash" assets through centers such as Moscow or Shanghai in which audits are limited because the auditors are in fear of their lives.

A third reason would be to exploit bailout opportunities. When some government gets suckered for a juicy bailout, the operations in question will suddenly acquire vast piles of dodgy assets and other dubious claims that were not there before. We saw this in late 2008, when AIG's London based credit default swap book suddenly became subject to bailout by US taxpayers, much to the impotent annoyance of the US authorities.

Meanwhile, the evils of managerial and crony capitalism will get worse. With business and finance becoming more global, shareholders' ability to control companies is becoming weaker, while the ability of management to hide income and assets (and even itself) in tax havens has become greater. Top corporate management is increasingly becoming a lottery, in which early success in the game of office politics entitles the winner to gigantic remuneration and a sybaritic lifestyle, all at the expense of an entity that, in the best case, more or less runs itself with the help of thousands of ill-paid drones, ideally mostly located in the Third World. Neither shareholders nor even governments have much hope of controlling these entities, not least because they increasingly have the latter in their pocket. Needless to say, this is not in any meaningful sense capitalism and could eventually spawn revolution when the long-suffering proletariat has finally had enough.

The crash of 2008 has spurred huge popular demands for tighter banking regulation, not unreasonably, but it now seems clear that the great majority of this regulation will be counterproductive. Proposals such as the "Tobin tax," a small *ad valorem* tax on trading, which would rein in the unhealthy trading dominance and rent seeking, are almost certain to founder on resistance from the banks themselves. Conversely, proposals to regulate credit default swaps or securitization to reduce their risks and distortions will run into severe headwinds and will lack the populist appeal to prevail. There will therefore also be no significant regulation of rent seeking trading, whether "fast trading" or in other forms.

There will also be no significant regulatory drive to reform risk management. This is partly because most regulators don't understand the problem, and partly because the industry doesn't want them to understand it and is expert at producing obfuscatory papers that throw sand in regulators' eyes if they get close to understanding it. The most likely outcome is therefore something like the current Basel 2 regulations, with a few tweaks at the edges, including their disgraceful favoritism towards the behemoths. That's what the big players want, and of course it helps greatly that the public's eyes glaze over whenever the words "banking regulation" are mentioned.

While the structure of financial services remains wholly unreformed, it is inevitable that crises and bailouts will occur again and again. The credit default swap market alone can be relied upon to blow up at regular intervals, leading to instances of blackmail like that of 2008, where the major players announce that they must be bailed out or civilization as we know it will collapse. Thanks to crony capitalism, those requests will generally be met with an open checkbook, although there may be the occasional attempt to take a hard line, at which point the collapse of confidence that accompanied the fall of Lehman Brothers will seem like a picnic.

On the political front, the politicians will find themselves more or less impotent in their attempts to rein in the financial services businesses, since the measures that would have some chance of working have little popular appeal or even understanding, and because the financial sector will have bought many of them up and neutralized most political opposition. The repeated bailouts and subsidies to the financial services sector will be unpopular, of course, and will result in political denunciations of capitalism and expanding but counterproductive government control over more and more of the economy.

★★★

As the real economy stagnates and then declines, there will come a point where even the financial services sector will eventually go into decline as well: the long-term future is therefore bleak even for the financial practitioners of New York and London. Declining income and high costs will combine to produce large reductions in headcount: functions will be eliminated, work will be increasingly outsourced to the Third World and profits to tax havens, remuneration will fall, and the weaker entities will go bankrupt or be merged into competitors. By the time the bloodbath is over, most practitioners will have been eliminated and those that remain will see their incomes fall by 80% or more.

This also promises a weak long-term future for the local beneficiaries from financial services incomes. Such losers would include local housing markets and those of the smarter resorts, together with the army of real estate agents, decorators, construction companies, lawyers, and other hangers on who benefited so outrageously during the bubble years.

Inhabitants of London and New York have spent the last couple of decades sneering at their provincial cousins, particularly those involved in the grubby world of manufacturing, while they enjoyed the good life. They won't be laughing when the "rust belt" has reached them also.

In New York, the "rust belt" effect will be severe but not overwhelming – it will be 1970s Cleveland rather than 1980s Youngstown. Many of the skyscrapers of the financial district and the luxury residential areas will become ghost buildings, as their predecessor buildings did in the 1930s, but they are unlikely to descend to the chain-round-the-facility-guarded-by-a-rottweiler-and-a-tattooed-thug state symptomatic of the worst industrial blight.

For London, it will be much worse: London will be the Youngstown, an excellent market for rottweilers, wire mesh, and tattooed thugs. Docklands in particular will revert to its 1970s squalor, albeit with some very expensive buildings scattered around. Few of the financial institutions that have prospered so lavishly in the London of the past couple of decades are British-owned, and those that are were excessively involved in the British mortgage market – an even bigger disaster than the US market because home values were even more outrageous at the peak.

Given that the financial sector will be downsizing anyway, will top management in Frankfurt, New York, or Tokyo want to keep its stable of expensive London whizzkids in order to continue participating in a market that was never central to their overall strategy and is now unprofitable? We doubt it. Even the Russian mafia may leave, although probably to Cyprus rather than Moscow. Whereas New York's downturn may produce municipal bankruptcy, given the crippling burdens under which British citizens already live, London's downturn has a fair chance of tipping the economy over into national bankruptcy. Going forward, British youth will have to find a new way to make a living – single-malt Scotch and tourism cannot support a nation of 60 million people.

★★★

The next three chapters describe a possible way out of this vortex of despair. We will work outwards from fixing Wall Street's risk management methods (and abandoning Modern Financial Theory) to making institutional and taxation changes that will reverse the structural deterioration in the performance of the financial services sector, to correcting the monetary and fiscal policies that have greatly exacerbated the adverse economic effect of the financial sector's failings.

Part Six

Charting a New Way Forward

15

The Math of Proper Risk Management

This chapter, a "how to" of proper risk management (and measurement!), is somewhat optional. In deference to our deficiencies in mathematical rigor, we have kept the mathematical discussion at the level of hand-waving, rather than getting serious. Nevertheless, some delicately nurtured readers find mathematics off-putting even at the hand-waving level, and we sympathize. All the same, if you can stand it, have a go – the subject of how quantitative risk management ought to be done is an instructive and useful one.

Before diving headfirst into the math of risk management models, there are some caveats we should never forget:

- The first is that the future is uncertain and always will be.[1] Only some of the uncertainty we face is quantifiable in any meaningful sense, and what is not quantifiable is often more important than what is. We must avoid the trap of thinking that what we think we can measure is all there is. We should also avoid the related trap, to which quantitative experts, bankers, and regulators are all especially prone, of overrating

---

[1] Going further, accurate prediction requires that we can predict the impact of factors such as future technological progress. But if we could predict those, then we could develop them now. Ergo, they are not predictable.

the importance of quantitative methods. Quantitative methods have their uses, but we need to be aware of their limitations.

- Precisely because the future is essentially unknowable, we should be wary about relying on any one quantification method. Since every method has own its strengths and weaknesses, relying on any one method leaves us exposed to that approach's particular weaknesses. It is better to be eclectic and use a suite of methods that complement each other. In this chapter we shall suggest a multiple "litmus test" approach for some particularly recalcitrant risk problems.

- Forecasts and risk assessments should be prudent and biased on the side of safety. This sounds straightforward, even trite, but is very difficult to achieve, because it requires that analysis be done in an environment where prudence is genuinely valued. This, in turn, requires a corporate and market structure that rewards prudence rather than penalizes it. In practice, as we have seen, modern risk managers are often pressured into "optimistic" don't-rock-the-boat assumptions and stress tests that are not nearly stressful enough. Forecasting and risk assessment under such pressures is essentially pointless.

Much real-world forecasting boils down to putting some arbitrary input, typically the most recent price, into an Excel spreadsheet and then extrapolating it to some ludicrous horizon period many years out. The very ease with which one can carry out such exercises means that they often involve very little thought, but take on a life and a spurious certainty of their own. Such "predictions" are naive in the extreme, and take no account of uncertainty or even their own past record of forecast errors, which might tell the forecasters something if they paused for a moment to reflect on them: typically, the errors in such predictions are so large that they drown any usefulness of the predictions themselves. Forecasting oil prices in particular has been a very entertaining mug's game. To give a well-publicized example, *The Economist* magazine got many sober nods of appreciation for its analysis in 1999, when it forecast oil prices of $5 a barrel, just before they began their long climb from the $10 they had at that point reached.[2]

---

[2] *The Economist*, "The Next Shock?" March 4, 1999. The article is well worth reading, just to see how wrong intelligent analysts can be: www.economist.com/opinion/displaystory.cfm?story_id=188181.

Such forecasts also ignore the ways in which forecasts become more degraded as the forecast horizon lengthens, as the world changes in ways that the forecasters had not and could not have foreseen. Forecasters should therefore avoid naive extrapolation, especially over long horizons, and they should take account both of the uncertainty inherent in any forecast and their own past failures. They may not wish to remind their paymasters of these, but should keep them crystal clear in their own memory banks.[3]

When forecasting prices or returns, it is generally much better to look at past patterns and incorporate these into the forecasts, especially patterns of mean-reversion by which prices often (and returns always) have a tendency to revert back from excessively high or low values – a tendency that simple extrapolation methods completely overlook. Even better is to build an underlying model, such as a model of the supply and demand for a commodity. Even then, one still has to be careful not to rely on naive extrapolation of the underlying factors on which demand and supply depend, and to be careful not to push the forecasts too far out into the future.

Another common error is to assume that the world follows simple linear Gaussian relationships. Leaving aside Gaussianity, the world is anything *but* linear, and forecasts based on linearity can be extremely inaccurate. The most one can say for linearity is that it might hold in the short run, as a rough approximation: so a particular variable – the volume of output, for example – might appear to be linear over a short period. However, the linearity will *always* ultimately break down. This is why naive extrapolation doesn't work.

One response to this sort of problem is to develop more sophisticated econometric models. We add more and more variables to some fairly linear regression equation, which typically lacks any plausible a priori foundation (so there is no particular reason to expect it to hold), then use it to extrapolate the variable of interest based on projections of input variables and estimates of the equation itself. But suffice it to say that, again and again, the apparently "best fitting" equations usually fail in their forecasts, often dismally; abundant evidence indicates that the predictive power of such models is no better than that of soothsayers

---

[3] Martin has forecast a level of 5,000 on the Dow Jones Industrial Index to readers on at least two dozen occasions since 2000. Still hasn't happened, but he's hoping!

or taxi drivers. To paraphrase one economist from many years ago, it's about time we took the con out of econometrics.[4]

The significance of nonlinearities was perhaps first appreciated by Henri Poincaré when he studied the famous "three body problem." If you have two planets in a solar system, you can predict their movements indefinitely. Now add a third, however small, such as a comet: at first, the new body will have no impact, but over time its effects become critical; and ultimately, the slightest changes in the size or location of the new body determine the behavior of the big planets. The basic idea is that as you project further out into the future, you need an increasing amount of precision about the dynamics of the system to compensate for a potentially increasing error rate; but, since there is a limit to that precision, this means that many dynamical systems are inherently unpredictable. Of course, a three body system is much simpler than those we seek to deal with in the "real world."

Poincaré's results were subsequently rediscovered by the meteorologist Edward Lorenz in the 1960s; he was attempting to forecast weather conditions a few days out and accidentally discovered that his simulations were acutely sensitive to very small discrepancies in the input parameters. This result later became known as the butterfly effect, whereby the fluttering of a butterfly's wings in the Amazon could set in motion a train of events leading, say, to a hurricane in Texas.

This chain of thought leads to chaos theory. A chaotic system is a particular kind of deterministic – that is to say, non-random – system with the property that a small change in input parameters can not only cause an arbitrarily large change in output, but can even cause the character of the system to change completely, changing from stable, say, to something wildly divergent and unpredictable, or back again.

To see a simple example of chaotic behavior, we set out below a chart of one of the simplest chaotic systems, the Logistic Map,[5] whose equation is given by:

$$x_{n+1} = rx_n(1-x_n)$$

---

[4] Leamer, 1983.
[5] May, 1976.

Logistic Map

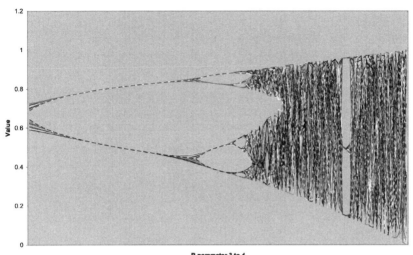

Figure 15.1 Logistic Map

This can easily be reproduced on MS Excel; you take 101 values of r, from 3 to 4 by 0.01 intervals, then set an initial value x_0 of 0.5, and copy-paste say 100 iterations of the above equation for each r value. Graph that lot (leaving out the r values and the x_0 values) and with a bit of twiddling of Excel's annoying graphing package, you'll get a picture like Figure 15.1.

The Logistic Map is a simple chaotic system. In particular:

- With r between 0 and 1, x_n converges on zero.
- With r between 1 and 2 x_n converges on the value $(r-1)/r$.
- With r between 2 and 3, x_n oscillates around the value $(r-1)/r$ before converging on it (very slowly indeed when $r = 3$).
- With r between 3 and $\sqrt{6}$ (about 3.45) x_n oscillates between two values forever.
- With r between 3.45 and 3.54 x_n oscillates between four values forever.
- With r between 3.54 and 3.57 x_n oscillates between 8, 16, 32, etc. values.

- From $r = 3.57$ the system is truly chaotic, with occasional islands of stability; for example x_n oscillates between three values around $r = 3.83$.
- From $r = 4$ the system diverges and x_n zooms off to plus or minus infinity.

These results show that chaotic systems can be very hard to predict: if the parameters governing the system (r, in this simple case, but also x_0 the initial value) vary just a little, it may suddenly change its behavior altogether, with its behavior after the change bearing no relation at all to its behavior before the change.

A second point to note is that even though a chaotic system might sometimes look random, it is not. Thus treating a chaotic price movement as random is not only in principle a category error, but may also produce very erroneous results.

We should also bear in mind that many of the factors affecting market movements are not random at all, but are simply unknown. The confusion of random and unknown is a central problem in much business forecasting, and the most common mistake in this area is to overlook the impact of unknown factors. Even business forecasters using the best probabilistic models to analyze situations in which they are inappropriate act surprised when reality produces results falling far out of line with outcomes their models anticipated.

Philosophically, failing to distinguish between the random and the unknown is an even greater category error than mistaking a chaotic distribution for a random one. Next week's weather may be largely random, subject to the vagaries of your location and the season of the year. However, next year's Gross Domestic Product is not so much random, as simply unknown. While certain factors on which the weather depends – whether there is a Katrina-like hurricane, whether the harvest will be good or bad – are random, the majority of factors on which next year's GDP depends are already "baked into the cake" by current production and marketing activities, current monetary and fiscal policies, and the current state of commodities, debt, and equity markets.

Since next year's GDP is mostly not random, we cannot assess it using probabilistic calculations. We certainly cannot assume that, if we take the standard deviation of GDP growth rates over the last 50 years, then the probability of next year's GDP lying more than three standard deviations from the mean is vanishingly unlikely. As 2008–09 has vividly demonstrated (and 1931 demonstrated before it), if policies and markets go dramatically wrong, GDP growth can easily fall far outside the range within which it normally moves.

Similarly, since economic conditions involve non-random factors, so too do earnings, interest rates, commodity prices, and stock markets. Even though the progress of the Dow Jones index may look like a random walk (actually, on closer inspection and comparison, it doesn't), the use of probabilistic methods to assess its movement, riskiness, etc. is a gross category error. Use of probabilistic methods, even sophisticated ones, that have apparently been verified by back-testing, can easily produce that most dangerous of all statistical artefacts: a prediction that is an apparent but not real fit to reality.

All is not however lost. Even the unknown can be estimated through fuzzy logic analysis to assess position risk and pricing, etc. Moreover, if we expand our stable of random distribution tools to include the Cauchy distribution as well as the Gaussian distribution, and have some idea of the possibilities that lie in between, we can get a much better estimate of how fat and how long the distribution's "tails" may be. Remember: it is in the tails rather than the body of the distribution that the risks lie.

To take a geopolitical example, consider the origin of World War I. The war was triggered by Gavrilo Princip's assassination of the Archduke Franz Ferdinand in Sarajevo, Bosnia on June 28, 1914, a mostly random event (albeit resulting from one of a number of Serbia-backed terrorist attempts during those years.) However, the assassination of the Austro-Hungarian Emperor Franz Josef's nephew alone did not cause the war, just as the isolated assassination of his wife Empress Elizabeth by an Italian anarchist in 1898 had not triggered war between Austria and Italy. If Franz Ferdinand had also been assassinated in 1898, there would have been at most an Austrian punitive expedition against Serbia, with no wider short-term consequences.

For European war to come, it was additionally necessary that the geopolitical conditions be conducive to it. The fuzzy logic "possibility" or "belief" of war breaking out was not zero in 1914, as it had almost been in 1898, because by 1914 Europe had divided into two opposing

alliances engaged in an arms race. In addition, there were secret trea-
ties between Britain and France, and secret war plans in the German,
Austrian, and Russian General Staffs, that made war more likely. That
"possibility" of war, dependent on both known and unknown factors
– so not fully apparent to contemporary decision-makers – was perhaps
30%. It had been higher, perhaps 50%, at the time of the 1911 Agadir
crisis, but had declined somewhat as the Anglo-German naval rivalry
had appeared to abate with the 1913 warship-building "holiday" proposal.

Without the random event of the assassination (or some other
equivalent random event), the 30% "possibility/belief" of war in 1914
would almost certainly not have led to war. There would have been no
casus belli allowing the General Staffs to trigger a pre-emptive war, and
so the European political situation might have continued improving,
until within a few years a general war might well have been as unlikely
as it had been in 1898.

Thus both random and non-random factors were necessary in
1914 in order for war to happen. Similarly, in the complex world of
economics, most events have both random and non-random (but often
unknown) components.

If factors affecting market moves are not random, then there is no
reason to expect them to obey probability's rules. Many apparent "fat
tails" in securities markets may be produced by the non-randomness of
some of the factors affecting securities prices. To the extent that markets are dependent on factors that are not random, they will not obey
probabilistic models and risk management that assumes probabilistic
behavior may well go seriously astray.

One can see similar issues in the housing finance market from 2003
onwards. In a stable market, losses on home mortgages will obey a
Poisson probability distribution, whereby moderate clustering of losses
can be expected. Provided house prices do not decline nationwide, and
none of the home loans are made on a fraudulent basis, probabilistic
models will predict losses on home mortgages quite well, although
even here Gaussian Value at Risk models will tend to underestimate
losses and have tails that are lengthy if not fat.

The US housing market of 2003–07, however, was not stable.
First, house prices were pumped up by excessively expansionary monetary policy, rising far above their long-term trend in almost all areas of

the country. That made certain a nationwide house price downturn, causing far greater losses than models anticipated. The size and duration of the likely price downturn was unknown, although certainly an appropriate simulation model would have included a random component, but the downturn itself from about 2004 on could be predicted with the utmost certainty.

Second, because of the long bull market in house prices, and the distorted incentives that Wall Street securitization had introduced into the housing market, it became attractive for mortgage market participants to write fraudulent loans. In the subprime area in particular, "liar loans" became attractive because they earned the mortgage broker a fee while obtaining a mortgage for the homebuyer, giving them the right to an asset that was apparently ever appreciating. Again, the epidemic of liar loans in the home mortgage market was an unknown but predictable result of loose money, ever appreciating house prices, and a home mortgage market with distorted incentives. Equally, appallingly high default rates on liar loans, once prices stopped appreciating, were not random; they were absolutely certain.

It is unsurprising that conventional risk management failed in a market in which non-random factors became increasingly important as the money-induced inflation continued. Not only did the mathematical models make assumptions about probabilities that proved to be untrue, they also assumed the randomness of factors that were in reality unknown.

A third form of non-random uncertainty is strategic uncertainty, or the uncertainty associated with economic games, which we discussed in Chapter 5. Perhaps the first point to understand about games is to be able to recognize one: we are in a game if we are wondering what other people will do, when their reactions affect us and vice versa.

What to do about games is altogether more difficult. In some cases, we can use game theory to tell us the economically optimal response as part of a Nash equilibrium, in which the parties involved each respond optimally to the other. But more often than not, an "optimal" response is impossible to determine, either because we can't find one or because there is more than one to choose from, and we can't tell what the parties concerned will go for. To make matters worse, there is abundant experimental evidence to suggest that people often do not go for the economically "rational" response anyway, but respond in accordance to still ill-understood behavioral norms. And then there are other games, such as games of chicken, where the outcome depends on bluff and counterbluff, force of personality, and other sometimes irrational factors whose impacts are impossible to predict.

On the other hand, trying to think through the interactivity of a game can be helpful to identify the range of possible outcomes, and so help to establish, for example, the likely worst outcome, which can then be fed into a stress test.

This kind of strategic uncertainty is particularly important for institutions whose operations represent a substantial share of a particular market – for example, Long-Term Capital Management in many derivatives markets in 1995–98. In such cases, the institution is no longer a "price taker" in the market but is interacting on a game-theoretic level with the other major market participants. Needless to say, purely probabilistic analyses of risk no longer apply in such cases.

Perhaps the worst responses to game uncertainty are to ignore it or to try to assume your way out of it by assuming arbitrary responses pulled out of thin air.

In many other situations we will be dealing with randomness in some form and in such situations we want to choose suitable random distributions and calibrate them properly. The key points to consider are:

- **Model risk:** We generally don't know which distribution to fit, and fitting the "wrong" distribution will produce errors. The best response to this problem is to select a variety of suitable distributions and check how they affect our estimates. The Gaussian is almost always a very bad choice; we need distributions that accommodate the fat tails that commonly characterize financial returns, and a much better choice is a stable Paretian. If we are dealing with extreme (very low probability, very high impact) events, we might use the distributions specified by Extreme Value Theory. In other cases, we might eschew fitting some off-the-shelf distribution and use the histogram of a set of returns actually achieved over some historical sample period, an approach known as Historical Simulation. In general, we should not be content with one model, but must add "litmus tests" to detect pathological risk profiles that appear artificially well-behaved in whatever single "best guess" model we choose.

- **Parameter risk:** Even if we think we know the distribution, any parameters of the fitted distribution are only estimated, not known, thus producing a second source of error. This can be a difficult problem to address and is usually glossed over by practitioners.
- **Sample risk:** When we calibrate the model, we need to choose a suitable data sample and sample period, and the former especially can make a very big difference to our estimates.

In addition, precisely because of the scope for estimation error, it is generally good practice not just to report an estimated risk measure, but also to report some indication of its precision. Perhaps the best such indicator is a prediction interval, which tells us that we can be 90% confident, say, that given the sample, model, and parameters, the unknown "true" value of our risk measure will lie in some specified range: the wider the interval, the less precise (and hence less informative) the estimate. One way to estimate such prediction intervals was suggested by Kevin using the statistical theory of order statistics, which deals with the properties of observations drawn from samples ordered from lowest to highest. We will skip over the details here; the important point is that these prediction intervals can be estimated.[6]

As an aside, if we wish to use probabilistic risk measures, and they do have their limited uses, then the Value-at-Risk methodology should be avoided: risk managers, please write out a hundred times, "The VaR is a discredited risk measure. I promise not to use it again." Where we wish to estimate a probabilistic risk measure, we should use measures like the Expected Shortfall or the Probable Maximum Loss instead.

To illustrate some of the issues involved, suppose it is August 19, 2009, a day we picked out at random, and we are interested in the next day's 99% Expected Shortfall for a portfolio invested in the New York Stock Exchange.

To deal with model risk, we consider two most commonly used models: a GARCH model with Gaussian errors, and a Historical Simulation model in which we estimate the Expected Shortfall from an historical sample of returns. To deal with sample risk, we use two alternative samples: the previous year's and the previous three years' daily returns. And, as per standard practice in this area, we gloss over the parameter risk

---

[6] Dowd, 2010.

in the GARCH model; parameter risk does not arise in the Historical Simulation approach because it does not use estimated parameters.

Estimates of the Expected Shortfall for the next day, August 20 2009, are shown in Table 15.1.[7] We see that estimates of the Expected Shortfall vary widely, and the Gaussian GARCH estimates are much lower (3.45% and 3.37%) than the Historical Simulation estimates (8.98% and 7.03%). This nicely illustrates how the Gaussian can lead to seriously under-estimated risks.

We also see that the Gaussian prediction intervals are quite narrow relative to the Historical Simulation intervals. This illustrates a further problem with the Gaussian, which we have not hitherto encountered: it can give spuriously precise risk estimates, a misleading sense that your risk estimates are much more precise than they really are. So, if we believed in the Gaussian, we would think that the 90% prediction interval, in the wider of the two cases, goes from 2.59% to 3.62%, whereas the corresponding Historical Simulation interval goes from a little under 6% to just over 10.5%. This confirms yet again that the Gaussian can be very treacherous.

Table 15.1: Estimates of Expected Shortfall for New York Stock Exchange, August 20, 2009

Model	Sample	Best Estimate of Expected Shortfall	90% Prediction Interval for Expected Shortfall
Gaussian GARCH	1 year's daily returns	3.45%	2.59% to 3.62%
Gaussian GARCH	3 years' daily returns	3.37%	2.87% to 3.58%
Historical simulation	1 year's daily returns	8.98%	5.91% to 10.52%
Historical simulation	3 years' daily returns	7.03%	4.85% to 8.09%

When dealing with randomness, there is also the all-important distinction between frequentist and Bayesian[8] probabilities. The former is objective probability of the "What is the probability that 1 in 6 balls in

---

[7] The figures in our examples are based on Dowd, op. cit.

[8] Propounded by the nonconformist minister Rev. Thomas Bayes (1764).

an urn is black?" type, and is the type of probability that most people are familiar with. The argument, in effect, is that either 1 in 6 balls in the urn is black, or some other number of the 6 balls is black, but we don't know which of these is true. The hope, then, is that if we can collect enough data and carry out suitable tests, our estimate of the probability that 1 in 6 balls is black will approach 1 if that hypothesis is true and 0 if it is not.

By contrast, Bayesian uncertainty is subjective, in the sense that it seeks to estimate probabilities taken as degrees of belief rather than objective fact, and to do so taking into account a user's prior beliefs. The argument here is that subjective beliefs matter, but the hope is that given enough accumulating evidence, the impact of prior beliefs will be drowned out by the evidence. Thus two individuals with different initial prior beliefs will, given enough evidence, eventually agree. However if the evidence is limited, they may not.

So my colleague might have been looking out of the window when the frequentist put the balls in the urn, but I took a sneak look and noticed that there seemed to be an awful lot of black balls going in. Consequently, his prior beliefs are quite open, whereas I am convinced that there is a fiddle. It will therefore take a lot of random drawings from the urn to persuade me that I am wrong. However, if evidence to that effect continues to build up, even I will eventually be forced to admit I was wrong, and concede that perhaps I need a new pair of glasses; while my colleague would have accepted the point much earlier. On the other hand, if I was right, then he was ignoring relevant information: he was just looking at the sausages coming out of the machine and ignoring everything else, including information about what was being fed into it.

The important point is that for the Bayesian, prior beliefs – that is to say, other bits of relevant information – matter. We would suggest that this Bayesian approach is much more relevant to risk managers, precisely because they have to (or at least should) take account of context, which the frequentist in his outer space zero-gravity laboratory ignores on principle.

One of the advantages of a Bayesian approach is that it allows us to specify our degrees of belief about the distribution we believe we face, so taking account of our beliefs about model risk.

A Bayesian approach can also take account of parameter risk, which is difficult to allow for in a standard frequentist paradigm: we specify our prior beliefs about the distributions governing parameter values, and can then sample randomly from these distributions instead of treating the estimated values of parameters as if they were their true values.

This sort of approach is easily implemented using Monte Carlo or "random number" analysis, a powerful approach that was first developed to solve the otherwise intractable analytical problems of the atomic bomb project and is now one of the mainstays of modern science, engineering, and, indeed, much of quantitative finance.

To take a simple example, let's say that we are fairly confident about the distribution that governs the random variable we are interested in, and let's say we feel we can also specify the distribution(s) that govern the random values of the parameters of that first distribution. We now calibrate the latter distribution(s) and then draw a single set of random parameter values. We use those parameter values to calibrate the first distribution and then draw a random value of the variable we are interested in from that calibrated distribution. This exercise, known as a simulation trial, gives a single simulated value for the variable of interest. We then repeat the trial many times over and thence obtain perhaps 10,000 simulated values of the variable we are interested in. We then draw up a histogram of these values and infer estimates of our risk measures from it.

To illustrate the potential usefulness of this approach in another context, suppose we are working for a pension fund and are interested in forecasts of future life expectancy. We take a mortality model (say, the CBD mortality model, one of the standard models in the field), set out our priors about parameter uncertainty (say, we assume a Jeffreys prior distribution, which is tractable, easily calibrated, and does not require strong assumptions), and write out a Monte Carlo program (don't ask!) that simulates the remaining life expectancy for an individual of a given age, for a given initial year, and over a specified future horizon period, both with and without taking account of parameter uncertainty.[9] We then calibrate the model against a chosen data set (say, we choose English and Welsh males) and, after a few minutes, the Monte Carlo routine produces the charts shown in Figure 15.2.[10]

---

[9] Cairns, Blake, and Dowd, 2006.

[10] For more on the longevity fan charts, see Dowd, Blake, and Cairns, 2010.

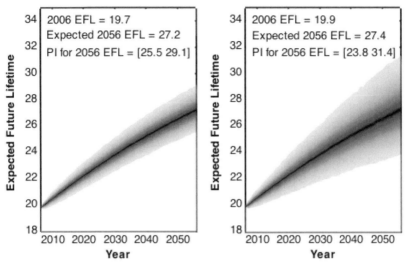

Figure 15.2: Longevity Fan Charts for 65-year-old English and Welsh Males

These charts, known as fan charts, give projections of the probability density functions for the future remaining life expectancy of 65-year-old English and Welsh males. The shading represents the likelihood of any given outcome – the greater the shading, the more likely the outcome – and give an easily understood visual representation of the quantifiable uncertainty involved, subject to the (limited) extent that we think we can quantify it. The bounds of the fan charts give us the 90% prediction interval for each future period over our forecasting horizon.

The life expectancy of a 65-year-old in 2006 is estimated to be a little under 20 years, but if we look at the chart on the left hand side, which ignores parameter uncertainty, we see that the same life expectancy 50 years out is projected to be 27.2 years, but this projection has a 90% interval spanning the range from 25.5 to 29.1 years. According to our projections, there is a 5% chance of life expectancy 50 years out being less than 25.5 years, a 90% change that it will be between 25.5 and 29.1 years, and a 5% chance of it being above 29.1 years. If we look at the right-hand fan chart, which takes account of parameter uncertainty, we see that central projection is much the same but the width of the prediction interval now widens dramatically, and spans the range from 23.8 to 31.4 years. The lesson (and one that often recurs in other contexts) is that if we ignore parameter uncertainty we can drastically underestimate the uncertainty we face. It is therefore important to take account of parameter uncertainty in our simulations.

One last point is worth stressing: however good a model might fit the historical data used to calibrate it, and however plausible its forecasts might appear to be, there is never any guarantee that a model will deliver good future forecasts: the world is changing all the time and the history of forecasting is full of examples where hitherto respectable models break down unexpectedly. A medieval actuary using the latest available models and data in 1347 would have completely missed the imminent approach of the Black Death, but at least would have had the consolation of probably not living too long to regret it. As the saying goes, forecasting is a difficult business, especially forecasting the future.

This example also illustrates the random/unknown difference mentioned above. Improvements in life expectancy appear to depend on two different types of factor. First there is the random factor of continued modest improvements in medicine and nutrition. Life expectancy from this cause can be expected to improve, but eventually with declining rates of improvement as the Law of Diminishing Marginal Returns takes hold. However, future life expectancy also depends on unknown factors. One is whether biotech research will come up with an effective aging-reverser, in which case the graph will bend sharply upwards as the aging-reverser is disseminated to the population as a whole. Another, sadly, is the possibility of a major nuclear or biological conflagration, in which case the curve will kink even more sharply downwards, as in the case of the Black Death.

Short of getting a crystal ball that actually works, the only respectable responses to this problem are to rely on alternative approaches running side by side – where one approach might pick up what another might miss – and never, ever, put forward any quantitative forecasting model without first establishing that it would have delivered reasonable forecasts had it been used in a past data sample. No model should be taken seriously until its developer has given you some reason to think that it would have worked reasonably well in the past, and even that is no guarantee of future performance.

Perhaps the best approach to dealing with non-random but unknown factors affecting markets is that of fuzzy logic. This is an extension of set theory originally devised by the Azerbaijani-American mathematician Lotfi Zadeh in 1964.[11] Underlying it is a departure from

---

[11] Zadeh, 1965. For further examination of fuzzy logic and its implications, we recommend Kosko, 1993.

Western Aristotelianism and one of its key principles, that something either is or is not; instead, it maintains that everything is a matter of degree. Fuzzy logic is therefore the mathematics of set classification of those objects that are typically neither fully one thing nor the other. In a black and white universe, a grey object is neither "black" (a member of the black set) nor "white" (a member of the white set). Under conventional Cartesian set theory, there were two possibilities: either (i) an arbitrary line would be drawn at which darker grey objects would be counted as black and lighter grey as white, or (ii) a third set would be created, of objects which were neither black nor white. Both were unsatisfactory – what about objects which were just faintly off-white, or very dark grey? What about polka-dot objects?

Fuzzy logic gets around this problem by introducing the concept of partial membership in a set. A grey object can be defined as being (say) 52% black and 48% white; a polka-dot object as being that percentage black that the polka-dots represent to the total area. The extent to which an object is a member of a fuzzy set is known as the "belief" that the object is a member of the set. Thus the grey object discussed above is black with 0.52 belief, and white with 0.48 belief. These fuzzy "beliefs" may also be thought of as resemblances between the grey object and idealized Platonic black and white objects.

The membership of an object in the union of two fuzzy sets is the higher of its memberships in each set. The membership of an object in the intersection of two fuzzy sets is the lower of its membership in each set. Thus the grey object above is 52% "either white or black." On examination, this makes sense; the grey object is not a very good example of either a white object or a black object, and a pure white or pure black object, being much better examples, would be 100% members of the union. Similarly, it is 48% "both white and black" – in this case a pure white object, being not at all black, or a pure black object, being not at all white, would be 0% members of the intersection.

The "beliefs" of fuzzy logic are not probabilities – there is not a 52% probability that the grey object is really black. Consequently, they are sometimes referred to as "possibilities," both to distinguish them from probabilities and to emphasize their similarities to probabilities in certain respects.

A nice feature of fuzzy logic is that it reflects the ways our thought processes actually work. For example, considerable psychological work has been done, asking subjects to rank armchairs, sofas, deck chairs, beanbags, etc. against the concept of "chair." It turns out that there is indeed a hierarchy of chairs, pretty consistent between different subjects, with only the most chair-like being susceptible to easy definition, and less chair-like members (stools, concrete ledges, beanbags) differing greatly from each other, bearing only a vague resemblance to the Platonic ideal chair, yet being sufficiently chair-like that they have a substantial percentage membership in the fuzzy set "chair."

The practical significance of fuzzy logic is that it leads to a powerful but simple and intuitive form of natural language programming, which has led to some remarkable advances, particularly in the area of engineering control systems. The first substantial industrial use was in an F.L. Smidth cement kiln in Denmark in 1978,[12] regulating the cement firing process, which resulted in an important saving in both energy and manpower. In 1987, a fuzzy logic control system for the subway in Sendai, Japan, was introduced; it saves 10% on energy costs, dispenses with human subway car operators, and stops within 7 cm of target, three times better than a human operator. Another notable achievement was a program to stabilize a helicopter in flight when it loses a blade, something that no human pilot or conventional program could do. Other applications include many automatic transmission systems, digital image processing, language filters on message boards, remote sensing, video game artificial intelligence, robot vacuum cleaners, and washing machines. Interestingly, the greatest industrial advances in fuzzy systems engineering have taken place in Japan and China, which were more accepting than the West of departures from the Aristotelian/Cartesian philosophical system.

Fuzzy logic allows us to analyze qualitative, ill-defined concepts that prevail throughout the business world in a way that reflects the fuzzy nature of the concepts themselves, and does not insert them into a Cartesian straitjacket. As has been discovered by control systems engineers, however, in order to be fully effective, it needs to be applied to situations where the decision being taken is an analogue one, with all options for, say, "size of advertising budget" being available, not an Aristotelian yes/no dichotomy of "make/don't make an acquisition." In the latter case, fuzzy logic analysis may provide ambiguous guidance – the fuzzy recommendation "52% make the acquisition, 48% don't"

---

[12] McNeill and Freiberger, 1993.

should *not* be rounded off into a 100% Cartesian execution of the deal! But this potential ambiguity reflects the essence of the problem and avoids a binary conclusion that is often an ill-judged over-simplification of real situations. Thus in most circumstances, fuzzy logic leads to improved decision-making by examining intermediate and tangential possibilities, and combinations thereof.

Fuzzy logic can readily be used to analyze risk and pricing, although by its nature the analysis produces fuzzy answers, a range of possible values, together with a "best guess." However, in many cases, where factors inputting into a valuation are unknown but not random, such a "range" valuation is the appropriate answer, not some spurious point estimate. A 1990s spreadsheet program Fuzicalc™ handled this analysis well; there is also a user-friendly Fuzzy Logic Toolbox in MATLAB.[13]

Another nice feature of fuzzy logic is that it easily accommodates the interdependence of events: if one feels that bad events are likely to happen together, we can easily build this into our analysis and produce estimates of tail events that reflect their interdependence. This can give us a good handle on tail fatness and can be used for risk assessment, valuation (e.g. options valuation), and other purposes (e.g. determining hedge positions). Fuzzy approaches also make it very easy to take account of any other distinctive features such as asymmetries, varying volatilities, and possible price jumps.

In these respects, fuzzy logic has a number of advantages over conventional statistical approaches:

- It is much easier to program.
- It does not require or depend upon hard and fast parameter values, such as values for correlations.
- It produces far better estimates of interrelated tail events than one would get by making the lazy assumption, as was done all too often in the run-up to the crisis, that bad events were uncorrelated.
- It will give answers that reflect the underlying fuzziness of the problem, and avoids imposing on it an inappropriate Cartesian precision.

---

[13] Fuzicalc™ Fuziware Inc., Knoxville, TN; for more on the MATLAB toolbox, see www.mathworks.com.

One final quantitative method that always has a place is stress testing or scenario analysis. Stress tests are one of very few widely used quantitative methods that have emerged well from the recent crisis. Indeed, with each successive crisis over the last decade or more, their stock has risen higher. At one level, stress tests are very primitive – motherhood and apple pie stuff, and subjective too – but those features are also their strengths. Properly used, they are ideal for flushing out the firm's vulnerability to external events. In the recent crisis, good stress tests would have exposed firms' vulnerabilities to the drying up of market liquidity, the rising credit spreads, the radicalization of correlations, and other highly damaging features of the crisis.

The key to stress tests are to get the "what if?" right; they are only as good as the scenarios they consider and how well they consider them. Nonetheless, it is possible to offer a few rules of thumb on the choice of scenarios:

- Risk managers should go over market history, and especially financial crises, and establish key historical scenarios. They should also consider plausible alternate histories – events that didn't happen, but could have – and not restrict themselves to historical scenarios alone.
- Stress tests should be stressful, but not excessively so. A mild stress event is not worth considering, but we don't want the firm to be crippled by the need to hedge against very extreme events. As a rule of thumb: if after careful analysis you think the probability of an event on a given day is less than 1 in 250,000, ignore it. 250,000 trading days is 1,000 years.
- A good rule of thumb is the "no suicide" rule: try to identify those scenarios that could bring the firm down if nothing was done about them, but which the firm could survive if it took suitable countermeasures. There is however no point worrying about stress events that the firm can do nothing to prevent, such as an asteroid impact or a nuclear war.
- Stress tests should take account, where appropriate, of interactions between market risk, liquidity risk, and credit risk.
- Stress tests should generally not be used in isolation, but are very helpful when combined with other forms of risk analysis.

Probably the most important single risk analysis that you can perform, if managing the risk of a firm with a large and active trading operation, is to install litmus tests to help detect instruments with pathological risk profiles. These are the biggest single danger to the firm's continued existence, because by designing instruments in which the tails are very "fat" (i.e. high probability of exceeding risk limits) or "long" (i.e. small but significant probability of losses many times acceptable risk limits), traders can make exceptional returns for themselves while nominally remaining within the firm's risk assessment parameters.

To guard against instruments with pathological risks, we suggest you have two tools available: Cauchy analysis and fuzzy logic analysis.

As discussed in Chapter 5, the Cauchy distribution is the most extreme of the class of stable Paretian distributions. Under a Cauchy distribution, "25-sigma events" such as occurred beginning in August 2007 occur every 2½ months, compared to once in the life of a billion universes under the Gaussian distribution. This is almost certainly too conservative, but its conservatism is precisely what we want, as the Cauchy distribution is the most sensitive possible test for instruments with very long tails, in which the possible loss may be many times the apparent risk.

The classic example of such an instrument is the credit default swap, in which premiums, typically in pre-crisis times of a fraction of 1%, are paid annually to insure against a risk of the entire principal amount. Cauchy analysis of a large portfolio containing many different instruments, including credit default swaps, will immediately flag the credit default swaps as a potential problem. That will enable risk managers to set trading limits for credit default swaps at a small fraction of those for other instruments, as is appropriate owing to their exceptional "long tail" risk. The traders will throw tantrums, of course, but the shareholders (remember them?) if not the management will thank you.

Fuzzy logic analysis is useful to detect instruments with exceptionally fat tails, in which multiple risk factors are potentially very highly correlated. Because fuzzy logic analysis assumes that the "belief" of multiple unlikely events is the minimum of their "beliefs" instead of the product, a portfolio with 100 instruments, each with a 5% probability of loss, will be shown by fuzzy logic analysis to have a 5% "belief" of total loss.

Fuzzy logic analysis will therefore "catch" tranched Collateralized Debt Obligations secured by large portfolios of mortgages, which we discussed briefly in Chapter 5. Conventional probabilistic analysis of the top 50% tranche of a portfolio of 100 subprime mortgages, each with a 10% probability of loss, will report that tranche to be very safe with the chance of loss less than 1 in 10^{20}. Fuzzy logic analysis will say there is still a 1 in 10 chance of total loss, even on this top tranche. Just as Cauchy analysis is the most sensitive test for "long tail" pathological risks, so fuzzy logic analysis is the most sensitive possible test for "fat tail" pathological risks. A fuzzy logic analysis of a portfolio with many different instruments including tranched collateralized debt obligations will immediately identify the tranched collateralized debt obligations as the problem, and enable you to set very small trading limits for them. Again, your shareholders will thank you even as the traders curse.

In summary, therefore, the wise risk manager will probably use a Paretian distribution analysis with alpha less than the Gaussian 2 as the "best guess" method to analyze the institution's risk portfolio – for example, the Levy distribution (alpha= 0.5) used by the Options Clearing Corporation is one possibility. However they will also carry out stress tests and further analyze their portfolio using Cauchy and fuzzy logic distribution analyses as litmus tests to pick up the pathological risks that traders and quants may be playing with. Finally, they will err at all times on the side of caution, and will take particular note of any markets in which their institution has a substantial market share, in which strategic uncertainty considerations may come into play.

Nevertheless, even if you implement the above recommendations it can all go horribly wrong, as we said at the beginning of this chapter. But at least when you emerge like Citigroup Chairman and former Treasury Secretary Robert Rubin on November 29, 2008 and say to the Wall Street Journal "Nobody was prepared for this,"[14] you will, unlike Rubin, have the satisfaction of knowing it is unreasonable to ask "Why the bloody hell not?"

---

[14] http://online.wsj.com/article/SB122791795940965645.html

16

Back to the Future – A New Vision of Finance

Alert readers will have already picked up some of the advice we would give investors and clients of financial institutions:

- take a longer-term perspective and return to investment rather than speculation;
- do not seek to "enhance" yields, because this always exposes investors to hidden costs and risks, while firms seeking finance should resist cutting corners on their financing costs, for the same reason; thus, both parties should be realistic in their expectations;
- avoid frequent trading, focus on static over dynamic strategies, buy and hold over activist portfolio management;
- pay more attention to costs and hidden charges, and work on the assumption that higher charges are usually a good signal of a bad deal;
- distrust commission-based salespeople;
- if you use derivatives, be clear why and use them only for risk management and not speculation;
- avoid complicated, opaque products; and

- do not take liquidity for granted and ensure that your liquidity is protected in a crisis.

Besides this motherhood and apple pie stuff, investors should also be careful of correlation-based investment and risk management strategies, which work well when not needed but are apt to break down when they are. This is *not* to suggest that they should give up on diversification. People understood diversification long before Modern Portfolio Theory, but they tended to practice it differently and more wisely. Diversification was assessed by committees of experienced practitioners, who took a long-term view and relied on their judgment rather than unreliable correlation estimates – a far cry from modern practices of modern fund management, with its obsession with short-term performance assessment.

Investors should demand transparency. Perhaps the most sobering lesson we have learned since the subprime crisis broke is the benefit of transparency in business dealings. Time after time, when a fiasco has occurred, a key contributing factors has been lack of transparency. Subprime mortgages, CDOs, and credit default swaps were all financial innovations that relied crucially on nobody asking too many questions. So too with the vast Madoff Ponzi scheme, involving some of the most sophisticated investors in the world, which rested on the same fatal human omission. Consider each of these:

- In the subprime mortgage case, investors were not given sufficient information on the contents of the mortgage pools in which they invested, but instead chose to rely on the debt ratings given by the rating agencies, which were churned out by models that ignored the most important risks involved. In the old North Country English phrase, investors were buying a "pig in a poke" and should not have been too surprised when the "poke" was opened and the pig turned out to be a big fat rat.
- Collateralized Debt Obligations were un-transparent in that investors were given inadequate information on the assets backing them, and were not informed about the extra liabilities that the banks had incurred off their balance sheets in separate securitization vehicles. This lack of transparency was a key contributor to the eventual collapse in the money market in September 2008.

- The credit default swap sneaked up on everybody, becoming a $62 trillion market, without anyone outside the business knowing much about it. As the Bear Stearns, Lehman, and AIG debacles revealed, these instruments also involved highly non-transparent credit risks of their own. As a holder of a CDS you don't know whether your counterparty has issued only a few of your CDS, in which case you'll probably get paid in a bankruptcy, or whether he has issued fifty times the outstanding debt you're trying to hedge, in which case you're unlikely to get paid.

- Lack of transparency was a key factor in the Madoff scandal. Thirty years ago, the professional investor would have wanted to know how Madoff expected to make his consistently high returns, and there were no options markets of sufficient size for him to claim them plausibly as sources of exceptional profit. However in the 2000s professional investors couldn't be so sure, because with derivatives there were an infinite number of arcane trading strategies that just might conceivably produce superior returns. Madoff was also very secretive about his trading secrets and most professional investors failed to ask the questions they should have.

Lovers of regulation have been claiming for a long time that the solution to the transparency deficit is additional government regulation. The Madoff case has surely shown that to be a false protection. The SEC, with over 70 years of legislation behind it, turned out to be incapable on repeated occasions, despite repeated warnings, of spotting a huge Ponzi scheme operating right under its nose. Giving the SEC a new transparency rulebook will merely add more bureaucracy and reduce transparency further, without protecting significantly against fraud, let alone simple gullibility or failure to take adequate account of risk.

If governments cannot be expected to provide foolproof transparency for investors, then investors must take care of the matter for themselves. A good general rule is that if you don't understand it, don't buy it. So don't buy second-hand mortgages, for example, nor slices of mortgages divided into incomprehensible securities packages. If investor demand for mortgage-based CDOs is removed, then banks will be forced to hold the loans involved on their balance sheet, which is where they belong.[1] Good old-fashioned bear-market skepticism can help a lot too.

In bond investment, demand simplicity. Complex credit structures offer too many opportunities for fraud or simply fudging, and the rating agencies are incapable of giving an accurate assessment of their merits. Hence, direct obligations of companies with published financial information and a straightforward business model should be preferred over messy conglomerates, let alone artificial debt structures. If as an investor you really wish to increase your risk to get a higher return, make sure that the additional risk is in the form of clearly visible leverage in an easily comprehensible situation. Similarly, when investing in international credits, demand obligations of countries like Brazil whose governmental systems are transparent and debt levels are well known, rather than countries like China where the entire banking system is masked by a fog of obfuscation and the political system is opaque.

Investors and other clients of financial institutions should also avoid buying products where the mechanism by which returns are achieved is not transparent. This "operating transparency" recommendation should extend not merely to the "black boxes" offered by Madoff and most hedge funds or those offered by unscrupulous derivatives dealers to unsuspecting clients (remember Procter & Gamble?), but should also include many of the artificial derivative-driven products that have in recent years become fashionable investments for retail investors.

A case in point is Exchange Traded Funds (ETFs), which are sometimes not what they seem to be. For instance, a short ETF may claim to track various stock and bond indices in reverse, generally achieved by taking a short position in the relevant futures contract. The whole structure is entirely above board; both the aim of the funds and the method by which the managers hope to achieve it are made quite clear. However, investors may not realize that, in order to track the relevant index, the ETF must be rebalanced periodically (usually daily) and that such rebalancing can introduce large tracking errors if the index being

---

[1] Borrowers who take out loans from banks should also insist on transparency when it comes to the potential securitization of their loans. Similarly, companies that deal with banks should insist that they be informed if the bank has any other direct interest in them; for example, whether the bank has taken a credit derivative position on them. Better still, borrowers and corporate clients should insist that their banks do not securitize their loans or take out credit derivatives positions on them at all.

followed is volatile. In one recent case, an ETF that shorts the Chinese market on a leveraged basis went down almost 50% over 2008, though without "tracking error"" it should have trebled in value. Thus an investor in late 2007 correctly assessing the overvalued state of Chinese shares and buying this ETF would have been rewarded by the nasty surprise of losing half his money, even though his market view turned out to be correct.

Investors can achieve transparency, and so sleep at night about their investments, but in order to do so they must demand it for themselves. No regulator can provide it.

★★★

As discussed in detail in previous chapters, the market isn't efficient. For investment managers, this is good news: Warren Buffett exists!

That's not to say that beating the market is easy; very few people do it, and even Buffett's record is questionable since the mid-1990s. Indeed, there are apparent counterexamples. When the Efficient Market Hypothesis was first popularized in the early 1980s, the record of the Value Line Investment Service was sometimes used to refute it. Over a 30-year period the stocks rated "1" by Value Line had on average outperformed those rated "5" by a huge margin – indeed they had outperformed them in each individual year, although on an annual basis there was some mixing in the middle. However, from the late 1980s, the outperformance more or less disappeared. It would appear at first sight that the Efficient Market Hypothesis had its revenge.

Not so fast. It turns out that Arnold Bernhard, the founder and 50-year boss of Value Line, died in 1988, and since 1985 the company has effectively been run by his daughter, Jean Bernhard Buttner. Apart from staging a messy ten-year family battle with her twin brother Arnold, she appears to have run the firm like Captain Queeg, terrorizing subordinates over trivia. Finally in November 2009, having, as Bloomberg put it "guided the company from a household name to near obscurity," she was banned by the SEC from further participation in the securities business over brokerage violations. In other words, the Efficient Market Hypothesis may have had its revenge, but it used an altogether human instrument to get it, in the form of Ms Buttner.[2]

---

[2] Sree Vidya Bhaktavatsalam and Christopher Condon, "Value Line Settlement Could Prompt Split as Buttner Reign Ends," *Bloomberg*, November 9, 2009.

The bottom line is that by understanding the market's behavioral anomalies and better estimating the unknown factors in particular businesses and the macroeconomic environment, an investment manager of above average knowledge, intelligence, and diligence can hope to obtain returns above the market average.

What is more, while it is trite to say that investors should study the great gurus and successful investors such as Benjamin Graham, Jack Bogle, and Warren Buffett, to learn what to do, they can also learn from studying bad investors. Such investors are common. By and large they are not the merely ignorant – the little old lady who never reads the financial press and doesn't attend parties where people talk about investments would perform exactly at the average, since her picks would be random. Instead, investment underperformers come in two groups:

- One, the less interesting, consists of the gullible, those optimistic souls who buy penny stocks, investing more whenever the possibilities seem most exciting; they are ones who follow the crowd, coming in as the market peaks, buying high and selling low. When you see everyone else doing one thing, it is time to think about doing the opposite.
- The other was represented by Martin's Oracle mentioned in Chapter 4 – the senior professional with superb market information but limited analytical capability.

Investors should also keep in mind that asset prices are often prone to bubbles when, to use Alan Greenspan's immortal phrase, exuberance becomes irrational. By definition, in such a period expectations become irrational and the tenets of the Efficient Market Hypothesis become even shakier than usual. As a side note, this is also true in periods of irrational fear, such as 1932 in the US, 1974 in Britain, and a few weeks in early 2009.

In such periods, investors' collective irrationality throws off valuation metrics such as discounted cash flow and price–earnings ratios. In bull markets, securities that had previously appeared excessively risky suddenly appear sound and are bid up in price – for example in the dotcom bubble. Similarly, in deep bear markets, securities that had been thought to be safe are now viewed as impossibly risky and so attract no bids – good securities are knocked down as much as bad, even though the bad in such periods have much greater risk of default. In a raging bull market, nothing is a bargain to a rational investor, in a deep bear market everything is. However, during such periods there are very few rational investors; even skeptics in a bull market are driven to pursue the "greater fool theory" for fear of being left out; conversely, even optimists in a deep bear market are frightened to buy what may be cheaper next week.

To deal with such periods, you should try to recognize them in progress for what they are and adopt a contrarian mindset, building up your war chest for when the market turns down and be ready to go bargain-shopping after it does. You should also benchmark indices against their long-term average, and change positions as prices deviate further from that average. This is not easy; the 1995–2007 period showed that equities can remain seriously overvalued for a decade, while the 1970s proved the same was true for undervaluation. Nevertheless, as the indices deviate further from their long-term averages, you should increasingly anticipate the market reversing itself and steel yourself against those calling on you to join the lemmings in their headlong final rush.

★★★

Financial systems in which the largest institutions last only a couple of decades before going out of business or being absorbed are inherently unstable; so, too, is a system in which a company calling itself *Long-Term Capital Management* can be set up, grow to enormous size and then collapse due to its own *mis*management, losing its capital in the process, all within five years.

We would therefore advocate the principle of the thousand-year bank.[3] The London merchant banks lasted for 200 years, which seems a reasonable risk management ambition, giving the system only a 0.5% probability of collapse in any given year. To get a banking system designed to last 200 years, given the inadequacies of risk management techniques, we must design it as if it was going to last 1,000. Since 1,000 years is 250,000 trading days, risk management systems must be

---

[3] Similarities to the ambitions of the late unlamented Reich are unintentional but unavoidable.

designed to survive 1 in 250,000 events, not merely 1 in 100 events. Catastrophes will happen, but if a bank's risk management system is designed for it to survive 1,000 years, it has at least an excellent chance of making it past 50 or 100, and might even last a few hundred, like the venerable Banca Monte dei Paschi di Siena, founded in 1472 and still going strong.

Everything else – governance and risk management systems, remuneration systems, career paths, and the nature of the bank's business itself – then follows from the "1,000-year-bank" principle.

To implement this principle, we must return to a system with reasonable levels of integrity, and this means we must find a way to place the costs of losses primarily on those who cause them. Traditionally, investment banks and London merchant banks were partnerships, with unlimited liability, in which creditors in a bankruptcy could go after the partners' assets. Being medium-sized institutions, the combined capital contribution of their partners was sufficient to fund their relatively low-risk operations, consisting primarily of advisory and underwriting work, with a modicum of brokerage and principal investment thrown in. It was recognized that the reputation of the institution was the main driver of its ability to attract business. If a house became known for shady dealing or over-trading, it would find itself losing the semi-tied corporate advisory relationships that were its bread and butter.

With the behemoths at their current size, however, the partnership structure is much more difficult to attain, since you don't want only billionaires to be qualified to run big commercial banks, and it would not be easy, at least in the short term, to see how the largest financial institutions could be reconstituted as family-dominated partnerships.[4] This said, it is perfectly possible to extend the liability of bank shareholders – to reintroduce the old practices of making bank shareholders liable for twice their shareholder investments – and to go back to partially paid up shares, both of which would give creditors assets to go after in a bankruptcy.

Various protections can also be built into banks' Articles of Incorporation, and would be if there was sufficient pressure from their clients. As well as preventing management from looting the institu-

---

[4] The issues involved in making large commercial banks operate on the partnership form are an urgent topic for research.

tion, these should also prevent shareholders from selling it crassly to the highest dodgy bidder in the next bubble. Japanese-style "strategic shareholders" from such long-term oriented institutions as pension funds might be an important help here, provided that their shareholdings can be suitably tied down for several decades. Thus the agency problems between shareholders and management must be dealt with in both directions. It would also be useful for the Articles to provide for a relatively high dividend payout, so that truly long-term shareholders can earn a decent return without undue reference to the stock's fluctuating market price.

All of these measures would serve to alleviate the now endemic moral hazard problems within institutions, reduce risk-taking at other people's expense, and take us some way back toward the tight and highly effective governance practices of a century ago.

Once the senior management is incentivized towards responsible risk taking, as opposed to the outright gambling of recent years, it will institute tight governance systems, which, in turn, will lead to effective risk management. A key to this is to recognize the limits of all control systems, and build in plenty of systems redundancy. Like building a nuclear power plant or a skyscraper in San Francisco, we should build in multiple safety systems so that one will save the institution if another should fail. We must seek to make our risk management systems proof against shocks larger than those likely to hit it in a normal human lifetime.

The risk management itself would shift away in focus from day-to-day fluctuations – these don't matter – towards the tail, those low-probability high-impact risks that pose the real threats to the bank.

Potentially, too, the risk managers, disgraced of late, can finally assume their rightful role in the institution. Their job is, or should be, to ensure that the institution is protected against unpleasant avoidable surprises. To fulfill that role, they need to have genuine influence and be listened to, by senior management most of all; at the same time, they also become the people whom, when disaster strikes, the CEO makes a point of pushing out of the window before jumping out himself.

There is a natural analogy here with the soothsayers of old: they too made their predictions and had unique status and influence, but heaven help them if they were wrong. In his *Histories*, Herodotus tells the instructive story of how Astyages, the evil king of the Medes, had had ominous dreams, which his soothsayers, the Magi, interpreted as foretelling that his grandson, the future Cyrus the Great, would eventually usurp his throne. So when Cyrus was born, he tried to have him murdered. Cyrus was secretly saved, however, and his grandfather later discovered that he was still alive. Astyages then consulted the Magi again to ask whether Cyrus still posed a threat to him, and they told him that he did not. Unfortunately for him, the original prophecy later came true – a self-fulfilling prophecy if ever there was one! – and Cyrus led the Persian revolt that overthrew him, but not before Astyages had had his revenge on the unfortunate Magi, whom he had impaled.

We are not suggesting, of course, that the impalement penalty should be applied to modern risk managers when they mess up. But it is important to drive home the point metaphorically if not literally: risk managers should have status and be taken very seriously by senior management, but this should come at a high price in terms of their own personal liability. Their wealth, their pensions, and even their future livelihood as risk managers should all be at risk.

A bank can also support its own risk management by reducing or staying clear of dangerous practices. The experience of the last two decades has repeatedly shown, that many of the risks to which institutions are exposed come from their trading activity, whether that takes the form of crude rogue trading or traders stuffing risk into the tails of their positions that then occasionally blow up and lose back the traders' earlier profits and more. But with senior managers and risk managers appropriately incentivized, trading would no longer look so attractive: the banks' trading activities would be markedly reduced, many trading desks closed down – after all, what is the point of banks' keeping exotic trading desks for the hedge funds to fleece? – and such trading as remained would be more tightly controlled.

For the same reasons, excessive leverage too would no longer seem so attractive either, and leverage ratios would fall to safer levels.

It is also in banks' interests to avoid pathological financial products like credit default swaps that cannot be reliably risk managed. It is not possible to set a position limit for such products that will satisfy traders without exposing the dealing institution to extortionate, possibly bankrupting risk; the apparently easy returns they generate in normal conditions will always tempt traders to increase their exposure and seek ways to get round the institution's risk management system by hook or by crook. Since such products cannot be safely managed, they must be identified as such and expelled from a reputable institution's sphere of business.

Our advice, therefore, is for banks to leave pathological products to the hedge funds – and don't let your bankers lend money to those hedge funds, nor your investment managers buy them! And if you are operating in a system where others are dealing in such products, limit the business you do with those institutions strictly. Better still, form an "Accepting Houses Committee" or equivalent organization, containing the highest quality houses, that can adopt rules preventing members from dealing in them and expel those that do so. It's not necessary to have regulation to drive pathological products from the market: the banks can do it themselves. In any case, regulators will always be extremely slow to spot them and liable to "capture" by those they regulate.

While on the subject of dangerous innovations, banks should also scale back on financial engineering. A well-run commercial bank has no real need for financial engineers in any case, and even investment banks will only have a limited need for them. Financial engineering's benefit to the global economy is highly questionable and the proliferation of financially-engineered products of recent years has brought few benefits and led to huge losses for society at large. As we have seen, one quarter's bad losses in late 2008 wiped out all the accumulated financial engineering profits of the last quarter century and saddled taxpayers with a bill for hundreds of billions, if not more.[5]

A new, risk-concerned management would therefore take a dim view of difficult-to-manage derivatives teams beavering away on products that almost no-one understands, which often turn out to be time-bombs. All those jokes about 25-year-olds producing financial hydrogen bombs no longer seem so funny.

---

[5] For those trusting souls who respond that the Troubled Assets Management Program in the end incurred only $100 billion or so of losses, we would suggest they consider the additional losses dumped on taxpayers by Fannie Mae, Freddie Mac, and AIG – not to mention the hidden time-bombs in the Fed's $2.3 trillion balance sheet.

In the long run, less opulent compensation for financial engineers, more aggressive audit and supervision policies for financial institutions' engineered assets, and, most importantly, the combination of a healthy cynicism about financial engineering and far fewer financial engineers, may put this genie at least half way back into its bottle.

Future levels of remuneration need to be (much!) lower and remuneration practices should recognize that current management are only stewards of an institution that is designed to outlive their grandchildren. This means moving away from rewarding short-term results and a move back towards greater reliance on salaries and much less reliance on bonuses. Such changes will greatly reduce the short-termist chicanery that has been so obvious in recent years – the manipulation of results, dodgy accounting, and so forth.

At the same time, it is important to make more use of deferred payments, in which payments are locked in for extended periods, and only paid out much later and, even then, assuming the institution is still in good shape. This would help to avoid the all too common situation where the institution is plundered or saddled with hidden risk exposures, and these problems only come out later when the parties concerned have escaped with their loot and cannot be touched. This would give the parties concerned a much stronger incentive to protect the longer-term health of their institutions.

At the top level, senior managers could be incentivized further toward this end by extending their personal liability, putting not just their past remuneration but all their wealth, including their pensions, at risk. The supreme incentive for key decision makers to take their stewardship seriously is the threat of personal bankruptcy, which should be ever present in a healthy financial system.

Banks also need experienced veterans with a memory of previous crises. Not only should the expectation for senior management be for service until at least the late 60s – no more retiring to count their winnings before the age of 50, thank you! – it will help further if there are more equivalents of the 1950s Morgan Grenfell chairman Lord Bicester, in office until 88 and providing sage if tetchy warnings from crises that occurred half a century or more earlier.

When GE acquired the investment bank Kidder Peabody in 1986, they forced the retirement of its 85-year-old chairman Al Gordon (Harvard Business School Class of 1925), who as a young partner had steered the firm through the 1929 Crash and its aftermath. There was no need to remove Gordon on grounds of incapacity – he lived to the age of 107, being active in the investment business until past 100, dying in 2009 and enjoying on behalf of his class Harvard Business School's first 75th and 80th Reunions. The new-look Kidder on the other hand managed to self-destruct within eight years, brought down by the huge losses of the Joe Jett "forward reconstitution" rogue trading scandal in 1994. Institutional memory *matters*!

The cumulative consequence of these changes on the industry would be profound and far reaching. For their part, the commercial banks would become zombified, metamorphosing into much less risky entities and going back to standard but useful retail banking activities. The idea of a "zombified" low-risk bank structure was originally proposed by Lowell Bryan, then the senior banking partner at McKinsey's, in a book written the last time a systemic meltdown happened, in 1988.[6] In our version of zombification:

- Lower levels of remuneration would discourage aggressive, entrepreneurial top management – the kind of management who wrecked the financial system – and slowly zombify senior management itself. Instead of competing ferociously for new and ever riskier ways of rent seeking, leveraging the huge pool of capital they controlled, the management cadre would over time collectively lose all initiative, competing un-aggressively, with capabilities only in the well-trodden, low-risk financial product groups that comprise 90% or more of the sector's economically useful transactions.
- Zombie management would go back to basics. The zombie banks would take a renewed interest in their clients, and go back to cultivating long-term relationships of mutual benefit. They would then think twice about breaking those relationships by securitization, because they would appreciate that retail credit risk is not just their bread and butter, but also their comparative advantage, and they would appreciate that securitization goes against the essence of good retail banking. Mortgage lending would revert back to the old Jimmy Stewart system.

---

[6] Bryan, 1988. See also Michael Quint, "A Bank Expert's Plan for Change," *New York Times*, August 22, 1990.

- These core banks would however be able to undertake management of investments on a fiduciary basis, act as trustees, and perform back-office and custodial functions, all of which would benefit from their soundness and unquestioned balance sheets.
- Being both cheaper and more customer-focused, in the retail markets the zombified banks would out-compete any banks whose distracted management remained on contemporary over-the-top pay structures.
- The zombification process would also kill off most of the zombies' trading activities. In well-established areas such as bonds, foreign exchange, top tier equities and straightforward derivatives, trading could be carried on by modestly paid staffs that would have neither the incentive nor the imagination to take great risks. "Principal trading," which in the current Wall Street consists largely of profiting from the firm's insider information and connections at the expense of its customers and the market, would no longer be a significant factor in the zombies' operations, because their controls would be too tight and their staff would not be capable of undertaking it profitably.
- Much of the recent financial services sector rent seeking would then largely disappear and its share of GDP would fall back towards the much lower levels of the past.

While the huge banks would become zombies, entrepreneurial skills and financial innovation would not disappear from the financial services sector. They would simply migrate to smaller institutions, such as the "boutique" investment banks, mostly established since 1995. These are in any case gradually taking an increasing share of the advisory business because companies wishing to do important transactions are discovering the conflict of interest disadvantages of having an advisor who is at the same time playing gigantic trading games with the stocks and bonds of their competitors and themselves.

Boutique investment banks would not be able to tap the rent-seeking opportunities from deploying enormous amounts of outside shareholders' money, and would never have the balance sheets of the current behemoths. They would however provide the full range of advisory services, as well as developing new financial products and providing value-added financial solutions in areas left fallow by the zombies. To the extent they required underwriting for a large financing, they would be able to obtain it from the zombies and from large passive pools of investment capital such as insurance companies and pension funds, both of which would make modest additional incomes from underwriting securities in which they would normally invest.

The great Lord Cromer, Governor of the Bank of England in the 1960s, once described the principal market advantage of the old London merchant banks as "prestige and standing": it certainly wasn't size or capital. If the boutiques get the best advisors, and start to do the most important deals, prestige and standing will accrue naturally to them, and we will see the re-emergence of good investment banking along traditional lines.

The current universal service behemoths will then find themselves in an untenable position – too costly to compete with the zombies and bad at retail banking anyway, and too cumbersome and conflicted to compete successfully with the new boutique investment banks. Since their excessive size would preclude them from being able to downsize to the scale of a viable investment bank, they would have two options. One would be to divest themselves of all the fancy stuff and go back to commercial banking – zombifying themselves, in other words. The other would be to abandon any pretence of advisory work and become a gigantic hedge fund, enjoying a lucrative but precarious existence for a few years until they took one excessive risk too many and vaporized.

As for the equity and hedge funds, these have shown themselves to be extremely shoddy investments, delivering very poor returns for very high charges, and one can only hope that investors, prompted if necessary by lawsuits from those whose money they are investing, will have long memories. For those considering investing in hedge funds, our advice is: don't – reputable low-charge mutual funds are much more promising.

17

A Blueprint for Reform

The restoration of a rational and stable financial system inevitably requires major reform on a number of fronts. History gives much guidance here and also a role model: the period we should seek to emulate is the nineteenth century. Then money was sound, the dominant currency of the time (the pound) was literally as good as gold, financial institutions were conservative and generally stable, and an altogether healthier financial ethos reigned.

It is very common these days to sneer at the gold standard: after all, it was Keynes who once dismissed it as "a barbarous relic."[1] We would suggest, on the contrary, that a gold standard or some suitably twenty-first century commodity equivalent[2] would be highly desirable, and put an end to the disastrous century-long experiment with fiat money and its attendant miseries of inflation and monetary instability. The fact that Keynes opposed the gold standard is a further reason to support it.

---

[1] Keynes, 1924, p. 187.
[2] See, e.g., Kevin's 1996 book, which following in the tradition of Irving Fisher's "compensated dollar" of a century ago and Friedman's "commodity reserve currency" proposal of the 1950s, discusses how a commodity-based monetary standard could be established to achieve price-level stability automatically, without relying on a central bank.

The nineteenth century model would also entail major reforms to financial institutions and the regulatory system: greater liability and greater responsibility, the repeal of deposit insurance and investor protection legislation, and the abolition of the big financial regulatory bodies such as the SEC and FSA. And, by nineteenth century standards, we really mean *early* nineteenth century standards: those that pertained to the period before the Bank Charter Act of 1844 and the Companies Act of 1862, when liability was very real.

As for the banking system, we would suggest that the role model is Scotland pre-1845, when the Scottish banking system was virtually free of state control, unhindered by a central bank, and equally admired and envied across the world – and copied by countries such as Canada and Australia.[3] In all three countries, free banking systems operated highly successful for very long periods of time. Indeed, the Canadian system was widely admired in the United States – and many US reformers in the late nineteenth century saw it as their ideal. The Canadian system was highly stable – apart from the failures of two small Alberta banks in 1985,[4] its last notable bank failure was that of the Home Bank of Canada back in 1923. There were no Canadian bank failures in the 1930s and, even after the establishment of the Bank of Canada in 1934, many still regard the Canadian banking system as the best in the world.

Our first choice environment would be one with a commodity standard, free banking (no central bank) and financial laissez-faire, restrictions on the use of the "limited liability" corporate form,[5] and the most limited government. Even if we don't return all the way to these early nineteenth century standards (and we can imagine the op-position!), we should still move as much as possible in that direction,

---

[3] See also, e.g., White (1984) or the readings in Dowd (ed, 1992).

[4] These were the Canadian Commercial Bank and the Northland Bank, both short-lived institutions that blossomed in the Alberta oil boom, over-expanded and then collapsed when oil prices fell in the mid-1980s.

[5] On the limited liability issue, we heartily recommend Campbell and Griffin (2006). To anticipate one obvious objection to our advocacy of laissez faire and the restriction of limited liability, we quote Campbell and Griffin: "limited liability under the Companies Act *was* not and *is* not the product of private negotiation in a market but of a public intervention ... indeed, in our leading company law textbooks the introduction of limited liability is often described as the result of laissez-faire, which is precisely what it was not" (p. 61).

though we would *not* advocate the reintroduction of the notorious debtors' prisons immortalized in the fiction of Charles Dickens! However, our proposed reforms herein are adapted to the "second best world" (if it's actually that; it may be about thousandth best of all the "parallel universe" possibilities) in which we live, with relatively large government, a fiat currency, and a central bank.

The most important institutional policy that must be solved is that of an excessively expansionary monetary policy. Simply making the monetary authority "independent" does not achieve this if the monetary authority retains its interactions with politicians and the financial community, both of which want loose money. The ideal to aim at is a hard money Fed, a Paul Volcker Fed.

Since we cannot expect a new Volcker to arise any time he is needed, and since politicians could not be trusted to appoint him if he appeared, we must "Volckerize" the Fed by statutory means. Legislation should change the Fed's legal structure and mandate so that even without a Volcker, price level stability is maintained – even with the feeblest political appointee at its head. The West German Bundesbank Act of 1958, pushed through by the disciplinarian Konrad Adenauer in a country with vivid memories of Germany's 1923 hyperinflation, provides a good model. The Bundesbank and the best-designed modern central banks have had a single overriding objective: the formulation of monetary policy to achieve and maintain stability in the general price level.

By comparison, the 1913 Federal Reserve Act gave the Fed unitary political control but a structure including twelve regional banks. It was thus hard to take decisions but easy for politicians to influence monetary policy. The Bundesbank Act did the opposite; the Bundesbank was nominally controlled by the German Länder collectively, so political meddling was almost impossible, while internally it was a single entity, providing for tight management control. A new Fed statute might borrow this structure of collective control by the states. This would provide Fed independence, while removing the requirement for the Fed chairman to report personally to Congress, where he can be browbeaten. Further independence from politicians and Wall Street could be achieved by moving the Fed headquarters physically away from Washington or New York – St. Louis, an agreeably geographically central location and a bastion of monetarism, would be an excellent choice. Remember, too, that the Germans established the Bundesbank in their conservative financial centre, Frankfurt, not in the then federal capital Bonn.

Even in our "second best world" we must extend liability for key decision makers, raise fiduciary standards, and reform both personal and corporate bankruptcy codes to reduce incentives to go into bankruptcy and give greater protection for creditors.[6]

There should be greater liability for corporate officers and the accounting and financial experts who advise them. Just as builders and engineers are held accountable if a building or a bridge collapses and people are hurt, there should some comparable standards of accountability if a firm collapses.

We also need major reform of corporate governance, relying more on the incentives created by extended liability rather than onerous systems of hard and fast rules with unnecessary and ineffective criminal penalties for non-compliance, of which the worst example is Sarbanes-Oxley, which subverts effective corporate governance by turning it into a huge compliance exercise.

Reforming the financial sector is more complicated. As discussed in Chapter 16, we have proposed changes in the industry that would "zombify" large commercial banks, turning them into low-risk institutions with a limited range of businesses. While it is, in principle, a bad idea for the government to be involved in the banking industry, the fact is that the government is already heavily involved – not least as the major shareholder in many large banks. This raises the question of how the government should manage this role, and we would suggest that the government should use it to push the industry in this direction, focusing in particular on basic functionality and the interests of the taxpayer – and, of course, on getting out of the banking system as soon as is feasible.

---

[6] We would also suggest reforms of bankruptcy rules as they apply to banks, to allow a fast track "Accident and Emergency" makeover to any future financial institution in difficulties, allowing it to be swiftly put back in operation with minimal disruption to everyone else. For some suggestions along these lines, see Dowd, 2009a, 2009b.

If any deposit insurance is retained for those banks, it should introduce some degree of depositor co-insurance to make depositors responsible, possibly with the exception of a very low ceiling of 100% insurance – say $10,000 and not for each *deposit*, but for each *depositor*. This would protect retail savers with large liquidity needs while preventing the brokered deposit phenomenon, by which most aggressive banks exploit deposit insurance and can attract money nationwide by providing marginally higher returns insured by the FDIC.

The other major element of state support for banks is the vexing issue of "too big to fail," the greatest moral hazard in the financial system. The doctrine of "too big to fail" needs to be repudiated altogether and safeguards must be taken to prevent bailouts in the future.

Of the major US banks and investment banks, only six now have assets of more than $1 trillion – J.P. Morgan Chase, Goldman Sachs, Citigroup, Bank of America, Morgan Stanley, and Wells Fargo. Below them there is a huge gap, with the next largest institutions, PNC Corporation and US Bancorp, having total assets of around $300 billion. Institutions of intermediate size – Merrill Lynch, Lehman Brothers, Wachovia, Bear Stearns, and WaMu – have gone bankrupt or have been absorbed into the behemoths. This strongly suggests that there is a break point at around $300 billion of assets – say, 2% of US GDP – at which financial institutions in times of stress such as 2007–08 become unstable and either agglomerate into tax-supported behemoths or fail.

Part of the solution is to provide a strong incentive for banks to shrink to a manageable size. We suggest an asset tax of perhaps 0.2% per annum placed on all agglomerations of financial institution assets larger than something like 2.5% of US GDP (currently about $360 billion). This would make the tax-supported behemoths uncompetitive in the long run, giving them a strong incentive to dis-assemble themselves into smaller entities that were not "too big to fail." Entities like Goldman Sachs would spin off maybe three to four hedge funds or private equity funds, of no systemic significance, and without the insider information on funds flows that comes with dominance. In addition a core entity would remain, with assets under $360 billion, that would function more like a traditional investment bank, although with capital of $20 billion or so (and lower leverage) it would still have ample firepower to underwrite and trade even the largest securities distributions.

We can also take measures to discourage the activities that are apt to lead to trouble. Four in particular stand out:

There is, first, the problem of excessive trading. A partial solution is a "Tobin tax"[7] on transactions, large enough to make much rent seeking trading (such as high frequency trading) unprofitable, but not so large as to remove liquidity from the market. A tax rate in the range of 0.05% to 0.1% ad valorem per trade would seem appropriate, applied to all trades. We are in general reluctant to recommend taxes, but in a second best system this has to be seen in the context where "good" activities are already heavily taxed.

A Tobin tax would wipe out the profits of much current trading activity, especially leveraged and high-speed trading: most of the traders' bonuses would then disappear and so would most of the traders too. Corporate finance, the creation of value by transactional skill, would once again become the dominant income stream, and its practitioners would in due course once again occupy the corner offices. By this means, financial institutions' focus would be reoriented towards the longer term and towards a proper appreciation of the financial services business's appropriate role in economic life.

Then there is the problem of what to do about credit derivatives, especially credit default swaps. There are, admittedly, good economic arguments for allowing lenders to lay off or share some credit risk, thereby managing it more effectively, but there are few good arguments for allowing short positions on unrelated entities. Bankruptcy is a necessary economic mechanism, albeit with a heavy social and economic cost to creditors and employees; it should not be artificially encouraged.

Our solution would be to require that any party benefiting from a default should have an insurable interest in the default, that is, they should have some loss that the transaction is meant to protect themselves against. There needs to some debate over the precise definition of insurable interest, of course, and the concept might need modernizing, but it makes no sense to have a system in which a party with no natural interest in a company can destroy that company using highly leveraged credit derivatives. If you want to destroy a company, you should have the decency to do it the old fashioned way in a fair fight, shorting the stock with no leverage and taking your chances, risk-

---

[7] Proposed by James Tobin (1918–2002), Nobel Memorial Prize in Economic Sciences, 1981.

ing possible ruin yourself if the stock price bounces back. Nor does it make sense to have a situation where creditors push for a company to be bankrupted, despite their natural interest to the contrary, because they have also used leverage themselves to short the company using credit default swaps In a rational system, the creditors should be trying to avoid bankruptcy, not cause it. An insurable interest requirement would solve these problems and kill most of the credit derivatives business: this can only be to the good.

This takes us to a third reform: transparency. Financial institutions should be required to disclose all relevant interest and positions in their derivatives positions, including any securitizations. By this we mean, on the one hand, that they should disclose their counterparties and the nature of their positions with them. So, for example, if a financial institution enters into a credit default swap position, that position would be disclosed to some central registration body. If a company has a loan with a bank, it can then find out if its own bank is "betting" against it via a credit default swap or has sold on its loan via a securitization; it can then, presumably, decide to take its future business elsewhere. On the other hand, any securitizations should be subject to "fingerprinting," allowing the investors to "drill" down into securitized positions to determine the precise nature of the underlying investments and the identities of the borrowers.[8]

Note, however, that this proposal would still allow banks to protect the confidentiality of their traditional activities and positions: the disclosures would only come into effect if positions were on-sold or incorporated into derivatives.

These changes need to be accompanied by restoration of sound accounting standards based on the principle that pertained previously, that assets can be written down, but must never be written up until they are sold. There needs to be an end to fair value abuses, most especially the disgraceful practice of giving positions fictitious "fair values" and paying bonuses on the basis of illusory profits created in this way.

On risk management, we would suggest financial institutions be required to use "best practice" risk management systems, to be determined by a committee dominated by people from outside Wall Street. We would suggest that this committee insist on highly conservative risk management practices, including high capital adequacy standards and

---

[8] See, e.g., Markowitz, 2009 or Gründl and Post, 2010.

the "litmus tests" proposed in Chapter 15. There would be flexibility in the precise risk management mechanisms chosen, but risk management that ignored "tails" or failed to take proper account of the various different types of pathological risks would not be permitted. There should also be strong risk disclosure requirements that would apply also to banks' "litmus test" results. In time, these statutory requirements would be replaced by a system of self-regulation, but today's bankers have proven that they can't be trusted to manage risks properly and, for the next generation at least, banks would have to operate under such constraints until they have become much safer and the bankers much more responsible.

Commercial banks benefiting from the remaining limited deposit insurance would be able to function perfectly well with simple accrual accounting practices, which would also have the advantage of making their balance sheets and accounting statements transparent. Investment banks would have more use for mark-to-market accounting methods, and should be free to use them provided increases in fair value are not brought through the income statement until the positions involved have been sold, and that bonuses are paid only on the basis of realized and not notional fair value profits. As for hedge funds, what they do is between them and their foolish investors, and is of no importance to society at large.

We would also suggest some tax changes. One is to remove the differentiation between interest and dividends, whereby interest is tax-deductible at the corporate level, whereas dividends are taxed at the individual level. Before President George W. Bush's tax reforms of 2003, dividends were taxed at total rates above 70%, when corporate and individual tax is taken into account at federal and state levels. This differential had the impact of encouraging excessive leverage and reducing dividend yields in 1998–2000 to little over 1%, well below their appropriate levels.

Being designed by the Bush administration, it is hardly surprising that the dividend tax reform of 2003 was botched. Rather than reduce the dividend tax at the individual level, which does nothing to remove the over-leverage tendency in corporations (and leaves dividends still tax-disadvantaged for institutional shareholders), dividends should continue to be taxed as ordinary income to the investor. However they should be tax-deductible for the corporation, so that only earnings retained in the corporation would be taxed. This would equalize the tax treatment of dividends and interest, so killing once and for all both the incentive and the excuse for excessive leverage. Executives and private equity groups who used leverage for their own enrichment would then have no encouragement from the tax code. Such reforms would also allow dividend payments to recover to much healthier levels.

We would suggest comparable reforms for the UK and, in addition, the abolition of the obnoxious non-dom tax break, which allows wealthy bankers to work in the UK but pretend they live elsewhere, so avoiding the heavy tax rates that everyone else pays.

Then there are the fiscal issues. There are major improvements that can be made in this area, even if we're not going to get our much preferred Coolidgean level of government.[9]

One would be fiscal responsibility legislation at the federal level. New Zealand pioneered such legislation with its 1994 Fiscal Responsibility Act. New Zealand's legislation provides for the government to report on its fiscal strategy, the current economic and fiscal situation, and the outlook over the medium and long terms. More important, it provides principles of fiscal responsibility that the government must consider but (in an unfortunate legislative wimp-out) not necessarily implement when developing its budgets.

These principles of fiscal responsibility were to:

- reduce total Crown debt to prudent levels by achieving an operating surplus each year until a prudent level of debt had been attained;
- maintain total Crown debt at a prudent level by ensuring that on average operating expenditures do not exceed operating revenue;
- achieve and maintain levels of Crown net worth that provide a buffer against adverse future events;

---

[9] Federal and state government expenditures totaled $9.8 billion in 1929, 9.5% of a GDP of $103.6 billion – federal expenditure was about a third of this. Spending had already risen to 17.2% of GDP in 1932, Hoover's last year – it was Hoover, not FDR who pioneered Keynesian deficit spending. It was 17.7% of GDP in 1940, the last year of peace, 26.2% of GDP in 1960, 30.4% of GDP in 1980, declined marginally to 29.2% of GDP in 2000, but had risen again to a new high of 32.8% of GDP in 2008. Source: Bureau of Economic Analysis, National Income, and Product Accounts, Tables 1.1.5 and 3.1.

- manage prudently fiscal risks facing the Crown; and
- pursue policies consistent with a reasonable degree of predictability about the level and stability of tax rates for future years.[10]

Despite the wimp-out clause, the Act has been highly successful. New Zealand's public debt to GDP ratio, which peaked at 77% in 1986 and was still 60% in 1994, was down to 24.4% in 2008 and the country has enjoyed solid economic growth with little inflation.

Clearly fiscal responsibility legislation along New Zealand's lines, or even a Constitutional amendment, would be helpful for the United States – although implementation would almost certainly require the additional mechanism of a line-item veto. That veto, implemented by Congress in 1996, was declared unconstitutional by the Supreme Court in 1998, so a constitutional amendment would be necessary to restore it. Nevertheless, for the US to preserve economic and fiscal stability, reform along these lines is essential.

Another reform specifically related to the financial markets is legislation prohibiting the federal government from guaranteeing housing finance. These guarantees have proved a hugely wasteful and damaging distortion of the housing finance market. Other countries, by arranging housing finance without such guarantees, have shown them to be unnecessary. Fannie, Freddie, and all the other members of their unnatural family need to be abolished.

In addition, the federal government should remove its tax subsidies, particularly the home mortgage interest deduction. The housing market has an inevitable tendency to descend at regular intervals into a speculative playground; at the very least this should not be at taxpayer expense. Citizens should be encouraged to accumulate assets in the banking system and the stock market, not in unproductive real estate, let alone in the vulgar ostentation represented by McMansions.

Internationally, the best possible reform would be the abolition of the International Monetary Fund and the World Bank. These have distorted global capital markets for more than 60 years. In the postwar years, they prevented the reestablishment of the highly effective and responsible system of development finance represented by the London merchant banks and their advisory capabilities. Today they provide generally bad advice to client countries and funnel large re-

---

[10] See, e.g., Scott, 1995.

sources through those countries' governments, thereby contributing enormously to their corruption and squalor. In addition, the existence of the World Bank and IMF provides legitimacy for the international bureaucrat class, which endlessly lobbies for ever more resources while shamelessly feathering its own nest. The result is that these gigantic institutions grow and grow, even at the best of times, and as we have seen all too clearly in the last two years, the temptation to turn to them in economic crises brings a danger of further highly damaging increases in unaccountable government drains on world resources.

Finally, there is the supreme task of restoring capitalism and reversing the repulsive cronyism that has now become all too rampant. This requires tackling the incestuous relationships involved and the revolving doors operating between Wall Street and the regulatory system, and between Wall Street and the government. In both cases, the key is to introduce rules that stipulate that neither regulators nor politicians can take Wall Street positions, remunerated or not, for a long period after they leave their regulatory or political positions. In fact, it wouldn't be a bad idea to stop the revolving door in the other direction, too: too many Wall Streeters have taken up powerful political positions where they can dish out goodies to their friends. We need more Main Streeters in positions of responsibility. And, as regards the politicians, we need reform to limit their freedom to take money from Wall Street.

The restoration of capitalism also requires one further institutional change, seemingly innocuous, but actually of great long-term importance. Some 50 years ago, institutional shareholdings represented only about 15% of quoted share capital, with about half held by individuals and the remainder held by bank trust departments and the like, investing on behalf of single individuals rather than deploying the capital of an amorphous mass. The estate tax, instituted in its modern form in 1916, had risen above 20% only in the infamous Herbert Hoover Great Depression-worsening tax increase of 1932. In the 1950s there were still many individual fortunes that had not been subjected to the tax, and hence held substantial percentage shareholdings in major corporations. Furthermore, even the less wealthy middle class retired to live on the dividends from their share portfolios; funded pensions were still fairly uncommon. The result was a capitalism in which the agency problems associated with the separation of ownership and control were held in tolerable check, because of the substantial individual shareholdings remaining and the power they exercised.

However, in a series of increases after 1932, the top estate tax rate by the 1950s had been increased in stages to as high as 77%. These tax changes did much first to corrode and then ultimately destroy the old shareholder structure; the family fortunes gradually disappeared, either to the taxman or to various "charitable" trusts that were no longer controlled by their beneficiaries. The percentage of funds managed on an individual basis shrank further as pension funds and mutual funds expanded, so that by 1980 institutional shareholders owned more than 50% of publicly quoted shares, a percentage that has trended gently upwards since.

Consequently, by 1980 the era of individual shareholder capitalism was over and managerial capitalism had replaced it.

This sea change was not obvious at the time. The general assumption in the 1970s was that the new institutional shareholders would wield their immense power in a suitable way – maximizing shareholder value, chastising management when it got out of hand and ensuring that the interests of all shareholders were adequately protected.

Unfortunately, this didn't happen, for reasons that are now all too obvious. The money managers at institutions were not titans of finance, moving markets at the slightest whim. They were instead middle level bureaucrats, well paid by the standards of the outside world but wholly reliant on the career structure within the investment management profession. With money managers needing to preserve their jobs through providing satisfactory investment performance quarter by quarter, they certainly weren't likely to endanger their positions through sticking their neck out in opposition to a powerful corporate management. Separating themselves from the herd and confronting corporate big shots, when in any case they spoke for only perhaps 5% of the company's stock, went entirely against the instincts of people whose closest equivalent in nature was the sheep.

Consequently, when institutions own majority shareholdings in most companies, and individuals (except for the occasional Buffett) are no longer significant, the structure that makes capitalism work breaks down. Since the managers of institutional money are not motivated to behave like the powerful shareholders they represent, they don't do so. As a result, management has a free rein to indulge in the "negligence and profusion" that Adam Smith famously deplored. Not only can it overpay itself, dilute the shareholders by excessive stock option grants, and pull the wool over shareholders' eyes by dodgy accounting, but it can also indulge in whatever Napoleonic expansion fantasies it pleases, regardless of the damage to shareholders' interests – unless the company's results become so appallingly bad that even the institutional sheep-holders turn feral.

Part of the solution is to turn the Modern Finance ability to create bizarre new securities back on itself and create a security that thwarts the Managerial Capitalism inherent in Modern Finance. A company whose shareholders wished to ensure good corporate governance could issue part of its capitalization in Founders' Stock, with the following characteristics:

- It is completely non-transferable (this must be locked up tight legally so some fast-buck takeover artist can't find a way to unlock it)
- It converts to common after 50 years
- For the first 45 years of its life, it gets an additional 1% per annum dividend above whatever is paid on the common, payable in common at the average price of the year/quarter.
- It has all other rights of the common, as to voting etc.

Founders' Stock would be attractive to college endowments and pension funds, which have a multi-decade time horizon and no conceivable need for liquidity. It could also be made available to wealthy individuals, particularly those in the founding families of the company, although in this case provision would have to be made for limited transfer on the death of the holder.

Holders of Founders' Stock would seek to maximize the long-term value of the company, since they would only lose by interim game-playing. They would also wish to avoid dilution of their holding through management stock options, destruction of its value through excessive management remuneration or possible bankruptcy through leverage, while they would be keen on substantial dividend payments. In other words, they would behave as traditional family shareholders. Their combined holding would be limited to 20–40% to preserve the liquidity and capital raising advantage of public company status. However in most circumstances they would collectively control the company in the same way as a founding family or a pre-1990 Japanese bank. Good traditional management and company employees would welcome their presence, since it would render the company secure against takeover, while long-term ordinary shareholders would soon find their returns enhanced through the controls the Founders' Stock imposed on management.

The second part of the solution to this problem is relatively straightforward, but it will take a long time. No amount of "better corporate governance" initiatives will change the incentives for the managers of institutional money sufficiently to turn them from sheep into watchdogs; any such efforts are essentially doomed, although if they can instill a little interim fear into corporate management and reduce its depredations, they will still be helpful.

Instead, we must re-create the world in which the majority of shares were held by individuals. Part of the answer is to be found in tax reform. Estate duty must be reduced, to a level no higher than 15–20%, in order to preserve family fortunes in their original form and prevent their dissipation in wasteful charitable trusts. In addition, income tax deductions for home mortgage interest and for charitable donations should be removed to divert the resources of the wealthy away from overpriced real estate and overdone "charity," and toward productive investment.

The other part of the answer is to make the big institutional investors take more responsibility. This requires changes along a number of fronts. A greater focus on the long term would certainly help, and institutional investors need to be pressured to commit themselves for long periods, so they take greater interest in their investments. Of course, it might also help that if Wall Street is drained of income potential, then the brightest minds might again go to the buy side, at which point they would vote more courageously and intelligently. Investing a multibillion pension fund ought to be the work of a superior intellect, but as the Efficient Markets Hypothesis says it might just as well be done by a drone, debunking such nonsense would no doubt help as well.

Restoration of shareholder capitalism by these means will take time. Only over a few decades will individual shareholdings rebuild to the point where corporate management has to take seriously the 82-year-old dowager owning 0.7% of their company who constantly nags the management demanding higher dividends, no stock options, and an end to wasteful corporate aggrandizement schemes. But over time and given the chance, the dowagers will once again take over from the bureaucrats and, assuming the government or the financiers don't manage to destroy it in the meantime, American capitalism will once again function properly.

18

Lessons to Take Away

We hope that this book, which has taken you at a brisk trot through 300 years of financial history, discussed the flaws in Modern Finance and modern economic policymaking, examined the recent crisis in detail, and made some proposals for improvements, has left you with a few well-defined conclusions.

The first is that Modern Financial Theory rests on unsound assumptions and should largely be ditched. Some of its main pillars – such as the Efficient Market Hypothesis, the assumption that returns are Gaussian, the belief that financial market risks are predictable, the belief that financial innovation is a good thing that helps make financial markets more stable, and so on – have been pretty much exploded. Modern Financial Theory also provided guides to action so false that they perverted the financial markets, causing trillions of dollars in losses, and damn near brought down the world financial system. However, its adoption as Holy Writ served the economic self-interest of Wall Street and in many cases was allowed to drive out previous superior analytical methods.

The failure of Modern Financial Theory extends to its favorite offspring, the discipline of Financial Risk Management. This has failed to come to terms with fat tails and even the most moderate of extreme events. It is senselessly wedded to the VaR risk measure, which peers myopically away from "bad days" and only works when risks are not particularly risky, and to correlation-based risk management strategies that break down when most needed. But going deeper, it is obvious by now that quantitative methods have been oversold and their limitations underappreciated. Most of modern quantitative risk management is in fact no more than an arcane cult that has helped to disguise risk-taking on a huge scale while pretending to do the opposite.

This said, there is still a need for quantitative methods, but there needs to be much more focus on the "tail events," where the real damage occurs, and much more humility in the face of what we don't know. Useful approaches include the use of stable Paretian distributions, Bayesian statistics, and fan charts. We also suggest that "litmus" risk pathology tests become standard practice. These might be based on fuzzy logic (which would catch "fat" tailed risks such as collateralized debt obligations), and Cauchy analysis (which would catch "long" tailed risks such as credit default swaps). In addition, genuinely stressful stress tests should be carried out. All of these would give us worst-case estimates on which good risk management needs to be based.

Another conclusion is that much of the practice as well as theory of Modern Finance is deeply flawed. The key is to return the structure of finance to that of a time when the practice of finance served the broader economy instead of just itself, and when financiers were both respectable and respected. We need the industry to return to the virtues of trust, integrity, and saving; a belief in the importance of the long-term and of long-term relationships; much lower and salary-based remuneration for practitioners, and far fewer of them; and a reversion in the financial services sector to dominance by bankers and corporate financiers rather than traders. Underlying all these and making them possible, we need the re-establishment of tight governance structures that force practitioners to serve their clients instead of ripping them off.

Nor should we forget that these spectacular failures took place against a backdrop of misguided economic thinking that not only enabled Modern Finance to run riot, but gave a spurious respectability to a range of profoundly damaging government interventions into the economy and paved the way for the emergence of crony capitalism. Perhaps most damaging is the philosophy of Keynesian macroeconomics, which sought to legitimize macroeconomic management by the state using the tools of activist monetary and fiscal policy, giving the state and its agencies enormous discretion to meddle with an economy that would be much better off left alone.

Monetary policy has led again and again to inflation and, as we write, to the prospect of renewed major inflation, even hyperinflation, as recent loose monetary chickens finally come home to roost. Over the last dozen years or so, loose monetary policy has also led to a series of highly destabilizing and damaging boom-bust cycles, leading to enormous misallocation of capital and the elimination of savings in the US. It is currently creating the basis of an even bigger and more damaging boom-bust cycle down the road.

These outcomes should persuade any thinking person that the monetary policy "experiment" – giving government control of our money – has failed. The very principle of monetary policy is unsound and the best money is that which manages itself. The best way forward is, therefore, to go back to some sort of commodity-based monetary standard. Failing that, a second best response is to give the Fed as much as possible a politician-proof governance structure and a tight mandate to pursue price stability as its single goal, thereby as far as possible "Volckerizing" it.

Loose fiscal policy has allowed the government to spend irresponsibly and grow to enormous size, gobbling about half of national income in Britain and close to that in the US. Out-of-control spending has also made the recent crisis immensely more damaging than it would have been. The burden it imposes on the economy, particularly the job-creating small business sector, threatens to bring down the nascent economic recovery and mire the US economy in endless stagnation. At the same time, most Western governments are rapidly building up vast amounts of debt and even greater unfunded obligations that future generations will be expected to pay. Those obligations are already so large that the bankruptcy of major Western governments appears inevitable in the years ahead.

We should remember that underlying the failures of Modern Finance is the failure of modern managerial capitalism. The basic weakness of the capitalist system, the problem of how to prevent management and powerful interest groups more generally from enriching themselves at everyone else's expense, has escalated to the point where the capitalist system itself is now in a major legitimation crisis, to use the language of our Marxist brethren. These interest groups have also taken over the state itself to a very significant extent, in the process turning modern capitalism into an ugly and corrupt system of crony capitalism that cannot be defended and is rightly reviled by the increasingly restive man in the street, who is called upon to pay for it.

Yet we would also argue that there is no feasible or desirable alternative to capitalism. State intervention is not the answer; meddling by corrupt and incompetent politicians is, indeed, a key part of the problem, and we don't need any more of that! Those who would defend the great principles of classical liberalism need to make common cause with the man in the street, who is being robbed blind like never before by an unholy alliance of venal politicians and financiers that are serving their own interests and lining their pockets.

The essential problem, consequently, is how to put capitalism back on its feet and restore its moral authority. Again, we would suggest that the answer is to look to the past – not to the twentieth century, but to the eighteenth and nineteenth centuries. This requires thoroughgoing reforms to corporate governance to make management both liable and accountable. A good starting point, particularly in the financial sector, would be to reconsider the demerits of the joint-stock form and the merits of the old partnerships, and think seriously about restricting or even repealing the limited liability statutes. Restoring free-market capitalism also requires rolling back the extensive apparatus of state intervention, with political reform to make government smaller and restore its accountability.

Nevertheless, as intellectuals we are drawn back to the core problem: of the need for alternative paradigms that will work. By 1771, when Joseph Wright of Derby painted the masterpiece on this book's cover, alchemy had become the subject of mockery and mild derision, having been replaced intellectually by the scientifically sound discipline of chemistry. We need a similar process in financial and economic theory, driving out not one but two groups of alchemists. One group is the deluded Modern Financial Theorists, whose panaceas must be replaced with a sound, reality-based structure of financial analysis and risk management. The other requirement for a new Age of Economic Reason is to abandon the philosopher's stone of universal government meddling sought by that sublime Paracelsus of economic alchemy – John Maynard Keynes.

Bibliography

Adams, J. (1995) *Risk*, UCL Press.

Arnuk, S.L. and Saluzzi, J. (2008) "Toxic Equity Trading Order Flow on Wall Street," Themis Trading LLC White Paper, December 17.

Artzner, P., Delbaen, F., Eber, J.-M., and Heath, D. (1999) "Coherent Measures of Risk," *Mathematical Finance*, vol. 9, pp. 203–288.

Bagehot, W. (1873) *Lombard Street*. (Republished by Echo Library, 2005.)

Bank for International Settlements (2009) *Quarterly Report*, September.

Bassi, F., Embrechts, P., and Kafetzaki, M. (1998) "Risk Management and Quantile Estimation," pp. 111–30 in Adler, R.J., Feldman, R.E., and Taqqu, M.S. (eds) *A Practical Guide to Heavy Tails: Statistical Techniques and Applications*, Birkhäuser.

Bayes, T. (1764) *Essay Towards Solving a Problem in the Doctrine of Chances*. (Republished by Cambridge University Press, 1958.)

Berkowitz, J. and O'Brien, J. (2002) "How Accurate are Value-at-Risk Models at Commercial Banks?" *Journal of Finance*, vol. 57, pp. 1093–1112.

Berle, Jr, A.A. and Means, G.C. (1932) *The Modern Corporation and Private Property*. (Republished by Transaction Publishers, 1991.)

Bogle, J.C. (2005) *The Battle for the Soul of Capitalism*, Yale University Press.

Bogle, J.C. (2009) *Enough: True Measures of Money, Business, and Life*, Wiley.

Bonner, B., and A. Wiggin (2006) *Empire of Debt: The Rise of an Epic Financial Crisis*, Wiley.

Bonner, B. (2007) "Goldman Sachs Was Wrong and 2 Million Families May Lose Their Homes," Daily Reckoning, November 14.

Bookstaber, R. (2007) *A Demon of Our Own Design*, Wiley.

Booth, P. (2009) "More Regulation, Better Regulation, or Less Regulation?" in Booth, P. (ed.) "Verdict on the Crash: Causes and Policy Implication," *Institute of Economic Affairs*, p. 157.

Borge, D. (2001) *The Book of Risk*, Wiley.

Bremner, R.P. (2004) *William McChesney Martin, Jr and the Creation of the Modern American Financial System*, Yale University Press.

Bryan, L. (1988) *Breaking Up the Bank – Rethinking an Industry Under Siege*, Irwin Professional Publishers.

Cairns, A.J.C., Blake, D., and Dowd, K. (2006) "A Two-Factor Model for Stochastic Mortality with Parameter Uncertainty: Theory and Calibration," *Journal of Risk and Insurance*, vol. 73, no. 4.

Calabria, M.A. (2009) "Did Deregulation Cause the Financial Crisis?" *Cato Policy Report*, vol. 31, no. 4, July/August, pp. 1, 6–8.

Calomiris, C.W. (2009) "The Debasement of Ratings: What's Wrong and How We Can Fix It," Mimeo, Columbia Business School.

Calomiris, C.W. and Mason, J.R. (2009) "Conflicts of Interest, Low-quality Ratings, and Meaningful Reform of Credit and Corporate Governance Ratings," mimeo, Columbia Business School, November.

Campbell, D. and Griffin, S. (2006) "Enron and The End of Corporate Governance," in MacLeod, S. (ed.) *Global Governance and the Quest for Justice*, Hart Publishing, pp. 47–72.

Chernow, R. (2001) *The House of Morgan*, Grove Press.

Cotter, J. (2001) "Extreme Value Calculations of European Futures Margin Requirements," *Journal of Banking and Finance*, vol. 25, no. 8, pp. 1475–1502.

Damato, K. (2001) "Investors Debate the Profitability of Much-vaunted Index Portfolios," *Wall Street Journal*, April 9.

Danielsson, J. (2002) "The Emperor Has No Clothes: Limits to Risk Modeling," *Journal of Banking and Finance*, vol. 26, pp. 1273–96.

Das, S. (2006) *Traders, Guns and Money*, FT Press.

Das, S. (2009) "Credit Crunch – the New Diet Snack for Financial Markets Part 1," *Wilmot* magazine, January, p. 37.

Diamond, D.W. and Dybvig, P.H. (1983) "Bank Runs, Deposit Insurance, and Liquidity," *Journal of Political Economy*, vol. 91, pp. 401–409.

Dowd, K. (1992) "Models of Banking Instability: A Partial Review of the Literature," *Journal of Economic Surveys*, vol. 6, pp. 107–132.

Dowd, K. (ed.) (1992) *The Experience of Free Banking*, Routledge.

Dowd, K. (1996) *Competition and Finance: A Reinterpretation of Financial and Monetary Economics*, Palgrave Macmillan.

Dowd, K. (2005) *Measuring Market Risk*, Wiley.

Dowd, K. (2009a) "Lessons from the Financial Crisis: A Libertarian Perspective," *Libertarian Alliance Economic Notes*, no. 111.

Dowd, K. (2009b) "The Current Financial Crisis ... and After," talk to the Paris Freedom Fest, September 13.

Dowd, K. (2010) "Using Order Statistics to Estimate Confidence Intervals for Quantile-based Risk Measures," *Journal of Derivatives*, February.

Dowd, K. and Hinchliffe, J.M. (2000) "Paternalism Fails Again: The Sorry Story of the Financial Services Act," in Dowd, K. (ed.) *Money and the Market: Essays on Free Banking*, Routledge.

Dowd, K., Blake, D., and Cairns, A.J.C. (2010) "Facing up to Uncertain Life Expectancy: the Longevity Fan Charts," *Demography*, February.

Dowd, K., Cotter, J., Humphrey, C.G., and Woods, M. (2008) "How Unlucky is 25-sigma?" *Journal of Portfolio Management*, vol. 34, pp. 76–80.

E-Finance Directory (2007) "A Look Back at NAR Housing Market Predictions," January 12.

Elliott, G. (2006) *The Mystery of Overend & Gurney: A Financial Scandal in Victorian London*, Methuen.

Euromoney (1998) "Caspian Securities: Bolstered Against the Asian Storm?" March

Fama, E. and French, K.R. (1993) "Common Risk Factors in the Returns on Stocks and Bonds," *Journal of Financial Economics*, vol. 33, pp. 3–56.

Fisher, R.W. (2008) "Storms on the Horizon," remarks before the Commonwealth Club of California, May.

Focardi, S.M. and Fabozzi, F.J. (2003) "Fat Tails, Scaling, and Stable Laws: A Critical Look at Modeling Extremal Events in Financial Phenomena," *Journal of Risk Finance*, Fall, pp. 5–26.

Friedman, M. (1960), *A Program for Monetary Stability*, Fordham University Press.

Friedman, M. and Schwarz, A.K. (1963) *A Monetary History of the United States, 1867–1960*, Princeton University Press.

Galbraith, J.K. (1954) *The Great Crash 1929*. (Republished by Mariner Books, 2009.)

Geithner, T. (2008) "Reducing Systemic Risk in a Dynamic Financial System," *Economic Club of New York*, June 9.

Graham, B. and Dodd, D. (1940) *Security Analysis*. (Republished by McGraw Hill, 2002.)

Greenspan, A and Kennedy, J. (2007) "Sources and uses of Equity Extracted from Houses," Federal Reserve Working Paper.

Grinold, R.C. (1993) "Is Beta Dead, Again?" *Financial Analysts Journal*, vol. 49, pp. 28–34.

Gründl, H. and Post, T. (2010) "Transparency Through Financial Claims with Fingerprints – A Free Market Mechanism for Preventing Mortgage-securitization-induced Financial Crises," *Financial Analysts Journal*, forthcoming.

Haldane, A.G. (2009) "Why Banks Failed the Stress Test," Bank of England, February.

Hanke, S. H. (2008) "Greenspan's Bubbles," *Finance Asia*, June.

Hanke, S. H. "Greenspan's Bubbles", available at www.cato.org (5 June, 2008).

Hanke, S. H. "Credit Feast and Famine", *Forbes* March 29, 2010, p. 168.

Hansell, S. and Muehring, K. (1992) "Why Derivatives Rattle the Regulators," *Institutional Investor*, September, p. 49.

Harr, L. and Harris, W.C. (1936) *Banking Theory and Practice*, McGraw Hill.

Hubbard, D.W. (2009) *The Failure of Risk Management: Why It's Broken and How to Fix It*, Wiley.

Hunter, R. (1999) "The Accounting Standard From Outer Space," *Derivatives Strategy*, September.

Hutchinson, M.O. (2006) "Sinking the Ship in a Flat Calm," *Financial Engineering News*, November–December.

IMF (2009) *Currency Composition of Official Foreign Exchange Reserves (COFER)*.

Issing, O. (2008) *The Birth of the Euro*, Cambridge University Press.

J.P. Morgan/Reuters, *RiskMetrics – Technical Document*, fourth edition, December 1996

Jones, S. (2009) "Of Couples and Copulas", *FT Weekend*, April 25–6, p. 35.

Kane, E.J. (1985) *The Gathering Crisis in Federal Deposit Insurance*. (Republished by MIT Press, 2003.)

Kaufman, G.G. (1988) "Bank Runs: Causes, Benefits, and Costs," *Cato Journal*, vol. 7, pp. 559–87.

Keynes, J.M. (1920) *The Economic Consequences of the Peace*. (Republished by General Books, 2009.)

Keynes, J.M. (1924) *A Tract on Monetary Reform*. (Republished by Prometheus Books, 2000.)

Keynes, J. M. (1931) *Essays in Persuasion*. (Republished by W.W. Norton, 1963.)

Keynes, J.M. (1936) *General Theory of Employment, Interest and Money*. (Republished by CreateSpace, 2009.)

Kipling, R. (1919) "The Gods of the Copybook Headings," *Sunday Pictorial*, October 26.

Kling, A. (2008),"Freddie Mac and Fannie Mae: An Exit Strategy for the Taxpayer", Cato Institute Briefing Paper No. 106, September.

Kosko, B. (1993) *Fuzzy Thinking*, Flamingo.

Kotlikoff, L.J. (2006) "Is the United States Bankrupt?" *Federal Reserve Bank of St. Louis Review*, vol. 88, no. 4 (July/August), pp. 235–49.

Kotlikoff, L. and Burns, S. (2005) *The Coming Generational Storm*, MIT Press.

Kynaston, D. (1995) *The City of London: A World of Its Own, 1815–1890*, Pimlico.

Kynaston, D. (2002) *The City of London: A Club No More, 1945–2000*, Chatto and Windus.

Leamer, E.E. (1983) "Lets Take the Con Out of Econometrics," *American Economic Review*, vol. 73, pp. 31–43.

Leeson, N. (1996) *Rogue Trader*, Sphere.

Lewis, M. (1989) *Liar's Poker*, Penguin.

Lewis, M. (2008) "The End," Portfolio.com, November 11.

Li, D. (2000) "On Default Correlation: A Copula Approach," *Journal of Risk Metrics*, vol. 9, no. 4.

Liebowitz, S.J. (2008) "Anatomy of a Train Wreck: Causes of the Mortgage Meltdown", Independent Institute Policy Report, October.

Macey, J.R. (2008) *Corporate Governance: Promises Kept, Promises Broken*, Princeton University Press.

Mackay, C. (1841) *Extraordinary Popular Delusions and the Madness of Crowds*. (Republished by Martino Fine Books, 2009.)

MacLeod, H.D. (1896) *A History of Banking in All the Leading Nations*.

Malanga, S. (2009) "Obsessive Housing Disorder", *City Journal*, Spring.

Mandelbrot, B. (1962) "Sur Certains Prix Speculatifs," *Comptes Rendus*, Paris Academy.

Mandelbrot, B. (1982) *The Fractal Geometry of Nature*, W.H. Freeman.

Markowitz, H.M. (2009) "Proposals Concerning the Current Financial Crisis," *Financial Analysts Journal*, vol. 65, no. 1, January/February, pp. 25–9.

Marshall, C. and Siegel, M. (1997) "Value at Risk: Implementing a Risk Measurement Standard," *Journal of Derivatives*, vol. 4, pp. 91–110.

May, R.M. (1976) "Simple Mathematical Models with Very Complicated Dynamics," *Nature*, June 10.

McNeill, D. and Freiberger, P. (1993) *Fuzzy Logic*, Simon & Schuster.

Meltzer, A.H. (2003) *A History of the Federal Reserve, Vol. 1 (1914–1951)*, University of Chicago Press.

Moyer, L. (2007) "Bear Stearns Bares its Soul," *Forbes*, August 3.

Murray, C. (2003) *Human Accomplishments: The Pursuit of Excellence in the Arts and Sciences, 800BC to 1950*, Harper Perennial.

Neal, L. "The Financial Crisis of 1825 and the Restructuring of the British Financial System", *Federal Reserve Bank of St. Louis Review*, May/June 1998, pp. 53–76.

O'Driscoll, G. P. "Money and the Present Crisis", *Cato Journal* Vol 29, No. 1, Winter 2009, pp. 167–186.

Palley, T.L. (1997) "How to Rewrite Economic History: The Boskin Commission," *Atlantic Monthly*, April 1997.

Partnoy, F. (1998) *F.I.A.S.C.O.: The Inside Story of a Wall Street Trader*, Profile Books.

Partnoy, F. (2003) *Infectious Greed*, Holt Paperbacks.

Powell, E.T. (1915) *The Evolution of the Money Market, 1385–1915*. (Republished by General Books LLC, 2010.)

Powell, J. (2003) *FDR's Folly: How Roosevelt and his New Deal Prolonged the Great Depression*, Three River Press.

Quint, M. (1990) "A Bank Expert's Plan for Change," *New York Times*, August 22.

Rebonato, R. (2007) *Plight of the Fortune Tellers*, Princeton University Press.

Reinhart, C.M. and Rogoff, K.S. (2009) *This Time is Different*, Princeton University Press.

Roll, R. (1977) "A Critique of the Asset Pricing Theory's Tests Part I: On Past and Potential Testability of the Theory," *Journal of Financial Economics*, (March), vol. 4, pp. 129–176.

Roth, D. (2009) "Road Map for Financial Recovery: Radical Transparency Now!" *Wired* magazine, February 2.

Sampson, A. (1973) "The Geneen Machine," *New York Magazine*, April 23.

Schlaes, A. (2007) *The Forgotten Man: A New History of the Great Depression*, Harper Perennial.

Scott, G. (1995) "New Zealand's Fiscal Responsibility Act," *Agenda*, vol 2., no. 1, pp. 3–16.

Shiller, R. (2003) *The New Financial Order: Risk in the 21st Century*, Princeton University Press.

Silk, L. (1990) "Savings Rescue: Figuring the Cost," *New York Times*, June 1.

Smiley, G. (2002) *Rethinking the Great Depression*, Ivan R. Dee.

Smith, A. (1776) *The Wealth of Nations*. (Republished by CreateSpace, 2009.)

St Louis Fed, FRASER (Federal Reserve System for Archival Research), *Federal Reserve Bulletin 1931–40*.

St. Louis Fed (2010) *The Financial Crisis: A Timeline of Events and Policy Actions*.

Steinbrück, P. (2008) "It Doesn't Exist!" *Newsweek*, December 15.

Stock, J.H. and Watson, M. (2002) "Has the business cycle changed and why?" Princeton University.

TABB Group (2009) *US Equity High Frequency Trading: Strategies, Size, and Market Structure*.

Taleb, N.N. (2007) *The Black Swan: The Impact of the Highly Improbable*, Random House.

Tett, G., (2009) *Fool's Gold: How Unrestrained Greed Corrupted a Dream, Shattered Global Markets and Unleashed a Catastrophe*," Little, Brown.

Thomson, R. (1998) *Apocalypse Roulette: The Lethal World of Derivatives*, Macmillan.

Timberlake, R.H. (1993) *Monetary Policy in the United States: An Intellectual and Institutional History*, University of Chicago Press.

Tobin, J. (1974) *The New Economics One Decade Older*, Princeton University Press.

Trollope, A. (1873) *The Way We Live Now*. (Republished by Oxford World's Classics, 2009.)

Wallace, A. (1980) "Is Beta Dead?" *Institutional Investor*, vol. 14, pp. 22–30.

Watts, R. (2009) "Goldman's Boss: We Do God's Work," *The Sunday Times*, November 8.

White, L. H. *Free Banking in Britain: Theory, Experience, and Debate, 1800-1845*, Cambridge University Press.

Wood, D. (2009) "Critics Attack Dynamic Provisioning Following Spanish Bank Results," Risk.net, October 30.

Xenos, S. (1869) *Overend, Gurney & Co. and the Greek and Oriental Steam Navigation Co.* (Republished by BiblioLife, 2009.)

Yahoo Finance (2010) "Goldman Sachs: Major Holders", January 8.

Zadeh, L. (1965) "Fuzzy Sets," *Information and Control*, vol. 8

Zingales, L. (2009) "Capitalism After the Crisis," *National Affairs*, p. 31.

Index